C [⟨ SO-ATJ-490]

THINKING,
THOUGHTFUL
WRITING

CRITICAL THINKING, THOUGHTFUL WRITING

Eugene R. Hammond

University of Maryland

SECOND EDITION

McGRAW-HILL BOOK COMPANY

New York   St. Louis   San Francisco   Auckland   Bogotá
Caracas   Colorado Springs   Hamburg   Lisbon   London   Madrid
Mexico   Milan   Montreal   New Delhi   Oklahoma City   Panama
Paris   San Juan   São Paulo   Singapore   Sidney   Tokyo   Toronto

This book was set in Zapf Book Lite by the College Composition Unit
in cooperation with The Clarinda Company.
The editors were Judith R. Cornwell, Susan D. Hurtt, and Bernadette Boylan;
the designer was Scott Chelius;
the production supervisor was Louise Karam.
R. R. Donnelley & Sons Company was printer and binder.

Cover credit: Sonia Delaunay, *GIRAUDON / ART RESOURCE, NY.*

CRITICAL THINKING, THOUGHTFUL WRITING

1 2 3 4 5 6 7 8 9 0 DOC DOC 8 9 4 3 2 1 0 9

ISBN 0-07-025917-8

Library of Congress Cataloging-in-Publication Data

Hammond, Eugene.
   Critical thinking, thoughtful writing
   Eugene R. Hammond. p. cm.
   Rev. ed. of: Informative writing. c1985.
   Bibliography: p.
   Includes index.
   ISBN 0-07-025917-8
   1. English language--Rhetoric. I. Hammond, Eugene. Informative
writing. II. Title.
PE1408.H323 1989
808'.042--dc19   88-21606

ABOUT THE AUTHOR

Eugene Hammond is a Wisconsin native with a degree from Oxford University. He now serves as Associate Chair of English and Chair of the Writing Group at the University of Maryland at College Park. His wife teaches chemistry and they have two young children.

To my partners in crime:
Ann Allen, Lucy Schultz,
Carolyn Hill, Betsy Cohn,
Sally Glover, Rosalie Gancie,
and the writing staff
at College Park

CONTENTS IN BRIEF

CONTENTS

PREFACE

Critical Thinking, Thoughtful Writing is a revised version of a book originally entitled *Informative Writing*. I chose the first title because I felt that
writing courses for a dangerously long time had, in the service of style
and organization, given short shrift to thoughtful content (well-selected
facts and careful inferences). Teachers and students who used *Informative Writing* appreciated its emphasis on substance, but they found most
original and useful "Facts, Inferences, and Theses" (Chapter 3), which
teaches students to build a thesis through their inferences; "Persuasion"
(now Chapter 6), which teaches the practical thinking skills of argument;
"Research through Careful Reading" (now Chapter 12), which teaches
students how to draw inferences as they read, and the Draft Review
Worksheets (now in Chapter 14) which teach students to be self-critical
as they revise.

    Critical Thinking, Thoughtful Writing, therefore, better describes the
originality and strengths of the book. In changing the title I am not suggesting that well-selected information is any less important. Selecting evidence well is one of the most crucial of the many thoughtful processes
that constitute writing. If students can become thoughtful in that area as
in many others, their writing course will once again be seen by them, as
it deserves to be seen, as the core of their curriculum and as the central
preparation for their professional lives.

    Chapter 1: "Where Do We Start?" This chapter helps students de-
termine what they value in "good" writing and then compare what they
value with the standards of their teacher and their classmates. It also
tries to get students to think about why they're taking this course.

    Chapter 2: "Telling Details." This chapter sends students out to search for details which can tell their readers something worth becoming aware of. Such a search is essential early in a course if we expect our students to substantiate their assertions habitually and effectively. The chapter is based largely on Ken Macrorie's ideas about telling facts (in *Telling Writing*), but it applies the principle of telling facts to all forms of writing—not just to narration and description.

Chapter 3: "Facts, Inferences, and Theses." This chapter includes several exercises in the most crucial skills for writers: distinguishing facts from inferences, drawing inferences from facts, and deriving theses from their inferences. Students will learn through this chapter how to use fact-inference pairs as a prewriting technique and how to use inferences as tools for organizing a paper.

Chapter 4: "Writing for a Reader." This chapter tries to get students to think seriously (as they write) about their readers, and particularly about their teachers, as complex readers-judges.

Chapter 5: "Systematic Patterns of Thought." This chapter focuses on a week-long exercise of practice in the so-called *rhetorical modes* (definition, cause-effect, problem-solution, comparison-contrast, etc.). It emphasizes the use of these strategies as tools for making your thinking clear to your reader. It concludes with advice for making essay exams easier by thinking of these organizational strategies first before beginning to answer any question.

Chapter 6: "Persuasion." All writing, I believe, is persuasive, but specifically persuasive techniques are more necessary when one's readers are not inclined to agree. This chapter explains induction, deduction, and Stephen Toulmin's model for combining the two, in practical ways so that students can make use of them. It also introduces the terms *ethos, logos,* and *pathos* as strategies of persuasion. And it explains the common fallacies in argument in terms of their misuse of either *ethos, logos,* or *pathos.* Carl Rogers's theory that only through care for one's reader is successful persuasion possible, concludes the chapter.

Chapter 7: "Paragraphing, Introductions, and Conclusions." This chapter uses a variety of exercises to help students develop both a conscious and an intuitive sense of how best to handle decisions about paragraphs, introductions, and conclusions.

Chapter 8: "Revision." This chapter offers a ten-question review form that can help a student revise any paper and a detailed checklist of revision strategies from rethinking, reorganization, and further research to tightening and choosing more precise words.

Chapter 9: "Sentence Sense." This chapter teaches students practical rules for punctuation. It does so through sentence imitation and sentence building exercises which teachers can use and then supplement to suit their students' individual needs.

Chapter 10: "Research in the Library." This chapter includes exercises which can be used in any library to show students the odd and often lively sources of information that they usually neglect when they head dutifully for the card catalog. It also includes guidelines (and a chart) for using the 1985 Modern Language Association format for parenthetical references and lists of works cited.

Chapter 11: "Research through Interviewing." The exercises in this chapter teach students to become comfortable with collecting information from other people. By mastering this skill, they will gain access to a much greater fund of information for their writing.

Chapter 12: "Research through Reading." This chapter leads students through the steps of drawing inferences as they read. It also offers practice in noting the uses of *ethos, logos,* and *pathos* (or what we might call "voice," "substance," and "attitude toward the reader") in what they read. It prepares students to write two kinds of assignments: rhetorical analyses and literary analyses.

Chapter 13: "The Writing Process." This chapter reviews the entire sequence of writing strategies that are taught throughout the book. The placement of the chapter does not mean that it should be studied last, but that it is not part of any sequence in the book and that a teacher can use it at any desired point in the course. Some may want to begin with this chapter, as it makes students conscious of the many steps and choices necessary to successful writing. There are advantages, though, to saving it for later in the semester (after one paper, or three, or four). After students have become more conscious of their own writing habits, they are much better judges of the usefulness of the advice offered here.

Chapter 14: "Suggested Assignments." This chapter includes nine assignments teachers may wish to use, each explained in a way that helps students proceed systematically from research to writing to revision. All the assignments require research of people, of places, of books, or of artifacts. None can be done in a student's room the night before it's due. Each assignment is accompanied by a draft review worksheet of questions which students can use to read each other's drafts and to make suggestions for improvement before a final draft is turned in.

Chapter 15: "What Next?" This chapter asks students to take stock of what they have learned and to think about how they will continue to improve their own writing after they leave this course.

The advantages of this text over others are:

1. The students practice every skill taught, so they will internalize more of what they learn.
2. Both exercises and assignments encourage observation, selection, and judgment: skills that will be necessary in any writing situation in which students will later find themselves.
3. Students finish the course knowing enough grammar to be literate representatives of our universities, colleges, and community colleges, but they learn grammar through practice and not through analysis.

4. Students read as much flawed work as they do models, so they are encouraged to develop their critical abilities.
5. Students for the most part write about subjects that they have come to know better than their teachers; consequently, they produce work that they're proud of, and they come to like writing.
6. Teachers using this book, after first becoming acquainted with it, need to do far less preparation than is usual in writing courses, since so many useful exercises are provided, and since much emphasis is placed on students taking the responsibility for their work into their own hands. This leaves teachers free to devote their energy to reading and responding to finished student papers, which is itself challenging and time-consuming work.
7. This text tries to understand and acknowledge the attitudes that both teachers and students have toward required writing courses. It doesn't pretend that we all love this work, but it does show how we can learn more about writing and at the same time enjoy it much more than we ordinarily do.

An Instructor's Manual, available from McGraw-Hill, provides a rationale for the approach this book takes to teaching writing. The manual also offers suggestions for the use of all exercises and assignments.

I'd like to say a special thank you to the following teachers and students (in addition to those I've cited in the text) whose ideas have made crucial contributions to the completeness and integrity of this book: Betsy Cohn, Lucy Schultz, Trudi Walsh, Tom Moore, Aletha Hendrickson, Tom Berninghausen, Betsey Blakeslee, Aimee Doyle, Jane O'Brien, Kathryn Riley, Tom Holbrook, Patti Rosenberg, Cristina Cheplik, Rowena Cross, Maria Lima, Vic Caroscio, Betty Day, Gerry Higgins, Ed James, Mary Kay Jordan, Craig Stoltz, Bobby Fong, Dawnelle Loiselle, and Leonard King, Kathleen Burke, and Jud Sage. Very useful comments and suggestions were given to me by the following reviewers, and to them I am also grateful: Joyce Durham, University of Dayton; Robert Garnett, Gettysburg College; Nancy Joseph, York College; Nancy Walker, Southwest Missouri State University; and Joseph L. Wheeler.

Eugene R. Hammond

CRITICAL THINKING, THOUGHTFUL WRITING

1

Where Do We Start?

Writing [is] the study of misunderstanding and its remedies.
I. A. Richards

Writing is the art of applying the seat of the pants to the seat of the chair.
Mary Heaton Vorse

Writing is an art that requires more soul and sweat than I'm willing to give.
student

Critical Skills and Attitudes for a Writer

Welcome to a course in which you will improve your writing through thoughtful practice. If you don't already have a pen you like to write with and plenty of paper you like to write on, pick them up in the next day or two. These, along with a typewriter or (if you are fortunate) a word processor, are the tools of our trade. With these tools in the next several weeks, you can expect to improve your writing in at least fifteen ways:

1. You'll become more observant.
2. You'll become a skilled collector and user of telling details.
3. You'll learn how to find what you need or want in a library.
4. You'll learn how to organize any chaotic mass of information.
5. You'll become confident (if you aren't already) about your grammar.
6. You'll master the use of commas, dashes, semicolons, and colons.
7. You'll learn to make every sentence in your writing count.
8. You'll learn to paragraph in a way that makes reading easier for your readers.
9. You'll learn to link your sentences smoothly.
10. You'll learn how to rethink and revise your first drafts.
11. You'll learn how to write effective introductions and conclusions.
12. You'll learn to write effectively to unsympathetic readers.

1

13. You'll learn to write with a voice that readers can recognize as yours.
14. You'll learn to write clear essays in class under pressure.
15. You'll learn to compare writing with, and to distinguish it from, other forms of communication such as talking, photography, and filmmaking.

You can accomplish all this even if, like most of us, you don't especially like to write. But there is one condition: that you *want* to improve your writing. If you don't want to learn, you might as well drop the course now, sell this book back, get into another course, and come back another semester when you're ready. You can succeed in this course if you're shaky about your grammar or if you think your writing is awkward. You can succeed if you think your aptitude is not for English but for engineering or computers. But if you're not curious, if you're not patient, if you're not willing to work hard, or if you're only taking this course because it is a requirement, you may have serious trouble with it. The work load in this course is going to fall not on your teacher but on you. Neither your teacher nor this book can tell you how to write better. You must decide for yourself that *you* want to improve. If you write badly now, it's not because you are not intelligent. It's because you haven't been *attentive* about improving your writing. That attention is where we want to start.

You can't learn to write if you don't want to learn. You also can't learn to write by studying about writing. You learn to write by writing—and by *thinking* while you write. In this class you will try to produce writing that you and your teacher and your classmates can genuinely admire. Much of your progress as a writer will come from practice—repeated papers in this class and others, repeated essay exams in this class and others, (and later, perhaps) repeated application letters that fail to get you a job, repeated memos that are sent back once you do get a job. You can practice writing, and gain some understanding of yourself, anytime you like by writing letters to friends or family, or by keeping a journal of your dreams, your conflicts, your decisions. But you can also practice, in this class, by writing assigned papers for your teacher and for your classmates and by doing the exercises suggested in this book.

The exercises in this book have been designed to enable you to practice and develop your writing skills one or two at a time until all the skills become part of your intuitive resources, thus improving your writing performance and giving you greater confidence as a writer. All the assignments, discussions, readings, and writing you do in this course will go into building your writing intuitions—intuitions for how to begin, how to organize, how to please your readers, and so on. Writing is a complex task which requires everything from getting your spelling right to making your voice distinctive enough to be heard. Writing any new assignment requires a combination of thought, hard work, and intuition. The more you can rely on intuition, the more energy you have left for thinking about matters that are really new.

One of the most profitable ways to build up your intuitions is to read your drafts aloud to friends. Every paper you write should also be silently read and commented on by several people before you turn it in. (Draft review worksheets have been supplied in Chapter 14 for every suggested assignment in this book so that your readers will have some guidance as to what to look for when they read.) Listen to what these readers suggest. As you do, you'll begin to notice how many choices you have, and make, every time you write. As the course progresses, you'll learn new options from your teacher, from your classmates, from me, and from your own increasingly good judgment. Your progress in developing both writing ability and confidence will be gradual but substantial.

In this course you will not simply be delivering enough words and sentences to reach your teacher's page limit. Nor will you be able to write any of your papers the night before it's due. You'll be thinking and taking notes about your subject from the day each paper is assigned. Also, you'll be trying to learn much more about writing than simply how to develop a good "style." You'll find that collecting information, sorting it out, drawing conclusions from it, and selecting only the best of your information and conclusions for your final draft are the most crucial writing skills. If you learn to present pertinent information clearly, you'll find that you have developed, without even trying to, your own style.

From the start, information will be your best friend. The more information you have, the better paper you can write. But once you have selected the information you most want to pass on, I hope you find yourself becoming concerned as well about your writing as a craft. You'll want to present the information you've selected as well as you possibly can. During this course you'll develop your own standards of what way is best—with your teacher's help, with the help of your classmates, and with the help of the advice in this book.

This book contains very few rules. If you think you'll do well in college, or in life, or in writing, by following infallible rules, you're mistaken. There are guidelines for most situations, writing or otherwise, but success lies in making the most of the options you have within these guidelines. Some so-called *rules* of writing were merely fashions which are now as obsolete as dress gloves and canes—"Never begin a sentence with *and* or *but*," "Never end a sentence with a preposition," "Never split an infinitive." Other "rules" of writing—"Grab the attention of your readers," "Outline everything you write"—are more precisely rules of thumb. They are useful in many cases, but not in all. The key to good writing is not learning to follow rules but learning what your choices are—choices in tone, in words, in paragraphing, in punctuation. Throughout this course you'll practice making choices. Your teacher and your classmates may make other choices than you make. Think carefully about their choices. But take seriously your own preferences too. Yours may be better in some cases. Theirs may be better in others. By the end of this course, you ought to have an excellent sense of how varied your choices are.

Throughout this book, I'll stop talking to you as often as possible to give you time to try exercises that will help develop your thinking about writing. You may interpret the exercise numbers that introduce these exercises as invitations to skip over to my next comments. If you do, though, you'll be squandering the money and effort you've invested in this course. My thoughts about writing may stay with you for six months (an optimistic estimate). But your thoughts about writing, as you discover them in these exercises, will stay with you for life.

Assessing Your Current Writing Ability

Exercise 1-1

All of you are starting this course with different writing strengths and different writing weaknesses. So before we can begin sensibly to work on improvement, we have to find out what your current writing abilities are. Perhaps you feel confident about your writing; more likely you do not. To let your teacher know your strengths and your weaknesses, *write*—as well as you can within the limitations of twenty minutes and beginning-of-a-course nerves—*a page or two about your training in English to this point and about what kind of writer you now are as a result of that training.*

- Be as specific as possible.
- You may write about just a single English class if you prefer.
- Cross out and revise as much as you wish. Don't worry about neatness.
- You might want to stop for a few minutes and take a few notes before you begin.

Assessing the Writing of Others

Exercise 1-2

For much of your life, you've handed in samples of your writing to be evaluated. Do you know what your teachers have thought about as they read that writing? Perhaps you should try on the role of evaluator yourself. Read each of the three items that follow, and after reading each, write at least four or five sentences in which you express your opinion about it. What do you like? What do you dislike? As you read, underline and make marginal notes so it will be easier to write your comments. When you've finished noting your opinions, try, in preparation for discussion, to give each of the pieces a quality rating between 1 (poor) and 10 (excellent).

The numbers adjacent to each paragraph have been added to make it easier for you to refer others to specific sections of your reading when you discuss your results. The first selection is a passage from a book about New Jersey.

From *The Pine Barrens*
John McPhee

There are twenty-five people in Hog Wallow. Some of them describe 1
it, without any apparent intention to be clever, as a suburb of Jenkins, a
town three miles away, which has forty-five people. One resident of Hog
Wallow is Frederick Chambers Brown. I met him one summer morning
when I stopped at his house to ask for water.

Fred Brown's house is on an unpaved road that curves along the 2
edge of a wide cranberry bog. What attracted me to it was the pump that
stands in his yard. It was something of a wonder that I noticed the
pump, because there were, among other things, eight automobiles in the
yard, two of them on their sides and one of them upside down, all ten
years old or older. Around the cars were old refrigerators, vacuum clean-
ers, partly dismantled radios, cathode-ray tubes, a short wooden ski, a
large wooden mallet, dozens of cranberry picker's boxes, many tires, an
orange crate dated 1946, a cord or so of firewood, mandolins, engine
heads, and maybe a thousand other things. The house itself, two stories
high, was covered with tarpaper that was peeling away in some places, revealing its original shingles, made of Atlantic white cedar from the stream
courses of the surrounding forest. I called out to ask if anyone was home,
and a voice inside called back, "Come in. Come in. Come on the hell in."

I walked through a vestibule that had a dirt floor, stepped up into 3
a kitchen, and went on into another room that had several overstuffed
chairs in it and a porcelain-topped table, where Fred Brown was seated,
eating a pork chop. He was dressed in a white sleeveless shirt, ankle-top
shoes, and undershorts. He gave me a cheerful greeting and, without
asking why I had come or what I wanted, picked up a pair of khaki trousers that had been tossed onto one of the overstuffed chairs and asked
me to sit down. He set the trousers on another chair, and he apologized
for being in the middle of his breakfast, explaining that he seldom drank
much but the night before he had had a few drinks and this had caused
his day to start slowly. "I don't know what's the matter with me, but
there's got to be something the matter with me, because drink don't
agree with me anymore," he said. He had a raw onion in one hand, and
while he talked he shaved slices from the onion and ate them between
bites of the chop. He was a muscular and well-built man, with short,
bristly white hair, and he had bright, fast-moving eyes in a wide-open face.
His legs were trim and strong, with large muscles in the calves. I guessed
that he was about sixty, and for a man of sixty he seemed to be in remarkably good shape. He was actually seventy-nine. "My rule is: Never eat except when you're hungry," he said, and he ate another slice of the onion.

The second selection is an article from *Ms.* magazine:

Professional Traveling (1983)

Jewell Parker Rhodes

Business travel can be treacherous when you're female and black. 1
Sooner or later, in neon script, the double whammy of racism and sexism hits.

One morning in Saratoga, I was nibbling a cantaloupe for breakfast 2
when a white colleague cracked a watermelon joke. "I thought y'all preferred to pick seeds," he said. A white couple at an Ivy League Club in
New York mistook me for a maid and asked me to clean their room—
despite the fact that my hair was neatly pinned, I carried a briefcase, and
wore my "intellectual" glasses and my three-piece pinstripe suit. A fellow professor at a convention in Detroit assumed I was a local black
hooker. Why? I wasn't near a bar. On one excursion South, I eschewed a
conference cafeteria lunch in favor of a hamburger diner; over relish and
onions, an ancient white man offered me five dollars if I took a trip to his
house: "Just for an hour." (He must have been recalling pre-inflation
days.) Needless to say, my professional performance lacked luster when
I delivered my paper during the afternoon conference session.

Like an innocent or a fool, I begin each trip with optimism, still de- 3
termined that race and sex not impede my performance and acceptance. My pretensions get depressed.

How potent is the subliminal irritation of being the only woman 4
on the businessman's shuttle between New York and Washington? Of
being the only minority at a professional meeting? Each trip represents
for me a lesson in alienation. Yet because I'm conducting business,
"networking," and trying to promote a career, I can't afford feeling alien
since it engenders mistrust and withdrawal. So each trip I'm vulnerable
anew.

Why *can't* business travel be pleasurable? I've read all the books 5
and articles on "how to dress for success." Wind me up and I conduct
myself with adequate charm. But after following all the advice, I find myself still belittled—*and* rendered less effective—due to the emotional and
psychological assaults.

Articles and books don't tell you how to deal with the loneliness of 6
being the only visible minority in a Midwestern town, or in an airport, or
at a meeting. Once I walked through a community for hours and never
saw another face with the slightest hint of brown. I did, however, spend
my evenings being interrogated by "well-intentioned" liberals who
wanted my opinion on every civil rights issue since the Civil War. Willy-
nilly, I am a spokesperson for my race.

Articles and books also don't tell you how to deal with sexual as- 7
saults beyond "carry a book to dinner." My rage gets dissipated only in a
Howard Johnson's hotel room, alone, with room service.

It becomes doubly hard to ward off sexual invitation when you feel 8 intense loneliness because nowhere else in the conference, the hotel, or the lounge, is there anyone who in the least resembles your sex or color. One loneliness begets another. Yet ward off sexual invitations you must—since the macho, conquering male abounds at professional meetings and since men compound their sexism with racist awe regarding your color. Any nonwhite characteristics can be viewed as exotic plumes.

Once, in the District of Columbia following a conference dinner, my 9 white male colleague and escort was nearly attacked by three black youths. Only a police officer delayed their action. Do you honestly believe I was at my professional peak the next day? And there also have been predominantly black conferences where sexist attitudes angered me so intensely I could barely function. I recall the time in Ohio when an African colleague called me in my hotel room at 1:30 in the morning so we could "discuss" improved relations between his country and mine. The rest of the night I didn't sleep.

In Atlanta, I spent a whole day shunning a black male's advances. 10 The bathroom provided my sole measure of peace. At dinner, I was enjoying my conversation with an author on my right when my ego-bruised pursuer shouted, "I'm a man too!" I groaned. I wanted to hide beneath the table. I'd forgotten that any public conversation between a male and female is seen as sexual.

What are the strategies for negotiating the sexist and racist trails of 11 professional meetings? I honestly don't know. A business suit doesn't necessarily serve as armor. A book doesn't shield one from all sexual encounters. I've tried wearing makeup and no makeup. I've tried dressing up and dressing down. I've tried the schoolmarm's bun and also the thick-rimmed glasses. Still sexism abounds. Superficial transformations don't negate discrimination. About my color, I can do nothing (nor would I want to if I could).

The best one can do is try to prevail with dignity. When I've been 12 the only woman at a conference, I search for minority colleagues— shared interests and shared culture sometimes bind. When I've been the only black, I search for women—women hug you when you're down and encourage you in your work. When I've been the only black *and* the only woman, I call long distance to reach out and touch a friend.

Sometimes humor helps. One year I dressed severely to compen- 13 sate for my baby face. I wore high heels to compensate for my lack of height. I felt every inch the professional. Yet at the academic convention registration, I was brusquely pulled aside. "Can't you read the signs? Student registration is to the right."

If they don't get you for race and sex, they get you for something else. 14

The third selection is from the preface to a book about plumbing for homeowners.

"Preface"
Care and Repair of the Plumbing and Heating System in Your Home (1963)
Charles Geiser

The purpose of this book is not to make a Plumber out of the Home [1]
Owner or Tenant, but to give the necessary information on the Care and
Repair of the Plumbing and Heating System, etc., WHETHER YOU EVER
DO ANY OF YOUR OWN REPAIRING OR NOT. THIS BOOK SHOULD BE
READ by the Home Owner, Tenant, Housewife, Maid, etc., in fact anyone
left to care of the Home during the Summer as well as the Winter sea-
sons. If the instructions are carefully followed, you will, no doubt, find
it a WONDERFUL HELP IN CASE OF SUDDEN OR UNEXPECTED RE-
PAIRS, in eliminating accidents, damaging property, unnecessary ex-
pense, etc.

DO NOT THINK THAT PARTS IN THIS BOOK ARE OLD- [2]
FASHIONED, or behind the times, DO YOU KNOW this book is being sold
all over the Country. About one third of the population live in Small
Towns, Farms, Villages, etc., and have no City Sewer, Gas, City Water, etc.,
U.S. Official Census 1960, Urban 125,268,759, Rural 54,054,425, Total Population 179,323,175. Where the majority have Gas or Oil for fuel, others
have to use Coal or Wood....

The author in a total of many years of experience, has come across [3]
some very sad accidents, and the remark that is usually made with a re-
gretting sigh, "IF I HAD ONLY KNOWN." There are many serious accidents that occur every year, especially DURING THE WINTER MONTHS,
simply because of the ignorance of the fact that the proper precautions
should have been taken, or because of the carelessness commonly called
"TAKING A CHANCE." Do not wait until the auto is missing before lock-
ing the garage door. Be prepared when it comes to looking after your
Plumbing, Heating, Ventilation, etc....

This book is written from practical experience (not technical or [4]
trade school experience) having been in the Plumbing and Heating
business for many years in Chicago, Chicago Suburbs, Colorado, Kansas, Wyoming, and Canada, so became acquainted with the many different State Laws, License, Examination Tests, Codes, Sanitary Engineering, etc.

You will find this book placed in many Libraries in the U.S., in the [5]
world's largest, in Washington, D.C.

MEMORIAL: The net proceeds from this book is being given to Or- [6]
phan Homes, Blind, Mental Institutions, Missionary Work. If you only followed one of the many items in this book, what you save on, for instance, on fuel alone during the Winter season (25–50 dollars) not saying

anything about the healthful results received, what you save, remember just a little for some charitable work.

    This book is written in the hope of helping and assisting the reader 7 along the lines for which it is intended.

Once you've taken all your notes, discuss with your classmates, in small groups or as a class, your opinions of these writings. You may all agree that one piece is terrible or that another is very good. But at the same time you should be giving your reasons for saying that one piece is good or that another is not so good. Your reasons undoubtedly will differ from those of your classmates. Perhaps some of you will even disagree strongly about whether a piece is good or bad. We have the same disagreements about movies, about politics, and about religion, so it shouldn't be surprising that we have these differences about writing.

Writing Priorities Survey

Exercise 1-3

The differences we have in evaluating writing are most often due to differing standards of what is important. So before we go too far in a writing course, we should try to find out what our standards are. The best way to start, perhaps, is to stop and write down what you look for when you read. List in your notebook the three things you think are most important in a piece of writing. Once you have three items, extend the list to five. These last two will be more difficult to come up with. Compare your decisions with those of your classmates.

    Now set aside these criteria and take the survey given in Table 1-1.

1. Mark with an H the three items that you think should have highest priority in this writing class.
2. Mark with an L the three items that you think should have lowest priority.

When you've finished marking your highest and lowest priorities, your teacher will survey the results in your class and tell you his or her current opinion. Note the totals, and compare your teacher's and the group's opinions with your own. My own H's the last time I took the survey went to "using supporting details," "developing a distinct tone of voice," and "becoming aware of one's readers." My L's went to "knowing precise verb forms," "spelling correctly," and "knowing correct manuscript form." Looking at my L's reminds me that I consider even these items important, though not as important as the others. In this course we'll be working on everything. You may, though, want to focus on weak areas while building up your strengths in all.

TABLE 1-1 Priorities: A Survey of Opinion

Writing Class Priorities	High-Rated		Low-Rated	
	Self	Group	Self	Group
1. Writing thesis statements				
2. Using supporting details				
3. Avoiding sentence fragments				
4. Knowing precise verb forms and subject-verb agreement				
5. Spelling correctly				
6. Punctuating correctly				
7. Drawing inferences				
8. Writing introductions				
9. Writing conclusions				
10. Developing a distinct tone of voice				
11. Observing one's subject carefully				
12. Writing logically				
13. Connecting sentences coherently				
14. Paragraphing clearly				
15. Learning to fear writing less				
16. Planning before writing				
17. Revising a first draft				
18. Using words precisely				
19. Becoming aware of one's readers				
20. Getting practice in reading				
21. Knowing correct manuscript form				
22. Being concise				
23. Learning to judge one's own work				
24. Other (specify) _____				

What we'll be learning in this course has long been called expository writing. I prefer to call it informative writing. I don't much like the term expository. No one outside of school seems to know what it means. And expository writing is usually considered the opposite of so-called creative writing. But all writing, not just fiction and poetry, is creative. Nonfiction is never a simple mirror of reality. It is always a *version* of ideas or events, of which there are many other possible versions. Nonfiction, no less than fiction, requires creative, thoughtful decisions about the selection of material, tone of voice, the interpretation of material, the arrangement of material, and the best way to persuade our readers.

You, and all your new classmates, will be writers, thoughtful writers I hope, in the professions you take up when you graduate. Because writing is private work, though, and so we rarely watch people do it, you may not yet realize how much of your time is going to be taken up with writing. Lawyers in television series spend their time in court. Police officers in television series spend their time making arrests. But Chicago lawyers and Detroit police officers and Los Angeles sales managers spend much of their time writing. Job announcements even for routine work often ask for written-communication skills. And promotions beyond college-exit jobs are almost always dependent on your communication skills. Schools and departments which test you exclusively through multiple-choice tests are (unintentionally) misleading you about your future. There are no multiple-choice tests after college. Whether you plan to be a teacher, an engineer, a marketing analyst, or a computer programmer, surveys show that you're likely to spend at least 25 percent of your working hours writing or planning writing—letters, reports on research, budget reports, grant proposals, business forecasts, press releases, speeches, management briefings, equipment justifications, technical bulletins (Faigley and Miller 560–61).[1] Much of the time you are not writing, you will be trying to be informative and thoughtful in other ways. What you learn in this course about writing will often help you to conduct business in person or over the phone. It will also help you to talk more clearly and specifically with your family and friends. Even if you never write for the rest of your life (an unlikely possibility), you'll find the thinking, research, and organizational skills in this course useful.

This book is shorter than some writing course texts because in this course *you* are going to have to do most of the work. Newspapers, your city council, your local courtroom, a person whom you choose to interview, and your library's books, magazines, and videotapes will all expand this textbook. At the end of this course you won't carry away a fund of propositions or rules. You'll leave with a willingness to work hard and a good set of writer's intuitions that will make you confident in attacking college and professional writing assignments.

---

[1] In this book I will acknowledge my sources, as I recommend that you do, by following the guidelines of the *Modern Language Association Style Manual* (1985). Whenever I quote or paraphrase material from another source, I'll add in parentheses at the end of my sentence the author or authors and the page or pages that I've borrowed from. Then I'll put all the details about the source in my Works Cited list on pages 360–366. Check the Works Cited list right now for the information about Faigley and Miller's article, so you can see how this reference system works, and then master it yourself for your own writing.

2

Telling Details

George Bernard Shaw once said that as he grew older, he became less and less interested in theory, more and more interested in information. The temptation in writing is just the reverse. Nothing is so hard to come by as a new and interesting fact. Nothing is so easy on the feet as a generalization.

John Kenneth Galbraith

Lloyd George [Prime Minister of England during World War I] was convinced that if the war could once be described in accurate language, people would insist that it be stopped.

Paul Fussell

Telling Details: The Basis of All Effective Writing

On March 14, 1983, Ruben Zamara, a negotiator for Farabundo Marti National Liberation Front, a coalition of five guerilla groups in El Salvador, complained about the progress of talks between the guerillas and the Salvadoran government: "Let's use fewer adjectives and more facts" (Hall B1).[1] If adjectives like "communist" and "imperialist" and "terrorist" were preventing communication from taking place in the 1983 El Salvador peace talks, so also do adjectives like "weird" or "interesting" or "terrible" hinder genuine communication when we write. Which of the two statements below, each taken from a student's paper about adjustment to college, tells you more?

- I share a dorm room 9 by 22 feet with a 6-foot, 4-inch roommate

---

[1] Here is my second parenthetical reference to the Works Cited list on pages 360–366 where you'll find the complete details about this article. Again I've listed in my parentheses the author's last name and the page number that the quotation appears on. This page number looks different because it's from a newspaper with pages numbered by section, A1–A20, B1–B14, C1–C16, D1–D12.

from Buffalo, two desks, a sink, and a set of bunkbeds. It's the
most space and the most privacy I've ever had.
- So far I haven't had as much of a problem adjusting to college as I
  thought I would have. I have met some interesting people, and
  some not so interesting people.

Photographers and filmmakers don't have adjectives like "interesting" at their disposal, so they make a profession of finding facts that
make their points. The photograph below, using a "telling" fact, could
replace many a written editorial. Every film you see is a continuous se-

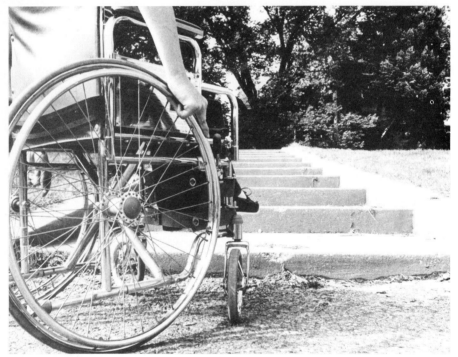

ries of telling photographs and incidents. Since most films try to tell, in
two hours, stories which would take thirty or forty hours to read, they
focus on crucial incidents. In the *Coal Miner's Daughter*, for example,
about the country singer Loretta Lynn and her husband "Doo," Doo's
bachelor character is presented to us in a thirty-second sequence in
which he tries to race his new jeep up an impossibly steep incline. The
task seems pointless, but Doo is stubborn—and he is finally successful. In
thirty seconds, the director has "told" us how stubborn (and yet finally
successful) Doo will be as a husband. Later in the same movie, when Doo
has for a long time been ignored by Loretta, we see him flirting with a circus
worker, and we "know" he's feeling sexually frustrated. Still later,

we see him surprising Loretta with a staked-out area for a new house, and we "know" that he is again feeling domestic and willing to please.

Published statistics are another familiar type of telling fact. *Harper's* magazine has for the past few years published a page of facts like the following at the beginning of every issue:

- Number of Iranian tanks that Iraq has captured and sold back to Iran: 150
- Total U.S. aid to Iowa farmers in 1986: $3,700,000,000
- Percentage of 18- to 24-year-old whites who voted in congressional elections in 1986: 22
- Percentage of 18- to 24-year-old blacks who voted: 25
- Portion of immigrants to the United States who settle in California: ¼
- Estimated number of babies sold in Naples, Italy, each year: 600
- Average price of a baby sold there: $40,000
- Number of cheerleaders in the United States: 600,000
- Percentage of recruited student athletes at Division 1 NCAA universities who graduate: 67
- Percentage of all students at those universities who graduate: 59
- Telephone calls made and received by Twentieth Century Fox chairman Barry Diller each day: 150

In a speech reprinted on page 233 of this book, Kathleen Hall Jamieson rightly warns us against being too easily persuaded by such telling statistics. But they undeniably provoke thought and by doing so encourage both writer and reader to look more deeply into the matter being statistically described.

Readers, no less than filmgoers or statistics collectors, appreciate facts that carry a clear message. Ken Macrorie calls these "telling facts" (32).[2] Others call them "telling" or "revealing" or "significant" details. If you become able—after this chapter, or by the end of this course—to find telling facts and use them in your writing, you will have mastered one of the most difficult skills (and the one requiring the most thought) in the art of writing. Decide now that you're willing to spend the time necessary to understand, collect, and use these telling facts. Here's a start.

Recalling and Writing Telling Details

Exercise 2-1

Think back to the home you grew up in. Write down some detail from your

---

[2] My second parenthetical reference in this chapter contains only a page number, not the name of the author, because I've already mentioned the name of the author in my sentence. Full details of the Modern Language Association guidelines for parenthetical references and for making up a works cited list are given in Chapter 10, "Research in the Library."

kitchen or attic or basement that would, by itself, give your teacher and class some idea of the character of either your father or your mother. Your response might be a single sentence, or two or three. Now compare your results with those of other people in the class (either by being called on in class or, in your next class, by checking a list selected by your teacher).

Have some of you succeeded in using a fact or detail to give us an idea of a parent's character? Be strict in your standards—you have nothing to lose if you don't succeed now, but you have everything to lose if you don't learn through your mistakes. Here are a few successful examples:

- One corner of our basement is a large paneled room with three fluorescent lights hanging from the ceiling and plenty of three-pronged outlets.
- As you walk through the living room into the kitchen, immediately you see the table set with four places, just as a top restaurant might look. It's only 3:30 in the afternoon.
- Opening the refrigerator door is always an adventure. On the top shelf are full and not so full cans of Miller Lite and Diet Coke. On the next, there are fifteen or twenty Tupperware containers which offend your nose if you peek into them. Hamburger expected to be cooked for dinner nights ago sits on the shelf slowly turning brown. The freezer looks like a perfect place for cross-country skiing.

This kind of success is rare. You'll undoubtedly find as you read each other's samples that details haven't come easily, and they haven't because there are two other ways to describe that come to the mind and to the pen much more readily.

There are three ways to describe a person or a place: by suggesting a *comparison,* by stating a *quality,* or by giving a *detail.* Comparisons can be helpful. The cross-country skiing comparison above gives us a vivid picture of a freezer in trouble, but comparisons do not always convey a clear image to a reader:

- As I entered the basement, I felt as if I were entering a dentist's office.
- Our kitchen looks like it came out of a magazine.

Stating a quality (through an adjective) comes most easily to us, but it is least helpful to our readers:

- The kitchen in my present house has a tendency to be a bit *sloppy* by the end of the day.
- I have always been overwhelmed by the *strong* and *dictative* atmosphere that the basement of my house possesses.
- Our attic is *weird.*

The value of almost any piece of writing depends not on its comparisons or on its assertions of qualities but on its details. A good letter of recommendation, written for you, for example, will make a much better impression with details about your performance than with adjectives like *intelligent, serious,* or *sensitive.* Every fact included in such a recommendation reflects the writer's interpretation of your character (since it is selected from hundreds of brief encounters you've had). But readers get a much clearer picture when they're given the facts, and they enjoy drawing their own meanings from them. The facts are therefore more persuasive than opinionated adjectives. Comparisons help if carefully selected, and qualities are sometimes a useful shortcut when we're in a hurry, but by far the most effective communication is achieved through details.

Qualities, Comparisons, Details

Exercise 2-2

Look at the following notes (not yet complete sentences) toward a description of a neighborhood. Which notes are statements of quality, which are comparisons, and which are details (or telling facts)? Which do you find most effective?

> Every kid should be raised in a ghetto. Predominantly white, Irish-Catholic neighborhood with a sprinkling of a few black-haired, tanned-skinned, Italians. Something out of an Irish Soap commercial. A Black, Oriental, or Jew nowhere to be found and Protestants treated like illegal aliens. One-way street so narrow one could spit across it (popular game). Stick ball, wise ball, half ball (called hemisphere), step ball—city games—make do. 23 row houses attached one to another on both sides of a 1-way street. Unread pages of the *Philadelphia Bulletin* blowing up and down the street making the ordinary trash somewhat more intellectual. Not unlike the floor of the N.Y. stockmarket during a bull market. 45 good Catholic families who have littered the street with over 150 children. Chalk designs on the street, crying babies, fighting children while parents do some city socializing on front steps. Ice Cream and Water Ice Trucks make their respective ritualistic appearances at 9:07 and 9:35. The sound of horns blowing accompanies the youth's shouts for the money from parents. The only universal sound emanating from households is the sound of the radio's baseball broadcast.
>
> The evening ends with the last out of the ninth inning. The final roundup of camaraderie and community of purpose or maybe plight. Young and old. Sporadic crying, yelling, laughing, and coughing. No air conditioning. The heat which for 12 hours bakes the city's concrete carpeting. A night with little promise of relief.

Has the writer found enough details to begin a paper about this neighborhood?

One more point. Not all details are telling. If I were to describe the room I usually teach in by saying, "The room is painted light green," I wouldn't have told you much. You'd have a much better picture if I noted, "The paint on the back wall is peeling, the ceiling is covered with water stains, and the exposed pipes rattle every time a toilet is flushed upstairs." Telling facts are facts which *tell* a reader something. They imply more than they say.

Attempting Telling Facts

Exercise 2-3

Take five or ten minutes to try to write some telling facts. Once you have a list, offer your attempts to the class to see what they think. Are the facts offered telling? Or ho-hum? If, after hearing from others a few successful telling facts, you decide that one of yours is clearly unsuccessful, offer it to the class as an unsuccessful attempt and see whether you can explain why it doesn't succeed. You can often learn more, at this point, from failures than from successes.

Here are a few good telling facts that students have come up with during the above exercise:

- She slogged through the mud path across the main quad to her next class. *(Implication: Students don't stay on the sidewalks and the college doesn't take care to pave the most convenient student routes.)*
- My father got out of his car, stopped to pick two daffodils in the front yard, and stepped into the house. *(Implication: He has not surrendered to the pressure to rush, rush, rush through life.)*
- When the grease that coats the top of the stove is splattered, it hits all four walls of the kitchen. *(Implication: The room is small, and its cooks are sloppy.)*
- He begrudgingly agreed to lend her $2 but then found that the smallest bill he had was a twenty. *(Implication: The richer a person is, the less likely he'll be generous.)*
- When he was introduced, his handshake was firm, but his palms were damp with sweat. *(Implication: He was nervous, though pretending not to be.)*

Of course, our efforts are not always so successful. Here are a few attempts that the class decided were inadequate:

- As he walked down the street, the beer and ale called out to him from the passing restaurants and bars. *(Not a fact.)*
- Giant "Eiffel Tower" steel electric-generators stand on a sweep of smooth bright grass. *(Not focused. What implication is intended?)*
- After two drinks, she could dance a fair polka; after three drinks, she was Polish. *(The second half is not a fact.)*

- The professor's desk was piled high with dusty books and papers. *(Perhaps a telling fact, but one used so often that it has become a cliché.)*

A common type of attempt at writing a telling fact follows:

- In the attic of the house I grew up in was a box placed so high I could not examine its contents until I was 8 or 9; then I discovered it contained dozens of letters, yearbooks, corsages—all sorts of artifacts from my parents' lives. They must have kept everything!
- My mother uses her own set of kitchen knives and keeps her knives in a special drawer so that no one else can use them. To her, the art of cooking lies in the right way of cutting.

In both cases above, a strong telling fact in the first sentence is weakened by a lame explanation or comment in the second sentence. Try, for now, to resist the urge to explain. In your writing later, you will, of course, be commenting on the facts you've selected. But that commentary is relatively easy, while finding facts that can convince is much more difficult. If you want to learn to be a good writer, you have to learn to *earn* the right to make a comment by starting with well-chosen details.

Writing Telling Facts from Direct Observation

Exercise 2-4

Coming up with a telling fact is difficult—thinking specifically is difficult—it means clearing out the cobwebs. But it's also difficult because so far you've been trying to recall telling facts rather than write them from observation. Telling facts are easier to collect than to recollect. So for homework for the next class, stop somewhere to observe for a while—allow yourself at least an hour—and write out five telling facts to bring to class. (It should be clear by now that the word *fact* is not limited to statistics; a fact is anything that can be observed.)

You can check your ability to find these telling facts by comparing yours, in your next class, with those of your classmates. One effective way to compare notes is to divide into groups of three or four in which you decide on the group's best five and worst five telling facts. Once a group has come to a decision, it can rejoin the class and read the facts chosen randomly. The class may then vote whether each example is or is not a telling fact. The class should vote the facts "telling" (when they have clear implications) or "boring" (when they call forth only a "so what" response). Finally, you might hand your facts in to your teacher to get a more experienced opinion.

Writing is never excellent or weak except in relation to whom we're writing for. Therefore, deciding whether a fact is telling or boring will always vary somewhat from person to person. Our response to any writing is colored by our past experience and our past reading, and in no two cases will that experience be identical. In the most extreme cases, some of us may miss the point of a telling fact because we're not at all familiar with the subject. But the experience of people living in the same culture is usually similar enough that your class will reach consensus about which facts are telling and which are not.

Many facts that a writer uses do their work (like supplying useful background information for a reader) without calling attention to themselves as telling facts. But telling facts are always worth striving for. The quest for them will keep any writer—a professional writer, a student A-writer, or a student D-writer—challenged while working on any writing assignment. Every paper needs strong details to support and explain its purpose. *No amount of correct or clever writing can substitute for a mass of telling facts in helping a writer achieve his or her ends.* If you didn't come up with five good facts the first time you tried for homework, try the same exercise again until you're more comfortable with selecting and writing them. Force yourself to sit quietly in a busy place and observe. Once you get the knack for finding telling facts, all your writing will be easier and more effective.

When we prepare well for writing, we first gather facts from observation (of places, people, books, newspapers, films) and then come to interpretations of the facts we've gathered. Sometimes, though, we write because we already have an interpretation, or opinion, that we want to get across. In such a case, we too often rely on our memory rather than firsthand observation to back up our opinions. And our memory offers, again too often, only vague recollections, as in one of the sentences that introduced this chapter:

- I have met some interesting people, and some not so interesting people.

We can't let sentences like that quit. They remain opaque to the reader, and three or four in succession, or six out of eight, will put the reader to sleep.

Searching for Telling Details in the Writing of Others

Exercise 2-5

Search the following passage for genuine details. Note where the writer has allowed herself to be satisfied with vague recollections.

> Some girls join sororities to increase their social interests, but a smart
> girl joins for a chance to better herself. She comes to the sorority to
> escape the anonymity of a large university. She works to become a
> person, an identity with feelings, instead of number 000-11-7777.
> Living with a large group of girls, she becomes more aware of others'
> wants and needs. By working with others, she learns to express her
> ideas and interests and become a leader. The sorority gives her the
> opportunity to work with the underprivileged and the disabled,
> helping her to grow mentally. As she works to become a part of the
> sorority, she grows stronger as an individual. With the support of the
> other members, she is fulfilled by the increase in her self-image.

There's a lot of feeling in this passage, but the message that gets through
to the reader is muddy. Don't let yourself be satisfied with such careless,
undetailed writing.

To see how you can build an essay out of specific details, you
might try, at this point, to write a description of a place that you think is
worth trying to understand better (see Assignment 1 in Chapter 14).
When I say "description," I don't want your mind to leap immediately to
"beauty." There's no point in writing fantasy like the following:

> My first glimpse of the beach was from a distance. I was standing on
> a hill gaping at what seemed to me the perfect beach. The scenic
> view looked like it belonged in a travel agency poster. There was a
> thick grove of coconut palms and a strip of virgin white sand that
> separated the trees from the deep blue Caribbean Sea.

You'll miss the whole point of a description assignment if you aim for
beauty. When you write a description, you should be aiming *not for
beauty but for honesty.*

```
DESCRIPTION ≠ BEAUTY

DESCRIPTION = HONESTY
```

What is your place really like? What makes it distinctive? How do people
use it? Places are distinctive—and thus worth writing about—only because people have made them so. People have conceived them, built
them, and perhaps neglected them. Now other people frequent them, or
pass by them, as quickly as possible. How? Why?

Your raw material for any description paper will be telling facts
that you collect by observing, patiently observing. Here is part of what
one student saw when she took a pencil and notebook to the back room of
a veterinarian's office where she had formerly worked as a receptionist:

The back room is filled with cages lining all four walls, stacked three and four cages high. The "E. E. box" (excremental exercise box), otherwise simply known as "the box," takes up most of the area in the middle of the room. Looking into the box, you can usually see one or two dogs curiously sniffing the urine-soaked newspapers. In one corner of the room, between two walls of cages, is a stack of donated newspapers which are constantly in use. Another corner has three steps leading up to the rear exit. Next to the rear door are stacked cases of various prescription dog food, sometimes stacked 6 to 7 feet high. At the bottom of the steps is a trashcan used to hide euthanized animals, each one placed in a trash bag, until they can be properly disposed of. In a third corner is a bathtub for bathing cats and dogs. Sticky jugs of flea shampoo are placed at random on the floor around the tub. Behind the tub is a concealed lavatory. The door to this 4- by 5-foot room rests on its lower hinges. Inside the lavatory, a dusty toilet with a cracked seat and no lid is camouflaged by more cases of prescription dog food, as well as cat food. A window fan, in the same tiny room, slowly rotating in a breeze of muggy summer air, is temporarily placed in the window above the toilet.

The writer's fresh interpretation of these details and others will of course be an important part of the paper she finally writes. But her interpretations will fall flat for the reader unless she has amassed many details like these to begin with. As we collect these telling details, we come to recognize meaning in the most ordinary details of our lives. When we include them in our writing, we offer the same pleasure of recognition to our readers.

This habit of observing patiently, of respecting what facts can tell us, and of seeking out the facts that resonate most will make all your paper writing more successful. Observation, after all, is not only useful in describing objects. When we read a book well, we underline various words, sentences, and paragraphs. By doing so, we implicitly acknowledge that these are telling words, telling sentences, telling paragraphs. They express, in miniature, much more than they actually say. If you were writing a paper on, say, Bob Woodward's *The Secret Wars of the CIA* (1987), you'd want to look back at your carefully observed underlinings to find telling quotations to use in your review. If you were to interview a woman in a nursing home, you would observe carefully how she acts and what she says. Some of how she looks would be telling; you'd be sure to include those details. Some of what she says would also be telling; you'd of course include that too. By seeking out telling facts and then drawing responsible inferences (conclusions) from them, you would be likely to write a fresh, honest, thoughtful paper.

Research of all kinds, then, is simply a form of observation, selected observation. The same keen observation, the same research methods, apply in analyzing a place, a person, a book, a table of statistics, a film, a magazine, a newspaper. It takes practice in each form of observation to look through the raw material and find what's significant, what's thought-provoking, what's of human interest. It takes practice in each to find the telling facts, and to determine the meanings that those telling facts reveal. Collecting information of any kind requires patience. You don't always find what you want right away. But the patient exploration the writer goes through each time follows the same pattern. And once you're confident that you can find evidence, you'll never again have to sit at your desk for hours staring at a blank page and worrying about how you're going to fill it.

Work at noticing telling facts until you can select them almost instinctively. Our ability to write telling facts is a reflection of our ability to discriminate, to select, to distinguish meaning from the lack of it. A couple of years ago, I was talking in the hall with a student who was trying to decide whether to take my section of English 101 or someone else's. Another student in the hall saw us talking and interrupted, "Are you taking his class? If you do, you should know—he likes details." That's a rumor I'd be happy to help spread. Telling details are the foremost tools of photographers, filmmakers, fiction writers, informative writers, persuasive writers, thoughtful writers—anyone who wants to get a point across economically and vividly.

3

Facts, Inferences, and Theses

As in other sciences, so in geography, careful, systematic, direct observation and description are preliminary to, and necessary for, any classification and explanation that may follow. The geographer in his study of any region, therefore, first of all systematically observes and records, usually onto a map, the patterns and arrangements of natural and cultural features. The second step, following observation and description, is the search for explanations as to why the region is as it is.

Vernor Finch and Glenn Trewartha

Most people would rather die than think, and most people do.

Bertrand Russell

Exercise 3-1
Review

Before starting this chapter, write out brief answers to the following questions:

1. What is an inference?
2. What is the difference between a fact and an inference?
3. What is a thesis statement?

You'll remember better the principles of this chapter if at the end of the chapter you come back and check what you've learned against these original opinions.

Inferences

As much as I have emphasized facts so far, I don't mean to suggest that facts are to be used by a writer without analysis, without commentary, without conclusions or judgments that the writer draws from those

24

facts. (It is an insecure lawyer or manager who stuffs a chaotic pile of facts into a brief or a report in the hope that some of the facts might convince.) We build a paper out of facts, but the resins that hold a paper together are the *inferences* that we can draw from the facts we put on paper. Inferences, I know, is a word that you either haven't heard before or are a little fuzzy about. You don't hear it much in everyday conversation—we take inferences for granted. But drawing careful inferences is crucial to becoming a good writer.

An inference is a judgment based on at least one fact. You drew inferences in Chapter 2 whenever you decided what you thought a telling fact "meant." Inference is very closely related to a much more commonly used term, implication. When a writer uses a telling fact—"Most of the people who fill the university's trash baskets are white, but most of those who empty them are black"—she is *implying* that there is some injustice here. When you or I read the same telling fact, we are likely to *infer* that there is some injustice. We're both going in the same direction—*from* the fact *toward* the idea of injustice—but the word used to describe the writer's action is *imply,* and the word used to describe the reader's action is *infer.* This chart may help:

S. I. Hayakawa, in *Language in Thought and Action,* has explained inferences so clearly that I'll call on him here to help me (41)[1]:

> An inference...is a *statement about the unknown made on the basis of the known.* We may *infer* from the material and cut of a woman's clothes her wealth or social position; we may *infer* from the character of the ruins the origin of the fire that destroyed the building; we may *infer* from a man's calloused hands the nature of his occupation; we may *infer* from a senator's vote on an armaments bill his attitude toward Russia; we may *infer* from the structure of the land the path of a prehistoric glacier; we may *infer* from a halo on an unexposed photographic plate that it has been in the vicinity of radioactive materials; we may *infer* from the sound of an engine the condition of its connecting rods. Inferences may be carelessly or carefully made. They may be made on the basis of a broad background of previous experience with the subject matter, or no experience at all. For example, the inferences a good mechanic can make about the inter-

---

[1] Now that you're in the habit of checking the Works Cited list on pages 360–366 when you see a number like this in parentheses, I'll stop offering you reminders. This is your last footnote.

nal condition of a motor by listening to it are often startlingly accurate, while the inferences made by an amateur (if he tries to make any) may be entirely wrong. But the common characteristic of inferences is that they are statements about matters which are not directly known, statements made on the basis of what has been observed.

Drawing inferences responsibly is a very important thinking skill. In this chapter, you'll practice "drawing" several kinds of inferences from several different kinds of facts.

Geologists and archaeologists are masters at drawing inferences. Most of the Western world in the eighteenth century believed that Noah, about 3000 B.C., had built an ark and survived a forty-day flood. Then James Hutton in the 1780s discovered clam fossils embedded in the granite of Scotland's mountains. Thinking about the fact of the embedded fossils, Hutton inferred that much of Scotland was at one time under water—not 5000 years earlier, as the biblical story of Noah suggested, but perhaps 6 million years earlier. Hutton's inference was a bold one in 1785, but much evidence discovered since his time has supported his claim (McPhee, *Basin and Range* 91–108). Geologists look at surviving artifacts from millions of years ago and try to interpret them, try to draw reasonable inferences from them.

Archaeologists work the same way. They sift through the remains of more recent times, the times since the human race made its appearance. Their method of working is well described by Craig Stoltz (3):

> Professor Joe Dent arrives to the first meeting of "Archaeology 451" with a plastic trash bag slung over his shoulder. He grabs the bag by the corners and shakes its contents onto the floor: several institutional memos, a Mozart Festival brochure, a Coke can. A small paper envelope imprinted with the name of an English industrial archaeology museum, a "Dear Friend" direct mail piece from an historical society, a black plastic cannister the size of a thread spool. A cellophane pipe tobacco packet, a twisted pipe cleaner, flecks of charred tobacco, and a scattering of papers, some handwritten, others typed, a few dittoed. Some are balled up.
>
> "This," says Dent, spreading the mess around with his foot, "is what archaeologists deal with—garbage." He's dumped onto the teacher's platform what has accumulated in his trash can since 7:30 that morning. The students of Archaeology 451 don't say much, but just look at the trash, their pens poised at their notebooks. They had planned on merely taking notes. "So what does this garbage tell us?" Dent asks. "Anything?" We begin to speculate, carefully at first. That Dent doesn't like classical music. No, that he doesn't like Mozart. Maybe he doesn't read brochures. Well, maybe he *reads* them but doesn't *keep* them. He's literate, we guess. He has a mild addiction to caffeine. No, practically everybody drinks Coke. At least he's not a

health nut—he smokes. But a pipe. A clean pipe. *Was* dirty, though. Probably a tourist type, with a decent camera. Those balled up papers—he has a temper. Or was bored. Maybe shoots baskets. Maybe shares an office. Or someone else put that trash in his can.

We continue for twenty minutes or so, leaping from fact to rickety inference, back to solid fact, on to other facts. Valid inferences, we find, are hard to draw: each must be checked in relation to other facts and inferences. After twenty minutes of pawing and grabbing, we know little about the man behind the garbage. Even this morning's trash, it turns out, doesn't yield many answers.

Archaeologist that he is, Dent has also brought in some "real" artifacts—the kind we'd planned on taking notes about. One is what we call an "arrowhead" of brown stone (later, we'll learn to call such things "projectile points"); another is an axe head the size of an open hand, a smooth finger-wide groove dividing it in two. Dent claims these are garbage too—cultural discards—but harder than fresh trash to draw inferences from: there are no other items with which to associate them. There is also a rectangular stone slab a-foot-and-a-half long and three-inches thick, half of its top face chipped an inch deep. This artifact has proved very difficult indeed to make assumptions about, Dent reports—to date, nobody has been able to figure out what it might have been used for. Such an item is known in archaeologist parlance as a "FRGOK": Funny Rock—God Only Knows.

"The archaeologist's real problem," Dent says, nodding back at the fresh trash scattered on the floor, is that "over time, almost everything disappears." If this trash were dumped outside, the paper and tobacco would decompose in a month; the plastic and metal would get kicked around, eventually buried, and biodegraded within a few hundred years. Even the gray plastic trash bags, always a target of angry environmentalists who complain that plastic lasts forever, would disintegrate within a millennium or two. So when archaeologists apply what may seem absurd scrutiny to chunks of stone, says Dent, holding the Funny Rock in his arms, it is not because they think these are the most telling cultural remains. They are not. It's because, most of the time, that's all a prehistoric culture has left behind. The rest has rotted away.

Drawing Inferences from Observed Facts

Exercise 3-2

Your teacher may not be so accommodating as to bring in the garbage, but a memorable way to practice drawing inferences is to draw them from the objects on your teacher's office desk, or from the notes on his or her monthly calendar, or from the contents of his or her pockets, purse, briefcase, or bookbags. Every item you note (e.g., an American Express card) is a fact from which you may draw a timid inference ("she doesn't like to carry lots of money with her") or a bold inference ("she's rich") or even— we hope—a responsible inference somewhere between those two.

It will help you sort things out in your mind when doing this exercise if you make a list down the left-hand side of a piece of paper of the items you've observed:

- a "J.C. Penney" tag
- five pens
- a pocket dictionary
- wire-rim glasses

Then, as you draw inferences, list those inferences opposite the facts with arrows between them:

- a "J.C. Penney" tag → doesn't spend much money on clothes
- five pens ——————→ writes a lot
- a pocket dictionary → not sure about how to spell
- wire-rim glasses ——————→ went to school during the 1960s

When you draw these inferences, do you have full confidence in them? What other facts would help you feel more sure?

At this point you should be noting that some of your inferences are timid and some are bold, that inferences with several facts behind them are more secure, that the inferences you can draw will differ from those of others because you start from different assumptions or you know more about a given subject. Most important, though, you should feel in your bones that from now on you can distinguish a fact from an inference. If you're ever confused in the future, all you have to remember is that all those things from the purse or pockets were facts. All the things you said about your teacher were inferences. When you've exhausted your teacher's patience with your "bold" inferences, do the same exercise with a volunteer student's backpack, or pair off with another student in the class and see how well you can infer things about each other using the objects each of you carries around.

Drawing Inferences from Statistics

Exercise 3-3

Now try the same exercise with a more revealing (or is it a less revealing?) kind of fact—statistics. The following is a breakdown of types of ads in two different magazines. Use Tables 3-1 and 3-2 (one at a time) to draw as many inferences as you can about the audience—in terms of age, sex, mar-

TABLE 3-1   Magazine 1   February 1988
Statistical Chart of Ads ¼ Page or Larger

Product Type	Full-Page Ads	Half-Page Ads
Cigarettes	11	
Public Utilities	2	
Cameras	3	
Beer/Liquor	4	2
Public Service	1	1
Food/Drink	18	4
Automobiles	12	
Health Care	5	5
Hair Care	20	6
Books	1	2
Bus/Railroad	2	
Insurance/Bank	8	1
Cosmetics	12	
Education	2	2
Computers and Electronic Products	2	
Airlines	3	
Home Care	2	1
Armed Forces	3	
Baby Products	1	
Clothes	3	
American Ass. of Retired People	1	
Magazines	2	2

TABLE 3-2   Magazine 2   February 1988
Statistical Chart of Ads ¼ Page or Larger

Product Type	Full-Page Ads	Half-Page Ads
Automobiles	2	
Public Utilities	4	
Airlines/Airports	7	
Hotels	4	18
Car Rental	5	4
Resorts	9	19
Computer Products	5	3
Luggage	1	2
Books	2	1
Food/Drink		1
Internal Revenue Service		1
Business Services	1	12
Conservation Societies		2
Public Service		4
Insurance/Bank	2	
Education	1	8
Jewelry		1
Furniture		1
Harmonica		1
Real Estate	10	2
Medical Insurance or Services	3	1
Ports/Cities/Counties	4	5
Entertainment/Dining		3

riage status, interests, and occupations—at which the magazine is aimed. Compare your results with those of the rest of the class, note what assumptions or background information led you to your inferences, and note whether your inferences tend to be bolder or more timid than those of your classmates.

You might want to guess what each magazine was; your teacher, by checking with the Instructor's Manual for this book, can tell you at the end of your discussion. You will have noticed again that some inferences made by your classmates are bold, some timid. Those who tend to draw timid inferences should try to take greater risks, to think a bit harder before writing. Those who tend to draw bold inferences need to seek out more evidence to justify the leap that they are asking their readers to make.

Combining Inferences into a Thesis

Exercise 3-4

For more practice in drawing inferences, this time noting how they can enable you to structure a paper, take a look at the photograph on the opposite page. Imagine that you are an archaeologist living in the year 2500, and you have found this photograph (see fig. 3-1) buried in a pile of rubble along the shores of the Gulf of Mexico. As a class, examine the photo in detail, and begin to list details—not judgments—about the picture along the left side of a sheet of paper. Once the class has noted ten or fifteen details, put on the right side of your paper, opposite each detail, any conclusions that you feel the detail might justify. Again, you're drawing inferences from the facts (details) you've noted. Once the right side of your paper is pretty full, describe at the bottom of your sheet the overall impression that you think the photographer of this picture was trying to get across. What do you think the purpose of the picture was?

You'll find, I think, that your interpretation of the photographer's purpose (i.e., your thesis) will be some kind of summation, or summation with qualification, of the inferences that you've listed on the right side of your paper. If you were to write out an analysis of this picture at this point, it would most naturally begin with a sentence stating the purpose of the picture, and that sentence would be substantiated by a listing (perhaps with some explanation) of some of the details you first put down on the left side of the page.

This exercise should help you see how most papers take shape. Your research begins with an examination of details, and yet your papers begin at the opposite end of the fact/inference/thesis sequence, with a summary of your inferences (a thesis).

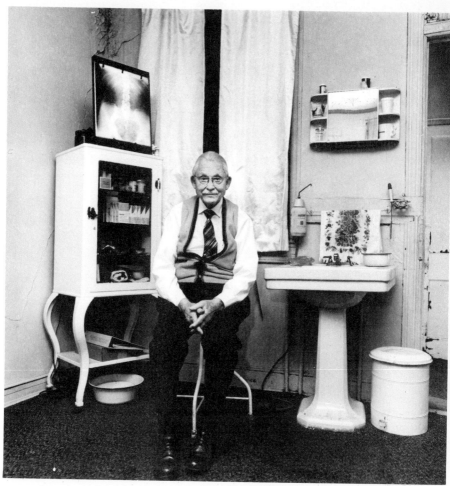

© *Joan Clark Netherwood, 1979*

Drawing Inferences and a Thesis from a Text

Exercise 3-5

You have practiced drawing inferences from objects you can see, from statistics, and from details in a photograph. Now you'll practice on the most
common type of information that writers draw inferences from—writing itself. Read the following advertising flyer that my sister-in-law found on her
car windshield in a shopping mall parking lot (I have changed the name
and location of the advertiser to preserve her anonymity).

  Your goal in this exercise is to come to some judgment about what kind of a person you think Sister Rebecca is. To prepare to make that judgment, draw any inferences about Sister Rebecca that you can from this flyer. Either circle your evidence and draw an arrow to the margin where you write your inference, or make a list like those you've been making in earlier exercises, with facts (in this case, words) on the left and inferences opposite on the right. Then, after looking over your facts and your inferences, write a sentence or two conclusion (thesis) giving your judgment of Sister Rebecca's character.

ESP
Reader and Advisor
Sister Rebecca

I will tell you your troubles and what to do about them. Don't let   1
other people confuse or mislead you. God helps all those who want to
help themselves. Through SISTER REBECCA all things are possible with
God's help on earth. I will show it to you! Advice on all affairs of life.

The Religious Holy Woman healer, God's messenger who will heal   2
the sick and the ailing, and remove all suffering and bad luck from your
body. She will call your enemies by name and tell you who to keep away
from. She is a religious and holy woman who will show you with your
own eyes how she will remove sorrow, sickness, pain and all bad luck.
What your eyes see your heart must believe. The touch of her hand will
heal you.

SISTER REBECCA has the God-given Power to Heal by Prayer. Are   3
you suffering? Are you sick? Do you need help? Do you have bad luck?
Are you unhappy, unlucky, and unable?

See SISTER REBECCA today. She guarantees to reunite the sepa-   4
rated and solemnly swears to heal the sick, and help all who come to her
and remove all evil spells. *She restores lost nature.*

She guarantees to cure you where others have failed. Will take the   5
sickness and pain away from you. One visit will convince you that she is
God's messenger on earth. SISTER REBECCA has helped thousands and
thousands and guarantees to help you, too. SISTER REBECCA removes
all pain. This religious healer will help you where others have failed. If
you suffer from alcoholism and cannot find a cure, don't fail to see this
gifted woman who will help you.

If you have done this exercise carefully, you should be able to imagine how you might paragraph an essay about Sister Rebecca.

The body of your paper would consist of several paragraphs, each emphasizing one of Sister Rebecca's character traits—her religious views, perhaps, her business sense, her intelligence, her own emotions, and her sense
of the emotions of her readers. The topic sentence of each paragraph could
be the most thoughtful inference you could come up with in each of those
areas, and each topic sentence could be followed by several sentences
quoting passages from the flyer which serve as evidence for your inference.
With an introduction that speculates about why such businesses exist in our
society (and most others) and a conclusion that shows some concern about
the lives of both Sister Rebecca and her clients, you would have an excellent paper, solidly researched, and very well organized, based on just one
page of evidence.

Fact-Inference Pairs as a Research Tool

Exercise 3-6

The pattern of moving from facts to inferences to a thesis applies to the investigation of any kind of raw material. In this exercise, we will practice fact selecting, inference drawing, and thesis forming using newspapers as data. Have someone in the class pick up twenty to twenty-five copies (one for each member of the class) of some newspaper that you're not familiar with. Pay for your copy, and then read your paper through, thinking of yourself again as an archaeologist. Collect twenty telling facts about the paper—not the telling facts chosen by reporters to tell their stories, but facts *about* the paper itself that tell us something about the paper's intended readers. Look for evidence of at least five different kinds: (1) facts about ads or the numbers of ads; (2) facts about the types of articles included; (3) facts about the arrangement of material—articles, pictures, statistics, ads—in the paper; (4) facts about the language used in the paper (that will lead to inferences about the assumptions, style or tone of voice preferred by readers); and (5) facts about the newspaper's own use of facts and inferences—what kinds do they use? in what proportion? Look also at the issues addressed on the editorial pages, the issues addressed and the tone of voice of the letters to the editor, or at anything else that strikes you about the newspaper. Your evidence is much more varied here than in any of the exercises above. If, at first, nothing "strikes" you, compare the paper with one with which you are more familiar, and you'll more easily see distinctive features. Again, place distinctive facts about the newspaper along the left side of a sheet of paper, and put your inferences about the paper's readers opposite on the right. Here are some examples:

Facts	Inferences
The *Seattle Post-Intelligencer* prints a story of an explosion that injured three workers in an Ilwaco factory on page A-11 and reports the story matter-of-factly.	Readers probably are more proud of industrial productivity than they are alarmed about industrial accidents.
A *Baltimore Sun* headline reading "Politicians' Egos on the Line" is set in special type.	The *Sun's* readers are interested in politics, but only superficially—in things like the psyches of politicians.
The *Village Voice* contains no reference to children or schools except a full-page ad for the Macy's parade and a small ad for a dance class.	The *Voice* is not a family newspaper. The Macy's parade must be an "in" event. If readers have children, they are precocious.
All the *Village Voice* ads for beer and wine are for foreign brands.	The readers have expensive tastes and are snobbish about what they drink.

Facts	**Inferences**
The *Village Voice* contains very few furniture ads, but four full pages of J&R ads for stereos and a full page of Crazy Eddie's stereos.	Readers all have stereos, but not much furniture.
The *Rutland Herald* publishes elaborate, detailed obituaries of people from all social classes.	Many readers probably know each other. It's a close-knit community.

The first list that anyone makes is likely to have some strong elements and some weak ones, so to get help in setting standards of quality for yourself, bring your first list to class, get in a group of three or four students, and decide what are the ten best fact-inference pairs you've come up with among you. The "best" ones will include facts not everyone would have noticed and inferences not everyone would have thought of. Now that you see more clearly what constitutes "quality" in fact-inference pairs, go home and upgrade your list, keeping your best pairs and adding new ones until your list reaches twenty-five. When you come to class again, look over your list, and write out a thesis statement (a summary of the points you'd like to make) for a paper you could write if you were asked to characterize the newspaper or its audience.

Here are some sample theses:

- The Friday, September 24, issue of the *New York Post* seems to indicate that it hopes to attract a wide variety of working-class people who are delighted with controversy, who are not politically knowledgeable, and who probably commute to work.
- The *Rutland Herald* addresses a group of rural, middle-aged, middle-class readers interested not only in local news but in international conditions. The majority of the readers are probably white and Protestant, and American by birth.
- The readers of the *Village Voice* see themselves as an exclusive, "in-the-know" group. They also see themselves as the champions of minorities and as politically "hip." They are most likely not your average New Yorkers, nor would they want to be considered so.

How did these writers come up with their theses? How did you come up with yours? They noticed the kinds of inferences that come up over and over again, and their theses were summaries of those inferences.

Compare your thesis with the theses of the other students in the class. You'll be curious to see not only how your judgments differ but how complex the theses are, how specific, how clearly thoughtful.

Next, ask your classmates how they would support their theses. Tell them how you would support yours. Now you should be able to see more clearly (1) how a thesis statement should be arrived at, after consideration of the evidence, and also (2) how to use evidence to support a thesis.

Paragraphing with Facts and Inferences

Fact-inference pairs can be used not only to arrive at a thesis that you can substantiate but also to help you paragraph your paper. Any inference that you've made three or four times could serve as the topic sentence, or main point, of a paragraph. Look at your list of fact-inference pairs, and collect a group with the same inference, or similar inferences. See whether, by listing all the facts together, you can make your inference more complex or thoughtful, as did a writer who was studying a copy of *The National Enquirer*:

Facts	Inferences (in Sum)
Eleven articles about general health issues (arthritis, asthma, cancer, stress, high blood pressure, weight loss, "beating the blues," digestion, hypnotism to treat health problems)	Readers very concerned about health problems. Apparently more given to worry than to action. Especially concerned with weight loss and energy. Very sedentary. Not willing to make major changes in their habits, although perhaps willing to make minor modifications. More oriented toward cures, especially miracle cures, than prevention. Not very skeptical of inflated promises for instant relief.
Cover article is "Top Experts Reveal Easy Way to Lose Weight While You Sleep"	
Eleven ads for diet and pep pills	
No articles about exercise or nutrition (or ads for health spas or exercise programs)	
Three ads for vitamins	
Ad with the heading "Lose Pounds Fast, Lose Bulges, Bumps and Inches Instantly"	
Ad with the heading "Instant Relief for Tired Aching Feet"	
Five cigarette ads, all for light cigarettes (Virginia Slims, Golden Lights, Barclay, Marlboro Lights, Raleigh Lights)	

This writer now has a point to make (the inference) and facts to substantiate that point that will make up a solid paragraph or two.

The Vulnerability of Inferences

Inferences that we draw are never wholly reliable. You'll note that even when the members of the class are all investigating the same newspaper, each member arrives at a slightly different (in some cases even a wildly different) thesis. Using the same newspaper and the same facts, some students will label the paper conservative, and others will label it liberal. Facts, even telling facts, can't yield 100 percent certain inferences. All inferences are personal—valuable, and yet vulnerable. Nevertheless, all inferences can be made more persuasive with the help of company. An inference substantiated by five facts is more reliable than one drawn from two. That's more reason for us to develop our ability to seek out the most pertinent, most telling facts.

As we learn to draw inferences, we must learn to draw responsible inferences. As we saw with the *Harper's* statistics, we cannot complacently assume that a single fact we've presented justifies the inference we'd like to draw. Occasionally, people will come up confidently proud with a telling fact that is implicitly racist:

- The clerk wearing a yarmulke put a dollar of his customer's change into his own pocket.
- Three California farm laborers were busy picking cabbages while three Mexicans snoozed under their sombreros.

One fact does not, of course, justify a conclusion. A single fact is always at least slightly unstable: from any fact, several (more or less probable) inferences can be drawn. Since several inferences can be drawn, we see the need for additional facts to limit the number of possible inferences. If the paint on my classroom wall is peeling, for example, it could be the maintenance crew's fault, or it could be the state legislature's fault. The added detail that state funds for the university have been cut back 10 percent per year for the past seven years might help to fix the inference and the blame. The quality of an inference depends, too, on the expertise of the person making it. A crack in a basement floor means more to a groundwater geologist than it does to a new homeowner.

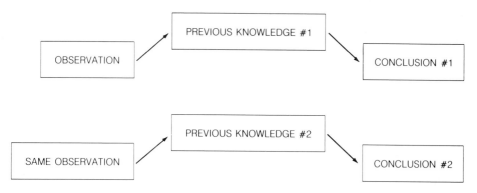

Since expertise is for the most part a matter of mastering more facts in a given area, we should be making a lifelong effort to become more expert in as many areas as possible so that we will be better able to interpret the new facts we face every day.

Just as knowledge differs from person to person and influences the inferences we draw, so do our assumptions. If, in the pocket of a married man in Exercise 3-2, three people saw a $60.00 grocery receipt, one person might infer that that man was a liberated husband, a second that he shares the grocery shopping with his wife, and a third that his wife made him go shopping this week. The first inference results from an assumption that "liberated" husbands are comfortable doing work that was traditionally expected of women. The second results from the assumption that the most shopping a husband might do is half of it. The third results from the assumption that all decisions about shopping in a marriage are made by the wife.

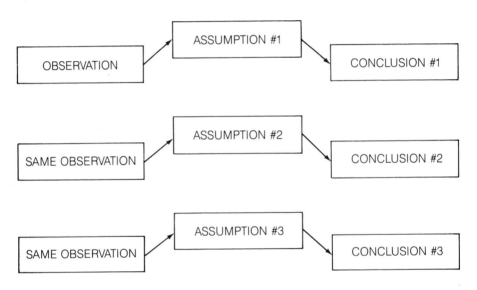

I mentioned in Exercise 3-4 that *a thesis is a summation, or summation with qualification, of inferences you've drawn about a body of material.* The qualification I mentioned there is often necessary because our inferences, like all inferences, are vulnerable. There may be evidence we haven't found yet that contradicts them. There may even be evidence that we're aware of that contradicts them.

Qualifying Inferences

Exercise 3-7

To remind yourself of the vulnerability of inferences, try this exercise. What inference, what interpretation, would we be inclined to draw from the following facts?

1. In January 1986, Mikhail Gorbachev proposed total nuclear disarmament by the year 2000.
2. The Central Committee of the Soviet Union's Communist Party passed a broad economic reform package in June 1987, giving up much of its total control over the Soviet economy.
3. Gorbachev took a number of steps in 1987 toward greater democracy and freedom of speech in the Soviet Union.
4. Gorbachev signed an Intermediate-Range Nuclear Forces (INF) agreement with the United States in December 1987 to destroy all intermediate-range nuclear missiles in Europe.
5. While he was in the United States to sign the nuclear missile treaty, Gorbachev agreed to release forty to fifty dissidents.

Should we be willing to write a paper using just these facts as evidence? What kinds of facts should we look for to more fully support our interpretation?

What if, as we search for more support, we also find evidence to contradict our interpretation? For example, that:

1. Intermediate-range missiles constitute only 4 percent of the world's nuclear arsenal.
2. The Soviet Union still has tens of thousands of dissidents that it will not allow to emigrate.
3. The Soviet occupation of Afghanistan continues.

What should we do about this evidence?

Often, when you have accumulated fact-inference pairs and you are eager to start drafting or even to turn your paper in, you'll realize that your inferences are still vulnerable and that your integrity and your desire for success demand that you search out a few more facts. Honesty is not always the best policy in life. But it is almost always the best policy in writing. If you concede that some evidence exists that complicates your position, your readers are much more likely to respect your position—and your intelligence—than they are if you naively ignore opposing evidence. Qualified inferences respond to readers' questions before they raise them.

Substantiating Assertions

You should see easily now that every assertion that we make imposes upon us a responsibility to substantiate it. When we make any assertion—*Tanya is a liar,* or *nuclear reactors are dangerous,* or *Napoleon Duarte is a dictator*—we usually make it because we've heard someone in our family, or on the news, make the same assertion. Too easily, we accept these assertions, these inferences, as facts. But any written asser tion is incomplete (and in most cases ineffective) until it is substantiated by facts. Substantiating our assertions is an acknowledgment that justice is more important than our desires.

Exercise 3-8

Look, one at a time, at the following list of reckless assertions. As a class, try to find four or five specific examples, specific details, that would substantiate these assertions so they would look less reckless. Note that when extreme assertions are made, evidence can easily be found both for and against them.

1. _____ is a racist campus.
2. There's no racism any more at _____.
3. The automobile is wrecking American life.
4. The automobile has finally made life worth living.
5. Men don't do their share of work in this society.
6. Men have far more responsibility than women in this society.
7. Young people are more ethical than old people.
8. Young people should learn from their elders.
9. *Fatal Attraction* (or a movie of your choice) was a great movie.
10. *Fatal Attraction* (or a movie of your choice) was a terrible movie.
11. Living in the suburbs is like not living at all.
12. The best American life is to be found in the suburbs.
13. Criminals commit crimes not because they are bad but because they've been injured by their families or society.
14. Criminals should be shot.

You'll now see that a reckless assertion is an insufficiently substantiated inference. Through this exercise you'll be learning to reveal yourself less recklessly in your own writing.

Facts and inferences are the building blocks of our writing skills. Any set of facts will yield at least slightly different inferences to every different writer. No two of us have the same experience, and our experience colors all our inferences. Nor do we share the same assumptions, which also color our inferences. We can thus *guarantee* that anything anyone writes—unless it copies both facts and inferences from another writer—is original. So don't waste any time worrying about whether or not your writing is original. At the same time, it will be pretty clear to others—to your teacher, and to your classmates—if you steal the inferences of someone else (whether a friend, or an expert you know, or an author). They won't carry your voice. They won't *sound like* your inferences. You'll of course borrow facts from other people. Facts are in the public domain. None of us can be expected to verify every fact we learn from others. But the inferences we make must remain our own. What we call intelligence in a person consists primarily of the facts at that person's command along with the thoughtfulness of the inferences that he or she consistently derives from those facts.

We are often advised by textbooks to write by starting with a subject (say, the automobile), trying to decide on an idea about the subject (say, "the automobile is harming American life"), then "factoring" that idea into at least three parts (say, "the automobile is harming American life by polluting our cities, by distracting our 16-year-olds from their studies, and by distracting all of us from walking through our neighborhoods and talking to people"), and finally trying to substantiate each of those ideas with facts and examples. This method of finding a thesis and then a factored thesis is a good place to start if we are writing an essay exam, the purpose of which is to show someone what we already know about a subject. But if we're examining any subject seriously, we're on very shaky ground when we start to write with "ideas." Most often, our ideas on sex roles, dorm life, gun control, automobiles, and other such issues are half-baked (more often quarter-baked) and based on the reflected opinions of parents and newscasters. The "ideas" we write down are surprisingly seldom our own, and surprisingly often contrary to our own feelings. Thesis statements cast in stone before a writer begins research and writing are dangerous invitations to muted or biased observation. And so we shouldn't allow ourselves to write "ideas," or theses, until they are earned with sufficient evidence. The first step in any assignment should be a search for the facts, the pertinent facts, the telling facts. Every fact you write down triggers an inference, which in turn may remind you that you have other facts at your disposal. And then the implications of those facts, in sum, will lead to an idea, a thesis, a proposition, that will always be more responsible than one arrived at through a deskbound search for an appropriate "topic" for a paper.

I'll be giving you a great deal of advice in this book about what you should take *out* of your prose. Now you know what you should put in— carefully selected facts and sound, thoughtful inferences.

4

Writing for a Reader

A reader doesn't read from an insatiable need to applaud.

source unknown

I now think more about the people reading my paper and try to make it so that it would sound clear to them. Before I used to write unspecific things because I expected people to know already what I was talking about.

student

The most important thing I learned in this course was not to be a "selfish" writer.

student

A good piece of writing closes the gap between you and the reader.

Linda Flower

Exercise 4-1
Review

Your interest in the issues raised in this chapter will be greater if you take a few minutes to respond to these two very different requests:

1. Describe two or three examples of a tone of voice that gets on your nerves.
2. List anyone who has ever read anything you have written.

Developing an Honest and Recognizable Voice

At least half the time that we pick up a book, we soon wish we hadn't bothered, as we are forced to try to digest statements like this one at the beginning of a book I bought to learn more about China:

> Right-wing disbelief and hostility or unreadiness to think or listen one
> can comprehend. It is part and parcel of a more or less coherent
> lengthy process of ideological socialization (Worsley 15).

Unfortunately, it is easy to see how such books come into being. The first drafts of our student works are all too often no more helpful than the sentence above:

> Stacey is my roommate at my dorm Queen Ann. I thought I would
> write about her because she is a wonderful person. We have a great
> deal of fun in anything we do. We help each other out if we have
> any problems. Our study habits are about the same. We get our
> studying done before we do anything else. Stacey and I have the
> same taste in just about everything. It's a nice feeling when you can
> relate and trust a person as I do Stacey.

Or, when we're asked to write a paper about a subject we know well, we deliver something like:

> The general notion of gymnastics brings to mind flips and swings on
> various apparatus. There exist various imposed requirements within
> men's and women's gymnastics which reflect the differences of these
> two sports. It is these requirements which make up the very essence
> which separates men's gymnastics from women's gymnastics. The diffi-
> culty of a woman's routine is set by a minimum requirement of one su-
> perior and two medium skills. Other skills are required for a routine, but
> they hold no difficulty value. The context of men's gymnastics is em-
> phasized by the philosophy that a man will be strong, forceful and fluid.
> The framework of men's gymnastics is built on these concepts and dic-
> tates a design such that the aspects of strength and swing can be
> stressed. These differences go beyond the superficial individuality of
> each event, and we can see that each sport seems to stress different
> points. It is this concept which indeed accounts for the wide differences
> between men's and women's gymnastics.

As Faulconbridge complains early in Shakespeare's *King John*, "Zounds, I was never so bethumped with words" (2.1.466). These passages fail, I'm afraid, to meet the standard for good writing established by the British Admiralty Pilots during World War II: "It should be intelligible to a tired man reading in a bad light."

Ken Macrorie has called the type of writing in the above examples "Engfish." One of my students who misheard the term calls it "Inkfish." Either is a good name for murky, bloated, pretentious language that results when a writer hasn't remembered that the job of a writer is to communicate. Swamped by writing like this, no wonder professors and students alike despair over the future of the written word. Writing like this keeps authors busy and paper companies solvent, but it communicates very little, and it enhances our lives not at all. When a television show doesn't tell us anything, we often sit and watch anyway because the flicker of light is calming. But when a writer doesn't tell us anything, we drop the book and fall asleep, because a printed page, as a printed page, is tiring. Many of us have self-destructively given up on books, not because books are incapable, even in this computer and television age, of entertaining us, informing us, and making us more human, but because we're not careful enough to be selective—to read only the best, and to avoid books published because an issue is temporarily popular or because (in school) a certain body of material, say, introductory psychology, needs to be "covered." Writers who provide these "demand" books often don't write their best because they don't have enough time to think through their subject carefully. And when, as readers, we look into three or four dull books (often textbooks) in a row, we sometimes too easily give up on books in general.

In this writing course, and after it, try to avoid adding to our pile of unreadable writing. Take your time when you write; give the reader something for her money, something for her time, something for her effort. That something is information, news, something she didn't know before, something that will help her live the rest of her life in a better way than she has to this point. That something is not just information but also your interpretation of the information. The reader may disagree, but she can only disagree if she knows what you think and if she knows the facts that have led you to think as you do.

Writing that stands out from the morass of words like those on the second page of this chapter is writing that sounds like it is being spoken by someone. Nevertheless, most of us hold back our personalities as we write. Some of our teachers have told us to keep our selves out of our writing. But even without that advice, we often write in voiceless language out of fear of revealing too much. We don't want people to recognize what we perceive as our ignorance or our lack of confidence about what we're writing. Our caution is not without reason. When we write (or talk), we do give our readers and listeners evidence (language) that they will use, whether we like it or not, to draw inferences about us.

Drawing Inferences about Writers

Exercise 4-2

To best understand how others will draw inferences from your language, practice drawing inferences yourself about the speakers and writers of the following passages, using only their language as evidence. I suggest that you circle the words or phrases that you find telling about the authors and draw arrows to some free space where you can write your inferences.

1. C-130 rollin' down the strip.
   Airborne Rangers on a one-way trip.
   Mission unspoken, destination unknown,
   Don't give a damn if they ever come home.
   Locked and loaded, ready to kill,
   Always have and always will.
   Squeeze the trigger and let it fly,
   Hit the bastards between the eyes.
   Before he died, I heard him yell,
   "Airborne Rangers are bad as hell."
   [U.S. Army Ranger chant (Harris 4.1–4.2)]
2. The ultimate revenge in this life, I think, is to come back to your high school as its commencement speaker. Imagine. Me. Not the president of my class, not the former chairman of the Latin Scrabble Club, not the head of the Keyettes (I think it was Nancy Immler, who would never go out with me). Not Goldie Hawn, with whom I once rode to the Hot Shoppe after the Bethesda–Chevy Chase game in the back seat of Pete Oldheiser's chopped-and-lowered Buick. Not Bob Windsor, the football player. But me, from the very bottom of my class. [Carl Bernstein, coauthor of *All the President's Men,* speaking at a high school graduation (5)]
3. I have never been in a strike before. It is like looking at something that is happening for the first time and there are no thoughts and no words yet accrued to it. If you come from the middle class, words are likely to mean more than an event. You are likely to think about a thing, and the happening will be the size of a pin point and the words around the happening very large, distorting it queerly. It's a case of "Remembrance of things past." When you are in the event, you are likely to have a distinctly individualistic attitude, to be only partly there, and to care more for the happening afterward than when it is happening. That is why it is hard for a person like myself and others to be in a strike. [Meridel Le Sueur, "I Was Marching" (229)]
4. On January 1, 1967, the Supreme Court of Arkansas will for the first time in a century seat four new judges, all at once. A majority of the seven. This impending influx of the uninitiated led me, some months ago, to turn from the question I so often put to myself, "What can my country do for me?", to a different question: What can I do for these novitiates who are about to outnumber me? That reverie led to this primer. I have decided, not without diffidence, to try to say to you four the sort of thing that I wish my late colleague, Judge Frank Smith, then in his thirty-seventh year on the court, had said to me when as an infant of only thirty-seven years all told I became his devoted associate on the bench. [George Rose Smith, introducing "A Primer of Opinion Writing"]

Writing reveals our charm, our goodwill, our intelligence, but it also reveals our anger, our snobbery, our sexism, our racism. Still, you can't write well if you're afraid of what your writing will say about you. You want to write more than just gradable noise on paper. You want to get used to your voice. You want to see what your voice reveals and then—during revision—make whatever modifications you feel are necessary. Only by practice, that is, by trial, and error, and criticism of our errors, can we develop confidence and get away from the voiceless writing that plagues both student and professional writers. But the payoff is generous. Checking on and working on our voices is one of many ways in which learning to write better helps us to become more generally mature.

It is remarkably easy to slip into voiceless language. The patterns of voicelessness surround us. You'll find a ready-made guide below (*"How To"* 104):

0. integrated	0. management	0. options
1. total	1. organization	1. flexibility
2. systematized	2. monitored	2. capability
3. parallel	3. reciprocal	3. mobility
4. functional	4. digital	4. programming
5. responsive	5. modular	5. concept(s)
6. optimal	6. transitional	6. time frame
7. synchronized	7. incremental	7. projection
8. compatible	8. third generation	8. hardware (software)
9. balanced	9. state-of-the-art	9. contingency

The table above is a guaranteed Inkfish generator. Pick any three-digit number, and you have a ready-made, impressive-sounding addition to your prose:

357: parallel modular projection
502: responsive management capability
793: synchronized state-of-the-art mobility

This writing may seem ridiculous, but if you don't start now developing a voice that you trust, you may find yourself writing it in six or seven years.

Rewriting Pretentious Prose

Exercise 4-3

There are no "functional incremental time frames" in the following letter I found in the files when I took over my current job. Nevertheless, the writer has resorted to Inkfish rather than communication. See whether you can repair the damage.

Dear Dr. Washington:
Receipt of your letter of August 2, 1974, with reference to the offering of English 103 and/or 171 to Susan R. Trowbridge is hereby acknowledged.

In view of the fact that she is currently out of the country and is not expected to return until after August the 20th, pursuant to my telephone conversation with your secretary, Ann Allen, I am requesting that the deadline for my daughter be postponed until after her return to enable her to exercise her option of taking either of the courses being offered.

Thank you for the courtesies extended and for your propitious consideration of this request!

Sincerely,

George Trowbridge, Consulting Psychologist (A concerned father)

What do you think of the writer of this letter? Rewrite the letter. Show Dr. Washington that you are indeed a "concerned father" and not just a consulting psychologist trying to show off your importance.

Since I've made you so self-conscious about voice in this chapter, you're probably concerned now about what voice is your natural voice. You can't achieve that natural voice by consciously trying to achieve it, so let's get at it another way.

Timed Writing

Exercise 4-4

Take out your notebook, begin on a new page, and write for ten minutes without stopping. You can write on any subject at all, but don't let your pen stop. Consider that attempt a warm-up. Now write again for ten minutes without stopping, again writing on any topic at all. For homework this evening, write three more of these timed ten-minute writings and see what you come up with. After the writing, make a note of anything that surprises you about what you wrote. Your teacher may want to look over and comment on one of the five timed writings that you've done.

You probably feel pretty awkward writing these timed writings. But as you practice them more and more often, you will find that they do several things for you. First, they show you that you are never without words. Second, they help you realize what your natural voice is. Third, they help you realize that writing can be used as a thinking technique: when you force yourself to keep your pencil moving, you'll find thoughts coming to your mind that you had forgotten were on your mind. (When you stop to take time to write, you have stopped to take time to think.) Finally, timed writings remind you that the first words off your pen are often not the best you can do and therefore that revision is a step in writing that should never be ignored. This timed writing doesn't often result in a final version that you'd be proud to hand to a teacher, or to anyone. But it can form the *basis* of a final version that can be handed in. Once you have something written down, you can begin to choose what you want to include in a paper. The choices you make, much more than the words you put down the first time, will determine your success as a writer.

Of course, your voice will not sound the same every time you write. Sometimes you're trying to soothe the feelings of the person you're writing to. Other times you're trying to move people to act or think more like you do. A variety of (honest) voices is at your disposal. Imagine describing your first week of college to a friend, to your parents, and to your writing class. Each description (if it's good) will sound like you, but each will select different facts, make different comments, and use different language. Similarly, your history papers, your astronomy lab reports, and your ethnographic studies in psychology will all sound something like previous work in each of those areas, but they should also sound (if the professor is to take any notice of you) something like you. We are assigned many roles to play in life, but our success and our integrity depend on our ability to give each of those roles the special stamp of our own character.

Many beginning writers, afraid of their own voices, feel that they could add some pep to their writing if they could just add some kind of "style," although they don't know quite how "style" is achieved. But you can't rush the steady climb toward a style you're proud of. Your style develops as your voice develops. And your voice can be only as sophisticated as you are. The more you learn, the more experience you acquire, the more you will have to offer in your voice. In a sense, your voice is dependent on your entire education, in and out of school. The more you learn, the more confidence, authority, and life your voice will carry.

In the meantime, we can achieve the best voice we're so far capable of not by adding some sort of style to our writing, but by subtracting elements in our writing that we share with everybody else. This is why we've been told so often not to use clichés like "hit the nail on the head" or "avoid it like the plague." Our use of a cliché tells readers that we understand life as well as most people do, but it doesn't tell readers our particular point of view on life. Conventions in writing are another form of clichés:

- This paper will discuss...
- The question of mercy killing is beyond the scope of this paper...
- In conclusion...

Many of the words and phrases which come most easily off the pen are the words that we all share, the ones that are not distinctive. Pruning these clichés from our drafts leaves us with the word combinations, and the fact-inference combinations, that are our own. Such pruning is, of course, more than verbal: it includes cutting out the comfortable, conventional repetition of ideas that often passes for thinking. The conventions are comfortable, but though we have come to expect conventional prose, we are quietly disappointed every time we read it.

Using conventions is the easiest way to get through life. If we get married too young, for example, we are likely to *imitate* fatherhood or motherhood instead of being good fathers or mothers. When we imitate, we tend to imitate only the surface features of fatherhood or motherhood. There is much to be learned, to be sure, from the way others have been fathers or mothers. But if we want to be distinctively good parents, we have to do what we think is best, adjusting our behavior regularly by checking with the established patterns. The same strategy results in effective writing. We should start writing by noting what we see and by writing what we think ought to be said. Later we can fit our observations and thoughts into one of the many conventional forms we have so that readers can make use of what we've learned. But if we start with a model in our minds and not with what we want to say, we are condemned to repeating old truths and to writing voiceless papers.

Robert Pirsig, in *Zen and the Art of Motorcycle Maintenance*, describes how writing became possible for one of his students only when she came to the seemingly simple recognition that she was free to start afresh. When asked to describe her college town, Bozeman, Montana, she at first couldn't think of anything to write about.

> She was blocked because she was trying to repeat, in her writing, things she had already heard....She couldn't think of anything to write about Bozeman because she couldn't recall anything she had heard worth repeating. She was strangely unaware that she could look and see freshly for herself (186).

Edward Hyams, in *The Changing Face of Britain*, looked freshly at a 50-square-foot creature, "automan," which rolls past each of us hundreds of times daily but which few of us have taken the trouble to think seriously about:

> The cheap, private motor-car is a great boon: it gives the ordinary human being seven-league boots: in the power of movement overland he becomes a giant; but giants, of course, take up more room than people of human size. A man in movement on his feet occupies, at any given moment of time, about four square feet of surface; but an automan—that man-motor-car creature which is more or less the typical inhabitant of a modern industrial country—at any given moment occupies something like fifty square feet.
>
>   To cope with the motor car explosion and its growing place in our lives we are forced to modify the shape of our cities to suit not man, but automan...and a town designed for automan cannot become a community of men, like a village or a small town (228).

The various subjects we take while in school often ask of us the same freshness. They want us to relook at everyday items which we have come to take for granted. For example, a physics textbook asks its readers to look freshly at a fountain:

> Streams of water form graceful arches as they rise and fall into a pond at the base of a fountain. Some streams rise steeply and fall sharply back to the pond. Other streams arch gently, do not rise as high as others, but fall farther away from their sources. You can easily understand these motions if you think of all curved motion as being simply straight line motion in two directions at the same time (Murphy 108).

Writers willing to look freshly and tell truths are not condemned to rehashing the same old stories, the same old issues. We have been given plenty of working room by our writing and our nonwriting ancestors. Our bookshelves (even in the so-called nonfiction sections) teem with fictions. As a nation, as human beings, we get very much used to the fictions by which we live—fictions about the family, fictions about good and evil, fictions about government, about race, about sexuality. When we write, unfortunately, we slip more readily into those fictions than we do into truth.

If we ask our readers what they want from our writing, their answer will seldom be *finesse* or *elegance* or even *clarity* but, rather, *likeness to the truth.* When a student reads his writing class a paper about the Olympics becoming an advertising event for the "official shoes," the "official beer," and the "official deodorant" of the games, the class gives the paper high praise, and when asked why they like it, they say, "Because it's true." Such praise is praise worth aiming for. Telling the truth is a service to other human beings trying to make sense of the world. For telling the truth, they'll call you original, and they'll marvel at your thoughtful, distinctive voice.

Becoming Conscious of Our Readers

Through the discussion of voice that has introduced this chapter, you're beginning to see, I hope, that writing succeeds or fails not because of its elegance but because of the way it affects a reader. When you write, you are not showing off, you are performing a service for a reader. When you think of yourself as trying to talk to someone as you write, then you will be likely to sound like someone when you do write.

One way to begin to think more seriously about your readers is to do some analyzing of groups of readers. Assignment 2 in Chapter 14 asks you to infer, from the way a magazine you choose is written and from the kinds of ads that it includes, what kind of readers that magazine is aiming at. You can make some reasonable guesses about those readers. But your guesses are of course only inferences, and the magazine in fact will have had many readers that you did not imagine. (You know yourself from your reading experience, particularly if you are black or a woman or both, that the readers envisioned by many of the writers we read did not include yourself.)

If we use the results of such a reader analysis carelessly and assume that the group that will read our writing is homogeneous (all alike), we can easily damage both the integrity and the quality of our writing. Because when we write for a stereotyped group, as television writers guided by Neilsen ratings often do, we too easily assume that we have to write *down* to that group. Although we claim in this country to believe in democracy, as writers we easily fall into the habit of distrusting our readers. "We forever hold back, on the theory that our neighbors are not so wise or remarkable as we are" (Mitchell C1). It's easy, once you've defined your readers as "college freshmen," for example, or as "university professors," to develop contempt for that group as a whole. But if you remember that every individual in that group will be very different and that any individual in that group might be you, you will be much more likely to write well. You will write *to* people, not *down to* them. To write well, we must learn to picture a reader—not a lump of readers, but one reader (at a time) in a large and diverse group.

You can improve your sense of readers substantially if you reflect for a minute on your experience reading a magazine to infer the possible characteristics of the people who read it. You yourself, as you were reading, were not, probably, the type of reader that the writers of the articles had in mind while they wrote. If we leave the title "readers" to the original readers of the magazine, your role might be better titled "overhearer." You are reading, but you're also overhearing and judging the whole process of writing and reading.

In many papers you write for a writing class, your teacher plays a very similar overhearing role. In writing a proposal paper, for example, you are supposedly writing to someone with the power to make the change you propose, yet your teacher is overhearing and judging the whole transaction. Similarly, in the persuasion paper in Chapter 14 (Assignment 7), you are supposedly writing to the classmate whose views you want to change. But again your teacher is overhearing. (Having an overhearer is not just a characteristic of writing in school: every time you write a business letter, your boss will be a quiet, or sometimes a not so quiet, overhearer.)

Teachers are not only overhearers, though. They are often cast in the role of being readers and overhearers at the same time. When you write a place description or a newspaper analysis or a research paper or a literary critique, you are writing to your teacher both as a reader (someone who wants to enjoy reading) and as an overhearer (someone who judges the quality of your writing). When other students read your work on draft review days, they take on the same dual role. (Even this role, though, is not unusual in life. The recipients of your business letters will quite naturally be making judgments about you as a writer and about what you're trying to do even as they respond directly to your message.)

Since the readers you will be writing for in this class will most often be your teacher and your fellow students, it will help to have some idea of how your teachers and your fellow students read simultaneously as readers and overhearers. To help you, I've collected some samples:

STUDENT 1: When I read another student's paper, if the grammar (word choice and punctuation) is poor, I have to spend too much time trying to figure out what the writer is trying to say. Therefore, the majority of my time is spent reading the writer's mind and I have less time to enjoy the paper.

STUDENT 2: When reading someone's paper I can usually tell if it's going to be good by the confidence of the writer. Whether the content is interesting or boring, I can enjoy a paper whose writer has the ability to include his own style and opens with an interesting introduction. A paper that is stifled by poor grammar or is boring because of an attempt to make everything grammatically correct or to write for an audience such as teachers (using large words that are vague) is not what I consider a good paper.

STUDENT 3: When I'm reading another student's paper I know it will be a good paper if it arouses some sort of feeling or response in me (such as sympathy or anger). If a paper can get me to think about that particular subject—it's a good paper. If I have absolutely no desire to go on reading, I know something is lacking in that paper. When I get the feeling that I can't wait to find out what's going to happen but at the same time want to savor every word and never finish reading—I know that's a good paper.

TEACHER 1: I always read a paper the first time for the content only, not marking anything. I always hope to read something I didn't know, or something old said or seen in a different way. It's so disappointing when the student sticks to the obvious details, the usual arguments. It means that she only tries to be acceptable instead of challenging herself to write something alive, worth reading by someone other than the teacher.

TEACHER 2: There are papers I read with frustration and say "Oh no, not this again—I've talked about this *19* times!!" But then, others make up for it—I *do* remember what the preceding paper was like (in spite of students who call my office to say "This is Jane. Jane Doe. I'm in your

8:00 English 101 class...") and thoroughly enjoy seeing Jane working on the details or cleaning up a particular grammar problem. And then I feel an *immense* satisfaction, a simple pleasure that something is working somewhere.

TEACHER 3: I usually read through the first paragraph quickly and if it is interesting, I continue reading. If it is not interesting, I throw it aside and tell myself I'll read it later. After reading through all the essays once (for content only), I then read through critically. Even though I try to be impartial, I cannot help responding more favorably to the ones that I enjoy.

In your one-on-one conferences with your teacher this semester, you'll see how your own teacher reads. And in draft workshops, you'll learn how your own classmates read. Think about what you learn from these encounters as you write. Anticipate your readers' needs and take care of them. Anticipate their assumptions and take them into account.

A genuine feeling for one's reader works surprising transformations in a writer's prose. Most poor writers are bound inside their own heads as they write. They make no imaginative leap to their reader's point of view. They see easily that their speech is a way of communicating, because they've known that most people listen when they talk. But if they haven't written many letters, most of their writing has been for teachers, and few students have taken the trouble to try to imagine what their teachers think as they read their papers. You know that readers come to a magazine article looking for information, for surprises, for clean, clear expressions of ideas. Well, your teacher will come to your papers looking for the same things, and she'll also make some comments to help you achieve them.

One of the first things that you'll have to learn if you want to improve your writing in this course is to overcome your contempt for your teacher as a reader. None of us would admit that we have contempt for our teachers, but if we stop to consider how little effort we often put into our papers and how much effort the teacher must put into reading them, we quickly realize that we really are showing contempt when we write. Keep in mind that your teacher wants to read some good material this semester. She takes no satisfaction in being a gradable-noise grader. Teachers, like any other readers, like to be informed, and they like to learn without going to too much trouble trying to figure out what you mean. See whether you can get your teacher to enjoy reading. It may be that you can if you provide some of the things that readers and teachers look for, such as:

1. Density of details
2. Challenging interpretations of details
3. Paragraphs in which every sentence is purposeful

4. Thorough research
5. Careful distinctions
6. Thoughtful introductions and conclusions

As a teacher reads, though, it's a rare paper that will delight him throughout. So at the same time that he is looking for items to praise, he'll be noting every obstacle to his comprehension of the paper. Every time he comes up against an obstacle, he'll explain to you why he found what you did an obstacle. You'll then begin to see that your punctuation, for example, and your paragraphing, and your organization are worth improving.

Of course, your teacher will not only read your essay but also grade it. Our society pays teachers (experts) to judge how well our students (candidates for jobs) have learned the necessary skills for these jobs. The teacher must step into that role of judge for five minutes each time he gives a paper a grade. But every other minute of the semester, including the time he spends writing comments on your papers, your teacher is an ally, a skilled reader trying to help you improve, trying to help you become not only a skilled writer but a skilled reader of your own work. Many students seem to forget that this all-but-forty-five-minutes-of-the-course teacher exists.

It helps to know how your potential readers read, but to become a skilled writer, you must also gradually acquire the knack of becoming two distinct people yourself when you write. One self is a writer who scribbles out a draft, does some revising, and then types up that draft. The second self is a reader who reads that draft as if he hadn't written it. Reading your draft aloud (advice I'm sure you'll resist) may seem childish, but it makes you acutely aware of basic needs of your readers. When you try to influence a reader through writing, you won't be there to smile, to demonstrate with your hands, to say "what I really mean is...." Your separation from the reader is reflected in the following diagram (Linton 27):

These gears show graphically that the actual words on the page are crucial. Only the writing, never the writer, gets to touch the reader. The writer must therefore depend on what she has transferred to the writing to do any communicating she wants to do. The first time you read one of your papers aloud in class, you'll want to change half your words, sentences, and paragraphs. It's not just a matter of hearing how your writing sounds but of becoming really conscious of your listeners. Once you're aware of your readers, you'll have much higher standards for your writing. You'll want to reveal at least one significant thing in every paragraph. You'll develop enough respect for your readers to believe that they will be convinced not by bullying but by a complete review of the information. You will remember that a reader wants to read rapidly, but wants to be mentally challenged.

All this effort to help your readers by becoming a reader yourself is much easier to undertake if you are working with a typed draft (or a draft on a word-processor screen). You're required to type your papers in a writing course not so much to make reading easier for your teachers as to enable you to *see* your work—to become a reader of your own writing, to develop your second self. Your second self will also grow if you write self-critiques of the papers you write in this course ("I am satisfied with this paper because..." or "I am not yet satisfied because..."). That second self will also grow as you read the drafts of papers by other students in your class. It will grow steadily in sophistication as the course proceeds.

As you develop your second self, your internal reader, you should see that you don't please an outside reader by trying to find out exactly what the reader wants. The reader often doesn't know what she wants. Editors don't know what they want until they see what a writer has delivered to them. Similarly, a teacher doesn't have a fixed form of exactly what he wants. He's looking to be surprised. He's looking for some work from you that is genuinely different, genuinely worth reading. Thinking about your readers, therefore, doesn't mean you should be pandering to their presumed tastes. It means that you should be crafting the work so well that they will have no trouble comprehending it. Our job as writers is to eliminate obstacles for readers.

What are the implications, then, of learning to respect the readers we write for? First of all, that respect helps us see the values that should guide us as we write: vitality, clarity, simplicity, and humanity (Zinsser 131). Vitality engages the reader's interest. Simplicity and clarity help the reader learn easily. Why humanity? Because we're human. Any understanding of our world is limited if we can't see the human dimensions of that understanding. Writing, like any other profession, requires both technical and human skills. Second, and very important, writing for readers we respect reinforces our respect for the craft of revision. No one can write in a first draft the kind of prose a reader would best understand. Our minds work too fast. They are too concerned during the first draft just with getting matters from brain to paper. The transition from first to final draft is best named, I think, the transition from "writer-based" to "reader-based" prose (Flower and Hayes 449–61). The first, incomplete step—writer-based prose—is not a sign that you're a poor writer. It is an essential step in the process toward excellence. This step is playful. It allows us to take risks, to try things out. It is also the best opportunity we have to think for ourselves. But a writer's patterns of thought should seldom be presented to readers in the order that they occurred to him. A lab notebook, for example, is writer-based: it reflects the sequence of research. A published scientific paper, however, must be reader-based: the research material must be reworked to fit into the experiences of the readers of the paper. Readers need time and space coordinates at the beginning of an essay. Readers need good transitions between paragraphs. Readers need contrasts signaled and quotations introduced. Readers are distracted by irrelevant details, unnecessary repetition, and faulty punctuation. *Readers, in short, expect the fruits of, not a record of, our research and thought.*

You have just finished a crucial chapter. Now that you're aware of a reader, that reader will keep you on your toes. Worrying about that reader will incline you to read your work aloud before you hand it in. As you read, you'll often be embarrassed, but that embarrassment is useful because it will teach you how to revise what you've already written and what to avoid the next time you write. Reading aloud will often make you wish you knew more about your subject; that's not a bad thing either. Reading aloud will also help you with your punctuation, since punctuation was once a system of breathing directions and still reflects the way we breathe as we speak. But the main value of reading aloud is in helping you see the voice that you project. To be a better writer, you'll have to develop that writer's voice. As you do, you will develop a sense of who you are, a sense of what tone you need for each writing assignment you're given, a sense of what words are appropriate for each writing assignment, and a sense of what effect your voice will have on your readers.

5

Systematic Patterns of Thought

I have many problems about writing essays but the biggest of which is organization.

student

The mind doesn't like chaos; ordering is its natural activity.

Ann Berthoff

Exercise 5-1
Reviewing Your Organizational Habits

1. Do you prefer to outline before you begin writing or after you've written out a draft?
2. Do you consider yourself generally an organized person? Why or why not?

Organization: Our Choice or Theirs?

Some of the professional writing you'll face after school will be expected to follow a predetermined order. If, for example, you plan to be a television screenwriter, you'll be asked to include in each episode:

1. Hooks (situations that viewers can identify with),
2. Laid pipe (background information on the characters),
3. Heat (tension),
4. Topspin (questions raised in the viewers' minds just before each commercial), and
5. Buttons (clever remarks made by characters leaving the scene).

If you're a personnel director, and you have to write a job description, you will be expected, most likely, to include sections on:

1. Scope of responsibility,
2. Specific duties, and
3. Personal requirements.

Some of your school papers must also follow a preestablished order:

1. An introductory paragraph which concludes with a thesis statement,
2. A series of body paragraphs that all begin with topic sentences, and
3. A conclusion in which you sum up your principal arguments.

If your paper is a biology laboratory report, you may be asked to use a structure like the following:

1. Title
2. Abstract
3. Introduction
4. Materials and methods
5. Results
6. Discussion
7. References

Most often when you write, though, you'll have to decide for yourself how to organize your material. It is you who decides how long you'll make your introduction, how many sections you'll divide your paper into, whether you'll use a formal thesis statement.

Organization is not a simple record of your thoughts. Neither is it a prearranged package, a method of "filling in the blanks." Organization is making order out of chaos. It results from decisions you make from the time you first start your research to the time, just before the final typing or revising on the word processor, when you may still be tinkering with scissors and tape. Organization will seldom be your first consideration when you write. The principal elements which a writer considers in preparing a paper are:

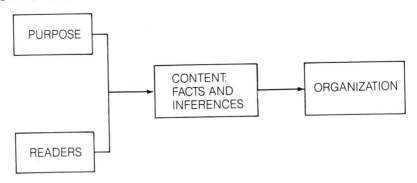

The decision to write starts in most cases in one of the two left-hand boxes. The writer starts either with a reader that wants something or with the purpose of conveying some information, or exploring a problem, or persuading a reader, or simply showing off. She then searches for content (facts and inferences) which will serve her purpose. Perhaps the facts she finds alter her purpose. But it is only after purpose, readers, and content are in mind that the writer faces the task of choosing an appropriate organization for her given purpose.

Choosing a Systematic Organization

Although organization is one of our later considerations as we prepare to write, it is a consideration that rarely works itself out easily. It is seldom easy to decide where to start. It is rarely obvious how many sections or paragraphs we will need. It *is* easy to catch ourselves writing "as I mentioned earlier." When other people complain about your organization, as they have complained about mine, they'll usually say that the piece isn't organized "logically." Although they use the word *logical,* they are only rarely talking about *induction* or *deduction,* the two forms of logic that will be examined in Chapter 6. What they mean, usually, is that the material hasn't been organized "systematically," in a pattern. Readers unconsciously expect patterns when they read, and if we can adapt our writing to the patterns they are familiar with, we can be much more easily understood. When we don't order our material in ways our readers unconsciously expect us to, we can easily bore or confuse them.

Exercise 5-2

To see how unsystematic ordering can distract attention from your message by disconcerting your readers, read the following sentences. Note what is odd about the arrangement of elements in these sentences, and suggest an order for them that would not distract readers.

- Our spaceship brought back from the strange planet a large animal, two small green people, and a soil sample.
- Cities are faced with countless problems, such as crime in the streets, littering, pollution, and traffic jams.
- Although the controversial speaker tried to proceed, stones thrown at the platform, annoying catcalls, and a barrage of rotten fruit brought an end to the meeting.

The Common, Systematic Thought Patterns

My guess is that in the previous exercise you've rearranged each of these sentences so that the most important item was saved for last. This order is called *climactic* order: the items mentioned are listed in an order that builds to a climax. Most readers find such an order systematic and satisfying. There are nine other kinds of order that are also systematic. Following is a list of what in my experience are the ten most common systematic thought patterns—ways of organizing material that we can put to the service of a variety of purposes in writing.

1. Chronological narration
2. Spatial description
3. Classification
4. Comparison-contrast
5. Definition
6. Cause and effect
7. Problem and solution
8. Assertion with examples
9. Assertion with reasons
10. Building to a climax

These useful thought patterns represent common ways of thinking. We find them, with equal frequency, in anthropologists' field notes, in grocery lists, in segments of the evening news. They are useful in writing because they are such common ways of thinking; no one really needs to be taught them. A reader is as likely to find a cause-effect sequence "logical" (that is, to find that he understands it) as the writer is, so it's a useful way to communicate. Since these thought patterns are common ways of thinking, they therefore become for us common *ways of*—or *strategies for*—*organizing* the facts and inferences we have selected to present.

1. Chronological Narration

This method of organization is the most common, and the easiest to write. It is almost always used to organize facts rather than inferences. Skill in using chronological order lies not in arranging one's facts in the correct order but in *selecting* those that convey the impression we want to convey. In reading the following examples, ask yourself why the writers selected the facts they did and what their overall purpose was. The first excerpt is from an introduction to a sign language textbook:

> The first permanent school for the deaf was established in Hartford, Connecticut, in 1817. It was many years later, after Thomas Hopkins Gallaudet had seen the establishment of a number of schools for the

deaf across the United States, that he also envisioned the
establishment of a college. This dream was passed on to his son,
Edward Miner Gallaudet, who was responsible for establishing
Gallaudet College, the world's first and only college for deaf students,
located in Washington, D.C. The charter for the college was signed in
1864 by President Abraham Lincoln (Riekehof 6).

From a chapter on functions in a mathematics textbook:

The Swiss mathematician Leonhard Euler (1707–1783) was the first to
adopt the expression $f(x)$ for the value of a function. He
systematically classified many collections of functions. Nevertheless,
it was not until the middle of the nineteenth century that the division
of a function into a domain and a rule occurred. This was the work of
P. G. Lejeune-Dirichlet (1805–1859) (Ellis and Gulick 22).

From a student response to Exercise 1-1, "Assessing One's Current Writing Ability":

My attendance at school was no more than following my brothers
and sister until the day I entered fifth grade. There I was rudely
awakened by a short, compassionate, but stern teacher who
demanded utter silence and total attention as she taught. My initial
response to Mrs. Brewer was that she would give in, and my friends
and I would rule once again, but she left no opportunity for an
overthrow.

From the diary of Mary Fish, who lived in New England during the American Revolution:

In the month of May, 1770, my dear and only daughter, Mary Noyes,
was taken ill of canker and worms. She was then a little more than
four years old, and although so young, would take anything that was
given her, if ever so bad to take. She would first taste it, and then
would say, it is not good, Mama. I told her the Doctor said she must
take it to make her better. She would then open her little mouth and
take anything, and would foment her throat over hot steam with great
discretion. She died on the 10th day of her illness...I closed her eyes
myself; and felt in some measure resigned, knowing that God could
give a good reason why he had thus afflicted me (Buel and Buel 61–
62).

Chronological order is clear, and usually necessary, not only in telling a
story but in explaining how to do something. A writer's purpose in explaining a process is generally to help others do the same thing or to
suggest a better way to do something commonly done carelessly. Here is
a brief example, about the process of writing:

The next day, after the dishes were washed, the bed was made, and
the Sunday paper was read, I began work on the first draft. I sat on

the couch, pen and pad in hand, coffee and cigarettes on the table, the 49ers game against the Giants on TV, surrounded by the notes I had taken. I wrote during the whole game. I then typed what I had, corrected errors, and reread it. I hated it. The quality I'd been hoping for just wasn't there. George read it and immediately saw that I hadn't reached what I had told him I was aiming for. I wasn't sure, though, that I wanted to change it then because I was getting tired of it. But I sat down anyway and in an hour and a half the paper had rewritten itself. I think it was rewriting while the problems were still on my mind that made the final draft work so well.

In explaining a process, the sequence of events needs to be interrupted occasionally, as this writer does in her last sentence, to give *reasons* for taking the path she is suggesting. (This is the first of many ways you'll see that these systematic thought patterns are used in combination.)

2. Spatial Description

This arrangement is used surprisingly seldom by writers. Though we often describe places to one another in our writing, we seldom need or want to give our readers the exact sense of standing where we're standing. We usually select details for their telling quality rather than for their precise arrangement in space, and then we organize those telling details in another organizational pattern such as comparison-contrast, classification, or assertion with examples. The following description, of the Bhotia river in the Himalaya Mountains by an Indian surveyor and secret agent named Hari Ram, is typical of most (318–319):

> At one place the river ran in a gigantic chasm, the sides of which were so close to one another that a bridge of twenty-four paces was sufficient to span it. This was just below or south of the village of Choksum. Near the bridge the precipices were so impracticable that the path had of necessity to be supported on iron pegs let into the face of the rock, the path being formed by bars of iron and slabs of stone stretching from peg to peg and covered with earth. This extraordinary path is in no place more than eighteen inches and often not more than nine inches in width and is carried for more than one-third of a mile (775 paces) along the face of the cliff, at some 1500 feet above the river, which could be seen roaring below in its narrow bed.

Hari Ram describes several details of spatial arrangement here to help us picture his experience, but it's fair to say that he, like most describers of spatial arrangements, has selected his details more for the meaning they convey than in an attempt to precisely recreate the scene in space.

3. Classification

Classification is the way our minds sort out the complexity of the world that surrounds us. We classify living things into plants, animals, and humans. We classify books into fiction and nonfiction. We classify families into lower class, middle class, and upper class. Some classifications are easy (plant, animal, and human). Some are vague and quite difficult to pin down (lower, middle, and upper class). You practiced your powers of classification every time in Chapter 3 that you tried to decide how many distinct inferences you could draw from the raw material you were examining.

Here is a passage from a physics textbook in which the author has gone through essentially the same process of classifying that you've been practicing:

> There are only two methods by which energy can be transferred between two points. The first method involves the transfer of matter. A falling weight can drive a stake into the ground. Electrons moving through a wire can transfer energy from one place to another.
>
>   The second method of energy transfer involves wave motion. All waves transfer energy. Sound waves transfer the energy of a vibrating string of a guitar to your ear. Light waves bring energy from the sun to the earth. Radio waves carry energy from a radio station to your home. Water waves can do tremendous amounts of damage during storms (Murphy 221).

Note that each of the two categories of energy into which energy transfer has been classified—transfer of matter and wave travel—are illustrated by a series of examples. Murphy has used assertion with examples (thought pattern 9) to help explain his classification.

This next example is from a mathematics textbook. Here the writers have used definition (thought pattern 5) to supplement their classification:

> A *function* consists of a domain and a rule. The *domain* is a set of real numbers, which are usually denoted by lower case letters *a, b, c, x, t,* etc. The *rule* assigns to each number in the domain one and only one number (Ellis and Gulick 16).

My final example is from a chemistry text. Here the author has also used definitions to make her classification clear. She also admits, as many classifiers do not, that the boundaries she has drawn do not always hold:

> Chemistry has traditionally been subdivided into four areas: organic, inorganic, analytical, and physical chemistry. Organic chemistry is the study of the compounds of a single element, carbon. Inorganic chemistry is the study of compounds of all the other elements. These

> divisions have blurred somewhat in recent years and there are
> subtopics, such as organometallic chemistry, being investigated by
> both organic and inorganic chemists. Analytical chemistry is the study
> of the methods used to determine the identity of the components of a
> mixture or a compound, and the relative amounts of each
> component. Physical chemistry is the study of the properties of matter
> and the development of theories that explain the observed properties
> (Segal 1).

Classifications are commonly used to sort out complexity, but they are
most effective in persuasive papers when you may classify several alternative actions or beliefs for the purpose of helping your reader choose
what you think is the best among several alternatives. If you've noted, for
example, that the only three ways to give integrity to college sports programs are to pay the players and not expect them to go to school, to stop
giving any special academic or financial help to athletes, or to develop
an academic and personal support staff which helps athletes fill their
doubly demanding responsibilities as students and athletes, you're well
on your way toward persuading someone to pay for an academic and
personal support staff.

4. Comparing and Contrasting

This is one of our most natural ways of learning, yet one that we must continually sharpen. Every day the world offers us nearly similar facts, inferences, definitions, titles, or theories that we must be alert to distinguish between. Try, offhand, for example, to explain the difference between

- an engineer and a scientist
- an Arab and a Moslem
- a politician and a civil servant
- a working mother and a working father
- intuition and instinct

Careful writers learn such distinctions when they're not already familiar
with them, and then they make those distinctions in their writing. The
following selection is from a sign language textbook:

> The Congenitally Deaf are those who are born deaf. The
> Adventitiously Deaf are those who are born with normal hearing but
> in whom the sense of hearing becomes nonfunctional later through
> illness or accident (Riekehof 7).

From a biology textbook:

> We live not on what we eat, but on what we digest (Moon 363).

From students' papers:

> The union soldiers went about their duties with such cold efficiency

that one might have thought they were *hanging their flag rather than a human being.*

The weekend journey across the border began for us at 16, when one of us had *secured a driver's license and, more important, a car.*

The many changes in our society are moving at a pace *too rapid for the elderly to keep up with and too advanced for the young to learn.*

The inferences you make that show that you are aware of such distinctions are much more impressive to teachers than simple inferences that don't demonstrate your awareness that the issues being discussed are complex. Often you use a comparison-contrast organization, in fact, to take your readers from a simple understanding of an issue to a more sophisticated one. Precisely that strategy is used by the authors of a 1936 geography textbook who are trying to distinguish "scientific geography" from most people's casual impression of the subject:

> It is not, to be sure, in the numerous *individual* features of regions that the geographer is primarily interested. Simply a catalogue of individual plants is not botany, nor is the listing of things to be seen within a region geography. Scientific study requires grouping and classifying and the tracing of origins and connections. When it is noted, for instance, in a study of a region's landscape, that there are repeating patterns of population distribution, drainage lines, fields, or any of the other very numerous features, and when these repetitions are discovered to have definite causal relation to other features (past or present) with which they are associated, there is then the beginning of scientific geography (Finch and Trewartha 5–6).

Most comparison-contrasts you make will be relatively brief, but you will also be asked regularly during your academic and professional lives to compare two items or ideas at length. Suggested Assignment 3, in Chapter 14, calls for just such a comparison, in this case of the readers of two newspapers. To make your comparison systematic, you need to call on your powers of classification as well as powers of comparison. Two items can be compared fairly only if you rate each by the same criteria.

Jeffrey Gagliardi, in the sample paper on page 291, compares the readers of the *New York Times* and those of the *Seattle Post-Intelligencer* in the areas of lifestyle, economy, and political preference. Joseph Greenawalt, in the sample paper on page 293, compares the readers of the *Seattle Post-Intelligencer* and those of the *Baltimore Sun* in the areas of interest in national and international events, business concerns, interest in sports and leisure, and political views. Each contrasts and classifies, but they have chosen different, though equally systematic, methods of organization. Gagliardi discusses the *Times* on all issues first and then discusses the *Post-Intelligencer* on the same issues:

1. **Introduction**
   Specific points about readers of the *Times*
   a. Lifestyle
   b. Economy
   c. Political preference
3. Specific points about readers of the *Post-Intelligencer*
   a. Lifestyle
   b. Economy
   c. Political preference
4. Conclusion

Greenawalt, on the other hand, uses his four issues as the principal structure and compares the two papers on each issue before moving on to the next:

1. Introduction
2. Interests in national and international events
   a. Readers of the *Post-Intelligencer*
   b. Readers of the *Sun*
3. Business concerns
   a. Readers of the *Post-Intelligencer*
   b. Readers of the *Sun*
4. Interests in sports and leisure
   a. Readers of the *Post-Intelligencer*
   b. Readers of the *Sun*
5. Political views
   a. Readers of the *Post-Intelligencer*
   b. Readers of the *Sun*
6. Conclusion

There is no law against Gagliardi's choice, but Greenawalt's pattern is generally considered more accessible to readers because it highlights the very specific contrasts by placing them right next to each other.

Why might a writer write a detailed comparison? Usually it is to understand each item compared a little better than we would if we analyzed it alone. But extended comparisons can also be used to indicate a preference, to help readers make a choice, or to help readers to understand something unfamiliar to them by comparing it to something more familiar.

5. Definition

We are all familiar with the term *definition*. In writing, students often use dictionary definitions to jump start their writing. Whatever the topic, the paper begins, "Webster's defines [topic] as...." Then the writer starts giving his own ideas. Save such definitions for when they're genuinely needed.

When are they needed? When you use a term that's unfamiliar to your readers, when you use a term that means different things to different readers, when you use a term in an unusual sense, or when you want to explain in detail what something is. A definition may be as short as a single word in parentheses. When I use the term *assertion* in this book, for example, I want you to remember that an assertion is also an inference, so I'll occasionally write:

assertion (inference)

Or a definition may take up a whole book. This textbook can be thought of, perhaps, as a 300-odd-page extended definition of the term *thoughtful writing*.

Textbooks are usually sprinkled with definitions. Bernice Segal in her chemistry book explains why:

> You will find in the course of studying chemistry that a great many new terms will be defined. The importance of learning the definition of each new term you encounter cannot be overemphasized. If you do not know the precise definition of a quantity whose value you are asked to determine, you will have difficulty with the reasoning required to solve the problem (2).

Every word we use we use not because it is "correct" in any absolute sense but because speakers of our language have agreed to use it in certain conventional ways. Scientists and dictionary writers try to be as precise as they can about terms—to do so, they write so-called *essential* definitions, like the following:

> Fishes are aquatic vertebrates, with either a cartilaginous or bony skeletons. They breathe by means of gills; are usually covered with scales; and have limbs in the form of fins (Moon 239).

An essential definition places the item being defined in a broad category, then shows how it differs from others in that category. In this case *fishes* are placed in the broad category *vertebrates* (animals having backbones) and then are said to differ from other vertebrates in being *aquatic* (living in the water). In this case the essential definition of the first sentence is reinforced with further contrasts, or distinctions: Fishes "breathe by means of gills; are usually covered with scales; and have limbs in the form of fins."

In practice, not all definitions are so rigorous. They draw on a variety of other thought patterns as they define.

Definition through Spatial Description:

> *The cell.* In most plants and animals the protoplasm is divided into very small parts called cells. These are merely the simplest units of

protoplasm of which the plant or animal is composed. A living cell usually consists of a tiny mass of protoplasm surrounded by a membrane called the cell wall. The central portion of the protoplasm, more active than the rest, is called the nucleus. The cell wall gives definite shape to the cell and the nucleus seems to regulate growth and reproduction. Cells are usually very minute, but are of innumerable shapes, varying with the special work they may have to perform (Moon 27).

Definition through Chronological Narration (from a Student Exercise):

One day when I was babysitting, the child, Andrea, became ill and I acted like an amateur. Andrea was four years old and I had been watching her since she was an infant. She attended nursery school at the time. Her mother worked and I would meet her at the bus and take her home after school.

On this one particular day she came off the bus and the bus driver told me she wasn't feeling well. I took her inside and called her mother's office. Her mother was in a meeting. By the time I got off the phone Andrea had gotten worse and was running a high temperature. I called my mother and she came over. My mother got her in bed and Andrea fell asleep. My mother told me what to do if she woke up and then left. A couple of minutes later, Andrea's mother called back and once she heard what was wrong, came home. I don't recall what happened between the time Andrea's mother left the office and the time she came home, but everything was under control by the time she got there.

On the basis of what I have written, I'd say an amateur is someone who hasn't had enough experience in his field to handle all situations. In my case, I had been watching Andrea for four years but I didn't know what to do once she became sick.

Definition through Contrast with the Usual Meaning of a Term:

Imagine that you have exerted great effort all day trying to remove a huge rock from your garden. Your muscles ache. You are very tired. In spite of all your efforts, the rock remains unmoved. You will say that you have worked hard all day. The physicist will say that you have done no work at all! According to the physicist, work is done only when a force causes an object to move some distance (Murphy 138).

Definition via Mathematical Formula:

The role of a manager can now be defined. His goal is to be efficient, and he is most efficient when he maximizes the difference between total costs and total revenues through time (Farmer 14).

Newly Created Definition to Make Solving a Problem More Efficient (Common in Mathematics):

> Let 1 be any nonvertical line in the plane and $P(x1, y1)$ and $Q(x2, y2)$ any two distinct points on it (Ellis and Gulick 10).

When you use a term your readers are unfamiliar with or when you want your readers to see a term in a different light than they usually do, a careful definition will serve your purpose and save them confusion.

6. Cause and Effect

This organizational pattern is relatively easy to use. Assertion of a cause-effect relationship is usually completed in one sentence:

> Our basic argument is that the way in which managers perform determines how productive, and hence how wealthy, any country will be (Farmer 13).

Then the writer goes on to discuss both the cause and the effect in detail.

Of course the establishment of a connection between a single cause and a single effect is difficult, except in science where through experiments scientists eliminate all possible additional causes. Thus, in science we have many clear causal chains, where cause 1 causes effect 1, which in turn causes effect 2, etc. Here's an example:

> A practical application of the expansion and contraction of gases and liquids is found in systems for heating buildings. The air directly around a radiator expands as it is heated. In this way, it becomes less dense than the cool air above it. The warm air rises and the cool air moves in to take its place. This results in circulation of air (Murphy 196).

Outside the realm of science any effect we see is likely to have had multiple causes and will itself in the company of other causes influence several new effects. The process is mind-bogglingly complex, but as human beings we try to make some sense out of it. Much of your learning in many subjects will stress cause-and-effect relationships.

An Example from Geography:

> By the time that classical antiquity drew to a close, as a result of the recorded travels of Greek scholars, such as Strabo and Herodotus, the empire building of the Romans, and the commercial enterprises of the Phoenicians, there had accumulated a considerable body of material relating to the earth's regions (Finch and Trewartha 1).

An Example from Sociology:

If a society is to function successfully and endure through time, certain conditions must be fulfilled. What are they?

First, individual psychological and biological needs must be met, and pivotal institutions (the family, religion, education, and so on) emerge to meet them. Second, new members, usually newborn babies, must be socialized, indoctrinated with the social values, and trained to occupy positions in the social structure. Third, behavior must be guided toward what is socially desirable, through norms and sanctions. Every society must have a system of control to regulate the expression of aggression, sexual behavior, and property distribution. There is no known society where people are allowed to rape, rob, or kill.

Fourth, for individuals to function in a society, interaction must be largely regular and predictable. There is always an element of uncertainty in interaction, but it is minimized insofar as the participants accept established norms or arrive at a consensus on new ones.

Fifth, the members of society must feel they belong to the group and are motivated to act according to its rules. The constellation of beliefs and values we call myth tends to meet this imperative. It sets social and individual goals, gives a sense of origin and purpose, and invests experience with meaning and value.

These two examples should remind you that when you write using cause-effect patterns, you should always keep in mind that there could be multiple causes of any effect you might be dealing with. If you ignore this complexity, you may sound very simple-minded.

7. Problem-Solution

This pattern is closely related to cause and effect, though it is more restricted in time. It deals with current situations and the means that might be used to cause an improved future. Problem-solution is a pattern fundamental to education, as this example from a physics textbook will indicate.

Suppose that you need to solve an equation for an unknown. For example, you may need to find the value of a in the equation

$$F = ma$$

To do this, the equation must be solved for a. We can do this by remembering that whenever any operation is performed on one side of an equation, the same operation must also be performed on the other side of the equation. In the present example, we first divide both sides of the equation by m. This gives us the equation

$$\frac{F}{m} = a$$

It is customary to place the unknown on the left side of an equation. Thus, our equation can be rewritten

$$a = \frac{F}{m}$$

and our problem is solved (Murphy 3–4).

Since one of the most common reasons for writing is a hope for some change, problem-solution is a commonly used pattern of organization— whether in single sentences, paragraphs, chapters, or whole books.

8. Assertion with Examples

This term is another way of saying "inference with details." The exercises you did in Chapter 3 all enable you to write paragraphs which consist of an assertion and several examples. Assertion with examples is the second most common thought pattern (after chronological narration). Since this whole book emphasizes assertions with examples, one example here, this time from a physics book, should be sufficient:

> Everything in the universe is in a state of motion. The earth itself is filled with moving things. The earth also spins on its axis. The earth and the other planets of our solar system orbit the sun. Our solar system moves through space as part of the Milky Way Galaxy. Stars and galaxies move away from one another (Murphy 31).

That should leave you spinning.

Assertion with examples is a pattern whose role is often to serve the other patterns. It is an easy pattern to recognize, and it should not be too difficult to use given the training you've had in this book.

9. Assertion with Reasons

Not all assertions we make need to be backed up by examples—often we substantiate assertions not with examples but with reasons.

A Brief Assertion with a Single Reason:

> We first must describe some important properties of real numbers, because real numbers, their properties, and their relationships are basic to calculus (Ellis and Gulick 1).

An Assertion with a Very Thoughtful List of Reasons:

> Biology is a required study in many schools, and we have a right to ask why it is considered so important that we are obliged to study it.

> In the first place there are few subjects that add so much to
> general culture by increasing the number of things in which we are
> interested and about which we should have information.
>
> Few people really *see* very much of the things about
> them—accurate observation is a very rare but valuable trait, and
> biology will greatly increase the powers of observation.
>
> Mere observation of facts is not enough, however, for one should
> be able to draw correct conclusions from what he sees. This ability to
> think and reason is one of the chief aims of the laboratory work in
> biology or any other science.
>
> Although these reasons for the study of biology are by far the most
> important, others can be mentioned which may seem more practical.
> It is the foundation of farming, gardening, and forestry and upon its
> laws are based the care and breeding of all domestic animals and
> plants.
>
> In even a more personal way, biology deals with the health and
> care of our own bodies—hygiene. It also includes the study of the
> cause and prevention of disease, the work of bacteria, and means of
> maintaining healthful surroundings—sanitation.
>
> One half of all human deaths are caused by germ diseases [this was
> written in 1921] and at least half of these could be prevented by proper
> knowledge and practice of hygiene and sanitation. This in itself is sufficient
> reason for interest in the study of biology (Moon 3–4).

Choosing the assertion-with-reasons organizational format means that
you are arguing deductively. Deduction will be explained in detail in the
next chapter.

10. Building to a Climax

If the nine organizational patterns above are merely servants to our purpose in writing, building to a climax is the servant of the servants. We
use it to organize narrations, descriptions, classifications, cause-effect
claims, problem-solution plans, examples, and reasons. I'll give just one
example, an account in a sociology book of the emergence of self-
awareness:

> As infants, we have no conception of ourselves as individuals, no
> notion that we are set apart from other individuals. Only as we
> interact with our mothers and others, bump up against things, find we
> have a name, are clothed and bathed, and feel the boundaries of our
> bodies, do we begin to be aware of a separate identity. Roughly at
> the age of two, we begin to use the pronouns "I," "me," and "you,"
> indicating that we are beginning to be conscious of ourselves and of
> other persons as separate individuals. This awareness grows as we
> acquire language and can participate in symbolic interaction.

We next learn to perceive roles and their relationships. As we observe and respond to others, they become meaningful objects that can bring us pleasure, pain, security, and so on. In order to win the responses we want, we learn to anticipate their actions by putting ourselves in their places—by taking the role of the other. In doing so we become objects to ourselves, able eventually to look at ourselves from outside ourselves, so to speak. Thus, we become aware of our moods and wishes and ideas as objects. We can then finally act toward and guide ourselves (Biesanz and Biesanz 84–85).

Writing and Recognizing the Common Thought Patterns

Exercise 5-3

To become more familiar with the systematic thought patterns available to you and to help you realize that those patterns are not infinite in number or complexity, try the following. Choose one subject from among the first three below.

First Class	Second Class	Third Class
Procrastination	Money	Confidence
The Elderly	Guilt	The Best Movie I've Seen Lately
High School Education	Marriage	Working Mothers

Write a brief (approximately one page) analysis of your chosen subject organized according to any one of the ten thought patterns:

1. Chronological narration
2. Spatial description
3. Classification
4. Comparison-contrast
5. Definition
6. Cause and effect
7. Problem and solution
8. Assertion with examples
9. Assertion with reasons
10. Building to a climax

When you've finished, write *a second analysis of the same subject,* using a second pattern of your choice. For example, if you wrote first an analysis of procrastination using a problem-and-solution organization, then write a second analysis, this time organizing, perhaps, according to assertion with examples.

During a class session, then, read, in turn, some of your papers aloud. After each reading by another student in the class, jot down (1) the method of organization you think the writer used and (2) a sentence or two explaining your decision. As soon as you've written down your estimates, compare them with those of other members of the class, and finally, ask the author what his or her intention was. You'll begin to see the variety of possibilities for organizing and the ways organizational patterns can be mixed with each other.

To reinforce your organizational sense, repeat the exercise a second and third time, each time choosing a new subject from a new column and writing about your chosen subject twice, using two different thought patterns. By the end of three classes, you will have used six patterns of organization, and you will have heard—from the rest of the class—the other patterns, and other ways of using the same patterns. You are building up your intuitive resources for organization.

All the thought patterns used in the exercise above are aids to readers. A definition makes clear a term that your reader may be unfamiliar with. Classification helps a reader sort a product or an issue into its important parts. A contrasting example helps a reader to see the subject you're focusing on more clearly. A cause-effect explanation helps a reader see *why* a certain event occurred. A narrative helps a reader see how certain issues might affect his or her life.

After this week of practice, you should be able to explain, better than a textbook can, what uses each pattern serves. You will also see that the patterns are not too complicated, and that they often overlap—we almost always use more than one pattern in any extended piece of writing. As you listen to the sketches written by others, you'll probably also be reminded of how important details and examples are in backing up any assertions that are made.

Recognizing Patterns in Everyday Messages

Exercise 5-4

Any message, no matter what its length and no matter where it's posted, will, if it wishes to be clear and persuasive, be grounded in an organizational pattern. The messages on cereal box panels and matchbook covers, in junk-mail circulars, on traffic signs, in department memos and political ads, and on medicine bottles were all written by someone, and each writer, often more intuitively than consciously, used some thought pattern to organize the message. In the examples below, try to determine the author's principle of organization.

From a Side Panel of a Box of Post Grape-Nuts

HERE'S HOW TO

GO GRAPE-NUTS®
cereal

OVER DANNON.®

½ container (½ cups) plain or vanilla-flavored DANNON® Yogurt
¼ cup POST GRAPE-NUTS® Brand Cereal
¼ cup (about) fresh, frozen or canned fruit*

Or use ½ container DANNON® Yogurt, any fruit flavor, and omit the fruit.

Spoon yogurt into dish. Top with cereal, then add fruit and serve at once. Makes 1 serving.

Sign on a Bathroom Door

MEN'S ROOM

Sign on a Staircase Door

FIRE DOOR
KEEP CLOSED AT ALL
TIMES TO PREVENT
FIRE FROM SPREADING

From the Side Label on a Bottle of Pepto-Bismol

Caution: This product contains salicylates. If taken with aspirin and ringing of the ears occurs, discontinue use. If taking medicine for anticoagulation (thinning the blood), diabetes, or gout, consult physician before taking this product. If diarrhea is accompanied by high fever or continues more than 2 days, consult a physician.

From the Inside Cover of *National Geographic*

> The National Geographic Society is chartered in Washington, D.C., in accordance with the laws of the United States, as a nonprofit scientific and educational organization. Since 1890 the Society has supported more than 2,350 explorations and research projects, adding immeasurably to man's knowledge of earth, sea, and sky.

The Lyrics for a Harry Chapin Song, "Cat's in the Cradle"

My child arrived just the other day.
He came to the world in the usual way.
But there were planes to catch and bills to pay.
He learned to walk while I was away.
And as he was talkin' 'fore I knew it, and as he grew
He'd say "I'm gonna be like you, dad,
You know I'm gonna be like you."

Refrain:

And the cat's in the cradle and the silver spoon
Little boy blue and the man on the moon
"When you comin' home dad?"
"I don't know when, but we'll get together then.
You know we'll have a good time then."

My son turned ten just the other day.
He said "Thanks for the ball dad, come on let's play."
"Can you teach me how to throw?" I said, "Not today."
"I got a lot to do." He said, "That's OK."
And he walked away, but his smile never dimmed.
And he said "I'm gonna be like him, yeah,
You know I'm gonna be like him."

Refrain

Well he came home from college just the other day
So much like a man I had to say
"Son I'm proud of you can you sit for a while?"
He shook his head and he said with a smile
"What I'd really like Dad is to borrow the car keys.
See you later, can I have them please?"

Refrain

I've long since retired. My son's moved away.
I called him up just the other day.
I said "I'd really like to see you if you don't mind."
He said "I'd love to dad if I can find the time.
You see my new job's a hassle and the kids have the flu
But it's sure nice talking to you."

> And as I hung up the phone it occurred to me—
> He'd grown up just like me.
> My boy was just like me.

Each of the messages above was organized according to some principle. And the longer the message was, the greater the chances that its organization could get out of hand. You'll begin to see, I hope, that even the brief papers you write for this class are complex documents, much in need of careful organization.

I don't claim that the thought patterns listed in this chapter comprise a complete list, or a closed system. Every textbook writer's list of organizational strategies differs, and many of these strategies overlap. But our inability to say "these are the only possibilities" should not lead us to despair of the strategies' usefulness. Keep your eyes open to whatever organizational strategies you find most common and most useful. If you find more useful strategies, add them to the list. In the meantime, this list is a valuable resource that you can turn to for any paper that you write.

Writing Patterned Answers to Essay Questions

Not being aware of these strategies for being systematic sets us back when we're writing a paper, but it sets us back most when we're trying to write an effective answer to an essay test question. When we're writing such an answer, the clarity with which we can present what we know becomes almost as important as what we know. Our instructors expect us not only to remember the course material but to be able to control it. But excitement or nervousness often leads us to write down all we remember at the moment, instead of setting time aside to try to organize an appropriate answer. A too-little-recognized part of our job in answering a test question is discovering what thought pattern the teacher is suggesting that we use.

Exercise 5-5

With the practice you gained in writing your six short organizational essays, look at the following questions—see if you can become expert at pattern spotting. For each question, decide on the principal organizational pattern expected, and mention also any secondary patterns that might be useful.

1. *History:* Compare and contrast the founding and development of the colonies of Massachusetts and Virginia. Be sure to discuss political, economic, social, and religious issues.
2. *Business:* Discuss three elements of risk that you discern in the business conduct of a public utility. Which is most serious?
3. *Biochemistry:* What are ketone bodies? Explain why and how they are formed in instances of starvation.
4. *Sociology:* How would you explain the differential earnings of men and women?
5. *History:* How did the concept of equality change in the period from 1607 to 1865? Be sure to trace the change through time.
6. *History:* What were the five most critical events leading to the Civil War? Be sure to explain thoroughly what each event was and why it led to the Civil War.

You should quickly become impressed with your ability to tackle the organization of a question even when you know nothing about the subject matter being questioned.

If you become an expert pattern spotter, half your work in answering essay questions is over. Once you recognize a pattern, you can make a quick outline. Here, for example, is an outline for question 4, which I think calls for an assertion-with-reasons response:

Men earned 40 percent more than women in the United States in 1983

- Because pregnancy takes many women out of the job market during crucial years of advancement
- Because many women are in a dependent role where duties are expected of them at home
- Because young boys are brought up to expect careers, while many girls are not brought up to expect them
- Because job discrimination and job segregation conditions still exist

Each of these reasons will need details or examples to back it up, but now we are ready to start writing, *trying* to keep our minds thinking—and not just filling in the blanks—as we do.

We can use this three-step method (choosing a pattern, then building an outline, and finally supporting the outline statements with examples) in writing any paper. The method short-circuits much of the work and time usually involved in writing. But it also short-circuits some of the thinking. On a test, when we've done most of our thinking before we begin to write, and where we have (we hope) the examples readily at our disposal, this three-step method can be effective. A paper not done on the spot, though, at school or on the job, will require much more research and thinking, and the longer but more thorough writing method detailed in Chapter 13, "The Writing Process," will serve us much better when we wish to present not just our current knowledge but a helpful and thoughtful piece of work.

6

Persuasion: Writing with Authority

The persuasion paper was the hardest because you couldn't just do research and write down a lot of facts. You really had to convince the reader that you were right.

student

Newspapers, television, movies, advertisements, parents, and friends, all, at one time or another, attempt to persuade you to accept a particular point of view. Theirs. If you are aware of the basic argumentative techniques, you may either use them to persuade others, or analyze how someone else has used them in an attempt to persuade you.

Joyce Middleton,
writing teacher

Unless you settle first the questions that are on your readers' minds, they won't listen to a thing you want to say.

Hubert Miller,
Nuclear Regulatory Commission

Writing...is an act of aggression disguised as an act of charity.

David Bartholomae

Earning, and Then Using, Authority

Most of us have very little faith that we are capable of changing another person's opinion or affecting another person's action. We have very little faith because we have no strategies in mind for influencing people. As a result, when we are asked to argue, we talk or write without thinking, and we produce something as muddled as this excerpt from a lab report

80

of an eighth-grade student trying to persuade her teacher that the melting point and the freezing point of a substance will be two different temperatures.

> Personally I think that, when a substance has a freezing point and/or a melting point in its graph measurements, that they don't equal each other. In other words, the heating points and melting points do not equal each other (their answers are different). The reason I think this is because when something freezes it pretty much always has air bubbles and when a substance melts it is a solid. So when weighing the substance the freezing point is heavier plus the freezing point is colder and the melting point is hot and they both can't be heated and melted at the same time, plus there is no movement in the frozen substance, but there is movement in a melted substance, so there is no way a freezing point and a melting point can equal each other.

(In fact, the melting point and the freezing point of a substance are identical—for water, for example, both are 32°F).

This student is floundering, partly because she is ill-informed, but partly because she is intimidated by the great knowledge gulf she sees as separating herself from her teacher. In order to persuade people, we must overcome that feeling of intimidation, and we do so by becoming well-informed, not only about our subject but about methods of persuading. It's up to you to become well-informed about your subjects, but I can help you a bit with the chief methods of persuading, first explained to us by Aristotle. They are *ethos* (appealing to us through one's "character"), *logos* (appealing to us through logic, usually with facts), and *pathos* (appealing to our emotions).

Persuasive writing is a form of selling. We in school sometimes pretend that we are above selling things, but just as Skippy peanut butter would be off the shelf in five years if Best Foods stopped advertising it, so, too, would our ideas be lost if we stopped speaking and writing on their behalf. So let's take a few pages out of the advertiser's book of strategy.

Discriminating Among *Ethos, Logos,* and *Pathos*

Exercise 6-1

How do the ads on the following pages try to get us to buy the products or ideas advertised? Take a few notes about the strategies you notice, and compare them with those noted by your classmates. Can you classify the strategies as using *ethos, logos,* and *pathos?*

A Bushel of Food
In a Package of Quaker Oats
And At One-Tenth the Cost

A 35-cent package of Quaker Oats contains 6221 calories—the energy measure of food value.

You would buy a bushel of ordinary mixed foods to equal that calory value. And that bushel would cost you ten times 35 cents.

Here is what it would take of certain good foods to furnish you 6221 calories:

To Supply 6221 Calories

In Quaker Oats . .	1 Pkg.	In Potatoes	21 Lbs.
In Round Steak . .	7 Lbs.	In Hubbard Squash .	65 Lbs.
In Hens' Eggs . . .	7 Doz.	In Young Chicken	20 Lbs.
In Cabbage	55 Lbs.	In String Beans . .	36 Lbs.

And here is what those calories would cost at this writing in some necessary foods:

Cost of 6221 Calories

In Quaker Oats . . .	35c	In Hens' Eggs . . .	$3.12
In Round Steak . . .	$2.06	In Fish about . . .	2.25
In Veal or Lamb . . .	3.12	In Potatoes	65c

Consider these facts in your breakfasts. The oat is the greatest food that grows. It is almost a complete food—nearly the ideal food. It supplies essentials which most foods lack.

At least once a day use this supreme food to cut down your table cost.

57 Cents
Per 1000 Calories

5½ Cents
Per 1000 Calories

50 Cents
Per 1000 Calories

Quaker Oats
Only 10 Pounds From a Bushel

Get Quaker Oats for exquisite flavor. They are flaked from queen grains only—just the rich, plump, flavory oats. We get but ten pounds from a bushel.

When such an oat dish costs no extra price it is due to yourself that you get it.

15c and 35c per Package
Except in the Far West and South
Packed in Sealed Round Packages with Removable Cover

5191

"— and Jim, don't worry about us"

"We're fine, really we are. The children are growing so fast. You'll be as proud of them when you come home as they are proud of you.

"As for those 'civilian shortages' you ask about—don't worry about us! If you could see me this minute, you'd know I'm simply basking in luxury. I'm writing this in bed—all tucked in under one of those beautiful Kenwood blankets Mother gave us when we were married. They are as soft and lovely as they were that exciting day when we opened our gifts. Remember?"

IF YOU, TOO, ARE FORTUNATE enough to own Kenwoods, take good care of them. They are more precious than ever now. You won't buy new blankets, of course, unless you *need* them...but if you do, don't assume you can't get Kenwoods until you have tried. Like other blanket manufacturers, we are largely engaged in war work. But we are making some blankets for the home.

Ask your favorite fine store to show you the new Kenwoods in all their fresh beauty, rich with soft, luxurious warmth. Their long-lasting satisfying service will make them treasured possessions through the years.   **KENWOOD MILLS, Albany, New York**

"I waited too long. My dealer didn't have a single Bendix Automatic Home Laundry left when I tried to buy one. And the factory had converted to war work.

"So I didn't get a Bendix. But I found that many I might have bought, had I inquired earlier, were serving Uncle Sam.

"They're scattered far and wide, by now—from this one in a USO club 'somewhere in Alaska' to the 55 on duty at the Maritime Training Station, Sheepshead Bay, N. Y. Not doing a *fighting* job, of course, but washing, rinsing and damp-drying *fighting clothes* at the turn of a single dial.

"So here's what I decided: If the Bendix I didn't get is serving boys in service, the dollars I didn't spend for it should be serving, too.

"And they *are* serving. I invested them in WAR BONDS—*extra* War Bonds in *addition* to those we buy each payday. Why not do the same—*all* you folks who *would* be buying Bendix Automatic Home Laundrys through these war years if they were available?"

★ **TO MORE THAN 300,000 BENDIX OWNERS:**
If your Bendix should need repair or servicing, call an authorized Bendix Automatic Home Laundry dealer or serviceman listed in the classified section of your phone book, or write **BENDIX HOME APPLIANCES, INC.**, South Bend, Ind. *The People who Pioneered and Perfected the Automatic "Washer."*

BENDIX
AUTOMATIC HOME LAUNDRY

This advertisement does not imply endorsement of our product by the Army, Navy or USO

The Changing Face of South Africa

South Africa is changing. Creating opportunities for all her peoples. In her social, political and economic life, reform is a reality. A new constitutional framework is in the making. And positive results are emerging from the ongoing consultations between Government and the leaders of all groups.

This is further evidence that the leaders of this multi-ethnic society are willing to work together to provide opportunity and achieve peace and prosperity. As a nation committed to the free enterprise system, South Africa has a lot to offer and a lot you can profit from.

So take a look at the changing face of South Africa. If you require any further information regarding progress and development in South Africa, do not hesitate to write to: The Minister (Information), South African Embassy, 3051 Massachusetts Ave. N.W., Washington, D.C. 20008.

Republic of South Africa-Looking forward to the future.

That's why it's good to know Mr. Goodwrench.

I get fast service from Mr. Goodwrench. To begin with, he greets me promptly when I bring in my van. But, above all, he knows I want my van back by the time he promises to get it back. That matters.

Mr. Goodwrench has GM training. And he works on GM cars every day. It stands to reason that he's the mechanic I should go to when I need service on my GM van or my car. Mr. Goodwrench is committed to reasonable prices that are competitive with those of other places I've gone to around here for service.

I want genuine GM parts and I know that Mr. Goodwrench seems to have a good supply of the parts I need. So whenever my van needs service, I watch for a Mr. Goodwrench sign. It's at more than 5,000 GM dealers. Across America.

Mr. Goodwrench works here

Let's have disposable retirement income, not disposable retirees.

Despite $700 billion in pension funds today, tomorrow could be less than golden.

More men and women are retiring, often years earlier, and

living to collect checks longer.[1] While inflation's share of those checks keeps increasing.

Can Social Security prevent disaster? At best, it's a partial answer. At worst, it may go broke unless its bite on salaries goes *much* deeper or its provisions change drastically.[2]

The burden is on private pensions. And we at Ætna Life & Casualty are convinced private pensions can help shoulder it.

Employers can't pull dollars out of thin air. So let's change tax laws that discourage small businesses from setting up pensions in the first place.[3]

Let's also give employees incentives to put a little extra into their company pension or savings plan. And—especially important for today's mobile work force—improve their pension vesting.

Neither last nor least, pensions should be better designed to stave off the munching of inflation. Ætna's acutely aware of this problem, and we're working on it.[4]

If you don't want the American dream of retirement to be permanently retired, use *your* influence with the powers that be —as we are trying to use ours.

Ætna
wants retirement to be affordable.

[1]America is crossing over to what's been called "the other side of the baby boom." The median age is shifting upwards, and with it the proportion of over-65's to the general population. In 1979 there were 5.4 workers to every retiree, as opposed to 7.5 to 1 in 1950, and by 2030 the ratio will be about 3 to 1.

[2]Social Security was never *intended* to be more than a basic system supplemented by private pensions and individual savings. The price for forgetting this has been high and promises to get higher: combined employer/employee FICA taxes on our grandchildren's salaries could reach 25%. Of course, there are alternatives. Social Security could increase the official retirement age,

pay benefits based on government-determined need, or simply *...reduce benefits in general!*

[3]Two-thirds of small businesses surveyed in 1978 offered no pension plans at all. One reason: Typically, big employers can write off 46¢ in taxes for every pension dollar they contribute, while most small ones can only write off about 20¢. In some cases,

they can't write off anything.

[4]Our real estate and participating mortgage separate accounts, for example, are designed to offer larger returns in the face of double-digit inflation. We've also helped fund the Pension Research Council's study of pensions and inflation.

LIFE & CASUALTY

Ætna Life & Casualty,
151 Farmington Avenue,
Hartford, CT 06156.

The party begins.

I can drive when I drink.

2 drinks later.

I can drive when I drink

After 4 drinks.

I can drive when I drink.

After 5 drinks.

I can drive when I drink

7 drinks in all.

I can drive when I drink

The more you drink, the more coordination you lose. That's a fact, plain and simple.

Still, people drink too much and then go out and expect to handle a car.

When you drink too much you can't handle a car. You can't even handle a pen.

The House of Seagram

The strategies employed by writers fall into precisely the same categories as do the strategies employed by these advertisers. Every writer who succeeds does so by using *ethos, logos,* and *pathos*—by presenting a trustworthy character, by substantiating all claims, and by influencing the reader's emotions.

Logos

Perhaps we should talk first about *logos,* or logic, since most people are afraid that they aren't competent in this area. The term *logic* includes a wide variety of systematic ways of thinking, specifically the ten common thought patterns discussed in Chapter 5. But the two most fundamental logical patterns are induction and deduction, referred to in Chapter 5 as "assertion with examples" (induction) and "assertion with reasons" (deduction). Induction and deduction are in fact never wholly independent of each other, but it is easier to understand them if we first assume that they can stand alone.

You have been practicing induction ever since Chapter 3—induction is the drawing of a reliable inference from a set of examples. If, for example, I were a Laplander who arrived in St. Louis and watched, for a few weeks, the way people worked and the way they were paid, I might notice the following: that doctors work hard and that they are paid handsomely; that judges work hard and that they are paid handsomely; that construction workers work hard and that they are paid handsomely. I'd surely draw the inference that Missourians who work hard are paid handsomely. I might check my inference, my inductive thinking, by looking at trash collectors. Since they work hard and are paid handsomely, I'd begin to think that my logic was foolproof. But if I then turned to shoe repairers, or mothers, or administrative assistants, who work hard but are not paid handsomely, I'd be very confused. Or if I were a well-schooled Laplander, I'd just realize that induction is never foolproof. Induction is our most common method of reasoning. And several examples are often enough to convince. But neither writers nor readers can ever be certain that a counterexample, or even many counterexamples, won't turn up.

I doubt whether you've heard the term *induction* very often, even though it describes the most frequent way we think. If I said "deduction," though, you'd probably think immediately of detectives, perhaps of Sherlock Holmes or of Magnum who often speak of making "simple deductions" from facts. These so-called deductions are, in fact, inferences, the products of inductive thinking. Genuine deduction is quite a different matter.

Both writers and readers are less conscious of deduction than of induction, but deduction can be very helpful. It is based on a logical device called the *syllogism*. A syllogism has three parts: a general principle (or common assumption), a specific example of that principle, and finally a conclusion.

General principle: All human beings die.
Specific application: My father is a human being.
Conclusion: Therefore, my father will someday die.

If you use this method of reasoning and your general principle is foolproof, then your conclusion is foolproof. Deduction thus seems to be a very powerful tool. But there's a catch. Very few general principles are as certain as the one—"All human beings die"—that I began my sample syllogism with. There aren't many principles (assumptions) that you can be sure your audience will share. Most human issues belong to the realm of the probable rather than the certain.

When I try to think of general principles that no one could disagree with, I fail again and again:

All people have a right to respect. *(Even criminals?)*
A human being, to be ethical, must regard people as intrinsically more
    valuable than animals. *(Does this mean that we can kill and eat an-
    imals without qualms?)*

Any such statement that I make *I* will call a general principle. *You* are more likely to call the same statement my assumption. If you make such a statement, *you'll* consider it a principle, while *I'll* call it your assumption. Deduction begins to look a little shaky.

Let's look at a few more examples. Suppose I wanted to argue that women should be drafted. The syllogistic structure of my argument might look like this:

General principle: Men and women are equal.
Specific application: Men are subject to the U.S. draft.
Conclusion: Therefore, women should be subject to the U.S. draft.

This one, like most attempts at deductive argument, is complicated. A reader might at first agree with my general principle, but once he saw my conclusion, he might go back, fairly, and ask me to define *equal.* Another reader might not want to listen because she feels that not even men should be subject to a draft. I'm stopped in my tracks because my readers will not accept my assumptions. Deduction is therefore fraught with risks. Readers can ignore your whole train of thought if they disagree with your assumptions. Still, deduction is useful for writers in fields like engineering or the law, where fixed codes exist, that is, where decisions are often based on "first principles."

General principle: Those guilty of second-degree murder should serve
    eight to ten years in prison.

Specific application: Donald Hyde has been found guilty of second-degree murder.

Conclusion: Therefore, Donald Hyde should serve eight to ten years in prison.

Deduction is also helpful when you can find some assumption that is shared by the person you want to persuade. If I, for example, wanted the principal of my daughter's junior high school to require three years of language study, and the principal was opposed to language study because he had never "used" the French he had learned but was also worried because the students in his school were having difficulty with English grammar and vocabulary, I might argue as follows:

General principle: Any study which improves students' grammar and vocabulary ought to be encouraged.

Specific application: The study of other languages improves students' mastery of English grammar and vocabulary.

Conclusion: Therefore, the study of languages other than English ought to be encouraged.

Since I had found for the basis of my deductive argument a general principle on which we both agreed, the principal would have to think twice before throwing out my suggestion.

Below are two letters to the editor of the *Los Angeles Times* responding to a court case in which the federal government (and specifically Surgeon General Dr. C. Everett Koop) attempted to force the parents of a child born with severe birth defects and brain damage to agree to have partially corrective surgery attempted. One writer emphasizes deduction in making her case, the other writer induction ("Letters" B2):

Deduction	Induction
Conclusion backed by general principles (assertion with reasons)	Conclusion backed by facts (assertion with examples)
The intervention of the U.S. surgeon general in the case of severely retarded and paralyzed Baby Jane Doe must be condemned quickly and completely.	The government lawyer says "what the family wants is not the issue here." Why? Will he take over Baby Doe's care? Who does he expect to care and love this poor suffering creature? Will society in its callous way take the place of caring parents?
By what right does Dr. C. Everett Koop presume to involve himself in the tragedy of this family? Is he a close friend or relative? Does he bear the cost of the child's care? Does he share the heartbreak of these parents?	I had a sister—born two years before me. She was made brain damaged by blood poisoning (before 5 years of age) when the scab of her smallpox vaccination was pulled off by a rusted suit button of a caring and loving uncle who was playing with her. She was confined to the Wrentham State Hospital in
No! Yet, he comes into their lives unasked, to challenge a decision that they have made with the help of their doctors, their family and their God. I pray that the courts will not allow	

Koop's unjustified, self-serving interference to continue.

Waltham, Mass. for 35 years.
She knew little family love after that. At first we had no transportation, and with seven others to care for, not the time. Did she know? We will never know. The state cared for her through the many convulsions—keeping her a prisoner in her room (for her own sake). She never roamed the beautiful grounds. Her care was protective and skillful. But there was a vacuum of life around her; she was not a contributor to society—just sick and alone and jailed. She mercifully died at 40 years. Not a life of my choosing certainly.

Baby Doe will have 100 times the agony my sister Pearl survived.

As I write this I am listening for the telephone to ring—announcing the birth of our second grandchild. I would *hate* for "our Lawyer" to intrude in this child's life.

Though induction and deduction can be explained separately, all thinking, all arriving at conclusions, contains elements of both. As you saw in Chapter 3, the inferences we draw from facts are never just a simple response to those facts. They are colored by assumptions (sex-role assumptions, assumptions about what certain categories of people are attracted to, assumptions about why photographers take photographs), that is, by deductive reasoning. And here in this chapter, when I gave a reason as the foundation of my deductive argument—"Any study which improves students' grammar and vocabulary ought to be encouraged"— that reason might be more persuasive if I added a few examples, that is, used inductive reasoning, to back up the reason.

Perhaps a diagram can clarify this point better than words can. Stephen Toulmin, in *The Uses of Argument* (1958), includes a diagram which helps us visualize the interconnectedness of induction and deduction (97–107). Two slightly adapted versions of that diagram follow:

The Simpler Version

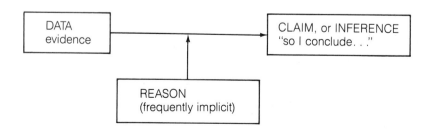

To take an example from the Sister Rebecca exercise (3-5) in Chapter 3:

My data is: Her name appears in all capital letters six times.
My claim, or inference, is: She is egotistical.
My reason for making the inference is: Only 2-year-olds, kings, queens, and people of great ego refer to themselves as if they were a separate person.

The More Complex Version

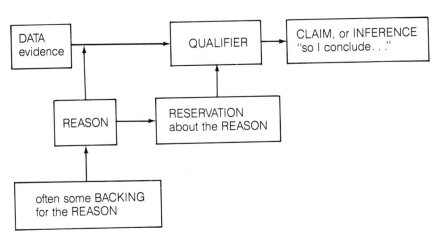

My data and *reason* are the same as in the simpler version.
My backing for the *reason* is contained in the following two examples: Queen Elizabeth is known to say, "The Queen is ready to dine." Evil Knievel once said on the Johnny Carson show, "Evil Knievel can jump that canyon—no problem."
My reservation is: But perhaps Sister Rebecca just wants readers to *think* she's a great person.
My qualifier, therefore, is: Sister Rebecca might in fact be humble, but so poor that she feels she needs to make herself seem great to attract customers.
So my modified claim now is: Sister Rebecca is egotistical, but perhaps she has to be egotistical to succeed in her line of work.

When you write with the care necessary to fill in all the boxes in this complex version of the Toulmin diagram, you are writing as responsibly as possible.

    Whether we emphasize induction (using examples) or deduction (starting from a common assumption), or consciously employ both as above, we hope of course to influence our listeners, but we must remember that our conclusions are never going to be certain. "Proofs" are not possible in writing. We all know the vulnerability of inductive arguments.

No matter how many examples we include, a counterexample can embarrass our argument. With deductive arguments, our assumptions are vulnerable. Advertisers can't prove that their products are best; similarly, we can't prove that our ideas or our proposals are best. Since *logos*, then, is always vulnerable, since it can't prove anything, we see why there's plenty of room for the two other means of persuasion, *ethos* and *pathos*, to play significant roles in our efforts.

Ethos

Ethos (the Greek word for "character") is our most powerful tool in writing. Every writer must employ logic, *logos*, before we'll trust him. But much of our trust comes not from a writer's logic but from other, less tangible qualities. Just as a musician wins a competition not only by playing the correct notes but by giving the musical phrasing "character," just as a salesclerk who is both knowledgeable and friendly earns more substantial commissions than one who is merely knowledgeable, so a writer with both a command of the material and a clear enjoyment of writing succeeds when a plodding writer doesn't.

A strong *ethos* does not come easily; you cannot fake an *ethos*. Everything you read, everything you write, every conversation you have, every experience you seek out contributes to the *ethos*, the voice, the character that is available to you when you write. You may do these things to enjoy yourself or perhaps to increase your ability to make friends and to find someone who'll want to spend a lifetime with you. But you're also working on your writing *ethos*. If your *ethos* building succeeds, some letter you write when you are 24 may get you the job you want; some memo you write when you are 34 will get you a promotion; some report you write when you're 44 will make you a well-respected leader. But thousands of hours of curiosity, and learning, and conversation will go into building the phrase, the sentence, the tone that will later come naturally at a time when you'll need it. If you can come through in your writing as a person of intelligence, integrity, confidence, and goodwill, you have done everything that *ethos* is capable of.

Whenever we write, we reveal ourselves—our intelligence or lack of it, our care or lack of it, our honesty or lack of it. When we revise and look at the "character" that emerges in an early draft, we can make adjustments in the way we wish to present ourselves. But we can't, once we hand in a finished copy, avoid responsibility for the character that comes through. Building up a trustworthy *ethos*, a trustworthy writer's character, is the biggest challenge we face as writers.

Pathos

Pathos (often thought of simply as an appeal to the emotions) does not have a great reputation. We're glad to acknowledge that we respect writers who are logical and writers whom we can trust. But we don't like to admit that writers succeed by making emotional appeals to us. *Pathos*, though, is not simply the raising of violent emotions in a reader. A writer can make an emotional appeal to the audience's sense of integrity, as John Kennedy did with his famous sentence, "Ask not what your country can do for you; ask what you can do for your country." But a writer needn't even be that dramatic to make good use of *pathos*. If we can reduce our reader's irritation and increase our reader's pleasure, we have employed *pathos* effectively. By not writing down to a reader, we make the reader more comfortable. By acknowledging the reader's point of view, we make the reader more ready to listen to ours. By using standard grammar and punctuation, we allow the reader to enjoy reading the substance of what we have to say.

Self-Checklist: Ethos, Logos, Pathos

Ethos	Logos	Pathos
1. Do I sound intelligent?	1. Are the facts I've used well-chosen?	1. Have I made a skilled use of emotional appeal?
2. Interested in my subject?	2. Are my inferences justified by my facts?	2. Have I shown a concern for the needs of my reader?
3. Well-informed?	3. Are my assumptions justifiable?	
4. Fair-minded?	4. Is my paper well-organized?	
	5. Is my purpose clear?	

Fallacies

While you try to use *ethos, logos,* and *pathos* in your own writing to make it effective, you should be becoming increasingly aware of the ways in which others, or you in your early drafts, misuse them. Misuses of *ethos, logos,* or *pathos* are usually called *fallacies* or *attempts to deceive,* although we often commit fallacies without intending to do so. Some of the more common writers' fallacies are the following:

1. Hasty generalization (weak induction: not enough facts considered). *Example:* "I can't write. I got D's on my first two papers."
2. The citing of illegitimate authorities (devious induction: use of an authority's opinion as a fact to reinforce an inference you want to make, when that authority's qualifications for offering the opinion are suspect). *Example:* "Dick Butkus and Bubba Smith think this beer tastes great."

3. Unstated assumptions (devious deduction: not stating the first principles of your arguments). *Example:* "He'll never graduate. He's an athlete."
4. Undefined key terms (weak or devious deduction: carelessness about whether the audience really knows what you mean). *Example:* "He's more qualified than she is. We'll hire him."
5. Inappropriate comparisons or analogies (weak or devious deduction: unstated general principle is that the two items compared are essentially alike). *Example:* "Since Napoleon made France strong again by attacking Austria and Italy, we should make the United States strong again by attacking Canada."
6. Unsubstantiated cause-effect claims (weak or devious deduction: unstated general principle is that your cause caused your effect). *Example:* "The English are a morose people because their weather is so cloudy."
7. A claim that there are only two choices (weak or devious deduction: unstated general principle is that there are only two possibilities). *Example:* "Either fight communism wherever it rears its head, or live in a world in which we have no friends."
8. Ignoring the point at issue (absence of *logos:* not constructing arguments that are to the point). *Example* from a paper on nuclear power plant safety: "A hydrogen bomb could destroy half of Connecticut."
9. The hurling of insults (misuse of *pathos:* trying to get readers emotional about irrelevant matters). *Example:* "You're not going to trust the word of a bureaucrat!"
10. Appeal to irrelevant emotions (misuse of *pathos:* this one is often very difficult to decide). *Example:* "No one who loves children can fail to put $25 in an envelope and send it to P.O. Box 47, New York, New York."
11. Exaggeration (abuse of *ethos:* readers won't trust a writer who overreacts). *Example:* "'You can't judge a book by its cover' is a very familiar saying, and probably the best one yet."

These are several of the many ways that you can annoy your reader or lose your reader's trust. The fallacies can be attributed to failures in *ethos, logos,* or *pathos,* but ultimately, all weaken *ethos.* They all weaken the reader's trust in the writer, and thus they weaken also the reader's willingness to take the action that the writer was hoping for in writing.

Detecting Fallacies in Argument

Exercise 6-2

Much of what passes for careful reasoning can be shown to be shallow if a few definitions are questioned. When I said earlier that I thought men and women were "equal," I should, if I wanted any real communication to take place, have explained what I meant by *equal:* Equal in strength? equal in dignity? equal in opportunity? Read, as another example, this exchange between Socrates and Hermogenes in Plato's dialogue *The Cratylus* (1.332). What fallacies of argument does Plato employ? Compare your answers with those of other students in the class.

SOCRATES: How would you answer, if you were asked whether the wise or the unwise are more likely to give correct names?
HERMOGENES: I should say the wise, of course.
SOCRATES: And are the men or the women of the city, taken as a class, the wiser?
HERMOGENES: I should say, the men.
SOCRATES: And Homer, as you know, says that the Trojan men called him Astyanax (king of the city); but if the men called him Astyanax, the other name of Scamandrius could only have been given to him by the women.
HERMOGENES: That may be inferred.
SOCRATES: And must not Homer have imagined the Trojans to be wiser than their wives?
HERMOGENES: To be sure.
SOCRATES: Then he must have thought Astyanax to be a more correct name for the boy than Scamandrius?
HERMOGENES: Clearly.

Exercise 6-3

Referring to the list of fallacies above if you need to, note what makes you uncomfortable about each of the following attempts to persuade.

1. I feel I can honestly say that motorcycles, in some instances, are safer than cars. How many motorcycle accidents have you heard of in which the driver went through the windshield or was speared by the steering column? In some motorcycle accidents the driver flies clear of the object he hit, as I did when I struck that woman's car.
2. Fidel Castro says that communism is the best form of government.
3. Birth control clinics are the cause of increased teenage sex.
4. If a thing can be produced without art or preparation, much more can it be produced with the help of art and care. (Aristotle)
5. If a thing is possible for inferior, weaker, less intelligent people, it is more so for people who are superior, stronger, and more intelligent. (Aristotle)
6. Buy Giant Panda hot dogs.
7. The virtues and corresponding works of a man are nobler than those of a woman. (Aristotle)
8. Those things are good which are one's own, possessed by no one else, and exceptional. (Aristotle)

9. It's time we take notice. The trend is now unmistakable. You need to understand *what it means!* Suddenly the United States no longer enjoys the highest per capita income of any nation. Sweden has now risen above us. The United States' world's highest living standard has *started on the way down.*

10. Most of the advanced nations of the free world—many of which are critical of America as supreme leader of the West—are suffering from faltering and divided leadership, lack of purpose, and lack of will to act unitedly against onrushing crises

Exercise 6-4

In order to ensure that you understand the ways in which you can easily offend, I suggest that you try to write a brief letter of complaint using *as many fallacies as possible.* Your letter will be given to other members of the class and rated according to how bad you've been able to make it.

All Writing Is Persuasive

In this chapter, I may seem to have assumed that persuasive writing is a distinct kind of writing. If there are distinctions among various "kinds," I think those kinds could be listed as follows:

Exploratory writing: writing to try to figure something out (a scientist's doodlings or a teenager's diary). Exploratory writing is not usually intended for others.

Expressive writing: writing primarily about one's own feelings and ideas (some poetry and literary prose). With expressive writing, it is assumed that the writer is interesting enough to have his or her thoughts, feelings, and language studied by others.

Informative writing: writing to help others learn what you know (reports, newspaper articles, radio and television news spots, letters, how-to books, much literature, bread-and-butter writing).

Scientific writing: writing to convince others that your ideas are correct (most academic writing, reports from national think tanks, philosophy).

Persuasive writing: writing designed to change people's attitudes or ideas or even actions (editorials, political speeches, commercials, sermons, proposals for action, lawyers' briefs).

While it helps to be able to see the differences above, most writers don't specialize in one kind or another. The principles of good writing—well-chosen facts, thoughtful inferences, clear organization, concern for one's reader, correct grammar and punctuation—apply as readily to one form as to another. Moreover, the distinction between the various kinds is often blurred. All four kinds that are intended for readers must be informative—persuasion won't succeed unless it includes reliable information, and even expressive writing provides information about the writer. All four public kinds also intend to be persuasive—scientific writing tries to convince readers that the writer's interpretation of the facts is correct, informative writing wants readers to believe that the information they've selected is worth the reader's time, and expressive writing wants readers to agree that the writer's thoughts are significant. *Ethos, logos,* and *pathos* will be useful to you not just in overtly persuasive writing but in any kind. Similarly, you can judge the quality of any piece of writing—whether a formal speech by Martin Luther King or a quick letter from your mother—by evaluating its *ethos, logos,* and *pathos.* But *ethos, logos,* and *pathos* are most useful as tools, of course, when they are most necessary—that is, when your expected audience is indifferent or hostile, when you must fully employ all your writing resources.

Planning to use *ethos, logos,* and *pathos* impressively may seem, at this point, to be a hopelessly complex task. But as you plan a persuasive paper, you can generally reduce your concerns to three: (1) to collect all the information you can about the subject (an aspect of *logos*); (2) to try to understand as well as possible how those opposed to you would think (an aspect of both *ethos* and *pathos*); and (3) to screw up the courage to take a firm stand (an aspect of *ethos*).

First, information, not cleverness, is your best ally. (Information, you remember, includes not only facts, statistics, and examples but the writer's own experience and the recorded opinions of authorities.) As psychologist Carl Rogers has noted, readers have a natural tendency to judge rather than to listen (284–89). We give our readers much less opportunity to judge if we refrain from throwing about our own judgments while we stay for a while with the facts. John McPhee, one of the most admired current writers of nonfiction, has successfully argued for the preservation of several wilderness areas, including New Jersey's Pine Barrens, by writing articles that simply describe life as it is lived in those areas. When we fail to be specific, readers with views opposite to ours usually stop listening, as when we assert, for example, that Carter had a better foreign policy than Reagan, or that Reagan had a better foreign policy than Carter. Specificity reduces the readers' opportunities to rush to judgment, thus allowing for some real communication, even if differences of opinion do continue to exist.

Second, to quote one of my students, "one cannot tell his reader that he is totally right and doesn't care how the reader feels." A reader whose beliefs or values are being threatened won't listen. Learning to write is (far more than we might expect) learning to understand other people. As John Stuart Mill paraphrases Aristotle, "He who knows only his side of the case, knows little of that" (36). Before you begin any argument of your own, try to write out a one-page argument from your reader's point of view. Then think in terms of values you might agree on. See whether you can find an assumption you share, as in the example of the uses of foreign language instruction a few pages back. What values make you most committed to your position? What values does your reader hold most strongly? Even if the reader knows the facts, he or she still needs nudging in your direction, usually because money, work, or time is involved.

Third, most of us are timid about making judgments, and therefore we don't write much in the margins of our books, or say much in class, or spell out our views to our elected representatives in government or even to our friends. It takes some courage to speak out rather than to just acquiesce to the opinions and actions of others. In order to have courage to make judgments, we first need plenty of information. But then we also need the courage to risk displaying our judgments—in discriminating between good work and bad, the correct and the incorrect, the moral and the immoral. We're all very careful (and we should be) to substantiate our assertions, but we should also encourage ourselves to be willing to stick our necks out, to make assertions. One of your goals for this semester should be to become more assertive—not in the sense that you aggressively state opinions without any facts but in the sense that when you've found enough facts, you feel confident in expressing your well-founded opinions.

7

Paragraphing, Introductions, and Conclusions

Paragraphing

A four-page paper, as you may well know from counting yourself, contains roughly 1000 words. A thousand words of chaos? Sometimes it seems so. We begin, of course, with an introduction and end with a conclusion, but what happens in between? The writer has given some organization to the 1000 words by ordering them into perhaps seventy-five or eighty sentences. But no writer could recall the seventy-five ordering decisions that went into arranging those sentences. Neither could a reader. However, if the piece is well organized, both writer and reader can spell out the ordering principles linking the paper's ten or twelve paragraphs. Paragraphs are the clearest, most memorable means a writer has to show a reader the steps in his or her thinking.

Paragraphing is, in the long view of history, a fairly recent convention of written communication. Until the seventeenth century, paper was too expensive to allow for such waste of space. But since that time periodic indenting has become a conventional way to avoid tiring the reader. Paragraphing is like punctuation in that it makes reading easier, though writers are freer to choose how they paragraph than how they punctuate. When we paragraph, we ask our readers to pause, take a half-second break, and think about all that's been said since we last indented before moving on. Paragraphing is much like picture taking. It's a way of selecting, focusing, emphasizing. Like a photograph, a paragraph can be

104

comprehended at a glance. Like a photograph, it allows the artist to highlight. Like a photograph, it shouldn't be shown to anyone but a relative until it contains something worth thinking about.

The conventional definition of a paragraph is that it is a group of sentences expressing a single idea. But a single idea is open to considerable interpretation (many paragraphs can comfortably contain three or four ideas as long as their arrangement is systematic). The paragraphs that writing teachers like most, and that readers of all kinds find easy to follow, consist of an inference or two (the topic sentence or sentences) followed by several examples. Here are two excellent examples from Paul Fussell's book on World War I, *The Great War and Modern Memory*. The first follows an assertion–with–examples pattern, describing a practice that would be unbelievable if Fussell didn't have the examples to back it up (27):

> One way of showing the sporting spirit was to kick a football toward the enemy lines while attacking. The feat was first performed by the 1st Battalion of the 18th London Regiment at Loos in 1915. It soon achieved the status of a conventional act of bravado and was ultimately exported far beyond the Western Front. Arthur ("Bosky") Borton, who took part in an attack on the Turkish lines near Beersheeba in November, 1917, proudly reported home: "One of the men had a football. How it came there goodness knows. Anyway we kicked off and rushed the first [Turkish] guns, dribbling the ball with us" (Slater 137). But the most famous football episode was Captain W. P. Nevill's achievement at the Somme attack. Captain Nevill, a company commander in the 8th East Surreys, bought four footballs, one for each platoon, during his last London leave before the attack. He offered a prize to the platoon which, at the jump-off, first kicked its football up to the German front line. Although J. R. Ackerley remembered Nevill as "the battalion buffoon" (57), he may have been shrewder than he looked: his little sporting contest did have the effect of persuading his men that the attack was going to be, as the staff had been insisting, a walkover. A survivor observing from a short distance away recalls zero hour: "As the gun-fire died away I saw an infantryman climb onto the parapet into No Man's Land, beckoning others to follow. [Doubtless Captain Nevill or one of his platoon commanders.] As he did so he kicked off a football. A good kick. The ball rose and travelled well towards the German line. That seemed to be the signal to advance" (Middlebrook 124). Captain Nevill was killed instantly. Two of the footballs are preserved today in English museums.

You will have noticed that while Fussell was using an assertion-with-examples organization, he also built—painfully—to a climax.

The next example follows a comparison-contrast (with examples) pattern in order to contrast model trenches in a London park with the real trenches in France and Belgium (Fussell 43):

The trenches I have described are more or less ideal, although not so ideal as the famous exhibition trenches dug in Kensington Gardens for the edification of the home front. These were clean, dry, and well furnished, with straight sides and sandbags neatly aligned. R. E. Vernede writes his wife from the real trenches that a friend of his has just returned from viewing the set of ideal ones. He "found he had never seen anything at all like it before" (112). And Wilfred Owen calls the Kensington Gardens trenches "the laughing stock of the army" (429). Explaining military routines to civilian readers, Ian Hay labors to give the impression that the real trenches are identical to the exhibition ones and that they are properly described in the language of normal domesticity a bit archly deployed: "The firing-trench is our place of business—our office in the city, so to speak. The supporting trench is our suburban residence, whither the weary toiler may betake himself periodically (or, more correctly, in relays) for purposes of refreshment and repose" (97).

The reality was different. The British trenches were wet, cold, smelly, and thoroughly squalid.

Note that neither of these paragraphs stands on its own. Though each is internally well ordered, they beg to be reunited with the paragraphs before and after them. Good paragraphs never stand alone comfortably. They are meant to lean on each other.

In my experience with student papers, the most common weaknesses in paragraphing are (1) using a paragraph as a series of unsupported assertions or (2) using paragraphs that are far too long or far too short. Long-paragraphers, by not making any decisions about linking, force their readers to organize the material themselves. Short-paragraphers are even harder on readers. Short paragraphs don't force a writer to do *any* linking, and thus that entire chore is left to the reader.

Over the years your teachers have probably asked you several questions about your paragraphs when they've commented on your papers. Their questions may have looked like the following:

1. What is the American Congress doing in the middle of a paragraph about France?
2. This seems to be a new idea. Why don't you begin a new paragraph?
3. Franklin's age certainly does not deserve a paragraph to itself.
4. One sentence doesn't make a paragraph. Doesn't this idea fit with the ideas above?
5. Does all this information belong together in the same paragraph?
6. This paragraph is very short. Can this information be combined with the information in some other paragraph?

We all know what to do, with a little thought, with comments like those above. Most paragraphing errors stem from carelessness rather than ignorance. There are other basic guidelines about paragraphs, however, that you may not be aware of. What are those basics?

1. If you write often enough, paragraphing will become intuitive for you. Until that time comes, some writers decide on their paragraphs in their outline or as they write their first draft. But it is not wrong, and it can often be fruitful, to "discover" paragraphs during revision rather than to compose them while drafting.
2. Your reader, in pausing briefly after each paragraph, naturally focuses most on the first and last sentences of paragraphs. These sentences (during revision) should not be wasted. They represent the writer's best opportunities for emphasis, and for clear transitions.
3. The first sentence of a paragraph need not necessarily sum up the paragraph: it is often more effective when it promises or simply piques curiosity. It might pose a problem which the writer proposes to solve. Or it might be a traditional topic sentence: a topic sentence assertion can, after all, tease a reader into wanting to know the specifics that support it.
4. At least as important as the paragraphs themselves are the bridges between paragraphs, the transitions that link what we've just read to what the writer would like us to read next. When not given a clear link, a reader will often quit rather than continue with any interest.
5. The best way, late in your drafting process, to see whether your work makes sense is to try to write a paragraph-by-paragraph summary of what you've written. Your attempt will quickly expose any irregularities in organization.

With these five guidelines in mind, you shouldn't need any paragraph "rules." Your future supervisors or printers or editors, or even the size of the paper you use, will tell you how frequently you'll be expected to paragraph.

Because we can't write paragraphs following set forms, it helps to practice paragraphing techniques until we become confident that we can control their flexibility.

Writing a Paragraph Outline

Exercise 7-1

Write a paragraph-by-paragraph summary of the following passage about kitchen knives. For each paragraph (numbered, for your convenience), sum up what the paragraph says *and* state how that paragraph serves the writer's purpose in writing the essay. Your finished summary should tell you whether the piece makes sense, and so of course you can use this technique with your own work to see whether your own writing makes sense.

From *The Supper of the Lamb*
Robert Farrar Capon

Unless you are wise in the ways of the world, you will be surprised 1
how hard it is to find a decent kitchen knife. Not because good ones are
unavailable, but because there are so many bad ones around that the
odds are against you. If you take what comes to hand, the chances are
you will get a knife that is too small, or the wrong shape, or that will not
hold an edge. In any case, it will cost more than it is worth.

How can that be, you wonder? How can it happen here in the land 2
of the better mousetrap, where quality merchandise always sells and the
makers of shoddy goods invariably wind up poverty-stricken? Ah, yes! I
shall spare you the chapters on aesthetic principles, personal integrity,
popular taste, and political mortality which a sufficient answer requires.
I give you only a new category by which to examine the assumptions of
your question. It is the concept of the Tin Fiddle.

Take the modern American bread knife. You undoubtedly own one: 3
shining stainless steel, slightly curved blade, and *serrated edge.* They are
sold, I suppose, by the millions. Yet if you remember your childhood—
your grandmother's house perhaps—or if you were lucky enough to pick
one up at a junk shop or a rummage sale, you have seen another, older
kind of bread knife: stained carbon steel, straight blade, and, most important of all, a *wavy* edge. Now *there* was a bread knife. It held an edge.
Better yet, its long straight blade came down flush with the board for a
full eleven inches. Best of all, with two wipes on a stone and six on a
steel, it would slice bread fresh from the oven. (Any knife that will not cut
hot bread is not a bread knife at all. If it will not let you have bread at its
best, how can it be worthy of the name?)

Now, what happened to that knife? I own an old one: It is on its 4
third handle. But the only modern copy of it I have ever seen was useless. It had a wavy edge, all right, but the blade was curved, the steel was
hopeless, and the whole thing was too short. Why can't the vast technological resources of America bring us up at least to the level of our grand-
mothers? That is where the tin fiddle comes in.

It is as if there were a conspiracy among violin makers (for what- 5
ever reasons) to provide the public only with violins made of metal. With
enough control of the market, and with advertising sufficient to arouse
the public's interest, they could reach the point at which no new
wooden violins were available.

It would meet with opposition, of course. Nobody who remem- 6
bered having heard a wooden violin would think the tin one as good. No
professional violinist would willingly play a tin fiddle. And there would
be an active market in old wooden violins. All that notwithstanding,

however, the tin ones would sell. With enough manipulation, the only thing available to the man in the street would be an instrument no professional would use: partly because some people never pay enough attention to hear any difference; but mostly because the people who really care about doing things well are not numerous enough to cut much mustard in the marketplace.

The serrated bread knife, therefore, is a tin fiddle, a con-job foisted 7 off on the nonprofessional public. So too are at least half the knives on the market, as well as a good percentage of the rest of the kitchen equipment sold for home use.

That knives should be used on boards, and not sink or counter 8 tops, goes without saying. Let me go further, therefore, and suggest that your cutting boards be numerous: a chopping block, if you can manage it, then a bread board, a fish board, and an onion board. Except for the chopping block, these can succeed each other in a kind of hierarchy. A new board is always a bread board; a retired bread board becomes a fish board (for filleting and skinning); and a retired fish board becomes an onion board. The principle is simple: At any given period in its life, a board will come into contact with nothing stronger than that for which it is named. A retired onion board, accordingly, becomes firewood. None of them, obviously, should ever see the inside of a dishwasher.

Finally, however, my protest. 9

I am against the electric knife personally, and against the electric 10 knife sharpener absolutely.

To take the latter first, it is one of the greatest tin fiddles on the 11 market. The only people who use it are people who don't care about knives. To begin with, it is not a sharpener, but a grinder. A well-treated knife, however—one kept abreast of its destiny by stone and steel—will never need grinding. (My father had a carving knife which he kept razor-sharp for thirty-five years with nothing but a steel. There was not a scratch on the blade. My knives are as sharp as his were, but not as beautiful. We are descended, you see, from men whom we shall be lucky if we match. There were giants in the earth in those days.)

The electric grinder is a dull tool. Its angles are usually too steep 12 for a long-lasting edge, it turns over a burr large enough to stop peas, and, in the hands of anyone but a genius, it will, in six short months, turn a die-straight edge into a series of gruesomely notched curves. Add to that the fact that it literally eats knives, and you have more than enough reasons for never bothering with it. Anyone who can use it well is already intelligent enough not to use it at all.

The electric knife, however, is a more complex problem. I grant you 13 that there are people who carve better with one than without. So far I allow it. I would rather see a roast sliced by electricity than mangled by a clown with a dull knife. I have watched beautiful roasts dismantled by inept carvers, and I know the anguish it involves. It would be less pain-ful—and neater—to see them kicked apart with a pointed shoe. I have also eaten Smithfield ham in great half-inch-thick slabs hacked off by a knife whose last sharpening took place at the knife factory. Anything that will spare mankind the torture of chewing its way through tough meat to searing thirst is on the side of the angels.

But for myself, I beg to be excused from the general stampede of 14 progress. By one of the ironies of fate, I do in fact own an electric knife. After brief use, it was placed on permanent loan to a friend. Not that it did not do what it was supposed to do—it did; and it was admirably ingenious in the bargain. It is just that, having learned the trade from experts, I found it gross, noisy, and unnecessary. When my father or grandfather carved, knife and hand were an inseparable unity; the whole process a silent display of grace. I could as soon imagine them with wires connected to their brains, as see them wanting cords to run their knives. I grew up with *artists*, you see—with philosophers who remem-bered that everything new is not necessarily better than everything old. The electric carving knife, therefore, makes no more sense to me than a motor-driven palette knife or a steam-powered violin bow. When Isaac Stern changes his ways, it will be time enough for me to think about mending mine.

It isn't stubbornness. It's just that, once you've seen giants, you 15 don't forget so easily.

After completing your paragraph summary, you can also note how each sentence contributes to the main idea of a paragraph by choosing one of the paragraphs above and explaining, sentence by sentence, how each sentence relates to the summarizing idea you've given for the para-graph. This task may seem complex at first, but if you force yourself to think, and if you compare your answers with those of other class mem-bers, you'll learn a great deal about how paragraphs help us structure our thinking.

Choosing, and Giving Reasons for, Paragraph Breaks

Exercise 7-2

In order to test your assumptions about how paragraphs are formed, read through the following essay by Fred Reed and decide where you would begin paragraphs if you were the writer of this essay. The sentences have been numbered to make class discussion about your choices easier. The paragraph choices made by Mr. Reed are identified in the Instructor's Manual.

Lean, Healthy, and Forty-Five
Fred Reed

(1) The anti-jogging column threatens to become a mainstay of such literature as we have, perhaps replacing Watergate memoirs. (2) As I imagine it, the anti-jogging writer packs his slanderous tendencies into a briefcase and goes to a place where jogging is committed—a trail along the Potomac, say. (3) He waits. (4) A jogger thunders by in $65 waffle rubber shoes, $68 jogging suit of parachute fabric crafted to reduce wind resistance, and Navajo jogger's sweatband. (5) He carries organic dextrose pellets and several pounds of electronics—an integrated-circuit wrist pedometer, a digital blood-pressure indicator and a solar-powered pulse-counter with built-in coronary alarm. (6) The well-equipped jogger has the circuitry of a small fighter plane. (7) He also has a certain amount of philosophical baggage. (8) He is jogging to find out Who He Is, information that he might have gotten from his wife or his driver's license. (9) He is Probing the Limits of Self. (10) The writer tries to make this sound ridiculous. (11) This is to misunderstand the jogger. (12) He is usually over 30, and has noticed that stairs are getting perceptibly steeper. (13) He is a bit disturbed by it, suspicious that something new has been slipped into the contract. (14) The moment of truth usually comes when he realizes they aren't really letting girls into college at age 14. (15) He looks uneasily around the office at men 10 years older. (16) They have smoker's cough, liver conditions, and look as though they are smuggling medicine balls. (17) In all important senses they are sessile. (18) At this point he acquires a deep desire to go white-water canoeing, to try rock-climbing or to go on a commando mission into Botswana. (19) By the end of the afternoon he is persuaded that he has only a few hours to live. (20) That evening he wheezes around the block while his wife shadows him in a rented ambulance. (21) There is something noble, tragic and silly in it. (22) The jogger lives for 30 years on a diet of lard and french fries, plugging up his arteries and taking years from his life. (23) Then he jogs to expand the arteries around the lard, getting the time back. (24) The anti-jogging writer sniggers at this inconsistency, as well as at the mystical hooha that surrounds jogging—the confusion of crumbling cartilage with enlightenment, the Oneness with Nature, and the High, which is in fact indistinguishable from the onset of flu. (25) The jogger tends to be a fiercely competitive fellow who is not about to be intimidated by God, metabolism, time and destiny. (26) He persists, that being what the fiercely competitive do best, and, lo, soon he is running five miles a day. (27) The American male believes that if a thing is worth doing, it is worth overdoing. (28) The children slowly forget him ("Ma, who *is* that guy...?"). (29) His knees fill with bone fragments and his kidneys begin to loosen, so he buys shoes. (30) By now he has noticed that running is work. (31) The jogger tries to conceal this behind a fraudulent jauntiness—"Yes, ran 40 miles today,

just didn't have time for a good workout. (32) Usually do it on one leg." (33) Yet it is most dreadful work. (34) Worse, it is boring. (35) The body really can be brutalized into condition, after which it will go on forever. (36) To have a reasonable expectation of cardiac arrest, one must run for hours. (37) The nirvana promised after Mile 5 doesn't materialize. (38) Stir-craziness comes. (39) He still doesn't know Who He Is. (40) Nobody but a thorough-going damned fool would suffer so much without an analgesic and a reward. (41) The analgesic is toys. (42) It is fun to get a new piece of running instrumentation—preferably with LEDs, the *sine qua non* of spiritual experience. (43) He may not go faster in his new, absurdly expensive, helium-filled shoes, but it is nice to unwrap them, like having an extra birthday. (44) The reward is showing off. (45) Face it: people get very little recognition in this anthill society. (46) It's a kick to be lean, healthy and 45, to be 11 miles into a run of 20, to be bounding along at an easy lope and sticking his chest out at the high school girls. (47) They never notice—they figure a fellow of 45 belongs in the Smithsonian—but there's hope that their mothers will come along. (48) And he feels so pleasantly superior to the majority, who would collapse at anything more arduous than relaxed breathing—among whom one inevitably finds, *heh heh,* the authors of anti-jogging columns.

Once you've made your decisions, defend them—first in a small group, then with the whole class. There will probably be much disagreement. The important thing, though, is that you can explain *why* you thought each paragraph division should be made. Your reasons for paragraphing, taken together with the reasons given by the rest of the class, should give you a good idea of how paragraphs are formed. People choose to paragraph for such reasons as length, unity, emphasis, and tone. At least one new reason comes up each time a class tries this exercise.

You may want to repeat this exercise using papers from other students in your class. Be sure, whenever you do this kind of exercise, to specify *why* you would begin a new paragraph in each place you have chosen, for it is in deciding *why* that you train yourself as a paragrapher of your own essays.

Coherence

Many of us are afraid that our writing within paragraphs isn't smooth enough, but we're not quite sure what *smooth* means. Clear signposts help, as in the following example (Kolb 16):

> The (attorneys) (state) that the (defendant) acquired additional property after the divorce hearing, and that (he) left a will. (They) (further state) that the court's ruling on the present motion will have a substantial effect upon the property rights of the plaintiff

and the defendant's heirs. If the divorce decree is not entered, the plaintiff would take the real property as tenant by the entirety, would have widow's rights in the after acquired property, and could dissent from the will. *On the other hand,* if the divorce decree is entered nunc pro tunc, the plaintiff could have a one-half undivided interest in the real property as a tenant in common, would have no interest in the after acquired property, and could not affect the will.

Two questions are involved. First, can a successor judge enter a nunc pro tunc decree involving the action of a predecessor judge? Second, is this a proper case for the entry of a nunc pro tunc decree? The answer to both questions is yes.

The writer above used signposts ("Two questions...First...Second..."), clear contrasts ("If...*On the other hand,* if..."), and parallel structure ("would take...would have...could dissent...") to make his work smooth. Smoothness only rarely requires formal connectors like *furthermore, however, moreover,* or *in conclusion.*

To see in greater detail how we most naturally connect our work, try the following exercise.

Exercise 7-3

Here is a set of data based on an article in the business section of a newspaper (Ross 5). The data, though raw, is complete and is in about the right order. Shape it into a piece of efficient prose, using whatever connecting words you need and paragraphing wherever you wish. Later we will compare your result with the results of others in the class and with the original.

past decade—supermarket chains deserting inner cities in alarming numbers—residents with no cars few or no alternatives to expensive convenience stores—number in Boston, Washington, and Chicago urban areas declined 28–50% in past five years—Community Nutrition Institute—new manual—how inner cities can maintain or bring back food markets—six case studies—including Santoni's Market in southeast Baltimore—offers practical guide—establishing food co-ops, farmers' markets—independently operated supermarkets—hints—limiting food assortment to 1000 or so staple items—selling products that cater to neighborhood needs—Do food-stamp users need appliance and camera equipment counters?—Sunday hours—wine and beer sales—minibus transportation—child-care centers—urge community to lobby local government—get a low-cost lease on adjacent city-owned property—use as parking lot—resurface sidewalks—high-powered street lights—available Community Nutrition Institute—Washington, D.C.

When you finish your smooth version, circle *every* word that you've added or altered. A comparison of the choices you've made could take an entire class period. You have hundreds of options to choose from as you link, but my guess is that you'll find that:

1. Your most effective link is repetition of a term or the use of a pronoun to replace that term.
2. When you do use connective words, your best choices are simple words like *and, but, or,* and *so.*
3. Parallel structure ("*limiting* food assortment...," "*selling* products...," "*avoiding* appliance counters...," "*providing* minibus transportation") is one of your most useful linking devices.
4. Only occasionally do you need blockbuster connectors like *moreover.*

Having completed the exercises in this portion of the chapter, you should now be more conscious of the writer's techniques—paragraph choices, choices of linking words, and choices of tone of voice—that hold writing together and make it sound "smooth." Since it is during revising that we make most of our decisions about how to ease our readers' passage through our writing, Chapter 8, "Revision," will include further advice about those decisions.

Introductions

Just as you guide the reader throughout the body of your paper using paragraphs, coherence, and transitions, you guide the reader at the beginning and at the end of your work with your introduction and your conclusion.

Exercise 7-4
Review

Before you read what I have to say about your introductions and conclusions, write in your notebook your current thinking about them:

1. What do you try to do in an introduction?
2. What do you try to do in a conclusion?

You can begin any piece of writing by introducing your credentials with a statement like:

> This 500-word essay which I am about to start is based on my
> knowledge of and experience in high school and college.

Is that too obvious? Too dull? Perhaps you're tempted to begin by philosophizing:

> For everything in life we all have two choices. As we have two sides to every coin, we have two sides like positive or negative, win or lose, profit or waste. Ohio State has made my life different than I had thought it would.

Is your reader following your reverie? Perhaps not. A third alternative is just to "sort of start writing," as the student who wrote the following did:

> On July 23, 1986, I was dropped off on a desert island. I was permitted to take three things along with me. The first thing I took was a knapsack full of government books. This would enable me to keep up with my studies in school. The next product I took along....

There are better ways. You'll find many lists in textbooks of what should go into a good introduction or what should go into a good conclusion, but I think you'll learn more by testing your own sense of what you like in an introduction or in a conclusion.

Exercise 7-5
Distinguishing Introductions, Conclusions, and Body Paragraphs

Look over the following paragraphs. Try to decide whether each is an introductory paragraph, a concluding paragraph, or a body paragraph from an essay. In the blank before each paragraph put an I if the paragraph is an introduction, a B if it is a body paragraph, or a C if it is a concluding paragraph. Once you've made your decisions, get into a group with three or four classmates and see if you all agree. If you don't agree, give your reasons for the decisions you made about the character of the paragraphs. Then share your group's results with the rest of the class. The original uses of these paragraphs can be found in the Instructor's Manual.

_____ 1. In the eighteenth century, an owler was a smuggler of sheep or wool from England to France. A few years later, the term was applied to one who sat up all night, now called a nightowl. But an owler today is one of the unusual breed of birders who do their stalking nocturnally. They often go alone, either because they prefer it that way, or because no one wants to tag along; there aren't that many people who enjoy the idea of hanging around a dim forest listening for somber owl hoots in the dead of night. (Neal Clark, "An Owling Primer," _Appalachia,_ December 1981.)

_____ 2. The so-called black land drain and the plight of the black farmer have surfaced as major issues among blacks only within the last decade. During the 1950s and '60s, the focus for black equality and justice centered on such issues as voting rights and desegregation of public accommodations. Yet, during the same period, the amount of black-owned land in the South, mostly farmland, declined precipitously from 12.5 million acres to 6 million acres. (Chet Fuller, "Living Off the Land," *Black Enterprise,* November 1982.)

____ 3. The rising price of land is a key factor behind the stagnation of the housing industry. In large city areas, the price of land for housing is rising by about 10 percent every year—leading to sharp increases in the price of houses, actually pushing them far beyond the reach of an average worker's purchasing power. ("The Dark Side of the Prospering Japanese Economy," *The East,* August 1982.)

____ 4. Parenting in any setting is not an easy task. Parenting abroad offers some uniquely challenging stresses and opportunities for parents. For families recently posted to a new assignment, complaints such as "I don't want to be here...These people are really weird...This place is the pits...I miss my friends back home" may prevail for weeks or even months as children adjust—or fail to adjust—to their new environments. Fortunately, most children not only make a successful adjustment but benefit greatly from the experience of living abroad. There are, however, five major areas in which problems surface again and again in child-rearing when families transport themselves overseas: teaching responsibility; relations with host country nationals; family communication; peer relationships; and returning home. These deserve special attention and consideration. (Joel Wallach and Gale Metcalf, "Parenting Abroad," *Foreign Service Journal,* June 1982.)

____ 5. Like confident parents who believe more in bloodlines than report cards, the supporters of dispute resolution have not been discouraged by the mixed reviews of evaluating academics. They remain confident that over the years, as mediation burrows its way into the court establishment, it will reach the goals that have been expected of it. To them, dispute-resolution programs have already proven one thing— that they can provide an atmosphere rarely found in the bullpens and back benches of the urban courthouse. "The bottom line," says Royer Cook, "is that people like the way they're treated." (John J. McCarthy, "Dispute Resolution: Seeking Justice outside the Courtroom," *Corrections Magazine,* August 1982.)

If your teacher lists on the board the reasons that you and your class-mates have given for your various decisions, by the end of the class you'll all have a thorough list of what you as readers expect in introductions, body paragraphs, and conclusions. That list should help you decide what to put in your own.

Exercise 7-6
Critical Reading of Introductions and Conclusions

You can learn to write better introductions or conclusions, too, by collecting some from various media to see how professionals go about that part of their business. Bring to class on a given day three or four of the following:

1. A textbook from another class
2. A newspaper
3. A magazine from your living room
4. A work of fiction
5. A how-tomanual
6. A cookbook
7. A piece of junk mail

Your teacher might add to this collection a scholarly journal and a nonfiction videotape.

Take all or part of class to read each other introductions and conclusions from these various media. Comment on the means used by each to hook readers in, and to let them go thoughtfully.

In the following boxes are four inviting introductions. If you become stuck while trying to write an introduction for one of your papers, read these over looking for ideas, then ask yourself two questions:

1. What do my readers need to know to understand what I want to say?
2. How can I interest my readers in what I want to say?

Something will click. Students are usually not too bad at introductions.

On June 27, 1957, *The New York Times* ran a brief story on page 3 titled "Non-whites Strike in Johannesburg." It stated that "on June 26 about half of Johannesburg's Negro, Asian, and Colored workers stayed at home for a one-day protest strike against South Africa's racial segregation. The action also was in support of a demand for higher wages." The writer noted that "the African and Indian National Congresses have claimed the strike as a 'significant victory.'" The rest of the story was devoted to the effects of the work stoppage. Stores were closed, transportation was slowed, and coal deliveries came to a standstill. We read stories of this nature daily, believing that we now know the facts, that we have come to an understanding of what has taken place. On a second reading, however, one begins to wonder if this sense of closure is due to thorough reporting or if it is an illusion created by smooth, confident rhetoric.

—An effective introduction to a student's paper. It doesn't state a specific thesis, but it makes us curious about an issue the writer wants to discuss. Such a strategy can be more effective than presenting a spelled-out thesis.

Everyone seems to agree that there is something wrong with the way science is being taught these days. But no one is at all clear about when it went wrong or what is to be done about it. The term "scientific illiteracy" has become almost a cliché in educational circles. Graduate schools blame the colleges; colleges blame the secondary schools; the high schools blame the elementary schools, which, in turn, blame the family. I suggest that the scientific community itself is partly, perhaps largely, to blame.

Lewis Thomas, introduction to "The Art of Teaching Science."

The weather satellite 22,300 miles out in space reveals a beautiful but deceptive picture of earth. The view we see is of a placid world floating peacefully in the blackness of space, patterns of white clouds winding like ornaments across the planet's disk. But we know how misleading that serene scene can be. Within those clouds, within the rest of the atmosphere so invisible, and beneath the surface of what we think of as a solid planet, lurk awesome energies that need only the proper conditions to unleash their havoc.

Kendrick Frazier, introduction to *The Violent Face of Nature.*

They gave me a party on my 80th birthday in August 1978. First there were cards, letters, telegrams, even a cable of congratulation or condolence; then there were gifts, mostly bottles; there was catered food and finally a big cake with, for some reason, two candles (had I gone back to very early childhood?). I blew the candles out a little unsteadily. Amid the applause and clatter I thought about a former custom of the Northern Ojibwas when they lived on the shores of Lake Winnipeg. They were kind to their old people, who remembered and enforced the ancient customs of the tribe, but when an old person became decrepit, it was time for him to go. Sometimes he was simply abandoned, with a little food, on an island in the lake. If he deserved special honor, they held a tribal feast for him. The old man sang a death song and danced, if he could. While he was still singing, his son came from behind and brained him with a tomahawk. That was quick, it was dignified, and I wonder whether it was any more cruel, essentially, than some of our civilized customs or inadvertences in disposing of the aged.

Malcolm Cowley, introduction to "The View from 80."

Conclusions

Conclusions are another matter. Good conclusions to student papershave in my experience been rare. Writer after writer resorts to a summary of exactly what they've said in the paper (as if I couldn't remember) or perhaps to a grand comment about how understanding just this issue may save the world. There is plenty of fertile ground between those two extremes, though rarely does anyone occupy it.

When you reach the point in your essay that you're ready to conclude, pick up your pen. Ask yourself, so what? Why have I bothered to write this paper? Before plunging right back in with an answer, take notes. Answer the *so what* question in several different ways. Then *select* the answer that is most promising and draft your conclusion. Simply because you've taken time to select the best at this point where most writers have allowed themselves to stop thinking and sail to the end, you'll startle your teacher with your results.

Exercise 7-7
Writing and Comparing Conclusions

One of the reasons we rarely improve at writing conclusions is that every conclusion is unique to a given paper and we can never compare what we've chosen to write with what someone else might have chosen. To help give you a rare opportunity for comparative practice, I've reproduced here a student paper from which the ending has been omitted. After reading through the paper carefully, write an ending based on how you think the writer-reader relationship in this paper should conclude. After you've read aloud your version and heard several other versions, jot down some observations about what a conclusion can do.

Sisu: the Word that Won a War
Aletha Hendrickson

One of the debates raging in Congress involves economic aid to the   1
Nicaraguan contra rebels. President Reagan pushes, Congress resists—
the public yawns. Reagan's strategy promotes fear of Communists on
America's doorstep. Fifty years ago another tiny country faced Soviet
domination: Finland, back door to Russia.

Considering that Finland shared one-half of its border with Russia,   2
that Russian manpower outnumbered Finnish forces 50 to 1, that Finland had no heavy industrial plants capable of manufacturing arms or
ammunition—why did Finland escape the fate of Poland, Hungary, Afghanistan and so many other overrun countries? What kept Finland
from becoming another Russian satellite?

I posed these questions to Helmi Juntunen, a Finnish-American, 3 who had served as a "Telephonist" in the Russo-Finnish war of 1939. "The main reason for Finland winning the Winter War of 1939," she said simply, "was *sisu.*" Although the term defies interpretation in any language, journalists were able to translate *sisu* in a way linguists could not. The press identified the essence of the Finnish character and graphically portrayed a valiant, victimized people. Writers were thus able to rally sympathy for the Finnish people, which resulted in immediate financial support.

Journalists reacted swiftly to the unprovoked and undeclared So- 4 viet attack on Finland. Stalin's troops crossed the Finnish border on November 30, 1939 (Soloveytchik 151); ten days later, *The New York Times* printed an appeal following an article on the Finnish Relief Fund, headed by former President Herbert Hoover:

Times to Accept Contributions
Contributions to the Finnish Relief Fund may be sent directly
to its headquarters in the Graybar Building, New York City, or,
if properly designated for that purpose, will be received by
The New York Times and forwarded to the Finnish Relief
Fund (*"Times* to Accept" 5).

That same issue covered Hoover's plea to 100 city newspapers "to act as agencies for collection of contributions" to keep down administrative costs ("Thirteen Bankers" 5). When dealing with Finnish aid, subsequent articles in the *Times* printed the full street address of the fund.

War news and articles generally emphasized the Finnish point of 5 view. Titles and headlines included: "Finns are Ready" (*Living Age*); "Fiery Finns, Hard to Rule, Quick to Fight and Intensely Proud of State" (*Newsweek*); "Finland's Fight for Freedom" (*Listener*); "Last Agony of Fighting Finland is Wrapped in the Beauty of Snow" (*Life*); "Help for Finland" (*The New Yorker*); "Finland's Snows Shroud Slaughter" (*Essay Annual*); and "Finland's Struggle" (*Contemporary Review*). When headlines mentioned both combatants, however, the Russians were generally portrayed negatively: "Finland—the Giant Killer" (*National Review*); "The Gangster Attack on Finland" (*Army Quarterly*); and "Attack on Finland" (*Queens Quarterly*).

Reporters and writers underscored not only odds against Finland 6 in its struggle, but the unfair advantage Russia took in its attacks. While previous treaties were "religiously" upheld by the Finns, Russians broke most of them (Sperling 1155). *Contemporary Review* compared the "utter incapacity and lack of preparedness of the Soviet military" with the "heroism and efficiency of the Finns" (Soloveytchik 151). Russians were described as "invading Reds" (152) and as "ruthless and murderous"

(Sperling 1158). Writers acknowledged Finland as the "immediate and direct victim of Stalin's aggression" (Soloveytchik 154). Statistics substantiated the David and Goliath aspect of the conflict: 180 million Soviets against 3.8 million Finns.

While Soviet nonmilitary achievements received little press space, 7 reporters treated readers to a crash course in Finnish political, cultural, and intellectual history. Finns possessed "the strongest and most truly national government" (Soloveytchik 157); women enjoyed positions of leadership. Though rooted in ancient folk-ways, though still three-fourths rural, Finland showed a "passion for education and self-improvement," having more university students and publishing more books annually per capita than any other country (Strode 7).

The press garnered swift support, causing Roosevelt to declare, 8 "American sympathy is 98% with the Finns" (Denny 42), despite a *Time* magazine article, "For Finland" which devoted 28 out of 63 lines to pro-Communist sentiment. *Time* noted that "intellectual Herman Shumlin...refused to let his production [of] *The Little Foxes*...give a benefit performance." As "pro-Finland stars and producers rushed...to castigate Mr. Shumlin[,] [s]omebody pointed out that Herman Shumlin was the only Broadway producer advertising in the *Communist Daily Worker*. It seemed that Mr. Shumlin had almost no friends except Leftish Lillian Hellman..." (16). Widespread involvement for Finnish benefits included: unions of stage, screen and radio; the Metropolitan Opera; the NBC Symphony Orchestra; Presidents Hoover and Roosevelt; investment bankers; "Right-Wing Socialists" ("Hoover" 16); Protestant and Jewish leaders, and the National Association for the Advancement of Colored People. Name dropping abounded: Tallulah Bankhead donated a week's salary, and Helen Hayes staged a benefit performance. The second screening of *Gone with the Wind* benefited the Finns ("For Finland" 17). Americans tended to link the Finnish cause with American patriotism, partly because of *The New York Times* coverage of a Carnegie Hall benefit performance which featured works by Sibelius, Handel's "Defend Her, Heaven," "Battle Hymn of the Republic," and the final selection, "The Star-Spangled Banner" ("Stage" 22).

Journalistic treatment of the Russo-Finnish War, then, spurred an 9 outpouring of sympathy and financial support from all segments of America: Hoover's appeal to 100 city papers to collect for Finland resulted in 1,200 responding. An Export Bank Loan to Finland soon followed even though Roosevelt and Congress had to tiptoe around the Neutrality Act. Aid usually took the form of civilian relief for men, women, and children routed from their bombed cities—but appeals for gas masks for civilians as well as for "1,000...Horses Now in War Service" were heard and filled ("Finland Seeks Gas Masks" 1). Such appeals were accompanied by a recitation of Finland's singular credit history— Finland was the *only* country current in its payments to the Bank. Journalists capitalized on the idea that investment in such a brave, deserving, honest people, with so much at stake, would not be wasted (or unpaid, should Finland survive).

Furthermore, journalists stressed more than the Soviet menace or the suffering Finns—they zeroed in on an aspect of the Finnish character which pried open American pocketbooks, as indicated in a subheadline in *The New York Times* one week after the early December bombing of Helsinki: "Drive is made out of respect for the 'quality' of the Finnish character" ("Thirteen Bankers" 5). That quality was summed up in the most wonderful of all Finnish words: *sisu. The Times Magazine* ran a major article, "*Sisu*, A Word that Explains Finland" to document the mystique associated with Finland (Strode 6–7). The author described *sisu* as "the Finn's minus as well as plus. It makes it impossible for him to compromise his ideals." He quoted Sibelius as saying that "*sisu* is a metaphysical shot in the arm which makes a man do the impossible" (7). Thus the fearless Finns dared to counter Soviet air power with skis and horses.

[The conclusion is omitted so that you can write one yourself.]

Works Cited

Bories, J. "Finns are Ready." *Living Age* Dec. 1939: 336–37.

Bruce, E. L. "The Attack on Finland." *Queen's Quarterly* 47 (1940): 48–53.

Delehanty, Elizabeth. "Help for Finland." *The New Yorker* 2 Mar. 1940: 50–51.

Denny, George V. "What Aid for Finland?" *Current History* Mar. 1940: 42–45.

"Fiery Finns, Hard to Rule, Quick to Fight, and Intensely Proud of State." *Newsweek* 11 Dec. 1939: 28.

"Finland, the Giant-Killer." *National Review* Feb. 1940: 161–65.

"Finland Seeks Gas Masks Here for Civilians; Orders 1,000 for Horses Now in War Service." *The New York Times* 11 Dec. 1939: 1.

"For Finland." *Time Magazine* 11 Mar. 1940: 16–17.

"The Gangster Attack on Finland." *Army Quarterly* Apr. 1940: 32–40.

"Hoover Appeals for a Finland Day." *The New York Times* 12 Dec. 1939: 16.

Juntunen, Helmi. Personal Interview 12 Mar. 1986.

"Last Agony of Fighting Finland is Wrapped in the Beauty of Snow." *Life* 11 Mar. 1940: 23–27.

Soloveytchik, George. "Finland's Struggle." *The Contemporary Review* Feb. 1940: 151–59.

Sperling, Rowland. "Finns Fight for Freedom." *The Listener* 14 Dec. 1939: 1155–1158.

"Stage Forms Group to Aid Finnish Fund." *The New York Times* 26 Dec. 1939: 22.

Stowe, L. "Finland's Snows Shroud Slaughter." *Essay Annual* 1940: 261–263.

Strode, Hudson. *"Sisu:* A Word that Explains Finland." *The New York Times Magazine* 14 Jan. 1940: 6–7.
"Thirteen Bankers Issue Appeal for Finns." *The New York Times* 9 Dec. 1939: 5.
"Times to Accept Contributions." *The New York Times* 9 Dec. 1939: 5.

Your own practice with introductions and conclusions will help you most in learning to write them, of course. So expect, during the semester, to see some of your introductions or conclusions reproduced and passed around to the class.

Introductions and conclusions, far more than any other aspects of a paper, test the writer's skill in understanding others. In an introduction you must bridge the gap between yourself and your readers. Because "shared context builds up between writer and reader as the piece proceeds,...the chances of losing, confusing, misleading, or frustrating a reader are at their greatest in the opening sentences" (Britton 21). An introduction, after providing that context, might end with a "thesis," but that's not always necessary. You may prefer to raise some questions or point out some crucial issues, saving your thesis, or message, for later. Whether you raise an issue, though, or state a thesis, your reader should know before long *why* you bothered to write this paper. An introduction has done its work if it shows that you respect your reader and that you know what you want to talk about. A conclusion has done its work if it shows that you know—and care about—the significance of what you've written.

8

Revision

Editing—which can be described very simply as the assembling and joining of selected pieces of film—is regarded by many directors as the creative peak of the entire film-making process, the preliminary shooting being largely a matter of collecting together the necessary materials to be assembled into a coherent whole.

Ivan Butler

Writing is committed speech—speech we are willing to polish, fix, and vouch for.

Dennis Drabelle

The rate at which one recognizes his own badness is the rate at which he grows as a writer.

John Ciardi

Now I see for the first time that discarded writing is not wasted effort.

student

Giving Yourself the Power of Two

Reviewing and revising what we've written, when we already have enough words on paper to fulfill an assignment, requires more effort and more patience than most of us are willing to give unless we're forced to. Yet this book attempts to force you to do just that—to make reviewing and revising a routine—because the practice you get in revising while you're in school will save you countless hours and serious frustration when you've left school and revision becomes necessary for your success and your livelihood.

Exercise 8-1
Review of Your Current Practice

How much revising do you do when you write papers or lab reports for school? What kinds of changes do you make?

124

Any piece of writing that you write in one session at your desk or word processor is the product of one person. A piece that you write out and then consciously revise becomes the work of two people, and it's often twice as good. During a first draft, a "discovery" draft, we are most curious to find out how much we have to say on the issue we've chosen to work with. We revise a bit during this draft as we change major ideas to minor ones, reorder our paragraphs, and occasionally change sentences, phrases, and words if they don't sound the way we want to sound or don't say what we want to say. But most successful writers take special pains during their first draft to ignore back-of-their-mind questions about words or sentences or even whole sections, special pains to suppress the reviser in them so that they can concentrate on finding the most interesting and appropriate facts and on interpreting those facts thoughtfully. But then as a deadline approaches, because they want to get their message across as clearly as possible and because they want to avoid embarrassment, they get very careful (even ruthless) not only about their facts, their inferences, and their introductions and conclusions but about their sentences and even their words.

Several recent politicians have tried to take their words back by saying that they "misspoke." But I haven't yet heard any writers excuse themselves by saying that they "miswrote." We can't take our writing back. Filmmakers, who know they can't take their films back ("I misfilmed?"), routinely spend six months editing until they have revised a film into the precise form that they want it to take. Of course, the filmmaker is hoping to make $20 million on a film, and you're only trying to please yourself, some of your classmates, and your teacher, so you may (understandably) decide to give less than six months to the task.

Revising, like the other aspects of writing, is a skill that improves with practice. At first, you'll probably feel awkward and unworthy of making judgments. If you're like most of us, you'll start by criticizing surface problems, like short, choppy sentences:

> This is a real story. It happened six years ago. I had a very close circle of friends. One day somebody proposed to climb a mountain. Actually a volcano. I was sure I was going to get lost. It was a terrible day and night for me.

Or an awkward repetition of words:

> When junior high school *started,* I *started* getting my first taste of real discipline.

Or poor grammar, word choice, or spelling:

> *Sanity* depends mainly on the way one *discipline* himself.
>
> I could *dare* his bet.

These things do matter, but it takes practice to break away from judging words, which is comparatively easy, and to start to judge the thought that went into your paper. Revision is not just changing a few words and fixing some punctuation, but looking back (*re-vision*) and making substantial changes in what we've thought or written. Learning to see the whole picture of what you are trying to say is one of the most difficult habits that you'll try to acquire during this course.

Student writers have a history of revising very little. Our habit of starting late often leaves too little time for revision. But even when we have the time, we change very little (1) because it's too much trouble to make changes, since a substantial change in one part of the paper often requires changes elsewhere, (2) because we've used all the lines on our paper with our draft, and there's no room to insert changes even if we want to make them, and (3) because even when we read over our work and are puzzled by a sentence or a paragraph, rather than change it, we decide that we must have had a reason for writing it that way the first time.

These excuses must be attacked head on. First, it's not difficult to allow time for revision. If we believe in its value, we will make time for it. Second, assuming that we're writing with pen and paper, we have to develop a strategy for leaving room for legible revisions. *Trying* to leave margins doesn't work for me (they get smaller and smaller as I go along). Writing on every second or third line doesn't work either (it distracts me from what I'm saying). What does work is a suggestion by Roger Garrison (24) that a writer draw a line down the middle of each page and draft only to the right of that line, thus allowing plenty of space on the left for questions, comments, and readable revisions. (See Figure 8-1.) Word processors, which make it easy to revise, eliminate the whole problem. They don't require any space to revise. Third, we're fools if we wholly trust the self that wrote our first draft, figuring "we must have had a reason." At this point we need some help from a person who is less uncritically fond of our work than we are.

By the time a paper has reached the clean-draft stage and is ready for full-time revision, the writer is not the best person to do the critical reading necessary to decide what should stay, what should go, and what should be added. The reading of a classmate, or teacher, or friend is fresher and will often help more because that reader has not become fond of ideas or phrases, as the writer has. When I submitted a draft of this book to editors at McGraw-Hill, they sent the draft out to six reviewers, all of whom sent me five to ten pages of compliments, criticisms, and suggestions. Those reviewers were trying not just to "fix" my work but to help me say best what I was trying to say. Some of their comments hurt when I first read them, but all the comments, particularly those that hurt, helped me to improve the final draft.

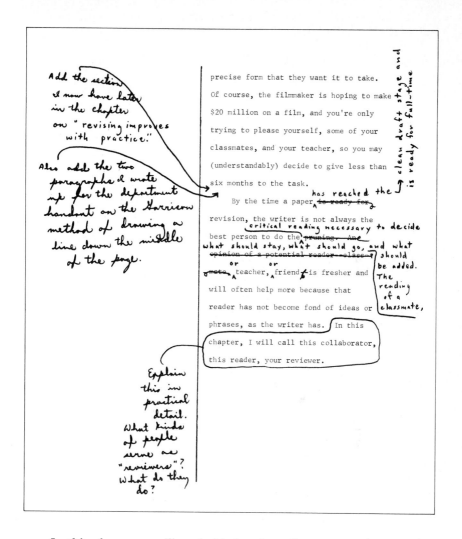

In this class, you will probably be given the opportunity to review the work of your classmates, in the process not only helping them see those particular papers more clearly but training you both in the skills of revising. For every assignment I've suggested in Chapter 14, I've included a sample rough draft and a set of questions which should help you review that draft. Following is a list of the broad questions which should be asked of any paper:

1. Is there enough fresh information here to make you glad you read this paper? What kinds of facts do you feel are missing? What further research do you think the writer should do?
2. Does the writer seem to have a genuine interest in the subject and a

good grasp of the information connected with it?

3. What are the most important assertions, or inferences, that the writer has made about the subject of this paper? Which inferences need to be made clearer or more specific?

4. What does the writer attempt to do in the introduction to the paper? Does the introduction provide the background you need to understand the analysis that follows?

5. Describe the writer's organizational strategy paragraph by paragraph. Which paragraphs don't proceed smoothly from the paragraph they follow? Note every point in the paper where you were temporarily confused.

6. Read over the concluding paragraph. What emotion does the writer try to leave you with? Can you make any suggestions for improving the conclusion?

7. What are two possible objections or points of view that you think the writer has naively neglected so far?

8. What thoughts or questions occurred to you as you read through this paper?

9. After reading this paper, what would you, as a thoughtful reader, now want to say about this subject? How has reading this paper affected your attitude toward the subject discussed?

Of course, the author of a paper is not bound to take all the advice that you give in answering these questions, nor are you bound to take all the advice that you get from others. *You* are responsible for your final decisions, and you may have reasons for disagreeing with some of the advice that you get. But even if you disagree, the comments from your reviewers will aid you in rethinking your paper, which is the purpose of revision. And ultimately, the goal of all this reading and rereading is not only to give you sources of advice but to make you a better reviewer of your own work—now, later in college, and as you write in your profession. Having become someone else's reviewer, someone else's reader, you should now be readier to become your own.

Self-Critique

Exercise 8-2

To be read on the day you hand in a paper. You may have thought when you typed up your paper last night that you were typing a "final draft." But no draft is ever final. A draft that we hand in is only a "deadline draft." We can't keep our work forever; a deadline forces us to quit. But that doesn't mean we could not have done better.

This time you're going to get one more chance not only to proofread but also to revise so that we can compare notes on what last-minute revisions people make.

First, take ten minutes just to proofread your paper, that is, to check for typing errors, spelling errors, and obvious errors in punctuation. When you finish, compare notes with the class on what you've changed. Check whether your habits are similar to those of your classmates. Which of you has the best strategy?

Next, take ten minutes to revise any parts of your paper you can without making major rearrangements (if a major rearrangement might be desirable, you can make a note to that effect at the end of your paper). Again, when you've finished, discuss with the class the kinds of changes you've made, and listen carefully to the kinds your classmates made.

Finally (even if there has not been enough time to complete the steps above), answer briefly in writing the following questions:

1. I am satisfied/dissatisfied with this paper because...
2. What have you learned about research from writing this paper?
3. What have you learned about writing from writing this paper?
4. If you were to start work over on this paper, what would you do differently?

Revision Checklist

When we revise, we attend not only to the major issues—adequacy of facts, thoughtfulness of inferences, clarity of organization, helpfulness of the introduction and conclusion—mentioned in the list above, but also to many "smaller" points that help us cleanse and clarify our work, often improving it from satisfactory to solid or from solid to distinguished. The items listed below (roughly in order of importance) are items that you'll want to check each time you revise. In fact, you won't think about them every time (you won't have the chance), but many of them will become part of your intuitive revising process.

1. Make reading as easy as possible for your reader by organizing your work clearly.

   • Check that your introduction makes clear your sense of direction and that your conclusion answers the question "So what?"

   • Check your organization by doing a paragraph outline of your paper to see whether it moves systematically.

   • Check the opening sentences in your paragraphs. Not all paragraphs need a topic sentence, but the first sentence should at least hint at the paragraph's direction of movement.

The movement of ideas (inferences) in any essay should be roughly clear from the way the paragraphs begin. Here are the extremely uninformative, and undisciplined, opening words of the paragraphs in an essay I received recently:

> The first item in...that struck me was...
> The following ad read as follows...
> I also enjoyed...
> I found it quite interesting how...
> The most interesting content in...to me was...
> The last items I have chosen to deal with are...
> I would like to say that viewing these newspapers was a good
>   experience for me.

But was it a good experience for the reader?

- Give your reader the results of your research, not a record of it. Take out references to what you are doing. Just do it. Skip words like those italicized below:

> There is a distinct difference between "professional" and
> "amateur." *First of all, I will give you my definitions for*
> *"professional" and "amateur."* A professional is a person that...
> *I'm reporting on a movie that* real movie hawks will enjoy the
> technical effects of.
> *The best inference I can think of is that* Baton Rouge parents
> care about their children.

- Check that you've used all your inferences to make worthwhile comments. Don't waste your reader's time or lose your reader's respect with inferences like that italicized below:

> Forty-five percent of the voters polled felt that the worst possible
> punishment for a crime is the death penalty. Fifty-five percent felt that
> a life sentence without parole is an even worse punishment than
> death. *These opinions vary to some extent.*

- Read through your draft to make sure that it reads "smoothly."

Confused	Clear
The Red Army then looted bicycles, telephones, washbasins, light switches, door locks, in an attempt to bankrupt the Germans.	The Red Army then looted bicycles, telephones, washbasins, and even light switches and door locks in an attempt to bankrupt the Germans.
After the end of the war the Soviets printed marks by the billion, creating an economic nightmare.	After the end of the war the Soviets printed marks by the billion, creating an economic nightmare in Germany.

- Parallel structure makes any similar set of ideas easier for a reader to comprehend.

Confused	Clear
Keith, my nephew, was only 13, skied like he was born on the slopes, fast, fluid, and he never fell.	Keith, my 13-year-old nephew, skied as if he was born on the slopes—he was fast, he was fluid, and he never fell.
The happiest moments in my life were getting married and having two kids, then see my two kids graduate from high school and college.	The happiest moments in my life were getting married, having two kids, and seeing my two kids graduate from high school and college.

- Make sure you've made your transitions in thought clear to your reader—often a simple "but" or "though" can help signal a contrast and make reading your work easier.

Confused	Clear
Before the strike had started, many industries had begun stockpiling steel. By the end of October 1959, those stockpiles had been almost completely used up.	Before the strike had started, many industries had begun stockpiling steel. By the end of October 1959, though, those stockpiles had been almost completely used up.

2. Identify for your reader the people, terms, and times that you want to talk about.

- Don't leave your reader stranded in time or space. Specify, near the beginning of your work, where and when the events you are talking about took place.

Confused	Clear
John Llewellen Lewis dominated the United Mine Workers for half the union's life.	John L. Lewis, an Iowa and Illinois miner, dominated the United Mine Workers from 1933 to 1960, more than half the union's life.

- Identify any wars or speeches or documents or organizations you refer to.

Confused	Clear
Chiang Kai-shek led the Kuomintang.	Chiang Kai-shek led the Kuomintang, a party founded by Dr. Sun Yat-sen in 1911 and challenged by the Communist party only after 1930.

- Define terms that the reader may be unfamiliar with.

Confused	Clear
Dr. Sun's party didn't appeal to Chinese peasants because most of his lieutenants were from Canton.	Dr. Sun's party didn't appeal to Chinese peasants because most of his lieutenants were from Canton, a rich coastal province with several large cities.

- Don't define terms that readers can be expected to understand. There is no need, for example, in an article for adults about birth control practices, to stop and define *conception.*

- Use a person's name the first time you refer to him or her in any paragraph. After that, you can switch to a short form of the name or to *he* or *she.*

Confused	Clear
In 1966, *he* gained new popularity in *his* party, and *he* entered the bid for the 1968 presidential nomination. To alter *his* reputation as a political loser, *Nixon* countered with a strategy aimed at settling the nomination in a series of presidential primaries. *He* won the first victory in New Hampshire easily. After *Nixon* had won most of the primaries, Governors Nelson Rockefeller of New York and Ronald Reagan of California entered the contest, but it was too late.	In 1966, *Nixon* gained new popularity in *his* party, and *he* entered the bid for the 1968 presidential nomination. To alter *his* reputation as a political loser, *he* countered with a strategy aimed at settling the nomination in a series of presidential primaries. *He* won the first victory in New Hampshire easily. After *he* had won most of the primaries, Governors Nelson Rockefeller of New York and Ronald Reagan of California entered the contest, but it was too late.

3. Be specific.

   - Don't leave details to the readers' imaginations.

     When stopped at the light at the intersection of Quesada and Dodge Streets, a driver could see *all kinds of interesting things going on* through the open windows of the hotel.

   Often in revision you'll see that you need more details. You may have written an error-free paper, but you may not have given us a clear picture of your subject.

   - Even when you're generalizing, make sure your statements are specific enough to be comprehensible.

> *It's funny how many different kinds of things there are of one thing.*
> Keats achieves *this* by *organizing the subject matter in a certain order*
> and *comparing it with something else.*
> Working at the Jersey City Medical Center *was certainly an*
> *experience in itself.*

More thought is all that's necessary to make these phrases more specific. Many writers, for example, have a fondness for unfocused words
like the pronoun *this* or the noun *thing:*

> The thing of it is, if you're onto a thing, it becomes a priority.

When you're tempted to use the word *thing,* remember the following
advice:

> *The Thing* was a movie made in the 1950s, starring James Arness as a
> monster with the cellular structure of a giant carrot. Only use the
> word *thing* to refer to the carrot or to the movie (in which case it is
> capitalized and underlined). If you use the word *thing* in your papers,
> your teacher will substitute the word *carrot.* If the sentence then
> makes sense, you are correct (King).

- Make your verbs as specific as you can. There are quite a few "easy"
  verbs in English—*go, make, have, do,* for example—that don't tax the
  writer's mind when they're used and that don't, therefore, engage
  the reader's mind. When you search for a stronger verb, you're in
  fact searching for a more specific verb.

  > books we *did* in class
  > books we *read* in class (*more specific*)
  > books we *studied* in class (*still more specific*)

- Learn the names for items you want to talk about. If you start talking
  to me about "the object blocking the tube when the tube was
  shaken" and you're really talking about a *cork,* I'm going to lose interest in the way you write. We all should be working constantly to
  expand our vocabularies, not so much to SAT words like *ineffable*
  and *callow* as to the names of everyday objects. Do you know what a
  mullion is, or a sill, a baseboard, a wainscot, or a socket? Do you
  know that a leather hat with a "thing sticking out" is a leather hat
  with a *visor?* Do you know the difference between asphalt tile and
  cedar shingles? between macadam and an oiled road? between elms
  and oaks and hickories?

- Not all specifics are interesting. Details from which no useful or appropriate inferences can be drawn lie heavy on the page if they appear in too much abundance.

  > The scoreboard can also be seen from any part of the field and keeps
  > the time, the score, the down, the quarter, timeouts, the number of
  > yards to go, and what yard the ball is on.

These are boring, not telling, facts. The reader asks, "So what?" But because our tendency to generalize is so strong, it is rare that we go wrong like this when trying to write specifically.

4. "Tighten" your writing until only the important words, phrases, and sentences remain.

Loose	Tight
There is a certain unfairness in that.	That's unfair.
A waiter can tell by the customers' actions and body language that they are impatient.	A waiter can tell by the customers' body language that they are impatient.

Every word, phrase, and sentence must earn its place, usually with the meaning it adds, but sometimes also by how it helps emphasis, rhythm, or grace. One way to get yourself to be more careful when you revise is to force yourself to reduce your draft by one-quarter, or one-third, or some other arbitrary figure (*this doesn't mean cutting out telling details*). Often your boss or your editor will do this cutting for you. It's excellent discipline, and it will lead you to making many qualitative, not just quantitative, decisions.

The following is an excellent exercise in tightening, adapted from Ken Macrorie's *Telling Writing* (60).

Exercise 8-3
Tightening

Strengthen the following paragraph by cutting it in half. You may rearrange the ideas if you wish. Think about what might make a good beginning and what might provide a sense of closure for the conclusion.

> Hands, did you ever notice how many different kinds of hands there are? I first began to notice hands when I found that all men's hands were not as large as my Dad's hands. They were large, strong, and forceful, yet always gentle like the man. His hand encompasses mine even now when he takes it gently yet firmly, as though providing it with a cover of protection against the outside world. But he has always been like that, strong and protective, yet gentle. When those hands hold a baby, the baby stops crying and is quiet as though calmed by their strength and gentleness. When those hands take a pencil and draw an idea, the lines are firm and confident. Other men seem to respond when they shake his hand to the friendliness and strength behind the handshake.

You see here that you've been forced not only to omit words but to rethink organization, to consider using parallel structure, and to decide what you most want to say. Tightening shows respect for the meaning of words and respect for our readers' time. It also helps us to specify, without unnecessary noise, the essence of what we want to say. Tightening teaches us one of the most useful writing skills: being selective—giving the reader not all, but the best.

5. Don't let yourself be satisfied with words that are only *close* to the meaning you want.

   • Check the meanings of words you're not quite sure of.

   > Ms. Winston is not sparing in the use of *acrimonious vituperations* against certain mental health practitioners; and in her case, this is *justifiably understandable.*

   The writer here, in an attempt to impress the reader with multisyllabic words, has achieved the reverse. How are *vituperations* different when they are *acrimonious?* Not at all. What does *understandable* gain by being modified by *justifiably?* Nothing. The writer isn't trusting the meaning of her words. She's trying to bowl us over with the mere sound of them. Her carelessness weakens her *ethos.*

   One of the most common carelessly used words is *revolve,* which must sound impressive to us, because it doesn't mean much and yet it is used frequently:

   > This essay will *revolve around* answering the question of whether studying at the University of Texas has been a positive or negative experience for me.

   > The world *revolves around* the word *survival.*

   What are these writers trying to say? What do the words say? If you catch yourself using larger words than you want, you can use a thesaurus to find simpler words. You could change, for example, *approximately* to *roughly.* If you do use simpler words, your writing may achieve the same virtue that the Canon 35-mm camera claims to have: so advanced, it's simple.

   • Remember that words have not only their strict meaning (called the *denotative* meaning) but also emotional colorations (called their *connotative* meanings). Even the names of cities—Paris, New York, Montreal, Liverpool, Dallas—call up emotions at the same time that they specify a place. We rarely make mistakes in connotation. We all know the difference in connotation, for example, between cheap and inexpensive. We all know the difference between crafty and intelligent. What we need to pay attention to during revision, though, is whether a word for which we have one connotation might have another connotation for our reader. I might think that *smart* has positive connotations, but some people don't, so I may well, in revision, when talking about my reader's favorite president, substitute *intelligent* for *smart.*

Making such a change is attending carefully to the *pathos* I'm using to persuade my reader.

- Finally, look for differences between spoken English and written
English as you review your final draft. *Really* should always be replaced. *Got* is oftenuspect. Even *this* must sometimes be questioned. When we're telling a story, we frequently say, "We went
down *this* road for miles." *This* is pointing to a specific road in the
speaker's mind, but to a reader *this road* is only *a* road. The correct
form in writing, unless the road has already been identified, is *a
road.*

6. Check your punctuation.

   - Review the rules for IC ; IC and DC , IC and IC ₒ DC in Chapter 9.
   Check that you've followed them in your paper.

   - If you have trouble writing complete sentences, read through your
   paper backward, sentence by sentence. When you read backward,
   you're less likely to miss fragments that don't sound too bad when
   they follow a good sentence.

7. Make revisions on the basis of your understanding of how English
grammar can best serve your meaning.

   - Check whether you've accidentally switched back and forth in your
   verb tenses (between present and past, for example) without any
   desire to change the time that you are referring to.

   - Strike out adjectives and adverbs that steal impact from your nouns
   and verbs.

     Many questions still remain unanswered.

   - Often you can strengthen your prose by making the subject you're
   writing about the grammatical subject of your sentence.

Foggy	Clear
To relieve academic pressures and personal problems one may encounter was another purpose of the Nyumburu Center being formulated.	The Nyumburu Center was established to help students relieve academic pressures and talk through personal problems.

   - Likewise, it often helps to make your verb active when you're describing an action.

Foggy	Clear
The pleasures of canoeing *were de-scribed* by John McPhee.	John McPhee *described* the pleasures of canoeing.

   - Check that your verbs match the number (singular or plural) of their
   subjects, even when a prepositional phrase has intervened.

     The *success* of my plans *depends* on you.

- Check that each pronoun you use refers directly to some noun that appears before it (a writer often doesn't notice whether pronouns agree with their antecedents until revision).

Foggy	Clear
He may use whatever *methods* he wants as long as *it* is effective.	He may use whatever *methods* he wants as long as *they* are effective.

8. Listen to the sounds of our language.

- Note the meaningless repetition of sounds.

    His *marks* improved *markedly.*

Many people are bothered by the repetition of sounds when they read through their own writing. Are there good reasons to avoid repeating a word or a sound? There are. A similar sound makes it seem to readers, if only for a moment, that they have come across a similar meaning. Then if the meaning is not similar, they have to sort out both meanings, and this takes time, if only a moment. But repetition is not necessarily an evil. Often, not only is it not awkward, but it serves your purpose.

The best guide to repetition is the end of Lincoln's Gettysburg Address (Macrorie 27):

> government of the *people*
> by the *people*
> and for the *people*
>   shall not perish from the earth

Lincoln chose to repeat *people,* his main idea. We'd think he was too much concerned with his own role as President if he had said:

> *government* of
> *government* by
> and *government* for
>   the people shall not perish from the
>   earth

If repetition is justified by your ideas, by all means use it. If it is only confusing, rethink your expression. Above all, don't make matters worse by going to a thesaurus for synonyms. Don't, in a paper about the actor Errol Flynn, call him Don Juan, then Casanova, then Romeo, then "the deceiver," then "Mr. Insatiable." Such "elegant variation" doesn't fool anybody. In fact, it calls more attention to the word we're repeating. Instead of looking for another term, what we should do is examine our thinking that has led to so much repetition. If you're repeating a reference to a person and that person is the subject of your paper, you should expect to be making repeated references to that person. If you're repeating an idea and the idea is worth repeating, it should stay in. If it is not worth repeating, perhaps some large-scale revision is needed.

9. Check to see that you've placed your emphasis where you want it.

- The principal place of emphasis is the end—the end of a sentence, the end of a paragraph, the end of a paper. When we read a poor ending, we have a strong sense of anticlimax:

   The audience of the eighteenth-century *Gentleman's Magazine* was intelligent gentry and merchants, although there were some exceptions.

The reason why a thesis seems to fit so well at the end of the first paragraph of a paper is that the end of a paragraph is an obvious point of emphasis. If you'd written the following introductory paragraph, you'd probably want to revise it because it ends on a quite unimportant note.

   Vietnam Tien-Phong, a very popular magazine back in my country, has continued its progress after 1975 in America and it has become the most sought-after bi-weekly magazine in the Viet community everywhere in the world. The reporters and editors serve the Vietnamese well with serious political views as well as with entertainment like novels, anecdotes, and jokes. The reporters work very hard. The magazine starts with a full page resume of the world's events.

Sentences have the same emphasis pattern as paragraphs. Linguists have recently—and tentatively—suggested that the easiest sentence pattern for a reader to follow is this one: given information first, new information last. Thus a skilled writer begins a sentence with a word or a phrase already familiar to the reader and then continues by adding something new about the subject:

   When Ted Taylor was growing up, in Mexico City in the nineteen-thirties, he had three particular interests, and they were music, chemistry, and billiards. His father had been a widower with three sons who married a widow with a son of her own, so Ted had four older half brothers—so much older, though, that he was essentially raised an only child, in a home that was as quiet as it was religious. His maternal grandparents were Congregational missionaries in Guadalajara. His father, born on a farm in Kansas, was general secretary of the Y.M.C.A. in Mexico. His mother was the first American woman who ever earned a Ph.D. at the National University of Mexico. Her field was Mexican literature (McPhee, *Curve* 8–9).

The circled words keep the reader on familiar territory, while the rest of each sentence moves on to new information. This pattern is by no means always necessary. But it *does* make the reader comfortable at the beginning of the sentence, and it leaves the reader free to *notice* what comes at the end, in the emphatic position.

- Emphasis also falls on the verb.

   She spends her days sewing patchwork quilts and blankets.

This sentence puts the emphasis on *spends,* not on the *sewing.* Thus, it deliberately makes her work seem like drudgery. An alternative— "She *sews* patchwork quilts and blankets"—calls more attention to her artistry.

10. Check over your paper to see what it looks like. Then revise with an eye to emptiness and fullness. If you have a brief paragraph, you may want to add details to it, combine it with another paragraph, or remove it entirely. If you have a paragraph that fills a whole page, you may want to eliminate weak sections of it or find places to divide it into two or three paragraphs of more readable length.

11. Check the spelling of any words you're not sure of. For this purpose, a speller's dictionary is far better than an ordinary dictionary, because you can look a word up *the way you spelled it,* and the dictionary will provide the correct spelling right after your spelling. I'd recommend *The Bad Speller's Dictionary,* by Joseph Kreivsky and Jordon L. Linfield (Random House, 1974).

12. Proofread carefully to ensure that you haven't left in any words you meant to take out, and that you haven't omitted words that you meant to use.

13. Check that the "style" that comes through in your work is the one that you'd like to come through. Efforts to inject some style by adding words or phrases usually backfire, but we should be concerned, as we revise, about the tone of voice that comes through. One alteration in tone that many inexperienced writers ought to consider is making their writing slightly stronger, slightly more confident than they're actually feeling. In a few cases this will lead to artificial haughtiness, but in most cases the alteration will reflect the confidence that the writer deserves but doesn't yet have. Inexperienced writers can easily find themselves hedging at every opportunity:

   An amateur *is thought of* as not knowing as much as a professional *to an extent.*

When we write something, we should legitimately think of ourselves as challenging our readers. A reader of the sentence above is left with nothing to think about. Most readers like to meet strength with strength. Unless they meet a strong writer, they don't want to give a work a strong reading.

14. Give your work a title that it deserves.

Let me quote an expert on this matter (and many others), Harry Crosby, who sees a "high correlation between the quality of a written composition and its title" (387–91):

> I have long believed that the shuttlecock process of finding an appropriate title stimulates creativity, unity, and significance. The writer starts out with a working title, writes a few pages, and then pauses to tinker with the title to make it fit what he has written. This helps him go back to writing with a sharper focus on what he is really trying to say. This back-and-forth process continues. If a good title emerges, the writer has evidence that he or she is developing a significant message expressed in a unified manner. If no title is possible, something is wrong.

Crosby notes several kinds of titles, among them:

Clever titles:
"Two Cheers for Democracy"—E. M. Forster
"The Scrutable Japanese"—Craig Spence

Titles which announce the thesis:
"We Scientists Have the Right to Play God"—Edmund F. Leech
"This Thing Called Love Is Pathological"—Lawrence Cusler

Titles which indicate the controlling question:
"What Is a Classic?"—Charles Augustin Sainte-Beuve
"What Does a Tune-Up Include?"—Charlotte Slater

Titles which indicate a specific topic:
"Desegregating Sexist Sports"—Harry Edwards
"Substitutes for Violence"—John Fisher

Titles which announce the general subject:
"On the Middle Class"—Steve Slade
"Historical Lessons About Great Leaders"—Arnold Toynbee

The first three types are admirable, and the fourth and fifth types get gradually weaker, but many titles on the papers I've received wouldn't even reach the bottom of this list. A good number of students use, as their title, the title of the assignment: "Description of a Curious Place"; "Persuading a Classmate." Another good number use no title at all. Look over the titles of the sample flawed essays in Chapter 14; you'll probably be embarrassed for the authors. Then think before you write a title; give your work a title that it deserves.

15. Review your work to eliminate the following frequently made word and phrase mistakes, often referred to as mistakes in *usage.*

accept, except: Accept is a verb meaning *receive willingly, except* is a preposition meaning *other than.*

I'd be pleased to *accept* the award in her honor.
The whole family will be there *except* Uncle Gus.

advice, advise: Advice is a noun, *advise* is a verb.

I appreciate your *advice.*
I *advise* you to take a long trip.

affect, effect: In normal use of these terms, both have the same meaning: *influence.* As a verb the word is spelled *affect,* and as a noun it is spelled *effect.*

Flower pollens don't *affect* me very much.
Grass pollens have a strong *effect* on me.

all ready, already: These are two different words. *All ready* means *prepared, already* means *before in time.*

The family was *all ready.*
Her father was *already* waiting.

all right: This is the correct spelling. *Alright* is not a word.

Fortunately, the people in the back seat are *all right.*

a lot: You haven't seen this phrase in print very often (because professionals and teachers have discouraged its use), so you may guess that it's spelled *alot.* It's not. *A lot* is two words, like *all right.*

among: See *between.*

amount, number: Amount is a measure of some mass that can't be divided into parts, *number* the measure of several items in a large group of items. (The difference between *less* and *fewer* explained later is based on the same distinction.)

The computer thief stole a staggering *amount* of money.
The bank robber stole an undisclosed *number* of twenty dollar bills.

as: See *like.*

assure, ensure, insure: All three words mean "to make certain, to make safe." Use *assure* with persons, *ensure* with things, and *insure* when talking about money.

I *assure* you I sent the check yesterday.
You can *ensure* quality if you treat your employees with respect.
You may *insure* the package if you wish.

between, among: Use *between* when dealing with two things, *among* when dealing with three or more.

The playoff race was *between* the Angels and the Twins.

The playoff money was divided *among* the Dodgers, Giants, and Astros.

can, may: *Can* means you are able to do something, *may* asks permission.

Can she climb that 10-foot wall?
May I offer an explanation?

capital, capitol: A state or country's *capital* is spelled with an *al.* That same state or country's *capitol* building is spelled with an *ol.*

cloths, clothes: Occasionally we might refer to more than one cloth as *cloths.* More often we are writing about what people wear every day and that is *clothes.*

He picked out several colorful *cloths* from the bazaar table.
He put his *clothes* on right after taking a shower.

conscience, conscious: Our *conscience* is the part of us that decides between right and wrong. To be *conscious* of something is to be aware of it.

My *conscience* bothered me after I refused to help.
I was never *conscious* that I had offended her.

contractions: There are many common contractions in English—*I'm, I'll, we'll, we're, you're, it's, can't, don't,* to name a few. Until ten or fifteen years ago, writers were discouraged from using them. In recent years, though, they are regarded increasingly as a more natural way to write. Be conscious, therefore, as you write of the level of formality you create as you choose, for example, between *I'll* and *I will.*

could have, would have, should have: These three phrases are often abbreviated to *could've, would've,* and *should've* when we speak. And then we sometimes assume that the spelling should be *could of, would of,* and *should of.* But all these pairs are helping verbs and therefore *have* is the correct form. *Of,* a preposition, doesn't belong in the middle of a verb.

With two more computers, we *could have* finished on time.
Sharon *would have* brought the ice if she had known that we
needed it.
We *should have* come before the dinner was served.

criterion, criteria: *Criterion* is a Greek word which has become an English word. It is one of very few words in English that still form their plurals in the original language rather than in English. Thus, we don't write several *criterions* but rather several *criteria.*

The most important *criterion* for a good play is that it entertain the
audience.I've based my overall judgment, though, on at least three
other *criteria.*

dessert, desert: This distinction at first seems easy. *Dessert* (accent on the second syllable) is the sweet we eat after a meal, a *desert* (accent on the first syllable) is a waterless land. But *desert* (pronounced just like *dessert* just to make things confusing) is also a verb meaning *leave.*

disinterested, uninterested: A *disinterested* person is uninfluenced by bias, an *uninterested* person would rather be doing something else.

> We expect Olympic judges to be *disinterested* observers.
> He was totally *uninterested* in the Olympics.

effect: See *affect.*

ensure: See *assure.*

except: See *accept.*

fewer: See *less.*

good, well: These two words mean the same thing, but *good* is used when the word serves as an adjective, and *well* is used when it is an adverb.

hear, here: Here is a place, *hear* is what we do when people speak to us.

insure: See *assure.*

its, it's: It's always stands for "it is." *Its* is possessive (like the other pronouns *her, his,* and *our*) even though it doesn't contain the apostrophe that we often associate with the possessive. Nouns have apostrophes when they become possessive, pronouns don't.

judgment: For no particular reason, *judgment* is the preferred spelling in the United States for the word that you might think should be spelled *judgement.*

know, no: These words sound the same but look so different that they should be easy to distinguish. *No* means *none, know* refers to knowledge.

> I expect *no* nonsense during this week at camp.
> I *know* you'll be good boys.

lay, lie: Lay/laid/laid means *to put or place.* It takes a direct object.

> Please *lay* the dress on the bed.
> I already *laid* it on the dining room table.

Lie/lay/lain means to rest or recline. It never takes a direct object. A common source of confusion is that the past tense of *lie* is *lay.*

> She *lies* down for a nap every afternoon these days.
> She *lay* down yesterday before 2:00.

lead, lead, led: Lead is a present tense verb, *led* is its form in the past tense, and *lead*—when pronounced like *led*—is the metal.

Today I'll *lead* you through the new computer manual.
Yesterday she *led* me through it.

less, fewer: Less refers to a portion of some general quantity, *fewer* to actual numbers.

There is *less* water in this lake than there should be to sustain large fish.
There are *fewer* students in this class than I expected.

like, as: Like and *as* have the same meaning. *Like* is expected when the word is a preposition, *as* when it is a subordinating conjunction.

He acted *like* a hero.
He acted *as* a hero might have acted.

loose, lose: Loose is an adjective with what you might think of as a hard "s," *lose* is a verb with an "s" that is *softer* and sounds like "z."

He always wears his tie *loose*.
Please don't *lose* the book I lent you.

may: See *can*.

number: See *amount*.

numbers: No one seems quite sure what the rule is about spelling out numbers. Any number from 1 to 10 can be spelled out and readers can follow with no trouble. But generally it is easier to read a number larger than 10 in its numerical form. The numerical form is only awkward at the beginning of sentences where a number can't be capitalized and therefore the spelled out form is preferred, no matter how large the number is.

past, passed: Most commonly this word is spelled *past*. It can be a *noun* meaning a time before now, an *adjective* referring to time before now, or a *preposition* meaning moving next to something. *Passed* is used, though, when the word is a *verb* indicating movement next to something.

My grandmother lives more than I would like in the *past*.
That rocker is a remnant from *past* times.
The grocery store is just *past* the movie theatre.
I *passed* the movie theatre on the way to the grocery store.

principal, principal, principle: The noun *principal* means the chief officer. The adjective *principal* means the most important. *Principle* is a noun which means either a general truth (the *principles* of the law) or moral ideas (she lives by her admirable *principles*).

The *principal* worked every weekend this month.
His *principal* reason for leaving was his fight with Jerry.

His behavior doesn't give me much confidence in his religious *principles.*

proceed, precede: These two words are never mixed up, but their spellings often are. *Proceed* means *continue* and has its two e's linked. *Precede* means *come (go) before* and separates its e's.

proof, evidence: Be modest about claiming that you've proven something. In most cases the matter you are discussing will never be resolved with certainty. What you've done is offer not proof but evidence.

quiet, quite: These words have *et* and *te* reversed, but they have very different meanings. *Quiet* is an adjective meaning *not loud, quite* is an adverb that can substitute for *very.*

raise, rise: We *raise* an object, we and objects *rise* without help.

They all helped *raise* the side of the barn.
The children wanted to watch the bread *rise.*

set, sit: We *set* an object somewhere, we and objects *sit* without help.

He *set* his book on the teaching table.
The flowers *sit* on the windowsill.

should have: See *could have.*

stationary, stationery: *Stationary* is an adjective referring to something that is not moving. *Stationery* is the paper we write letters on.

supposed to, suppose to: It's difficult to say these two words carefully because the last sound of *supposed* is the same as the first sound of *to.* So inexperienced writers often think there is no *d* on *supposed.* The *d* is necessary, though, because *supposed* is a passive voice form of the verb *suppose.* Memorize this spelling. *Used to* is often misspelled for precisely the same reason.

She's *supposed to* be here before 6:00.

than, then: These words are pronounced somewhat similarly, but they are quite different in spelling, meaning, and grammatical function. *Then* refers to time, and *than* makes a comparison.

Then he swept into the room after keeping them waiting 45 minutes.
He's less prompt *than* he used to be.

there, their, they're: *They're,* like all contractions, can be spelled out as *they are.* *There* refers to a place. *Their* is a possessive pronoun similar to *his* or *her.*

They're expected tomorrow from Milwaukee.
My wife keeps her keys *there* whenever she's out of town.
They sold *their* children's bikes last week.

till, until: Both these words are respectable, but note their spellings. *Til,* which you might regard as a third choice, isn't a word.

too, to, two: These words sound alike. *Two,* the number, is rarely confused with the others. But *too,* meaning too much, and *to,* a preposition (*to* the store) or part of an infinitive (*to* arrive), need to be carefully distinguished.

try to, try and: When we speak, we frequently use phrases like *try and accomplish, try and get, try and find.* There is no real *and* intended. In writing, the more precise forms of *try to accomplish, try to get, try to find* are expected.

used to, use to: It's difficult to say these two words carefully because the last sound of *used* is the same as the first sound of *to.* So inexperienced writers often think there is no *d* on *used.* The *d* is necessary, though, because *used* is a passive voice form of the verb *use.* Memorize this spelling. *Supposed to* is often misspelled for precisely the same reason.

> He's less prompt than he *used to* be.

utilize, use: Both these words mean the same thing. There's nothing wrong with the shorter word *use* so it is usually a better choice.

where, were: *Wh* has a harsh sound, *w* alone a softer sound. *Where* refers to an (unknown) place, *were* is a verb referring to past time.

> *Where* are our friends living since they left?
> They *were* living in a very dirty apartment until last week.

whether, weather: As in the above example, *wh* has a harsh sound, *w* alone a softer sound. *Whether* refers to a choice we have, *weather* to the raininess or sunniness of the day.

> I can't decide *whether* to get married.
> The *weather* is bound to get worse before it gets better.

who, whom: *Who* and *whom* mean the same thing, but are correct or incorrect choices depending on whether they are used in a subjective or objective case slot in a sentence. If you don't know the grammatical rules for determining the case of a noun, choose *who* or *whom* by comparing them with the more familiar *he* and *him.* Where you would use *he,* use *who.* Where you would use *him,* use *whom.*

who's, whose: *Who's* means who is. *Whose* doesn't.

> *Who's* home?
> *Whose* watch is this behind the couch?

woman, women: *Woman* refers to one adult female, *women* to more than one.

would have: See *could have.*

your, you're: *You're* means you are. *Your* doesn't.

> *You're* the best friend I have left.
> I like *your* brother.

A BRIEF REVIEW OF REVISION – courtesy of Michael Berheide

1. Avoid redundancy. It should be avoided. It is repetitive and redundant; that is, redundancy should not be used. So stay away from redundancy and repetitiveness.

2. Personally attacking the proponent of an argument does not refute the argument, you idiot.

3. There are two types of people in the world: those who continually divide the people of the world into two types, and those who do not. Try to belong to the latter type, and avoid "overclassification."

4. Always check for spelin erors.

5. Try to keep, somewhere near the predicate of your sentence, so the reader does not have to look all over for it, your object.

6. I really don't think that your personal feelings should be used as if they were arguments—it just doesn't seem right.

7. It is not advisable to ever split infinitives.

8. I really don't know whether to tell you to be "wishy-washy" or not. Some say yes, others say no. Who's to decide?

9. If you had not made your verb tenses agree, you will have wished that you do.

10. Fragmented sentences: no good. And this sentence no verb.

11. Some people think that simply stating the converse of an argument refutes it, but this is not true.

12. Don't you think that asking lots of rhetorical questions is silly?

13. One should assiduously strive to disencumber an exposition of obfuscatory and vestigial verbiage.

14. Colloquialisms and trite expressions should be avoided like the plague. And it is not hip to use slang, either.

15. Avoid redundancy. It should be avoided. It is repetitive and redundant, so avoid it.

9

Sentence Sense: Making Grammar Your Ally

My grammar is not that hot, in fact it's not even warm.

student

I had grammar viciously driven into my head for eight years.

student

I find training in grammar to be quite a bore, especially with all the emphasis placed on subjects like dangling modifiers, etc., which really don't play a major role in my life in my opinion.

student

I am a good writer. Writing usually comes easy to me. I have a quality of sensitivity so the papers I write usually represent that quality. Although writing comes easily to me, grammar does not.

student

My high school training in English consisted of several poorly taught classes and one that was well-taught. The teacher for my junior year was the head of the school's English department. She was a very strict lady who preached nothing but grammar. For most of the semester we were bombarded with pronouns, clauses, participles and more. I admit that I hated every minute of it. But now I realize she was the only teacher who took the time to concentrate on grammar. Other teachers, most likely bored by the subject, skimmed over grammar in order to do more interesting things. Even though I hated her and the course, I learned more than I did in my other high school classes. Today I am more at ease when writing because of that class.

student

Exercise 9-1

Self-Assessment: Common Punctuation Errors

The following sentences are punctuated improperly. Revise each and explain in each case why your revision is correct.

- I hope to become an accountant when I graduate, sometimes I look in the classified ads to see what qualifications most companies want their accountants to have and all of the ads I read wanted a college degree.
- Teaching for example, is a career where there are just too many people with degrees in this field.
- College offers a variety of topics to learn from, for instance people who are interested in rocks and have been collecting them all their lives, can major in geology.
- The listing didn't include; however, the schedules for services in any other religious faiths.
- "Several hundred persons turned out Sunday at Marlboro College," several hundred is a lot for Rutland.
- The *Rutland Herald* and the *New York Daily News* have different types of readers, however, they both serve their readers in the same manner.
- It was our first chance to break open the game and put a few runs on the scoreboard; against the first-place team.
- People begin to congregate at the Rendezvous early in the evening it is mostly a light crowd.
- He heard me looked over smiled and started walking to the car.
- In a world that is constantly changing, and more and more is being discovered. There will always be something new to learn.

If you can correct the punctuation in all the sentences above with little trouble, you probably don't need the rest of this chapter. If you had some difficulty, though, with these revisions, this chapter should help fill in the gaps in your knowledge of grammar and punctuation, and by doing so improve both your confidence and your performance.

Exercise 9-2

Self-Assessment: Grammar and Punctuation Terms

Before beginning the review of English grammar and punctuation in this chapter, test yourself to see what you already know. What rules do you re-member for using:

1. A comma?
2. A semicolon?
3. A colon?

How would you define:

1. A sentence?
2. A clause?
3. A phrase?

In most college courses, a substantial part of our study time is spent learning the vocabulary of the field—*norms, sanctions, stratifica-tion,* and *diffusion,* for example, in sociology; *genus, species, in vitro,* and *in vivo* in biology. If it weren't for grammar, the number of terms you must master for a writing course would be very few: *fact, inference, the-sis, ethos, logos, pathos, paragraph, introduction, conclusion.* But even dreaded grammar increases the list of essential terms only to about twenty-five, as listed in Table 9-1.

You've reviewed subjects and verbs so many times by this point in school that I'll assume you can pick them out of any sentence. Most of the other terms should at least sound familiar, though you might be hard-pressed to explain them. The two items in the list below that most people refuse to learn are gerunds and participles, yet we use gerunds and participles almost every time we talk or write. It's time to learn what they, and the other basic elements of sentences, are.

TABLE 9-1   Terms Essential to Studying Grammar

Basic parts of speech	Sentence elements
Nouns	Subjects
Verbs	Verbs, or predicates
Adjectives	Objects
Adverbs	Phrases
Conjunctions	Noun phrases
	Verb phrases
	Prepositional phrases
	Verbal phrases
	Clauses
	Independent clauses
	Dependent clauses
Conjunctions	**Verbals (Demoted Verbs)**
Coordinating conjunctions	Gerunds
Subordinating conjunctions	Participles
Conjunctive adverbs	Infinitives
Relative pronouns	

What Is a Sentence?

The most important knowledge that you as a speaker and writer of English should have is a sense of what a sentence is. In English, as in most other languages, the basis of a sentence is a relation between a noun and a verb, a relation between matter and energy. Einstein's theory of relativity, $E = MC^2$, tells us that all life consists of matter M and energy E. Very conveniently, sentences, too, consist of matter (a subject, or noun) and energy (a predicate, or verb). Readers don't want to hear about matter without energy, or energy without matter. They'll accept:

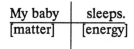

My baby	sleeps.
[matter]	[energy]

or

The nuclear reactor	is leaking.
[matter]	[energy]

But they won't accept:

My baby.	
[matter only]	

or

	Is leaking.
	[energy only]

Intuitively, we realize that to say something meaningful, we have to include some matter, and we must give that matter some energy. Nevertheless, students (and others) often enclose collections of words between a capital letter and a period that are *not* sentences:

1. Knowing what you can do and cannot do.
2. A person of always good intentions.
3. Which I liked a lot, because it gives you the feeling of being in college.

The writers of these collections of words are having difficulty getting their ideas across either (1) because they don't know what a *subject* is, or (2) because they don't know what a *verb* is, or, most likely, (3) because they don't know that *a sentence must contain an unsubordinated subject and verb.* Perhaps you are able to see the errors in the above sentences, but still you don't know what I mean by that last phrase, "unsubordinated subject and verb." You probably wrote, in answer to the questions that open this chapter, that a sentence is a "complete thought." Well, what makes a thought "complete" (in English, and also in Swedish, Swahili, or Sanskrit) is an unsubordinated subject and verb.

Destroying a Sentence by Adding to It

Exercise 9-3

Write out, on a sheet of paper, the following sentence:

> Dr. Schulte stayed with her patient all night.

We all know that we could destroy this sentence by taking away either the subject or the verb. But can you *add* a word in front of this sentence that will destroy it as a sentence? Try.

How many examples did the class come up with? If none, then look at the following partial list of words that would work:

after	before	when
although	if	where
because	since	while

You might, for now, want to think of these words as *sentence destroyers*. In fact, they are known as *subordinating conjunctions*.

Repairing a Nonsentence by Adding to It

Exercise 9-4

Use a subordinating conjunction at the beginning of the sentence "Dr. Schulte stayed with her patient all night," and then finish the thought in some way that satisfies you.

Read your new sentences aloud in turn. Now you may be able to see why these sentence destroyers have the name *subordinating conjunctions*. They are *conjunctions* because they *connect* things, in this case the first part of the sentence to the last part. They are *subordinating* because they make the first part of the sentence *subordinate* to, or *dependent* on, the last part of the sentence.

Discovering an Independent Clause

Exercise 9-5

From your last sentence take away your sentence destroyer and "Dr.

Schulte stayed with her patient all night," and note what's left. Is what's left a sentence? Yes. Its subject and verb don't have a subordinating conjunction in front of them. They are an *unsubordinated subject and verb.* Compare your sentence with those of the rest of the class.

Clauses

You now should be able to understand easily one of the most useful terms in English sentence structure: a *clause. Because Dr. Schulte stayed with her patient all night* is a clause. And *Mr. Schulte made breakfast for her* is also a clause. What makes a group of words a clause? A clause is a group of words that contains a subject and a verb. But clauses come in two types that are punctuated very differently. The two types are dependent (or subordinate) clauses and independent (or main) clauses. An independent clause is a complete sentence. It can stand on its own. Dependent clauses have subjects and verbs, but they also have a subordinating conjunction, so they can exist only as parasites, attached to an independent clause.

One last point. Dependent, or subordinate, clauses are not necessarily subordinate in the importance of the ideas they convey. The idea in a dependent clause can be as important as, or even more important than, the idea in the independent part of the sentence. (For example: "I'll stop by to see you Friday *if I finish my paper.*") Subordinate clauses are subordinate, or dependent, only in grammatical terms, not in terms of meaning.

Adjectives and Adverbs

I'm sure you noticed that you used words other than nouns, pronouns, verbs, and conjunctions in the sentences you've written. Almost all of those words, and groups of words, can be classified as either adjectives or adverbs. For the moment, let us say simply that adjectives help us understand nouns, and adverbs help us understand verbs (adverbs, in fact, do more than this).

Exercise 9-6

To see what adjectives and adverbs are, let's take advantage (as we will throughout this chapter) of those among your classmates who have learned these grammatical terms before and who remember pretty well how to use them.

Take a basic sentence. I suggest:

The coach traveled.

Tell us *which* coach traveled by adding a word or a group of words to this sentence. Compare your suggestions. All your additions—whether single words, or prepositional phrases, or clauses—will be serving as adjectives.

Now return to the base sentence:

> The coach traveled.

Can you tell us something about *how, when, where,* or *why* the coach traveled by adding a word or a group of words? Again, compare your suggestions. All your suggestions this time—words, prepositional phrases, or clauses—will be adverbs.

Those of you who added single-word adverbs may have noticed that most of them end in -*ly*. Charles Dickens spoofs writers who rely too much on adverbs in a passage from *A Tale of Two Cities* when he describes an indictment against the character Charles Darnay, who is said to have "wickedly, falsely, traitorously, and otherwise evil-adverbiously" revealed English secrets to the French king (93).

The main reason for learning the difference between adjectives and adverbs is to know whether to write *She rode smooth* or *She rode smoothly,* or *He wrote good* or *He wrote well.* In most cases, an adjective has a plain ending, while the adverb with a similar meaning ends in -*ly*.

Adjective	Adverb
happy	happily
sure	surely

But in one very common case, that of the adjective *good,* the form changes entirely:

Adjective	Adverb
good	well

Because so many people don't know the difference between adjectives and adverbs, we often hear on television, "He pitches good in relief" or "She skates good under pressure."

In adding adjectives and adverbs to our base sentence, some of you, instead of adding single words or phrases, probably added whole clauses, such as *when the season ended* or *because she needed a left-handed pitcher.*

Enriching Sentences with Clauses

Exercise 9-7

Now all of you should try to add a clause.

> The coach traveled...

Compare your answers. What, again, is the definition of a clause?

Enriching Sentences with Prepositional Phrases

Exercise 9-8

I'm sure that some of your adjectives and adverbs in Exercise 9-6 were neither clauses nor single words but prepositional phrases, like "in the car" or "past the pub" or "after the game." Prepositional phrases are for most people the easiest part of English grammar to remember. But quickly to make sure that you *all* know how to use prepositional phrases, add any one you please (a new one if you used one last time) to our base sentence:

> The coach traveled...

How many different prepositions did the class come up with? There are forty or so in all. A good list, with sample objects attached, follows:

about the winner	*concerning* your father	*over* the hedge
above the garage		*past* the sign
across the pond	*down* the sewer	**since* the war
*after breakfast	*during* the heat wave	*through* the woods
against the brick	*except* vegetables	*to* Arkansas
along the street	*for* your uncle	*toward* the clock
among the players	*from* your aunt	tower
around the corner	*in* a box	*under* the sink
at the game	*inside* the chest	**until* Saturday
*before dinner	*into* the pool	*up* the hill
behind the house	*like* her husband	*upon* demand
below the high-water mark	*near* the cliffs	*with* my friend
beneath the window	*of* the plumber	*within* an hour
beyond hope	*off* the chimney	*without* any worry
by the farmer	*on* the plate	
	outside the tavern	

Distinguishing Subordinating Conjunctions from Prepositions

Exercise 9-9

You may have noted that some prepositions (*after, before, since,* and *until*—marked with an asterisk above) can also be used as sentence destroyers (that is, subordinating conjunctions). How can you tell, in a given sentence, whether a word like *before* or *after* is a preposition or a subordinating conjunction?

Prepositional phrases have a nice ring to them: *under the table, without regret, during the play*. Prepositional phrases are not clauses because they have no verb—just a preposition, an object, and often an adjective or two modifying the object. Prepositional phrases play a peripheral role in a sentence: they help explain nouns and verbs; they don't act themselves.

The <u>purpose</u> of the rule <u>is</u> to protect the committee's members.
    subject   *verb*
        prepositional phrase
The <u>success</u> of my plans <u>depends</u> on you.
    subject   *verb*
        prepositional phrase

Also, prepositions desperately need their objects. Prepositions and their objects are so closely connected that it wasn't until the thirteenth century that prepositions were separated from their objects when people wrote. A twelfth-century writer, if he used modern spelling, would have written "inthetree" or "behindthebush."

Phrases

Prepositional phrases are the most common of several kinds of *phrases* in English sentence structure. A phrase is a group of words not easily separated that *does not include a subject-verb pair.*

A noun with its modifiers is sometimes called a *noun phrase:*

The old school will be torn down.
A good leader could solve our problems.

A verb with its helping verbs is often called a *verb phrase:*

Refugees *have been helped.*
Victory *might be achieved.*
John *can be bribed.*

These helping verbs (and combinations of them) can be used along with the main verb of a sentence to form a *verb phrase:*

am	*has*	*could*
is	*have*	*will*
are	*had*	*would*
was	*should*	*shall*
were	*may*	*do*
be	*might*	*does*
being	*must*	*did*
been	*can*	

Participles, gerunds, and infinitives also introduce phrases, but we need to review them before we look at their phrases. Steel yourself while we look first at those common but strangely named grammatical animals, participles and gerunds. There are two bizarre paradoxes in sentence structure. One, you've already seen, is that you can add a word to a complete sentence and by doing so make the sentence incomplete. The second paradox is that you can take a verb's "verbness" away from it by adding -ing. Watch.

Participles

Exercise 9-10

Fill in the blank below with any word you choose. You may add words within the brackets, too, if you wish.

_____ing [   ], Gary left for the park.

When you compare your suggestions, you'll find that every word you suggested for the opening blank is a verb, but that each new word you created—*running* or *laughing* or *coughing,* for example—is clearly not the verb in the sentence. *Left* is the verb. Your newly created word is an adjective modifying *Gary.* Thus a *present* participle (there are *past* participles too) is a base verb plus -ing which acts as an adjective.

If you added words within the brackets, you created not just a participle but a participial phrase.

Past Participles

Exercise 9-11

Fill in the blank below with any word you choose.

The _____ ed mother looked out the window.

Again, comparing suggestions, you'll find that you filled in the blank with a verb but that your newly created -ed word is an adjective (a past participle) modifying *mother.*

Omitted -ed Endings

I read an article call "Trouble for Dad."

Your ear probably tells you that *call* above should be *called.* But it may not. And you probably don't know why it should be *called. Called* is not the subject of the sentence; *I* is. It's not the verb; *read* is. It's not the direct object; *an article* is. *Called* is a participle, one of those verbs demoted to adjectives. It is easy to recognize *-ing* participles, *present* participles like *driving* in the phrase *a driving rain.* But equally important, though a little harder to recognize, are *past* participles.

a *crumbled* brick
a *renewed* contract
a *broken* twig

We talk about a *washing* machine, a machine in the act of washing, but we also speak of *washed* clothes, where the washing is already completed.

Most past participles end in *-ed.* But some end in *-en,* and a few are very irregular. (Common past participles which don't end in *-en* or *-ed* are *bent, bet, hit, held, hurt, lost, made, rung, sung, strung, struck,* and *taught.*) All have the same form of the verb (called the "third principal part") that you use when you say "I have *fixed,*" or "I have *broken,*" or "I have *run,*" or "I have *joked.*" Past participles are frequently used in English:

Ruth bought 60 acres of *cultivated* land.
The stone structures in London, *blackened* by coal soot in the nineteenth century, are now being cleaned.

Here are a few common errors related to the use of the past participle (or its identical twin, the verb form that follows the helping verb *have*):

Wrong: The college buildings were in the *old-fashion* design.
Wrong: Here in college I have been *force* to study more.
Wrong: I've *notice* some changes in myself.

If you make similar errors, try to check over your writing, after you have everything else straight, to see whether some of your participles, and verbs following *have,* aren't missing their *-ed.*

Gerunds

Gerunds, unfortunately, look just like present participles. They also are made up of a basic verb plus -*ing*.

Exercise 9-12

Fill in the blank in the following sentence with any word you like. You may add words within the brackets, too, if you wish.

_____ing [   ] pays off in the long run.

Compare your answers. You all filled in a verb, but you wound up with a subject for your sentence, a gerund. If you added words in the brackets, you created not just a gerund but a gerund phrase.

Gerunds are frequently used as subjects of sentences.

> *Swimming* exercises every muscle in the body.
> *Writing* is less difficult when you write regularly.

You might remember the difference between participles and gerunds by remembering that a gerund is a verbal noun and that a participle is a verbal adjective.

You've just seen in action a very important grammatical principle: once a verb has -*ing* added to it, it is no longer a verb. It's been demoted to a mere *verbal*—a participle or a gerund. Many sentence fragments that we write are fragments because we've included only a verbal, not a verb, in what we thought was a sentence:

> *Wrong:* Lauren *having* the best earned run average of all our pitchers.

The only way a verb with -*ing* added to it can regain the status of a verb is with the aid of a helping verb from the *is* family—*is, are, be, been, was were, am:*

> *Correct:* Lauren *is having* her best year as a pitcher.

Converting Verbs into Participles and Gerunds

Exercise 9-13

To give you some idea of how versatile these -*ing* forms are, try returning to your base sentence:

> The coach traveled.

Now, convert the verb into a participle modifying the coach and add a new verb to the sentence. Compare your sentence with those of your classmates. Then convert the verb into a gerund and make a statement about the coach; e.g., *Traveling is a coach's curse.*

Just to make sure that you can recognize when a verb plus *-ing* is still a verb, take our base sentence and alter the verb so that it contains an *-ing* form that is still a verb.

Participles and gerunds are both called *verbals*—not verbs but *verbals*. A verbal is a sort of verb that has been demoted to noun or adjective status. There is one other kind of verbal, the *infinitive*. Compared to participles and gerunds, infinitives are easy. They're marked with an extra word, *to: to knit, to see, to travel.* Like the other verbals, infinitives cannot serve as *the* verb in a sentence.

> I   want   to study.
> ___ _____
> *verb infinitive object*
>   To breathe freely is a sign of health.
>   _____   ___
>   *infinitive subject   verb*

Converting Verbs into Infinitives

Exercise 9-14

To practice just for a moment, take our original sentence, convert *traveled* into an infinitive, and add a new verb. Note how the verb ending changes. Try another example:

> The mayor of Atlanta attends many dinners.

Now alter this sentence to indicate that the mayor only plans to be at these dinners. Again, note how the verb ending on *attends* changes. Also note the ending on *plans*. The practice of adding an *-s* ending to a verb attached to a third-person-singular subject doesn't apply to an infinitive because an infinitive is not the verb in the sentence.

While the verbals—participles, gerunds, and infinitives—have been demoted from main-verb status in the sentence, they still retain some of the characteristics of verbs: they are often accompanied by direct objects or modified by adverbs or adverb phrases:

> At Lodi, near Medea, fifteen rebels attacked workers
>   repairing   the railway.
>   _____   _____
>   *participle   and its object*
> A conference of specialists in cultivating   rice will be held
>   _____   ___
>   *gerund   and its object*
>   Tuesday in Calcutta.

Decisively defeated   in the New Hampshire primary,
its adverb participle   another adverb, this one a prepositional phrase

Howard Baker was forced to withdraw as a candidate for
the presidency.

A verbal with its adverbs or objects is called a *verbal phrase.*

Parallel Structure

The exercises that you've just completed will help you write with more
variety in your sentence structure. You should now be able to see many,
many options that you have when you write your sentences. But sentence variety is not as important as it is sometimes said to be in writing.
In fact, sentence similarity, or similarity of sentence patterns, is an often
neglected virtue. Repetitive, or parallel, structure within and among sentences is one of the writer's principal tools for achieving coherence, clarity, and a pleasing rhythm. Few of the devices available to the writer are
as helpful, as frequently applicable, as strengthening to style as parallel
structure. The ease with which the English language doubles its subjects, its verbs, or its phrases or clauses makes parallel structure a fluid
way to write.

Exercise 9-15

If you practice imitating parallel structures in the writing of others, the
rhythm of parallel writing will soon come naturally to you.

Model: The town stopped noticing National Suicide Day because they had
absorbed it into their thoughts, into their language, into their lives.
(Toni Morrison)

Sample imitation: The boys stopped practicing basketball because they had
pushed sports out of their afternoons, out of their summers, out of their
concerns.

Your imitation: _____

_____

_____

Model: Her blindness has limited her to puttering in the garden, walking to
the mailbox, and listening to the radio.

Your imitation: _____

_____

_____

_____

Model: Without the mitochondria in our cells, we would be unable
       to move a muscle, to drum a finger, to think a thought. (Lewis Thomas)
Your imitation: _____

_____

_____

Punctuation

With a knowledge of the basic elements of grammar reviewed above, you
can learn all the important rules for punctuation. Punctuation is your
readers' best friend. It helps words on a page sound as much as possible
like the human voice. So you owe it to your readers to punctuate as
clearly as possible. Erratic punctuation distracts a reader the same way
that backstage stage-crew voices distract an audience at a play. In both
cases the "noise" is clearly unprofessional, and it prevents the listener
from concentrating on the main event.

Exercise 9-16
Punctuation Review

To review your abilities and preferences in punctuation, try to reintroduce
the punctuation into the following passage, from which all punctuation has
been removed (McPhee, *The Pine Barrens,* 11–12):

> I asked Fred what all those cars were doing in his yard and he said
> that one of them was in running condition and that the rest were its
> predecessors the working vehicle was a 1956 Mercury each of the
> seven others had at one time or another been his best car and each in
> turn had lain down like a sick animal and had died right there in the
> yard unless it had been towed home after a mishap elsewhere in the
> pines Fred recited with affection the history of each car of one old
> Ford for example he said I upset that up to Speedwell in the creek
> and of an even older car a station wagon he said I busted that one up
> in the snow I met a car on a little hill and hit the brake and hit a tree
> one of the cars had met its end at a narrow bridge about four miles
> from Hog Wallow where Fred had hit a state trooper head-on
>
> Fred apologized for not having a phone after I asked where I would
> have to go to make a call later on he said I don't have no phone

because I don't have no electric if I had electric I would have had a phone in here a long time ago he uses a kerosene lamp a propane lamp and two flashlights

You may be able to punctuate the above passage correctly even if you don't know many rules of punctuation. Your ear will help you punctuate if you are a frequent reader. But if you do make some mistakes, or if you find your ear unreliable, you can only learn punctuation if you learn the rules. So whether you need them or whether you just want a quick review, here are the rules for punctuation in English, each introduced in connection with a common writing problem.

Common Problems in Punctuation

1. Comma Splices and Fused Sentences

The most common grammatical fault in our writing is the so-called *comma splice*. One reason we have trouble with it is that we don't know what *splice* means. *Splice* is a word used regularly only by sailors and Boy Scouts. To splice is to join, usually to join two pieces of rope. Here's a rope splice:

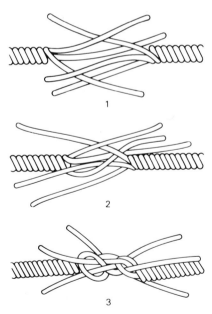

Sequence of steps in making a short splice

A comma splice is the use of a comma rather than a semicolon or a period to join two complete sentences.

> I haven't decided how many kids to have, there are a lot of factors to consider when we decide to have kids.

> She is capable of doing the work, that is what is so puzzling.

> In New York, Philadelphia, and Baltimore, the sugar refineries ran out of raw sugar, this led to the layoff of 15,000 workers.

Sentences, of course, shouldn't be joined by a comma. If there's a complete sentence on both sides of a comma, the comma should be replaced by a semicolon:

> She is capable of doing the work; that is what is so puzzling.

Or the comma should be replaced by a period and a capital letter:

> She is capable of doing the work. That is what is so puzzling.

A comma is only useful in sorting things out within a sentence. It has no use between sentences.

Occasionally, writers join two sentences without using even a comma.

> I am glad I chose this school it is now my home.

Such a sentence is called a *fused sentence. Fused*, like *splice*, is a technical term. When two wires from separate electrical circuits come too close to each other, the heat generated can melt the wires and join them together so that the circuits are no longer distinct and useful. Similarly, in a fused sentence, the two distinct sentences are damaged because they are brought so close together that readers can't tell them apart.

Comma splices and fused sentences are both often called *run-on sentences*. But *run-on sentence* is a much misunderstood—and feared—term. When you write a long sentence and worry about whether it's a "run-on," you're usually worrying needlessly. *Run-on* is a technical term for the error of joining two complete sentences with no punctuation, or with a mere comma. There's nothing wrong with a long sentence as long as it's punctuated correctly.

> In New York, Philadelphia, and Baltimore, the sugar refineries ran out of raw sugar; this led to the layoff of 15,000 workers.

When a sentence is finished, shut it up with a period or with a semicolon. Don't leave its gates wide open (with no punctuation) or even half open (with a comma).

2. Sentence Fragments

You may not feel quite confident yet about your ability to locate and avoid comma splices and fused sentences, but I want to mention one more common problem—the sentence fragment—before trying to clear up all three. *Fragment* is a more common word than either *splice* or *fused*. A fragment is a broken part of something—part of a vase, part of a hammer, part of a sentence. Here are some common types of sentence fragments:

> Because each person's definition of success is different.
>
> Something I could be proud of.
>
> All of which is prepared by the infamous hospitality crew.

Comma splices and sentence fragments are related errors. A comma splice is too much of a good thing (two sentences between a capital letter and a period); a fragment is too little of a good thing (not even one sentence between a capital letter and a period). In both cases, inexperienced writers usually go wrong because they don't know which connectors—sometimes conjunctions but often pronouns—make a sentence or clause grammatically dependent, and which allow a sentence or clause to remain grammatically independent.

3. Punctuation with Connectors

To clarify in your mind the distinction between independent and dependent clauses, review the following list of common connectors.

1. *Personal pronouns—he, she, it, they,* etc.—do not make a sentence dependent.

   > Jeff is a bum. *He* stole my football yesterday.

   The sense of the second sentence does depend on the first sentence having been there, but the second sentence is grammatically independent. It is not wholly independent in meaning, but it's a rare sentence in any piece of writing whose meaning is *wholly* independent of what comes before and after. Punctuation decisions must be based not on meaning independence but on grammatical independence.

2. So-called *demonstrative pronouns,* pronouns that point out (*this, that, these, those*), are like personal pronouns (he, she, it, they) in that they do not make a sentence dependent.

   > Perry left home yesterday. *This* was fine with me.

3. *There* and *here,* in the constructions *there are* and *here are,* do not make a sentence dependent.

   > I have six brothers. *There* are four living right here in Portland.

4. *Conjunctive adverbs* (a list follows) do not make a sentence dependent.

also	likewise	then
besides	immediately	therefore
consequently	moreover	similarly
finally	instead	thus
first	nevertheless	still
otherwise	now	on the other hand
on the contrary	meanwhile	in fact
furthermore	sometimes	
however	indeed	

I won the mile. *Now* I feel that I can quit racing anytime.
Business is booming. *Still* I worry about our loans.

For all but the shortest conjunctive adverbs, like *now* and *still* above, a comma is normally used to separate the conjunctive adverb from the body of the sentence:

Finally, our rosebush is blooming. The petunias, *however,* won't bloom for another week.

Conjunctive adverbs get their name because they act as adverbs—they tell *how, when, where,* or *why*—while at the same time they serve as conjunctions, making connections clear.

5. There are two kinds of connectors, *subordinating conjunctions* and *relative pronouns*, that *do* make a clause dependent. They really must be memorized so you can distinguish them from conjunctive adverbs.

Subordinating conjunctions		Relative pronouns
after	though	that
although	even though	who
because	whereas	whose
before	as	whom
if	whenever	which
since	till, until	
when	unless	
where	as if	
while	as though	
so that	as much as	
wherever	as long as	
how	in order that	
whether		

Elizabeth is home *because there was a fire at the library.*
I know a lawyer *who works every Saturday in a Boulder legal aid clinic.*

To see what these sentence destroyers can do, compare the following examples:

When caffeine ($C_8H_{10}N_4O_2$) is burned in a limited supply of O_2, the products are CO, H_2O, and NO; all are gases.
When caffeine ($C_8H_{10}N_4O_2$) is burned in a limited supply of O_2, the products are CO, H_2O, and NO, all *of which* are gases.

Which is a sentence destroyer. Even *of which* will do the trick, and so "all of which are gases" can't stand alone. It must be connected to a whole sentence with a comma.

These conjunctions are often given little respect. We have studied nouns, verbs, adjectives, and adverbs a hundred times. But the connectors, the conjunctions, are the keys to clear punctuation, for they give us the keys to knowing whether our subjects and verbs are subordinated or not.

The common definition of a sentence as a "complete thought" doesn't help us much in punctuating. But when we keep in mind that a sentence is an "unsubordinated subject and verb," we realize that recognizing clauses, independent and dependent, is the key to punctuation. When clauses are linked, and most sentences link clauses, they are linked in very predictable ways:

Independent clause	;	Independent clause
Dependent clause	,	Independent clause
Independent clause	o	Dependent clause

The first two of these three rules are absolute. The third rule does have exceptions. When the concluding dependent clause is not essential to understanding the meaning of the independent clause, a comma should precede the dependent clause.

> Samantha is one of the better players on the team when her competitive spirit is engaged, as she demonstrated against Paul VI and other tough teams.

There is properly no comma before the dependent clause "when her competitive spirit is engaged" because the independent clause is not intended to be understood without it. But there is a comma before the dependent clause "as she demonstrated against Paul VI and other tough teams" because that clause is not essential, though it adds a nice detail. Your ear is a more reliable judge of punctuation on this issue than it is on most.

Let me give several examples of each of these three basic punctuation rules:

• IC ; IC

> I like pizza; Kathy likes hot dogs.
> I wonder where our neighbors found the money; perhaps they've been robbing banks.

Of course, you can always use a period and a capital letter in the place of a semicolon.

• DC , IC

> When Errol paints his house, we'll celebrate.
> Unless he loses, Jack will still be arrogant.

In sentences of this type, the comma serves as a sort of warning that now the independent (or main) clause is coming.

- $IC_0 DC$

    We'll celebrate when Errol paints his house.

    Jack will still be arrogant unless he loses.

In these sentences no comma should intrude because the independent clause is not intended to be understood without it.

4. Punctuation with *And*

If you now have the punctuation of independent and dependent clauses straight, you've learned the most important part of this chapter. I'd now like to introduce a less frequent but still common punctuation problem: punctuation with *and*.

I've said that IC ; IC is correct. And, of course, IC . IC is correct. But there is a third way of connecting independent clauses—that is, with a comma and a so-called *coordinating conjunction* (this is the last conjunction that you'll meet). The coordinating conjunctions are *and, but, or, nor, for, yet,* and *so,* but the most common by far are *and* and *but*. These conjunctions (connecting words) are called *coordinating* rather than *subordinating* conjunctions because they do not subordinate. They leave the two things they connect grammatically equal.

    John loves Abby, *and* Abby loves John.

    The government gives, *and* the government takes away.

    I like pizza, *but* it doesn't like me.

Exercise 9-17

And, of course, can be used to connect many things other than independent clauses. To give you some idea of the variety possible, finish, with the rest of your class, the following sentence:

    George bought a hammer and...

When you've finished completing the sentence, decide whether you should put a comma after *hammer*. When you compare your answer with your classmates' answers, you'll see how easily any of the grammatical parts of our sentences can be doubled. Some of you doubled the object (*George bought a hammer and some nails*), some the verb plus the object (*George bought a hammer and returned the lumber*), and some the subject, verb, and object (*George bought a hammer, and Maria bought firewood*). Only in the last case do you need a comma before the *and*. *Only when* and *is connecting two entire independent clauses do you need to put a comma before it.*

So, our earlier rule is revised:

IC(;)IC *or* IC(, and)IC

Here's another way to look at it:

verb	(and)	verb
phrase	(and)	phrase
object	(and)	object
	but	
IC	(, and)	IC

5. Interrupting Words, Phrases, and Clauses

How many times have teachers or editors told you that you must use a comma both *before* and *after* a certain word, or phrase, or clause. Do you know why? The principal use of commas (e.g., DC , IC) is to highlight the independent clause in a sentence. And that's the same reason why you use a comma before and after any *interrupter* of the independent clause.

Independent, Interrupter, Clause

Peter, *however,* is the one you can depend on.

Jessica, *you may remember,* was our first choice.

The rule might be stated as follows: "Use a pair of commas to set off material that adds information without affecting the meaning of the rest of the sentence" (Raymond and Goldfarb 49). Using one comma but not both is a common mistake:

Wrong: The prison system, he believes attempts to be fair.
Wrong: Barbara soon made friends, or at least acquaintances of her
own age.

Deciding where to put the second comma depends on our being able to pick out the sentence's independent clause. The second comma follows the interrupter; it comes just before the flow of the independent clause resumes.

Correct: The prison system, he believes, attempts to be fair.
Correct: Barbara soon made friends, or at least acquaintances, of her
own age.

There are a number of *types of interrupters:*

- Single-word comments, including conjunctive adverbs:

The Kangfu Textile Company in Shanghai will, *incidentally,* start production in November of medical elastic stockings.

- Nouns, with their modifiers, giving further information (called *appositives*):

  El Arish, *the main depot for Egyptian forces in the Sinai peninsula,* was the last bastion to be attacked.

- Participial phrases:

  Raiders of the Lost Ark, written and produced by George Lucas and Stephen Spielberg, offered the same style of appealing adventure as the 1973 movie *The Sting.*

- Adjective clauses:

  The Jordanian fighter plane, *which was built in Seattle, Washington,* was intercepted while flying in international air space.

- Words that express an alternative:

  A new hat is an extra, *if minor,* responsibility.

- Long prepositional phrases:

  Will the Soviets now try, *under cover of the world's preoccupation with Middle Eastern events,* to reassert their sway over Hungary?

A problem that many writers take to their graves is being unsure of which phrases and clauses are interrupters and which are not. For example, consider this common maxim:

People who live in glass houses shouldn't throw stones.

The clause *who live in glass houses* is not set off by commas. Why? Because the independent clause, the main part of the sentence, doesn't have the same meaning if that clause is eliminated:

People shouldn't throw stones.

We need the clause *who live in glass houses* to know what people the writer is talking about. Note the contrast in the following sentence:

Bill, who spent last year in Thailand, plans to begin study at the University of Wyoming in the fall.

This sentence makes sense without the interrupting clause. The clause is not necessary to our knowing who Bill is. Therefore, it is a genuine interrupter and merits two commas. The difference between noninterrupting and interrupting clauses goes by several names—*restrictive* versus *nonrestrictive,* for example, and *defining* versus *commenting*—but I like best the distinction *identifying* versus *supplementary. Identifying* clauses make it possible for us to know exactly who or what the noun preceding them is. *Identifying* phrases and clauses should not be separated from their main clauses with any punctuation. *Supplementary* clauses give interesting information, but not information necessary for identifying the noun that they follow. *Supplementary* words, phrases, and clauses need two commas to show that they are supplementary, to acknowledge that they are interrupters. To see how the two are commonly used and to make yourself confident of the way they are punctuated, try the following exercise.

Exercise 9-18
Phrases and Clauses: Identifying or Supplementary

Make the following statements more specific by adding an appropriate phrase or clause in each of the blanks. Decide whether your additions should be separated from the main clause by commas.

Women _____ have power _____ .
The Exxon station _____ ordered a sign _____ .
The veteran _____ raised a flag _____ .
An earthquake _____ killed 700 people _____ .

When your clauses are *supplementary,* when they *interrupt* the main flow, they'll have been set off by two commas. When your clauses *identify* the nouns they follow, they'll fit right in without any punctuation.

If you've understood the IC ; IC and DC , IC and IC $_0$ DC rules, and if you've understood the "interrupter" rules, you should from now on be able to punctuate that troublesome word *however.*

> The list, *however,* didn't include the rest of the family: Mary, Louis, Carol, Ralph, and Theresa.
> I ran out of gas; *however,* soon afterward a passing motorist gave me a ride.

However is the most commonly used conjunctive adverb. It is surrounded by commas when it interrupts a single independent clause. But when it introduces a second independent clause, it will have a semicolon before it, dividing the two independent clauses, and a comma after it, separating the *however* from its own independent clause.

6. Introducing a Quotation

The key to deciding what punctuation is appropriate when introducing a quotation is, once again, understanding where the independent and dependent clauses begin and end.

When punctuating a lead-in to a quotation, you have three choices: a comma, a colon, or no punctuation at all.

> He summarized his views on revision in this way: "A writer's principal work is rewriting."

> He summarized his views on revision by saying "A writer's principal
> work is rewriting."
> He said, "A writer's principal work is rewriting."

What is the difference between these three lead-ins? Why the need for different punctuation? Sentence structure. In the first example, the grammatical
sentence is complete before the quotation begins. The colon says, "Wait,
there's more, even though the grammatical sentence is complete." In the second example, the structure of the sentence before the quotation is not complete. We must add an object for *saying*. *Saying* what? Since the gerund *saying* needs an object to be completed, we can't pause, so we use no
punctuation. The quotation serves as the object of the gerund *saying*. (A
quotation always serves grammatically as a noun in a sentence.)

What about the third example? The use of the comma in the third
sentence is a matter of convention. *She said* or *he said* is so common in
English that it gets its own rules. To be precise, we should say:

> He said that "The writer's principal work is rewriting."

That the writer's principal work is rewriting is a noun clause, a clause
which is acting as a noun, the object in the sentence. But the expression
is so common that we save ourselves trouble and skip the *that*. When we
do, we replace it with a comma.

Punctuating a Quotation

1 . When the sentence structure is complete before the quotation, use a colon to
    introduce it.
2 . When the sentence is continuing, particularly when the quotation is the object of
    a preposition, or a participle, or a gerund, no punctuation is needed.
3 . When a *that* is skipped after *said,* use a comma to replace the *that* and introduce
    the quotation.

Note: The same rule that governs the use of colons in quotations
governs their use elsewhere too. We all "know" that a colon introduces a
list, but not every list needs a colon. What about the following?

> The Rossborough Inn is used by faculty, staff, and alumni for:
> conferences, luncheons, banquets, cocktail parties, and wedding
> receptions.

The colon here is intrusive. It blocks the path from a preposition (*for*) to
its objects (*conferences*, etc.). The structure of the sentence is not complete at *for*. A colon would be appropriate if *for* were given the object *the
following*.

> The Rossborough Inn is used by faculty, staff, and alumni for the
> following: conferences, luncheons, banquets, cocktail parties, and
> wedding receptions.

Punctuation Rules and Guidelines: A Final Review

1. The key to punctuation is locating the sentence's independent clause.
2. IC;IC.
3. DC,IC.
4. IC$_0$DC (except when the dependent clause takes a surprising turn of thought or sounds like an afterthought).
5. I ,int., C.
6. IC, and IC.
7. A colon builds anticipation. Use a colon to introduce a quotation or a list *if* the structure of the sentence is already complete.
8. The purpose of most commas is to highlight the main clause of a sentence: to signal the end of introductory phrases or clauses, to separate out interrupters, or to signal the beginning of afterthought phrases or clauses. A comma is also used to separate in lists of three or more items (e.g., apples, oranges, and bananas). And commas can be used at our discretion to indicate pauses for emphasis.

Punctuation conventions have shifted many times in history as writers and publishers have tried to find the most flexible system for making their meanings clear. When Thomas More wrote in the early sixteenth century, he simply used a virgule (/) anytime he wanted his reader to pause:

> First yf he have cause to fere / yet fereth he more than he nedeth /
> For their is no devill so diligent to destry him / as god is to preserve
> hym / nor no devill so nere hym to do hym harme / as god is to do
> hym good / nor all the divelles in hell so strong to invade & assawte
> hym / as god is to defend hym / yf he distrust hym not but faythfully
> put his trust in hym / (153)

Within a hundred years, though, the virgule was replaced by a four-part breathing system: a comma (,) meant a short breath, a semicolon (;) a slightly longer breath, a colon (:) an even longer breath, and a period (.) a full stop. Our current uses of these four marks are partly related to the sixteenth-century breathing standard, but in the eighteenth century, their uses were firmly tied to sentence structure. The eighteenth century has bequeathed us the rules we've worked through above, such as IC ; IC and DC , IC. But the virgule, or a new form of it, the dash, is coming back. Even in the eighteenth century it could be found in the novel *Tristram Shandy* by Lawrence Sterne:

> —My mother, who was sitting by, looked up,—but she knew no more
> than her backside what my father meant,—but my uncle, Mr. Toby
> Shandy, who had been often informed of the affair,—understood him
> very well. (3)

Sterne used the dash to reinforce commas, which we no longer do. The wonderful thing about the modern dash is that it is so flexible. We can use it to substitute for a period:

> You may say that this business of marking books is getting in the way of your reading. It probably will—that's one of the reasons for doing it.

For a colon:

> Consider some of the things the blues are about—work, love, death, floods, lynchings.

For a semicolon:

> One day I absentmindedly started crossing the street without looking up or down—the street was empty.

For a comma:

> In order to communicate with the dying, we must ourselves understand—and try to feel—the process of dying.

For opening and closing parentheses:

> So I walked on and on—horses were too expensive—until I had wandered beyond railways, beyond stage lines, to a land of "varmints" and rattlesnakes.

When you're not sure how to punctuate, try a dash. It may not win you any prizes, but it won't get you into any trouble either. Then head back to this chapter for a quick review of the more sophisticated comma, semicolon, colon, and period.

7. The Apostrophe

The apostrophe is often confusing to people who write infrequently because we don't need it when we talk, so we are careless about learning it for when we write. One of the apostrophe's uses is simple. It fills in for missing letters in contractions:

> *it's* for *it is*
> *you're* for *you are*
> *let's* for *let us*

The second use is equally simple. When a noun is converted to an adjective (as *Tom* is in the phrase *Tom's pipe*), 's is added to the noun. If the word already ends in *s* (*boys, gloves*), a simple apostrophe is added to make the word possessive (i.e., to make it an adjective): *boys', gloves'*.

One of the most frequently made errors is using 's to indicate the plural when a simple *s* will do.

Wrong: I was at San Francisco State for two year's.
Wrong: There were 300 student's in my first college class.

The other case where writers tend to use an unnecessary apostrophe is in the possessive pronoun *its*. This word has no apostrophe. But because it indicates possession, we just itch to stick one in: we want to write *it's* or even *its'*. Resist the urge. You don't have the urge to put an apostrophe in *his* or *her* or *our* or *their*, do you? Well, *its* is in the same family.

her house	our house	its house
his house	their house	

Its needs an apostrophe no more than *his* or *her* or *their* or *our* does. *Its* is a good clean word without any little squiggles above the line. Save your apostrophes for converted nouns that need them.

The survey of grammar in this chapter is by no means complete. Nor is it 100 percent reliable (the very mention of the word *grammar* triggers the association *exceptions*). But the exercises and checklists here are a solid foundation and are intended to be practical: they cover the grammar you need to know to punctuate correctly, and they are brief enough that you shouldn't be afraid to come back to them anytime your confidence needs a boost.

10

Research in the Library

The assignments were interesting, but involved a very lot of work and research for some of them.

student

I learned the most from my research assignment because (1) it taught me how to use the microfilm, (2) it helped in my organization problems, and (3) it helped me to take advantage of the libraries.

student

Why didn't someone teach me about these approaches to writing research papers back in high school? They wanted research papers but didn't tell us how to approach the job mentally....I never heard until now that actually developing the thesis or the purpose and approach of the paper was such a lengthy, active process. I thought that I must be dumb....So, I'd pile up the facts and try to organize them into paragraphs and hope the teacher would think I had said something new or meaningful.

student

Exercise 10-1
Review

Before you begin this chapter, write a bit about your research experiences in the past and what you found valuable or frustrating about them.

Research: The Way We Find Raw Material for Our Papers

Research is *not* looking into the encyclopedia and copying out some information appropriate to your topic. It is *not* taking twenty books out of the library and picking out pieces of each to pull together into a term paper. It is *not* "changing" the words of your sources into your own

176

words so that you can hand in a paper. Research is bringing the knowledge of the past to bear on problems of the present. It is delving into
libraries and other storehouses of information to find facts from which
you draw inferences. If and when you become a professional researcher,
it will be very important that you find *all* the important facts and *all* the
important sources of information before you begin to write. The purpose
of professional research is to arrive at the soundest possible judgments
based on the best information available.

But while you're an undergraduate, you will be assigned research
papers because your teachers value curiosity, reflection, and creativity,
and they know that you can increase those skills only if you practice
them. Thus when you search a subject, it's important for you to find representative facts, but by no means all of them. Your teachers will be most
interested not in your command of the subject you've studied but in the
curiosity, reflection, and creativity with which you draw inferences from
the facts you find. The facts you'll find are of several kinds.

1. The fact that something happened:

> In February 1965, President Lyndon Johnson ordered the first
> bombing raids into North Vietnam (Kearns 261).

2. The fact that someone said something:

> Sir Thomas Browne, a seventeenth-century father of eleven: "I could
> be content that we might procreate like trees, without conjunction, or
> that there were any way to perpetuate the world without this trivial
> vulgar way of union: it is the foolishest act a wise man commits in all
> his life" (Browne 79).

3. Statistical facts:

> The population of Kenosha, Wisconsin, in 1970 was 78,805
> ("Kenosha" 5, 760).

4. The fact that some authority interpreted a given fact in a given way:

> Eleanor Roosevelt thought early in 1952 that Adlai Stevenson would
> make a good president, but she doubted whether he could get the
> Democratic nomination (Lash 206).

The sources for all four kinds of facts must be acknowledged, as
I've done above. What can't be acknowledged, because they can't be borrowed, are the inferences you draw from these facts. Your paper will be
shaped by these inferences. *You* are the thinker (and the selector) at
work in the history of information and ideas. When you finish a research
paper, you will understand a subject much better than you did when
you began, partly because you've found so much more information, but
primarily because you've been forced to draw so many inferences, to

make so many judgments, about the facts that you've found. If you're afraid to draw inferences (because you're underinformed), that will come through in the hesitant or dependent voice you project in your paper. On the other hand, if you report your interpretations with confidence, your readers will quickly recognize your success in making sense of the material you've worked with.

Though the term *research paper* usually means "library research paper," library research isn't, of course, the only way to locate information. When you do research, you are looking for firsthand information, and libraries are only one source of it. Other sources include:

1. Interviews
2. Corporation records
3. Court records
4. City, state, or federal records
5. Museum holdings
6. Letters in your grandparents' attic
7. Films, television videotapes, and radio tapes or transcripts
8. Old copies of books, magazines, or newspapers in secondhand stores
9. Computerized databases with clever names, like NEXIS, for business information, or BIOSIS, for information in the biological sciences (A database is a huge computer-memory collection of information. You can select data for examination by typing in the key words for the subject you're interested in.)

Looking at a videotape of the June 5, 1953, *CBS Evening News* or at a January 1918 edition of the *San Francisco Chronicle* makes you feel like you're reliving history and (often) makes you feel like writing about what you feel so that you can share the feeling with others. The thrill just isn't there when you look up "World War I" or "McCarthyism" in the encyclopedia.

When you are asked to write, to write anything, the first thing that should pop into your head is *research*—you have to search somewhere for the facts from which you will draw your inferences. That research can often be completed without the help of a library. When a student decides to write about the Campus Health Center, he goes there to see what he can see, to collect any facts about it that are telling. When a book reviewer reads through a book she's just been sent by a publisher, she underlines passages that strike her as good, or bad, or unusual, and then when she starts writing, she looks back at her carefully observed underlinings to find telling quotations to use in her review. When a journalist interviews the owner of a successful racehorse, he observes carefully how the person acts and what is said or unsaid. Your purpose in practicing this research, this patient, thoughtful observation (besides that of learning more for yourself), is, most often, to help your teacher and classmates understand the subject of your research a little better than they did before.

Libraries

Research, wherever it starts, though, often takes a writer to a library, simply because so much of our history—documents, newspapers, magazines, audiotapes, videotapes, books, academic studies—is deposited in libraries. I know you've been told before that there are "treasures" in your library, but most of us don't believe that line because what we've found—encyclopedias, summaries, and thirdhand accounts with all the human details removed—hasn't made us eager to return. General encyclopedias are useful for looking up people, places, and terms with which we're not at all familiar. "Heraclitus," perhaps, or "Odessa." They help us learn, but they rarely offer an invitation to study or to think. Many of the encyclopedia and other thirdhand accounts are dull, not just because they're thirdhand stories, but because writers so often write badly. If you were to spend a day reading randomly in the library, you'd probably spend five out of seven hours with bad—or at best mediocre—writing. But during the other two hours you might also find:

1. A firsthand account of World War II (or the 1929 stock market crash) in *Time* magazine
2. Social thinking about birth control in 1911 in *The Yale Review*
3. *National Geographic* articles about Iran dated 1985, 1980, 1975, 1968, 1960, 1953, 1947, 1943, and 1932
4. Poems by Australian or African poets
5. Firsthand accounts of life in prison, or in Colorado, or in El Salvador
6. Local, national, and international newspapers, on microfilm, dating well back into the nineteenth, and occasionally even the eighteenth, century
7. Microfilmed document collections—e.g., in my library, *The Archives of George Allen and Company, 1893–1915,* or *Contemporary Newspapers of the North American Indian,* or *Records and Briefs in the United States Cases Decided by the Supreme Court*
8. Videotapes of 1940s detective films (Films and videotapes in libraries are—perhaps surprisingly—underused, because they're not easy to return to for patient examination; books—thanks to libraries—are easy to find and use, so they get most of the attention.)

If you get interested in Americans in Paris in the 1920s, you can probably find sixty books in your library on the subject, some to be flipped to the side quickly, others so absorbing that you won't want to leave.

You'll do yourself a great favor if you make your local library a familiar resource. Take the library tour at your library to learn its main features, but stick around after the tour is over and watch a few tapes, look over some old documents, browse through some old magazines. You may feel, once school starts, that you're too busy to "shop" in the library, but you can always procrastinate on a paper or on anything else you're doing in the library by finding your favorite shelf and taking down a book or a magazine.

Because libraries collect so much chaotic information, useful and seemingly useless, well written and poorly written, they need a system to organize it and make it possible for users to find what they're looking for. The Chinese, who formed libraries as early as the sixth century B.C., divided their collections into "classics," "history," "philosophy," and "literature." Our modern libraries are fuller, and therefore our classification systems are more complex. Almost all U.S. libraries organize their collections using either the Library of Congress classification system or the Dewey decimal classification system.

The Library of Congress (LC) system uses letters of the alphabet to classify holdings, and the Dewey decimal system uses three-digit numbers:

The Library of Congress System

A	General Works
B	Philosophy, Psychology, Religion
C	History and Auxiliary Sciences
D	History and Topography (except North and South America)
E–F	History: North and South America
G	Geography and Anthropology
H	Social Sciences: Economics, Sociology, Statistics
J	Political Science
K	Law
L	Education
M	Music
N	Fine Arts: Architecture, Painting, Sculpture
P	Language and Literature
Q	Science
R	Medicine
S	Agriculture
T	Technology
U	Military Science
V	Naval Science
Z	Bibliography and Library Science

The Dewey Decimal System

000–099	General Works
100–199	Philosophy
200–299	Religion
300–399	Social Sciences
400–499	Language
500–599	Pure Science

600–699	Technology (Applied Science)
700–799	The Arts
800–899	Literature
900–999	General Geography and History

These systems were developed during the 1870s—the Dewey by Melvil Dewey for the Amherst College Library, the Library of Congress by Charles Cutter for the Library of Congress—and although both systems have proved useful enough to last more than a century, neither is *so* good that it has driven out the other. Today you'll find that most college libraries use the Library of Congress system and that most public libraries use the Dewey system. The systems are used to classify a library's holdings not only in books but in magazines, films, tapes, and microforms as well. Thus the call number for the book *Cosmos,* by Carl Sagan, in the LC system is as follows:

```
QB44.2
.5235
```

The call number for the videotaped television series of the same name is this:

```
VIDEO CASSETTE
QB 981
.c83
```

And a related journal, *Space Sciences Review,* has this call number:

```
Q81
.577
```

    More important than trying to remember what call numbers are associated with what subject is becoming familiar with your library's principal rooms. These vary from library to library, but in general you'll find that you want to know:

1. The catalog—until recently almost always a *card* catalog, now increasingly on microfiche or at a computer terminal
2. The book stacks
3. The reference room
4. The periodicals room
5. The nonprint media room

To get a sense of the layout of these rooms in your own library, you might try the following exercises (or similar exercises specific to your library). If you are stumped at any point, ask a librarian for help. Librarians know well how complex a research task can be, and they welcome the opportunity to teach us how to use the library efficiently.

Exercise 10-2
The Catalog and the Book Stacks

1. Recall that the catalog contains not only title cards and author cards (or microfiche notes) but also subject cards. Find the call number for a book about U.S. agriculture written during the 1920s. (Try the 1950s if there are none from the 1920s in your library.)
2. Locate your book in the stacks, and write down the floor and the shelf where you found it. (If you don't find it, ask a librarian how you can find out where it might be, and explain to your class what you learned by asking.)

Exercise 10-3
The Reference Room

1. Go to the reference section of your library, and browse to see what's available. Find a book in the reference section that you'd like to spend more time with, or one that leads you to an interesting book or magazine elsewhere in the library. In class the next day, identify and describe the book that helped you so that others will realize that it's available. Also mention at least two other books from the reference section, perhaps less intriguing, but at least useful.
2. What is the call number and location in the reference section of *The New York Times Index?* of the *Reader's Guide to Periodical Literature?* What is the earliest date for which each is available?
3. By using *The New York Times Index,* identify two articles written for *The New York Times* in 1964 about inflation. Give the dates and a brief description of each (the *Index* will give you all this information).

The Periodicals Room

Libraries use the term *periodical* to refer to newspapers, magazines, journals, and any other kinds of reports that are published "periodically," at regular intervals.

Exercise 10-4

1. The list of the periodicals that are available in your library is usually called the serials list. (Serials is a term that includes all periodicals, and

also reports and journals that come out in series but not at regular intervals.) Using the serials list, find the call number of *Time* magazine and
note the date of the earliest *Time* that is owned by your library.
2. Look up (on microfilm) *The New York Times* from the day that one of
   your parents was born. In class the next day, describe, using two or three
   examples, the world into which your parent was born.
3. Introduce yourself to *The Yale Review,* a magazine that is still published,
   but that was in its glory from 1911 to 1920. During those years, *The Yale
   Review* contained articles on everything you could think of, from homosexuality to real estate holdings by railroads to new discoveries in radiation. Look at the library's serials list to see where *The Yale Review* is
   located in the library. Once you find it on the shelves, leaf through one
   of the 1911–1920 volumes (or the earliest volume your library has), and
   read an article that catches your interest. (If your library does not carry
   The Yale Review, try some other magazine published during the 1930s
   or earlier.) While you read, take some notes, including at least the following:
   a. The author's main point
   b. Two or three assumptions of the author that you can detect
   c. Four or five fact-inference pairs that the author uses
   d. The *ethos* that the author presents
When you're finished with this article, stop in the reference room and
check the *Readers' Guide to Periodical Literature* to see if you can find at
least one other article by the author of your article, or at least one other
article written on the same subject during the same decade. After finding
this second article and reading it, note briefly the difference between the
two articles. In class the next week, compare your notes with those taken by
others in your class.

Exercise 10-5
The Nonprint Media Room

Browse through the separate nonprint catalog, if there is one, or the central
catalog, if not, and pick out a videotape that you've never seen before.
Check it out, watch it, and note whether the tape was fiction or nonfiction,
persuasive or informative, well-made or ill-made. Compare your results
with those of your classmates.

Research Strategies

You may already have written research papers that you've learned from
and been proud of. If so, you know that an invitation to write another

library research paper is an opportunity to learn yet another subject well. On the other hand, you may never have written a research paper, or you may have written several that you didn't much care for. If you are in this "other hand," let's start fresh this time and make the most of the opportunity.

First, it helps to recognize that any long paper is not written through the use of only one or two skills. There are many constituent skills in research-paper writing. Let's consider several of these one at a time.

1. Following a Curiosity Trail

When you start work on a research paper and your subject has not been specified for you, indirection can often serve you as well as direction. As I was preparing this chapter, for example, I decided that I wanted to use as an example an opinion by Eleanor Roosevelt. I'm not sure why I chose her; I suppose it was because I've always admired her. I liked the *Eleanor and Franklin* show on television, and I knew there was a book of the same name, so I thought I'd look the book up in the card catalog. First, though, I wondered whether I could find an opinion of hers more easily in the *Encyclopaedia Britannica* (which I could look at in the reference room, on the same floor I was on). The very brief article there on Eleanor Roosevelt didn't tell me much (it didn't mention any of her opinions), but it recommended two books by Joseph Lash, *Eleanor and Franklin* and *Eleanor: The Years Alone.* Now I felt more confident going to *Eleanor and Franklin* because I could be more sure that it was a respectable source. So I headed for the card catalog (still on the second floor) and looked up Joseph Lash. He had written several books on Mrs. Roosevelt during the 1960s and 1970s, and he had also made a cassette or two (held by our library) talking about the books. I copied out the call

numbers
E807.1	E807.1	E807.1
.R572	.R573	.R574

I might be able to use, but I also noticed that Lash was born in 1909 and that

he had written a book back in 1936 called *War Our Heritage:* JX 1953 .L33 That

sounded like a pacifist book by a very young man, and I've long been intrigued by the philosophical passions Americans of the thirties seem to have had—I've seen nothing like them in my lifetime: the passions I knew during the sixties were more political than philosophical. So after I picked up a couple of E807s on the fourth floor, I stopped on the third floor to pick up the JX book. Before I looked at *Eleanor and Franklin,* I paged through *War Our Heritage.* Sure enough, it was a pacifist argument, with a preface by a World-War-I-era pacifist, much older, who explained how he thought pacifism had changed since his youth. If I were responsible for a research paper later this term, I'd have had the beginnings of an idea for a paper—a comparison of the pacifist attitudes of 1930s students with those of 1910s students. I'd look into the preface writer, Bruce Bliven, to see whether he'd written anything else. I'd note anybody else whom Lash mentioned or footnoted in his book. But mostly I'd look into my favorite sources—newspapers and magazines, of 1915, say, and 1935 (using *The New York Times Index* and the *Readers' Guide* to look up "Pacifism")—and find some contemporary thought on the subject.

The only difficulty in following a curiosity trail is starting it. The trails don't begin very easily in your own brain, even if you're a naturally curious person. Suggested Assignment 5 in Chapter 14 starts you with the issue of *The New York Times* published on the day of your birth. But you can start a curiosity trail almost anywhere in the library—in an article about the effects of railroads on Chicago's urban planning that you find in a book in the reference room called *The Encyclopedia of Urban Planning* (Arnold Whittich, McGraw-Hill, 1974), in an article about acid rain in Norway from a magazine that you pick up in the periodicals room called *Research in Norway*, in a short videotape that you find lying around in the nonprint media room called *Basic Film Terms*. Once you pick up a book or a magazine or a tape, you've started on your curiosity trail, and you can follow the trail in whatever direction you like. Make your research a genuine search, a search which heads in a direction that fascinates you.

2. Finding Information Systematically

This second search strategy is much more thorough and direct than following a curiosity trail. A systematic search begins not at the card catalog but in the reference room. Welcome to the world of indexes. It seems at first forbidding, but you'll soon appreciate what it can do for you.

I'd like to introduce you here to two reference books for looking up current issues, two reference sources for looking up historical issues, and one very useful source for background information on any subject. Once you've located and used these books and checked into the books near them on the reference shelves, you'll leave any sketchy advice I can offer far behind you.

When you have a paper assignment that requires you to study a topic of current controversy, two excellent books you'll probably want to turn to are *Public Affairs Information Service Bulletin* (*PAIS*) (New York: Public Affairs Information Service, Inc., published yearly) and *Bibliographic Index* (New York: H. W. Wilson, published yearly). *PAIS* is most useful when you're looking for statistics or when you're writing on an issue with public policy implications, for it indexes articles, books, and pamphlets in all fields, as long as they bear on public policy decisions. Here's a typical excerpt (521):

Public relations

† Maddalena, Lucille A. A communications manual for nonprofit organizations. '81 222p bibl il chart index (LC 80-67965) (ISBN 0-8144-5606-5) $17.95—*Am mgt assns*

INSTRUCTIONAL MATERIALS. See Education - Instructional materials.

INSULATION

Hirst, Eric and Raj Talwar. Reducing energy consumption in low-income homes: evaluation of the weatherization program in Minnesota. bibl tables *Evaluation R 5:671-85 O '81*

Smith, Gaines. Stormy weatherization: billed as models for the rest of the nation, mandatory insulation programs in Oregon are models of special-interest politicking. *Reason 13:31-9 F '82*

United States. House. Com. on Small Bus. Subcom. on Antitrust and Restraint of Trade Activities Affecting Small Bus. EPA [Environmental Protection Agency] proposed rulemaking on chlorofluorocarbons (CFCs) and its impact on small business: hearing, July 15, 1981. '81 iv + 202p bibl tables chart (97th Cong., 1st Sess.) pa—*Washington, DC 20515*
Synthetic compounds used widely in the refrigeration industry and in insulation.

INSURANCE
See also
Annuities.

I learn here (after checking abbreviations in the abbreviation key at the front of the volume) that I can find information on insulation policy in *Evaluation Review,* Volume 5 (October 1981), pages 671 to 685, in *Reason: Free Minds and Free Markets,* Volume 13 (February 1982), pages 31 to 39, and in a published 202-page July 15, 1981, hearing of a congressional subcommittee entitled "EPA Proposed Rulemaking on Chlorofluorocarbons and Its Impact on Small Business" (which should be available in my library's government documents collection). Perhaps one of these sources will prove valuable and interesting; perhaps this source, or one of the others, will mention another possible source or even include a bibliography of further sources.

A second current-issues index, potentially even more valuable than *PAIS*, is the *Bibliographic Index*, which lists any bibliography (with more than fifty citations) published during a current year either separately or as part of a book, pamphlet, or periodical. If you find an entry here, it may well lead you to a single article or book that can give you your entire list of possible sources, and thus you will have more time for your note taking and writing. I imagined that my subject was Argentina, for example, and looked up "Argentina" in the 1982 *Bibliographic Index* and found (33):

ARECUNA Indians
  Thomas, David John.   Order   without   govern-
  ment; the soc. of the Pemon Indians of Vene-
  zuela.   (Ill.   studies   in   anthropology,   no   13)
  Univ. of Ill. press '82 p250-6
ARGENTINA
                       History
  Walter, R. J.   Argentina;   1862-present. Hist
  Teach 14:313-26 My '81

              Politics and government
  Rodríguez, Celso.   Lencinas y Cantoni; el po-
  pulismo cuyano en tiempos de Irigoyen. Edi-
  torial de Belgrano '79 p345-67 annot
ARGENTINE painting. See Painting, Argentine
ARGUMENTATION. See Oratory
ARHAR. See Pigeon pea

ARID regions
    See also
  Deserts
ARID regions agriculture
    See also
  Dry farming
ARIDIZATION of land. See Desertification

ARISTOCRACY in literature
  Stanton, Domna C. Aristocrat as art; a study
  of the honnête homme and the dandy in 17th
  and   19th   cent.   French   literature.   Columbia
  univ. press '80 p279-300
ARISTOTLE, 384-322 B.C.
  Hardie, William Francis Ross. Aristotle's ethical
  theory. 2nd ed Oxford univ. press '80 p430-7
  Sober, E. Evolution, population thinking, and
  essentialism. Philos Sci 47:382-3 S '80

---

about
Aristoteles. La poétique; le text grec avec une
  traduction et des notes de lecture par Roselyne
  Dupon-Roc et Jean Lallot; pref. de Tzvetan
  Todorov. Seuil '80 p463-5
Warterlow, Sarah. Nature, change, and agency

I don't read Spanish (an obvious handicap when trying to write about Argentina), so I'll have to ignore Celso Rodríguez's article, but I will expect to find a considerable list of sources of Argentinian history, 1862 to the present, in *History Teacher* magazine (I decoded "Hist Teach" by looking it up at the beginning of the *Index*), Volume 14 (May 1981), pages 313 to 326.

When you're trying to locate historical events or historical attitudes toward issues, the most efficient indexes to turn to are *The New York Times Index* and the *Readers' Guide to Periodical Literature. The New York Times Index* notes every article that appeared in *The New York Times* during a given period. As I glanced through the July to September 1916 *Index*, I came upon "Georgia," and the entries there, though only briefly described, would seem to offer the beginnings of a cultural history of sex, ethnic, and political relations of the period (152):

GEORGE, V., King of England (continued)—
    success, Sept. 7, I., 1:8; issues procla-
    mation with regard to property of British
    subjects in enemy countries, Sept. 9, 3:5.
GEORGE, Charles E.—wife applies for ali-
    mony and counsel fees pending her suit
    for divorce, July 9, I., 6:8.
GEORGE, John Valance—death, Aug. 17,
    11:3.
GEORGE, E. WARREN (freighter,) *see*
    SHIPBUILDING.
GEORGIA—Editorial on passage of bill per-
    mitting women to practice law, July 31,
    8:4; Atlanta Journal charges that T. E.
    Watson is in a scheme with Louisville &
    Nashville R. R. to capture State Govt. in
    primaries and support H. M. Dorsey for
    Gov., Sept. 11, 3:7; Dorsey attacks ex-
    Gov. Slaton and charges that Jews have
    raised a fund to defeat him because of
    Frank case, Sept. 12, 3:3; Dorsey nomi-
    nated for Gov., Sept. 13, 1:4: editorial,

> Sept. 14, 6:3; letter by ex-Gov. Slaton re-
> plying to charges of Dorsey, Sept. 16,
> 10:6; final returns give large majority to
> Dorsey, statement by Gov. Harris, Sept.
> 20, 5:4.
>
> GERARD, (Amb.) James Watson—letter to
> A. von Briesen of Amer. Physicians' Ex-
> pedition Committee commending work of
> hospital in Germany, July 9, I., 14:1;
> plans to take rest in Scandinavia, July 11.

These entries are quite easy to read. The first editorial on women practicing law can be found, the *Index* says, in the July 31 (1916) *Times* on
page 8, starting in column 4. Although *The New York Times Index* only
locates articles in *The New York Times,* the dates of its articles often indicate where information can be found in other papers. Here, for example, I would expect that an editorial on women practicing law could be
found in *The Atlanta Constitution* on or near July 31, 1916. I'd be curious
to compare the perspective in the two editorials.

To get further historical information from weekly and monthly
magazines, our best source is the *Readers' Guide to Periodical Literature,*
which indexes articles in by no means all our periodicals, but in about
200 of our most popular and most respected ones. *Readers' Guide* entries look much like the entries in the other indexes, as you can see in
this example from the March 1957–February 1959 volume (1610):

> RAILROADS, Toy
>   For after-Christmas railroading. il Sunset 120:
>   54 Ja '58
>   Now you see it, now you don't. J. C. Gon-
>   zalez. il diag Am Home 59:94-5 D '57
>   Roll away blackboard and train table. R. G.
>   Smith, jr. il Workbench 14:18-20 N '58
>   Toymaker puts a new train on the tracks.
>   il Bsns W p 116-17+ Je 29 '57
>   *See also*
>   Railroad models
>
> RAILROADS and state
>
>   United States
>   Can technology solve our railroad problems?
>   address, May 5, 1958. A. E. Perlman. Vital
>   Speeches 24:565-8 Jl 1 '58
>   Make room for competition. Farm J 82:86 Ag
>   '58

Railroads: from overlord to underdog. R.
Bendiner. Reporter 19:19-24 Ag 7 '58
Railroads: the track ahead. il Newsweek 51:
78-80 Ja 20 '58
Things are looking up for the railroads. il
U S News 45:73-4 Ag 1 '58
  See also
Railroads—Federal aid

RAILS (birds)
Clapper rail. H. M. Hall. il Audubon Mag 60:
72-5 Mr '58
Singing wood-rail. A. F. Skutch. il Audubon
Mag 61:20-1 Ja '59 (to be cont)

RAILTON, Arthur R.
Detroit listening post. See issues of Popular
mechanics magazine

RAILWAY express agency
Express stop? Bsns W p 18 Ja 3 '59
Expressman's burden. Newsweek 53:53 Ja 5
'59

One of these articles (in *The Reporter,* Volume 19, pages 19 to 24, August 7, 1958) indicates that railroads are declining, another (in *U.S. News & World Report,* Volume 45, pages 73 to 74, August 1, 1958) that their future is looking up. Here, again, is the beginning of a problem I could investigate. If I wanted to find out what more thorough studies (longer than two to five pages) of the railroads suggested in 1958, I'd turn first to *PAIS* from that year or to the *Bibliographic Index* of that year. I'd soon have plenty of material to try to interpret. If I wanted a current update on railroads, I could turn to *PAIS* or the *Bibliographic Index* for the most recent year, or I could perhaps decide to pay for a computer search (most computer search services combine the resources of several indexes), using *railroad* and perhaps *future* as my key words. As I write, more and more of these indexes are being computerized, and some (Infotrac is now available in my library) are now free. A librarian will be happy to teach you how to do a computer search and will help you decide on key words and subject headings most appropriate to your needs.

The reference sources I've recommended so far plunk you down in the middle of a problem and trust you to interpret ("inference") your way out of it. If and when you feel lost, you can probably gain great comfort from some item you'll find in the last reference source I'd like to mention: Eugene P. Sheehy's *Guide to Reference Books* (Chicago: American Library Association). Unlike the indexes we've been talking about, this book isn't an alphabetic list of people, places, and subjects, but a field-by-field guide to helpful reference books. When I looked up "Canada" in Sheehy, two of the items I found listed were *The Oxford Encyclopaedia of Canadian History* and a book by William Matthews called *Canadian Diaries and Autobiographies* (Berkeley: University of California Press, 1950), which is said to list 1276 published and unpublished works. When I looked up "Biochemistry," I found, among other things, *The Encyclopedia of Biochemistry*, for nonspecialists, that might help me find my bearings.

Too much time spent in the reference room makes me desperate to find a book with a story that continues from one page to the next. On the other hand, too much time in a week of issues of *The New York Times* makes me want a reference book to help me put what I've read into some kind of perspective. Your search strategy will depend on your subject, but you should plan to be moving back and forth between the reference room, the catalog, and the stacks where your books and magazines are. The step you'll be tempted to skip is visiting the reference room, so I recommend that you leave your jacket and your papers in the reference room to make sure you keep coming back.

3. Note Taking

Writers are sorters. The quality of a paper you finally produce will depend to a great extent on your ability to decide what is worth noting and what is not. The notes you take reflect your intellectual achievement as a sorter.

As you read, you'll begin to see facts you'll want to use, quotations you'll want to use, opinions of others you'll want to use and comment on. Either copy them out in the library, or make photocopies of the pages you want to quote from (dimes for the copying machine are crucial tools of the contemporary researcher). *Each time you select or copy out a fact, a quotation, or an opinion, ask yourself, "So what?" Your answers to that question will begin to build your stock of inferences.*

Exercise 10-6
Drawing Inferences from Your Research Sources

Imagine that the following five items were articles that drew your attention while you were doing your research. Draw as many inferences as you can about the reporters, the issues discussed, and the cultural climate at the time that these articles were written. Compare your inferences with those of your classmates. When you do your own research, use the same method to build the stock of inferences that will yield *your* point of view about the material you have researched.

1. From the *Los Angeles Times,* June 2, 1944, page 5, a caption below a picture:

   > On Warpath—Sporting mustache and cigar as in his Guadalcanal glory days, when he downed 26 Jap planes, Marine Major Joseph J. Foss of Sioux Falls, South Dakota, is again on duty in the South Pacific. He heads his own squadron of Corsairs which bear the insignia of a royal flush in spades with the joker a winged fighter smoking a large cigar.

2. From the *Los Angeles Times,* June 2, 1944, page 5, an article:

   ### Deluded Japs Still Long Way From California Coast

   > New York, June 1, UP. Japanese forces on Wake Island thought they were fighting off the California coast where they soon would establish a beachhead, Lt(jg) Jerome Langer, 26, of Brooklyn, Coast Guard LST navigation officer and first man back from the May 17 landing, said today.
   >   The Japs were told that they would be joined by forces from the "Pearl Harbor base" for the California landing, he said. They lost their sense of direction, he explained, because commanding officers ordered troop transports to sail in circles for hours at a time.

3. From the *Los Angeles Times,* June 2, 1944, page 5, an article:

   ### Negro Promoted

   > Naples, June 1, AP. Lt. Colonel Benjamin O. Davis, Jr., New York City, commander of an all-Negro fighter group in Italy, has been promoted to colonel.

4. From the *Charleston Daily Courier,* December 19, 1864, page 1, a notice:

   > Important If True—A gentleman who arrived from Macon Saturday evening informs the Augusta "Constitutionalist" that a report was in circulation at Macon that General Hood assaulted the enemy's works at Nashville, carried them, and was in possession of the city. The rumor also states that General Cheatham was killed at the head of his corps in the streets of the city near the capital.
   >   Our readers can take these reports for what they are worth. They may or may not be true. We are disposed to believe that Nashville has fallen into our hands, as Hood had the city closely besieged at last accounts, and was preparing to assault the works.

5. From the *Los Angeles Times,* June 1, 1944, page 6, an article:

Nazis Confirm Lynching of One American Flyer

London, May 31, UP. A Berlin dispatch to the Stockholm newspaper Dagens Nyheter said today that official German circles had confirmed the mob lynching of an American airman shot down in Central Germany.

The dispatch also quoted German authorities, in the first official comment on the reported shooting of 47 British and Allied airmen at a German prison camp, as denying that any airman was lynched after once becoming officially a prisoner of the German government.

The dispatch said that an "infuriated crowd" killed the one surviving crew member of an American plane which crashed at an unspecified German village. It added that official German circles claimed the lynched American had been aboard a plane which machine-gunned a crowd of churchgoers, killing several women, old men, and children.

The alleged confirmation of the lynching of the American followed the German propaganda hysteria pace set recently by Propaganda Minister Goebbels himself, when he wrote in the Nazi party organ that the government could no longer protect "terror" raiders from the "mad fury" of the German population.

Many writing instructors suggest that you note facts, quotations, and comments on 3- by 5-inch or 4- by 6-inch note cards. They might be right. Note cards can easily be arranged and rearranged. But they are also heavy. And they are difficult to carry under your arm. And I never have them sitting around my room. So I prefer to use paper—full-size paper. I keep all my notes—facts, quotations, opinions, references, photocopies—on a series of loose-leaf papers that might be termed a "research log." Instead of buying note cards, I've bought a scissors and some paper clips. So when I want to arrange and rearrange my notes, I cut my large paper, shift pieces of it from stack to stack, and clip slips of related notes together.

Reference notes, those separate notes detailing fully the publishing information about any source you might draw from in your paper, can easily get out of hand as you proceed with your research. I've often been advised to copy out the complete entry, for example,

Lash, Joseph P. *Eleanor: The Years Alone.* New York: W. W. Norton, 1972.

for every book I look at so I won't be missing any information when the paper is completed and it's time to type up my works cited list. That recommended method is thorough, and it is necessary in preparing a scholarly work like a dissertation. But I found as an undergraduate, and still find now, that it saps my energy and my curiosity. I like to move fast while I'm researching, flipping from book to book to journal to magazine to newspaper. So I use a shortcut which I recommend, with caution, to you. When I decide that I'll probably use a quotation, I copy it out, and I put only a brief reference—(Lash 298)—after it, as follows:

Eleanor Roosevelt's comment on John Kennedy in 1960:

> "Here is a man who wants to leave a record (perhaps for ambitious personal reasons as people say) but I rather think because he really is interested in helping people of his own country and mankind in general." (Lash 298)

I may never use this quotation in my paper. If I don't use it, I won't have wasted time copying out the full publication information. If I do use the quotation in my final draft, then after I complete the draft and have stopped worrying about the quality of the paper itself, I can return to the book (if I still have it) or to the library's card catalog (if I don't) and look up the information I need to complete this entry in my list of works cited.

   If any class time can be made available, you should bring twenty or twenty-five notes—quotations, other facts, your comments—to class on a specified day well before your paper is due and compare with your classmates the kinds of notes you've taken and your reasons for taking the notes you have. You'll get several useful tips from your classmates.

4. Keeping the Subject Covered to a Reasonable Size

Only time and experience will help you do this. It is obviously difficult to cover the war in Vietnam or the life of Margaret Mead in three to ten pages. But that doesn't mean that you have to restrict yourself to the battle of Khe Sanh from 12:00 to 4:00 p.m. on February 25, 1968. You can write about large events or whole lives by discussing them through typical events or representative examples. You could look, for example, at criticism of our war in Vietnam in your 1967 student newspaper, in the 1970 *Times* (of London), and in the 1973 debates in Congress published in the *Congressional Record*. Similarly, you could look at Margaret Mead on her first trip to Samoa in 1925, as a prominent professor of anthropology in 1957, and as a television personality in 1965. Almost any large issue or whole life can be brought within a reasonable compass if you examine three or four representative examples.

5. Evaluating Your Sources

As a student, you can't always tell whether the sources you quote from are reliable or not. The fact that they've been published and the fact that they've been bought by your library help establish their reliability, but these facts are no guarantee of either accuracy or sophistication of judgment. Looking up reviews in a review journal from the field you're investigating might help, but reviews can often have racist, sexist, patriotic, or old-boy-network biases. As you get to know certain fields (black history, for example, or computer design), you'll gradually come to realize whom you can trust and whom you can't in those fields. Do try to get to know the political conditions in the fields you write about, but because papers are due early and often, you'll often, in the meantime, just have to use your own judgment of the *ethos, logos,* and *pathos* employed by the authors you're reading when you try to assess their value.

6. Ensuring That Your Work Is Your Own

The point of doing a research paper is to arrive at *your* interpretation of events or people or productions that we all are aware of (or could be aware of, if we kept ourselves informed). You fail to achieve that interpretation if you rely heavily on someone who has already interpreted the same events. When we read a persuasive interpretation of some event, it's difficult in most cases to form an alternative interpretation, so the best defense against borrowing the ideas of others is not to read them. Look as much as possible at firsthand sources of information, not at later interpretations. Try, as often as possible, to work with periodicals rather than books. Inevitably, though, you will come across some interpretations (even in newspaper accounts). Just remember that "_____ thinks _____ " is, to you, just another piece of evidence, a fact that you must in turn draw your own inference from.

You know you can't use any opinions of others, word for word, as if they were your own. For example, suppose you were writing a paper about ecology and you came across the following passage:

> Nature is, above all, profligate. Don't believe them when they tell you how economical and thrifty nature is, whose leaves return to the soil. Wouldn't it be cheaper to leave them on the tree in the first place? (Dillard 65)

In most schools, if you turned in a paper which used the words above without a note and without quotation marks, you'd fail your course and be put on academic probation. You'd be just as guilty, though, if you wrote the following, in an attempt to "change a few words":

> Nature is wasteful. Just because its leaves return to the soil doesn't make it economical and thrifty. Wouldn't it be cheaper if the tree just kept its leaves all year round?

In order to avoid danger, and in order to force yourself to do the thinking that a research paper is supposed to elicit from you, you should (if you want to use this passage) do one of the following:

1. Quote it all, acknowledge your source with a parenthetical reference—(Dillard 65)—and full information in your works cited list, and then comment on the quotation from your own point of view.
2. Summarize the quotation in one sentence, acknowledge your source as before, and *comment* (as before) on Dillard's point of view from your own point of view.

A library research paper requires a serious investment of time and thinking. There are no legitimate shortcuts. Shortcuts like plagiarism short-circuit learning, and they are a breach of trust.

7. Incorporating Quotations

One of the recurrent worries of writers of research papers is how to handle quotations: we worry about what to quote, about taking quotations out of the author's context, and about blending quotations into our own writing. The principal guidelines to follow are that (1) you should use quotations as evidence, not as a continuation of your own argument, (2) you should identify every quotation, and (3) you should follow up each quotation by explaining its significance.

Exercise 10-7
Punctuating Quotations

To practice the mechanical rules for introducing quotations in your work, answer the questions below, and compare your answers with those of your classmates. Perhaps your teacher can put a couple of answers for each question on the board.

1. How would you punctuate your sentence if you were using footnote style and you wanted to quote from page 296 of Ralph Ellison's *Shadow and Act,* where he says that in Harlem "it is possible for talented youths to leap through the development of decades in a brief twenty years"?
2. How would you punctuate this same quotation if you were using not footnotes but parenthetical references with a "List of Works Cited" at the end?
3. If you want to quote the words "this is no dream" from page 296, and you know that "this" refers to Harlem but your reader doesn't, how can you make it clear to the reader?
4. If you want to quote the line "a world so fluid and so shifting that often within the mind the real and the unreal merge, and the marvelous beckons from behind the same sordid reality that denies its existence" from

page 296, but you think the quotation is too long, and you don't think that the part about the real and the unreal merging is so important, how can you shorten and then punctuate your quotation?

5. If you wanted to quote Robert Capon's whole paragraph about the electric knife sharpener (Chapter 7, page 109-110), how would you place it on the page?

8. Acknowledging Sources

You may have the impression that the purpose of writing research papers is to learn the forms for what used to be footnotes and bibliographies and what are now parenthetical references and works cited lists. That is not their purpose. Research papers are assigned so that you can practice investigating a mass of material, determining what is important in that material (a crucial skill), coming to a conclusion about the material, and organizing the selected material to help a reader. Learning accepted forms for acknowledging sources is far less important than these four skills, but you should nevertheless become aware of the basic conventions for acknowledgment.

Conventions for acknowledging sources have been shifting significantly this past decade, but they have now settled down, and I'm confident that your children will be using the same "new" forms that you are beginning to use now. First in psychology but now in almost all fields, footnotes are being replaced by parenthetical references, and bibliographies by a final list of works cited. The official guides to acknowledging sources are now the *Publication Manual of the American Psychological Association* (1974) for social science subjects, the *Council of Biology Editors Style Manual* (1972) for sciences, and the *Modern Language Association Style Manual* (1985) for humanities subjects. In this course we will follow the Modern Language Association guide.

The aim of parenthetical references is to be as simple as possible. The parentheses that enclose your reference are placed just before the final punctuation mark in the sentence in which you refer to the work being acknowledged. In most cases the reference includes just the author's last name and the page on which the material you are referring to originally appeared:

(McCauley 25).

If two books or articles by McCauley appear in your works cited list, your parenthetical reference must distinguish the two works:

(McCauley, "Pollution Control" 36–40)
(McCauley, "Hospital Costs" 16–21)

If two McCauleys appear in your works cited list, you must distinguish between the two people:

(Michael McCauley 36–40)
(Patricia McCauley 17–24)

If you are quoting from an article whose author is anonymous, your parenthetical reference should include the title—shortened—in the usual place of the author:

("Hospital Costs" 14)

If you have mentioned the author in the sentence where your parenthetical reference is to appear, your reference need only indicate the page or pages:

(36–40)

The system is wonderfully simple, as soon as you get used to seeing numbers without p. or pp. before them and knowing that those numbers refer to pages.

Every parenthetical reference is a promise to the reader that full information about this source will be found in your list of works cited. Therefore, when you've finished your paper, make a list of all the works you've cited, get all the bibliographic information you need, and make up, in alphabetical order by authors' last names, your list of works cited.

9. Putting Together Your Works Cited List

When listing books, the three principal parts of your entry should be (1) the author's name, (2) the title of the book, and (3) the place of publication, publisher, and date of publication. Each of the three principal parts is separated by a period.

McPhee, John. Basin and Range. New York: Farrar, Straus, and Giroux, 1981

Note that the author's last name comes first, that titles are underlined, that a colon comes between the place of publication and the publisher, and that a comma comes between the publisher and the date of publication. When the entry requires more complicated information, the required order is as follows: (1) the author's name, (2) the title of the part of the book written by the author, (3) the title of the whole book, (4) the name of the editor or translator, (5) the edition of the book, (6) the number of volumes in the book, (7) the place of publication, publisher, and date of publication, and (8) the pages within the larger work that the author's work covers.

When you are listing periodicals in your Works Cited list, the required order is (1) the author, (2) the title of the article, (3) the name of the periodical, (4) the volume number of the periodical if it is published no more frequently than quarterly, (5) the date of publication, and (6) the pages within the periodical that the author's work covers. Here is an entry for an unsigned article in *Time* magazine:

"A Fighter Pilot Turned Negotiator." Time 10 Oct. 1983: 35.

Note that titles of articles are placed in quotation marks, that the titles of newspapers, magazines, or journals are underlined, that a period follows the title of the article, that no punctuation comes between the magazine and its date, that all months except May, June, and July are abbreviated, and that a colon comes between the date and the page numbers.

Table 10-1 is a chart that covers the most usual possibilities that you'll come across in your research, but Murphy's law of research guarantees that you will turn up a source that fits no model that I predict here. When you do, just make your best guess based on the principles explained here. The purpose of systems of acknowledgment is not to drive writers crazy but to serve readers by being clear, convenient, and concise.

To keep works cited conventions from taking on greater importance than they deserve, I'd like to conclude this chapter not with talk about those conventions, but with a comment on inferences. We consider our research papers finished, and we begin to feel genuine pride in them, when we are confident of our inferences, confident, that is, of our interpretations. It is those thoughtful interpretations, and the well-selected information on which we have based our interpretations, that make the difference between drudgery (halfhearted term papers) and challenging intellectual work.

TABLE 10-1   Checklist for Works Cited Format

BOOKS	
One author	McPhee, John. Basin and Range. New York: Farrar, Straus, and Giroux, 1981.
Two authors	Raymond, James, and Ronald Goldfarb. Clear Understandings. New York: Random House, 1982.
Editor	Cooper, Lane, ed. The Rhetoric of Aristotle. New York: Appleton, Century, Crofts, 1932.
Author and editor	Fielding, Henry. Tom Jones. Ed. Sheridan Baker. New York: Norton, 1973.
No author identified	College Park Grammar Review Worksheets. Raleigh, N.C.: Contemporary Publishing Company, 1980.
Second or later edition	Strunk, William, and E. B. White. The Elements of Style. 3rd ed. New York: Macmillan, 1981.
One of several volumes	Keller, Helen Rex. The Dictionary of Dates. 2 vols. New York: Macmillan, 1934.
Article that is included in a book	Babbitt, Irving. "Burke and the Moral Imagination." In The Burke-Paine Controversy. Edited Ray B. Browne. New York: Harcourt, Brace, & World, 1963: 149-156.

MAGAZINES AND NEWSPAPERS	
Signed article in journal appearing quarterly or less frequently	Gebhardt, Richard. "Imagination and Discipline in the Writing Class." English Journal 39 (1977): 26–32.
Unsigned article in magazine appearing monthly or more often	"A Fighter Pilot Turned Negotiator." Time 10 Oct. 1983: 35.
Signed newspaper article	Zinsser, William. "Why Johnny's Teachers Can't Write." The New York Times 12 Nov. 1978: F30.
Unsigned newspaper article	"Another Icy Blast Moves In." Houston Chronicle 19 Jan. 1984: 1.
Newspaper editorial	"Politics of Earth, Air, Water." Editorial. The Christian Science Monitor 30 Jan. 1984: 13.
Book review	Rosenfeld, Harry. Review of O Albany, by William Kennedy. The Washington Post Book World 29 Jan. 1984: 1.

ENCYCLOPEDIA ARTICLES	
Signed article	Thorn, R. J. "Solid-State Chemistry." McGraw-Hill Encyclopedia of Science and Technology, 1982 ed.
Unsigned article	"Lipid." The Encyclopedia Americana, 1982 ed.

UNPUBLISHED MATERIALS	
Doctoral dissertation or master's thesis	Jordan, Mary Kay. "The Effects of Peer Review on College Students Enrolled in a Required Advanced Technical Writing Course." Diss. U. of Maryland, 1983.
Photocopy	Walsh, Mark, and Martha Walsh. "The Farm." Unpublished manuscript, 1969.
Lecture	Ellison, Ralph. "A Writer's Life." University of Notre Dame, 4 Apr. 1968.
Interview	Miller, Kathleen. Personal Interview. 17 Jan. 1984.
Television or radio program	Robertson, Pat. "The 700 Club." WTTG, Washington, D.C. 5 Feb. 1984.

11

Research Through Interviewing

At first I was scared, but I enjoyed interviewing someone. It made me and him feel important.

student

Nothing so animates writing as someone telling what he thinks or what he does—in his own words.

William Zinsser

Exercise 11-1
Review

Answer the following question in your notebook:

What qualities would you expect to find in a good interviewer?

In most kinds of writers' research, the first steps are the easiest: browsing through books related to your topic, sitting back to watch a movie through the first time before you review it, walking through a farmers' market watching the customers and the sellers while jotting notes in a notebook. But when your writing is to be based on an interview, the hardest step comes first—asking a stranger to set aside an hour to sit and talk with you. (Asking for the first interview of your life is also harder than asking for any later ones.) Once you've screwed up your courage to ask for an interview, though, the interview itself and writing a paper based on it will come more easily. The interview, if you have well-prepared questions, is almost always more enjoyable than you would have guessed, and writing a character sketch involves, as usual, selecting the best material, drawing inferences, searching for a focus and organization, testing your ideas in a first draft, and revising that draft until it makes good sense.

Before you ask for an interview, stop to ask yourself whether you have picked up some bad habits without even having started writing. First of all, most published interviews are interviews of "famous" people, and as readers we're not very demanding about what we're willing to listen to from them. If an interviewer can get Eddie Murphy to say anything, we'll probably pay money to read it. The writer doesn't have to ask skillful questions or select very carefully what she'll print and what she'll edit out. Writers of interviews with famous people often earn their salaries more for their ability to "get" interviews than for their ability to write or edit them well. The person you interview for this class will *not* be famous, so you'll have to ask good questions, and you'll have to select very carefully what to present your readers with. You'll have to both interview and write well.

The second bad habit you may have picked up is the laziness of printing an interview as a disjointed set of questions and answers, as in the following excerpt from an interview with British novelist E. M. Forster (Cowley 28):

> INTERVIEWERS: While we are on the subject of the planning of novels, has a novel ever taken an unexpected direction?
>
> FORSTER: Of course, that wonderful thing, a character running away with you—which happens to everyone—that's happened to me, I'm afraid.
>
> INTERVIEWERS: Can you describe any technical problem that especially bothered you in one of the published novels?
>
> FORSTER: I had trouble with the junction of Rickie and Stephen. [The hero of *The Longest Journey* and his half brother.] How to make them intimate, I mean. I fumbled about a good deal. It *is* all right once they are together....I didn't know how to get Helen to Howards End. That part is all contrived. There are too many letters. And again, it is all right once she is there. But ends always give me trouble.
>
> INTERVIEWERS: Why is that?
>
> FORSTER: It is partly what I was talking about a moment ago. Characters run away with you, and so won't fit on to what is coming.
>
> INTERVIEWERS: Another question of detail. What was the exact function of the long description of the Hindu festival in *A Passage to India?*
>
> FORSTER: It was architecturally necessary. I needed a lump, or a Hindu temple if you like—a mountain standing up. It is well placed; and it gathers up some strings. But there ought to be more after it. The lump sticks out a little too much.
>
> INTERVIEWERS: To leave technical questions for a moment, have you

ever described any type of situation of which you have had no
personal knowledge?

FORSTER: The home-life of Leonard and Jacky in *Howards End* is one
case. I knew nothing about that. I believe I brought it off.

INTERVIEWERS: How far removed in time do you have to be from an
experience in order to describe it?

This form doesn't require the interviewer to be a writer; it only requires
that the interviewer own a tape recorder. Such an interviewer may well
have asked good questions, but he's provided no writer's consciousness
to guide us along, helping us see connections, highlighting the interviewee's most important character traits. Although you're practicing a
new research technique in this chapter (interviewing), you'll bring to the
character sketch you finally write all the writing skills you've shown in
your earlier work—selecting and organizing your material, interesting
your reader in the subject, showing that you understand the implications of what you've written.

Your first step is to choose the person you'd like to interview. Start
thinking of possibilities now, and tell someone—soon—who it is you
plan to interview so that you will begin to believe that you will actually
do it. Your interview will work best (believe it or not) if you don't know
the interviewee at all, or if at all, only by sight. Also, you should probably
interview a person at least 40 years old—old enough to have developed
a perspective about what life means to her, or to him. I recommend that
you interview someone who has chosen a path you don't plan to follow—a roofer, a bus driver, a mother of seven, a fire fighter, someone
who has grown up in another country. I highly recommend going to a
nursing home to find your interviewee. Most people in nursing homes
are happy to talk. They have a wealth of experience, they have plenty of
time, and they will have more free time a week later when you need to
check a few things or ask a few more questions. You might bring along a
small present to thank the interviewee with after the interview.

Whether you interview a person in a nursing home, though, or a
busy working person, you'll be surprised how often people respond en-
thusiastically to the idea of talking, if only for a short time, about themselves. If the first person you ask doesn't want to talk or doesn't want to
take the time, just thank her anyway and try someone else. You're not a
reporter whose story will be incomplete until he has talked to a key witness. You're just a writer looking for *an* interview, and any interviewee
will do. If your first try results in a refusal, your second one is not likely
to.

In class, before you actually face your interviewee, you can practice
several techniques that will make the process of interviewing and writing
easier and more effective.

Preparing Questions for an Interview

Exercise 11-2

Bring to class ten sample questions that you might bring to an interview. When class begins, pass your list to a neighbor and take a list from a neighbor. Choose the three questions of those ten that you think will elicit the most interesting answers. Pass the list along again, and take a different list. See if you'd choose the same three questions as the person who reviewed the list before you. Then, with your classmates, share the best questions and explain, in each case, *why* those questions were designed to bring out the best information. Take good notes, and feel free to use any of these questions in your own interview.

Practice Interview

Exercise 11-3

Practice interviewing your teacher. (Instead of, or in addition to, interviewing the teacher, you and your classmates may want to interview each other or a person selected by your teacher.)

Use the expanded question list you now have to conduct a group interview of your teacher. Take notes on all questions asked, not just your own. Note how your teacher responds, just as any interviewee will respond. Some questions she will refuse to answer, some she will answer matter-of-factly, some she will enjoy talking about. When you note an area that she is interested in, abandon your question list and follow up the provocative area. (Your teacher will probably comment on the way you are interviewing at the same time that she is answering your questions.)

When the interview is over, write up (either in class or at home) a character sketch of your teacher. If all the sketches are compared, you will see a variety of choices—for introductions, conclusions, quotations, organization. The following are some instructive samples from a teacher interview:

1. *Opening sentences:* Do these start the reader off well?

   - Cristina Cheplick left her friends and family to come to America to live with her husband.
   - Many questions come to mind when you talk to someone who has emigrated from another country.
   - "My parents wanted me to be a doctor, but I wanted to teach," said Cristina Cheplick.
   - "Life is a series of hassles," C. Cheplick said about life in Romania.

- Cristina Cheplick began to learn English in 5th grade, and read her whole book in a week.
- In 5th grade, Cristina was introduced to the English language; consequently, at the age of 28, she is an English teacher.
- Cristina Ionescu was born in a hospital in the Romanian town [sic] of Transylvania, which is near her hometown of Cluj.
- Cristina Cheplick is a woman who has already experienced more than most people have.
- Cristina Cheplick has chosen the lifestyle of the U.S. instead of the one in Romania.

2. *Telling facts:* Are these good ones?

- When she talks to friends from Romania, they don't ask about the government here but about food: "Do you have to stand in line for cheese?"
- Cristina smiled when she showed off the Romanian valentines her friends sent.
- Even though her own country has its problems, she still looks back on it with fondness.
- She saw *The Sound of Music* ten times, and even knows the dialogue by heart.
- It was a zip for her to read an English novel, she was so taken by the language.
- She went to all the movies she could and learned everything that she could about English culture. She met a visiting American and married him.
- In Romania, she lived in a two-bedroom apartment with the rest of her family.

3. *Using quotations:* Are these well chosen?

- "It's a land where people vote with their feet," said Mrs. Cheplick, quoting her husband, "everyone wants to leave."
- Eight years of English and college gave her a good background to come here: "Everyone is poor and has to stand in line."
- "My marriage enabled me to leave, but that's not why I married."
- The national paper is only five pages long, due to government censorship. "When my mother saw the *Washington Post,* she thought it was the news for the entire year."
- The question that seems most prominent is: "How are people in America different from the people in your country?" This was the question that Mrs. Cheplick was asked. She replied that the big difference is the demeanor of the people.
- She emphasized it (the happiness of teaching English in America) through her enthusiasm and detailed descriptions. "Romania," she says, "is a very poor country."

4. *Paragraphing:* Would these paragraphs make a substantial contribution to a paper?

   - She took the bus to her teaching job every morning, and returned in the evening. On her return trip, she witnessed the long line of citizens already waiting in line for the morning bread, cheeses, and other needs. When she retired for the night, she would sit up in bed, and read the 5-page *Scinteia* published by the gov't.
   - C. Cheplick is an English teacher at the University of Maryland. She used to live in Romania until her marriage. She hopes to be an American citizen soon. She dresses in sweaters and slacks and ruffly blouses. The main difference she sees is the carefree attitude of Americans. America is a completely different world. Cristina smiled when she showed off her Romanian valentines.
   - Her college education was free, with an agreement to work for the government. She took eight years of it in grade school and four in college. What a life!

5. *Choosing a focus:* Note how many choices you have.

   - *Being practical:*
   Mrs. Cheplick picked her occupation in Romania, knowing that teachers and doctors made the same amount of money.
   - *The linguist:*
   All of her life, she has had a love for different languages. Many a time, she would go to the movies to try and pick up some of the languages. Many times in class she would read ahead, just for the fun of it.
   - *The happy teacher:*
   An English teacher from Romania? Sounds like a contradiction in terms, but C. Cheplick, Freshman English teacher at the University of Maryland, is very happy in America teaching English. She emphasized it through her enthusiasm and detailed descriptions.
   - *Seeking a new life:*
   She was refused entrance to the party government. She left her family and friends to try to make a new life with her husband in a strange new country. She knew she would never have a successful career in Romania.
   - *Appreciating the new life:*
   Cristina left Romania to come to teach in America. She has much more freedom and enjoys the freedom of expression. Also, she does not have the everyday worry of where the next meal is coming from.
   - *Hard times:*
   Mrs. Cheplick recalls the time when she was on a bus in Romania, and "the driver shut the doors on a person." People are rude and discourteous.
   - *Hard worker:*
   C. Cheplick began to learn English in the 5th grade and read the whole book in a week. She was always ahead of her class and studied for two years solid to get into college to study English.

Comparing Written and Video Interviews

Exercise 11-4

Use videotapes to learn interviewing techniques. Like the papers you'll write for this class, segments from *PM Magazine, 20/20,* and *60 Minutes* are successful because they are written to inform and entertain audiences—several of these ten- to twenty-minute segments try to reveal the predominant character trait of a person, making that person come alive for the viewer.

1. View a videotape which features a particular individual (the person does not have to be famous). If possible, get a copy of the script.
2. As you watch, keep in mind the following questions:

   • How does the introduction try to gain your interest?
   • What is the scriptwriter's focus?
   • How does the writer move (i.e. make transitions) from one revealing fact to the next?
   • *How* and *where* do quotations fit into the script?
   • Why is the ending provocative (if it is)?

The writing process is very much the same for a television script and for an article. Writing for presentation on paper must, however, be more descriptive than writing for a television script, because a camera can capture for the viewer what a reader—unless told—never sees. Note, in the tape you've chosen, how the camera shots (description) aid in emphasizing points made by the narrator.

   If you've done Exercises 11-2 and 11-3, you should be well prepared to start now on your interview. Take your master list of questions and meet your interviewee at a scheduled time and place. Bring a small tape recorder if you wish and if your interviewee doesn't mind. A tape recorder will give you much (perhaps too much) raw material to work with and prune. But don't feel that you need a tape recorder. You'll be well prepared for writing, and you'll save yourself hours of tape-listening time later, if you just bring two or three pencils and plenty of paper. Since you won't want to write down everything, your pencil will serve as a natural instrument of selection. Inevitably, both you and the interviewee will be nervous for the first few minutes, but soon you'll be talking freely. The questions you'll ask will depend on you and your interviewee and on the quality of the question-list selection you did in class, but there are some general guidelines you can follow:

1. Be sure to ask not only *what* the person has done but also *why* she has done it. You can be sure that the reader reading your sketch will con-

sistently be asking, "Why?" Anticipate the question.

2. When you come upon any area that your interviewee is clearly interested in, ask more questions about that area. It may well be a key to the person's character.

3. Don't be afraid to stop and write something down to keep it from being lost. Your interviewee won't feel ignored. He'll be glad that you're being careful.

4. When you run out of good questions, leave, even if you think you'll need more information later. You can plan on being back in touch, at least by telephone. You haven't had your last chance at research yet.

5. As soon as you're on your own, fill out your abbreviated notes so that you can understand them. Two hours after the interview, your notes will be puzzling. Two days later, they'll look like hieroglyphics.

When writing time comes, remember that, as with any other assignment, you are both a researcher and a writer. In this assignment, specifically, you are both an interviewer and a writer. Now that you have the raw material for a paper, it's your job to pull that material into shape: to *select* (don't fill your pages with everything you heard); to draw inferences from the facts you've discovered; to decide on a focus, an introduction, and a conclusion; to find a scheme of organization; to introduce your quotations skillfully and balance your emphases on quotations and commentary; to make sure you've provided enough breadth and depth of information; to omit irrelevant biographical details; to check for inaccuracies. As your draft begins to take shape, you'll find that you can't do all these tasks yourself, that your interviewee is still necessary. If you return to the interviewee, you can, in ten to fifteen minutes, ask the questions that you now know are important, though you didn't see their importance when you were only a first-time interviewer.

As you rework the final draft, there are some larger questions well worth asking. Have you found something that your readers wouldn't expect? Have you challenged your readers' assumptions? Have you told us something about human nature? If you have, we can now see a little better behind our human masks.

12

Research Through Careful Reading

Reading is not simply a matter of gathering data, but also, and simultaneously, a matter of going through a sequence of moves which the writer has controlled for the purpose of leading the reader to assent. The skill of critical reading, it goes without saying, is one of understanding when one's assent has been earned.

John T. Gage

Writing is both knowing conventions and knowing where to flaunt them. Reading is knowing conventions and knowing how to recognize when, how, and why they have been broken.

Alan C. Purves

I have been told that reading helps.

student

Exercise 12-1
Review of Your Reasons for Reading

Before you begin this chapter, answer the following question in your note-book:

> When you casually pick up a book or a magazine what is it that makes you keep reading?

Drawing Inferences While Reading (Reading between the Lines)

Whenever we read, we expect our writer to take us a step beyond our current situation. (When we're writing, of course, we should keep the

209

same in mind—that we are trying to take *our* readers a step beyond *their* current situation.) Reading, like writing, is a naturally reflective activity. Rarely do we just soak in something that we're reading. Most of the time we implicitly comment on what we read while we read. Of course, when we're distracted or tired, our eyes may be running over the pages, but in those cases we're not really reading.

Your reading has been becoming more thoughtful throughout this course. Back in Chapter 1, you read the work of some professionals, and you wrote down your sense of what was strong or weak in that writing. In Chapter 3, you read Sister Rebecca's advertisement and drew inferences about her. In Chapter 5 you read several excerpts from textbooks noting the patterns by which they organized their material. In Chapter 7 you wrote a paragraph outline of Robert Capon's essay on Kitchen Knives. Throughout the course you've been reading and judging sample essays in Chapter 14. On draft review day, you've been reading and judging the work of your classmates. And throughout the course, you've been reading and judging your own work as you revise. In addition, you may frequently have been asked to write in class about your reading assignments. Perhaps you've even kept a journal of notes on what intrigued or puzzled you about your reading during the semester. All these exercises have helped to make you a more active reader. In this chapter, though, we'll try to become more self-conscious of what we do when we read thoughtfully.

Any piece of writing you pick up will consist primarily of facts (selected by the writer) and inferences (made by the writer). Here are two examples from Rachel Carson's book, *Silent Spring* (1962):

Fact: Since the mid-1940s over 200 basic chemicals have been created for use in killing insects, weeds, rodents, and other organisms described in the modern vernacular as "pests."

Inference: To adjust to these chemicals would require time on the scale that is nature's; it would require not merely the years of a man's life but the life of generations.

As readers, we can simply take all this in, adding the facts to our memories and accepting the inferences as helpful insights. *Or* we can do our own thinking, our own drawing of *readers' inferences* about the facts and inferences as we read. (See Table 12-1.) Our inferences are called "readers' inferences" because we are drawing inferences not about the author's subject but about the author as a writer: her interests, her aims, her prejudices, the reading and research that prepared her to write, the cultural expectations of her society, the readers she intended. The author's fact and inference above become, for the reader, two facts about the author from which the reader can draw inferences.

TABLE 12-1   Drawing Readers' Inferences

Author's Fact
Since the mid-1940s over 200 basic
chemicals have been created for use
in killing insects, weeds, rodents,
and other organisms described in the
modern vernacular as "pests."

Reader's Fact (About the Author)	Reader's Inference (About the Author)
The author has checked government records to get these statistics.	The author has been responsible about providing evidence. She probably decided to use statistics because that's the only language that is persuasive to those who don't seem to care about environmental issues.

Author's Inference
To adjust to these chemicals would require
time on the scale that is nature's; it would
require not merely the years of a man's life
but the life of generations.

Reader's Fact (About the Author)	Reader's Inference (About the Author)
The author makes a bold predictive inference here about the future.	The author is trying to use her expertise as a biologist and her sensitivity to biological time to scare us. Her statement is so extreme that perhaps she is exaggerating.

Drawing Readers' Inferences

Exercise 12-2

An active reader draws a large number of readers' inferences while reading. See if you can draw ten such inferences as you read the following article. Bring your list to class. You and your classmates can compare lists—either in small groups or as a class. You should be able to refer to sentences, words, or phrases in the article to back up your inferences. (Throughout this chapter, the paragraphs of the reading selections have been numbered to make it easier for you to refer to them in discussion or in your writing.)

From *Silent Spring* (1962)
Rachel Carson

The history of life on earth has been a history of interaction 1
between living things and their surroundings. To a large extent, the
physical form and the habits of the earth's vegetation and its animal
life have been molded by the environment. Considering the whole
span of earthly time, the opposite effect, in which life actually
modifies its surroundings, has been relatively slight. Only within the
moment of time represented by the present century has one
species—man—acquired significant power to alter the nature of his
world.

During the past quarter century this power has not only increased 2
to one of disturbing magnitude but it has changed in character. The
most alarming of all man's assaults upon the environment is the contamination of air, earth, rivers, and sea with dangerous and even lethal
materials. This pollution is for the most part irrecoverable; the chain of
evil it initiates not only in the world that must support life but in living
tissues is for the most part irreversible. In this now universal contamination of the environment, chemicals are the sinister and little recognized partners of radiation in changing the very nature of the world—
the very nature of its life. Strontium 90, released through nuclear
explosions into the air, comes to earth in rain or drifts down as fallout,
lodges in soil, enters the grass or corn or wheat grown there, and in time
takes up its abode in the bones of a human being, there to remain until
his death. Similarly, chemicals sprayed on croplands or forests or gardens lie long in soil, entering into living organisms, passing from one to
another in a chain of poisoning and death. Or they pass mysteriously by
underground streams until they emerge and through the alchemy of air
and sunlight, combine into new forms that kill vegetation, sicken cattle,
and work unknown harm on those who drink from once pure wells. As
Albert Schweitzer has said, "Man can hardly even recognize the devils of
his own creation."

It took hundreds of millions of years to produce the life that 3
now inhabits the earth—eons of time in which that developing and
evolving and diversifying life reached a state of adjustment and
balance with its surroundings. The environment, rigorously shaping
and directing the life it supported, contained elements that were
hostile as well as supporting. Certain rocks gave out dangerous
radiation; even within the light of the sun, from which all life draws
its energy, there were short-wave radiations with power to injure.
Given time—time not in years but in millennia—life adjusts, and a

balance has been reached. For time is the essential ingredient; but in the modern world there is no time.

The rapidity of change and the speed with which new situations 4 are created follow the impetuous and heedless pace of man rather than the deliberate pace of nature. Radiation is no longer merely the background radiation of rocks, the bombardment of cosmic rays, the ultraviolet of the sun that have existed before there was any life on earth; radiation is now the unnatural creation of man's tampering with the atom. The chemicals to which life is asked to make its adjustment are no longer merely the calcium and silica and copper and all the rest of the minerals washed out of the rocks and carried in rivers to the sea; they are the synthetic creations of man's inventive mind, brewed in his laboratories, and having no counterparts in nature.

To adjust to these chemicals would require time on the scale that 5 is nature's; it would require not merely the years of a man's life but the life of generations. And even this, were it by some miracle possible, would be futile, for the new chemicals come from our laboratories in an endless stream; almost five hundred annually find their way into actual use in the United States alone. The figure is staggering and its implications are not easily grasped—500 new chemicals to which the bodies of men and animals are required somehow to adapt each year, chemicals totally outside the limits of biologic experience.

Among them are many that are used in man's war against nature. 6 Since the mid-1940's over 200 basic chemicals have been created for use in killing insects, weeds, rodents, and other organisms described in the modern vernacular as "pests"; and they are sold under several thousand different brand names.

These sprays, dusts, and aerosols are now applied almost univer- 7 sally to farms, gardens, forests, and homes—nonselective chemicals that have the power to kill every insect, the "good" and the "bad," to still the song of birds and the leaping of fish in the streams, to coat the leaves with a deadly film, and to linger on in soil—all this though the intended target may be only a few weeds or insects. Can anyone believe it is possible to lay down such a barrage of poisons on the surface of the earth without making it unfit for all life? They should not be called "insecticides," but "biocides."

The whole process of spraying seems caught up in an endless spi- 8 ral. Since DDT was released for civilian use, a process of escalation has been going on in which ever more toxic materials must be found. This has happened because insects, in a triumphant vindication of Darwin's principle of the survival of the fittest, have evolved super races immune to the particular insecticide used, hence a deadlier one has always to be developed—and then a deadlier one than that. It has happened also because destructive insects often undergo a "flareback," or resurgence, after spraying, in numbers greater than before. Thus the chemical war is never won, and all life is caught in its violent crossfire.

Along with the possibility of the extinction of mankind by nuclear 9 war, the central problem of our age has therefore become the contamination of man's total environment with such substances of incredible potential for harm—substances that accumulate in the tissues of plants and animals and even penetrate the germ cells to shatter or alter the very material of heredity upon which the shape of the future depends.

Some would-be architects of our future look toward a time when it 10 will be possible to alter the human germ plasm by design. But we may easily be doing so now by inadvertence for many chemicals, like radiation, bring about gene mutations. It is ironic to think that man might determine his own future by something so seemingly trivial as the choice of an insect spray.

All this has been risked—for what? Future historians may well be 11 amazed by our distorted sense of proportion. How could intelligent beings seek to control a few unwanted species by a method that contaminated the entire environment and brought the threat of disease and death even to their own kind? Yet this is precisely what we have done. We have done it, moreover, for reasons that collapse the moment we examine them. We are told that the enormous and expanding use of pesticides is necessary to maintain farm production. Yet is our real problem not one of *overproduction?* Our farms, despite measures to remove acreages from production and to pay farmers *not* to produce, have yielded such a staggering excess of crops that the American taxpayer in 1962 is paying out more than one billion dollars a year as the total carrying cost of the surplus-food storage program. And is the situation helped when one branch of the Agriculture Department tries to reduce production while another states, as it did in 1958, "It is believed generally that reduction of crop acreages under provisions of the Soil Bank will stimulate interest in use of chemicals to obtain maximum production on the land retained in crops."

All this is not to say there is no insect problem and no need of con- 12 trol. I am saying, rather, that control must be geared to realities, not to mythical situations, and that the methods employed must be such that they do not destroy us along with the insects.

The problem whose attempted solution has brought such a train of 13 disaster in its wake is an accompaniment of our modern way of life. Long before the age of man, insects inhabited the earth—a group of extraordinarily varied and adaptable beings. Over the course of time since man's advent, a small percentage of the more than half a million species of insects have come into conflict with human welfare in two principal ways: as competitors for the food supply and as carriers of human disease.

Disease-carrying insects become important where human beings 14 are crowded together, especially under conditions where sanitation is poor, as in time of natural disaster or war or in situations of extreme poverty and deprivation. Then control of some sort becomes necessary. It is a sobering fact, however, that the method of massive chemical control has had only limited success, and also threatens to worsen the very conditions it is intended to curb.

Under primitive agricultural conditions the farmer had few insect prob- 15 lems. These arose with the intensification of agriculture—the devotion of immense acreages to a single crop. Such a system set the stage for explosive increases in specific insect populations. Single-crop farming does not take advantage of the principles by which nature works; it is agriculture as an engineer might conceive it to be. Nature has introduced great variety into the landscape, but man has displayed a passion for simplifying it. Thus he undoes the built-in checks and balances by which nature holds the species within bounds. One important natural check is a limit on the amount of suitable habitat for each species. Obviously then, an insect that lives on wheat can build up its population to much higher levels on a farm devoted to wheat than on one in which wheat is intermingled with other crops to which the insect is not adapted.

The same thing happens in other situations. A generation or more 16 ago, the towns of large areas of the United States lined their streets with the noble elm tree. Now the beauty they hopefully created is threatened with complete destruction as disease sweeps through the elms, carried by a beetle that would have only limited chance to build up large populations and to spread from tree to tree if the elms were only occasional trees in a richly diversified planting.

Another factor in the modern insect problem is one that must 17 be viewed against a background of geologic and human history: the spreading of thousands of different kinds of organisms from their native homes to invade new territories. This worldwide migration has been studied and graphically described by the British ecologist Charles Elton in his recent book *The Ecology of Invasions*. During the Cretaceous Period, some hundred million years ago, flooding seas cut many land bridges between continents and living things found themselves confined in what Elton calls "colossal separate nature reserves." There, isolated from others of their kind, they developed many new species. When some of the land masses were joined again, about 15 million years ago, these species began to move out into new territories—a movement that is not only still in progress but is now receiving considerable assistance from man.

The importation of plants is the primary agent in the modern 18 spread of species, for animals have almost invariably gone along with the plants, quarantine being a comparatively recent and not completely effective innovation. The United States Office of Plant Introduction alone has introduced almost 200,000 species and varieties of plants from all over the world. Nearly half of the 180 or so major insect enemies of plants in the United States are accidental imports from abroad, and most of them have come as hitchhikers on plants.

In new territory, out of reach of the restraining hand of the natural 19 enemies that kept down its numbers in its native land, an invading plant or animal is able to become enormously abundant. Thus it is no accident that our most troublesome insects are introduced species.

These invasions, both the naturally occurring and those dependent 20 on human assistance, are likely to continue indefinitely. Quarantine and massive chemical campaigns are only extremely expensive ways of buying time. We are faced, according to Dr. Elton, "with a life-and-death need not just to find new technological means of suppressing this plant or that animal"; instead we need the basic knowledge of animal populations and their relations to their surroundings that will "promote an even balance and damp down the explosive power of outbreaks and new invasions."

Much of the necessary knowledge is now available but we do not 21 use it. We train ecologists in our universities and even employ them in our governmental agencies but we seldom take their advice. We allow the chemical death rain to fall as though there were no alternative, whereas in fact there are many, and our ingenuity could soon discover many more if given opportunity.

Have we fallen into a mesmerized state that makes us accept as 22 inevitable that which is inferior or detrimental, as though having lost the will or the vision to demand that which is good? Such thinking, in the words of the ecologist Paul Shepard, "idealizes life with only its head out of water, inches above the limits of toleration of the corruption of its own environment....Why should we tolerate a diet of weak poisons, a home in insipid surroundings, a circle of acquaintances who are not quite our enemies, the noise of motors with just enough relief to prevent insanity? Who would want to live in a world which is just not quite fatal?"

Yet such a world is pressed upon us. The crusade to create a 23 chemically sterile, insect-free world seems to have engendered a fanatic zeal on the part of many specialists and most of the so-called control agencies. On every hand there is evidence that those engaged in spraying operations exercise a ruthless power. "The regulatory entomologists...function as prosecutor, judge and jury, tax assessor and col-

lector and sheriff to enforce their own orders," said Connecticut ento-
mologist Neely Turner. The most flagrant abuses go unchecked in both
state and federal agencies.

It is not my contention that chemical insecticides must never be 24
used. I do contend that we have put poisonous and biologically potent
chemicals indiscriminately into the hands of persons largely or wholly
ignorant of their potentials for harm. We have subjected enormous numbers of people to contact with these poisons, without their consent and
often without their knowledge. If the Bill of Rights contains no guarantee
that a citizen shall be secure against lethal poisons distributed either by
private individuals or by public officials, it is surely only because our
forefathers, despite their considerable wisdom and foresight, could conceive of no such problem.

I contend, furthermore, that we have allowed these chemicals to be 25
used with little or no advance investigation of their effect on soil, water,
wildlife, and man himself. Future generations are unlikely to condone
our lack of prudent concern for the integrity of the natural world that
supports all life.

There is still very limited awareness of the nature of the threat. This 26
is an era of specialists, each of whom sees his own problem and is unaware of or intolerant of the larger frame into which it fits. It is also an
era dominated by industry, in which the right to make a dollar at whatever cost is seldom challenged. When the public protests, confronted
with some obvious evidence of damaging results of pesticide applica-
tions, it is fed little tranquilizing pills of half truth. We urgently need an
end to these false assurances, to the sugar coating of unpalatable facts. It
is the public that is being asked to assume the risks that the insect con-
trollers calculate. The public must decide whether it wishes to continue
on the present road, and it can do so only when in full possession of the
facts. In the words of Jean Rostand, "The obligation to endure gives us
the right to know."

Drawing Inferences from a Writer's Facts

One of the readers' inferences that we might draw about Rachel Carson
in the selection above is that she is not hesitant to explain what she
thinks are the implications of the facts she presents. As readers, we can
draw our own inferences, but if we do, we must compare them with
hers. Other authors prefer to engage their readers by using only telling
details (usually in narrative or descriptive form) and then allowing readers to draw their own inferences not only about the author as a writer
but about the subject of the writing itself.

Exercise 12-3

See how many inferences you can draw about the family and the society described in the passage below, the opening pages of Richard Wright's *Native Son*. Again, bring your list of inferences to class, and compare your results with those of your classmates. As always, be prepared to point to the evidence for your inferences (you may want to underline such evidence).

From *Native Son* (1940)
Richard Wright

Brrrrrrriiiiiiiiiiiiiiiiiiiinng!   1

An alarm clock clanged in the dark and silent room. A bed spring   2
creaked. A woman's voice sang out impatiently:

"Bigger, shut that thing off!"   3

A surly grunt sounded above the tinny ring of metal. Naked feet   4
swished dryly across the planks in the wooden floor and the clang
ceased abruptly.

"Turn on the light, Bigger."   5

"Awright," came a sleepy mumble.   6

Light flooded the room and revealed a black boy standing in a nar-   7
row space between two iron beds, rubbing his eyes with the backs of his
hands. From a bed to his right the woman spoke again:

"Buddy, get up from there! I got a big washing on my hands today   8
and I want you-all out of here."

Another black boy rolled from bed and stood up. The woman also   9
rose and stood in her nightgown.

"Turn your heads so I can dress," she said.   10

The two boys averted their eyes and gazed into a far corner of the   11
room. The woman rushed out of her nightgown and put on a pair of
step-ins. She turned to the bed from which she had risen and called:

"Vera! Get up from there!"   12

"What time is it, Ma?" asked a muffled, adolescent voice from be-   13
neath a quilt.

"Get up from there, I say!"   14

"O.K., Ma."   15

A brown-skinned girl in a cotton gown got up and stretched her   16
arms above her head and yawned. Sleepily, she sat on a chair and fum-

bled with her stockings. The two boys kept their faces averted while their mother and sister put on enough clothes to keep them from feeling ashamed; and the mother and sister did the same while the boys dressed. Abruptly, they all paused, holding their clothes in their hands, their attention caught by a light tapping in the thinly plastered walls of the room. They forgot their conspiracy against shame and their eyes strayed apprehensively over the floor.

"There he is again, Bigger!" the woman screamed, and the tiny one- 17 room apartment galvanized into violent action. A chair toppled as the woman, half-dressed and in her stocking feet, scrambled breathlessly upon the bed. Her two sons, barefoot, stood tense and motionless, their eyes searching anxiously under the bed and chairs. The girl ran into a corner, half-stooped, and gathered the hem of her slip into both of her hands and held it tightly over her knees.

"Oh! Oh!" she wailed.   18

"There he goes!"   19

The woman pointed a shaking finger. Her eyes were round with 20 fascinated horror.

"Where?"   21

"I don't see 'im!"   22

"Bigger, he's behind the trunk!" the girl whimpered.   23

"Vera!" the woman screamed. "Get up here on the bed! Don't let 24 that thing *bite* you!"

Frantically, Vera climbed upon the bed and the woman caught hold 25 of her. With their arms entwined about each other, the black mother and the brown daughter gazed open-mouthed at the trunk in the corner.

Bigger looked round the room wildly, then darted to a curtain and 26 swept it aside and grabbed two heavy iron skillets from a wall above a gas stove. He whirled and called softly to his brother, his eyes glued to the trunk.

"Buddy!"   27

"Yeah?"   28

"Here; take this skillet."   29

"O.K."   30

"Now, get over by the door!"   31

"O.K."   32

Buddy crouched by the door and held the iron skillet by its handle, 33 his arm flexed and poised. Save for the quick, deep breathing of the four people, the room was quiet. Bigger crept on tiptoe toward the trunk with the skillet clutched stiffly in his hand, his eyes dancing and watching every inch of the wooden floor in front of him. He paused and, without moving an eye or muscle, called:

"Buddy!"   34

"Hunh?"   35

"Put that box in front of the hole so he can't get out!"   36

"O.K."   37

Buddy ran to a wooden box and shoved it quickly in front of a gap- 38
ing hole in the molding and then backed again to the door, holding the
skillet ready. Bigger eased to the trunk and peered behind it cautiously.
He saw nothing. Carefully, he stuck out his bare foot and pushed the
trunk a few inches.

"There he is!" the mother screamed again.   39

A huge black rat squealed and leaped at Bigger's trouser-leg and 40
snagged it in his teeth, hanging on.

"Goddamn!" Bigger whispered fiercely, whirling and kicking out his 41
leg with all the strength of his body. The force of his movement shook
the rat loose and it sailed through the air and struck a wall. Instantly, it
rolled over and leaped again. Bigger dodged and the rat landed against a
table leg. With clenched teeth, Bigger held the skillet; he was afraid to
hurl it, fearing that he might miss. The rat squeaked and turned and ran
in a narrow circle, looking for a place to hide; it leaped again past Bigger
and scurried on dry rasping feet to one side of the box and then to the
other, searching for the hole. Then it turned and reared upon its hind
legs.

"Hit 'im, Bigger!" Buddy shouted.   42

"Kill 'im!" the woman screamed.   43

The rat's belly pulsed with fear. Bigger advanced a step and the 44
rat emitted a long thin song of defiance, its black beady eyes
glittering, its tiny forefeet pawing the air restlessly. Bigger swung the
skillet; it skidded over the floor, missing the rat, and clattered to a
stop against a wall.

"Goddamn!"   45

The rat leaped. Bigger sprang to one side. The rat stopped under a 46
chair and let out a furious screak. Bigger moved slowly backward toward
the door.

"Gimme that skillet, Buddy," he asked quietly, not taking his eyes 47
from the rat.

Buddy extended his hand. Bigger caught the skillet and lifted it 48
high in the air. The rat scuttled across the floor and stopped again at the
box and searched quickly for the hole; then it reared once more and
bared long yellow fangs, piping shrilly, belly quivering.

Bigger aimed and let the skillet fly with a heavy grunt. There was a 49
shattering of wood as the box caved in. The woman screamed and hid
her face in her hands. Bigger tiptoed forward and peered.

"I got 'im," he muttered, his clenched teeth bared in a smile. "By 50
God, I got 'im."

He kicked the splintered box out of the way and the flat black body 50
of the rat lay exposed, its two long yellow tusks showing distinctly. Bigger took a shoe and pounded the rat's head, crushing it, cursing hysterically:

"You sonofa*bitch!*"   51

The woman on the bed sank to her knees and buried her face in 52
the quilts and sobbed:

"Lord, Lord, have mercy...."   53

"Aw, Mama," Vera whimpered, bending to her. "Don't cry. It's dead 54
now."

Locating Assumptions While Reading

Some writers, especially those who have come to be regarded as authorities, use fewer facts than you've noticed in the two previous readings. A writer who has become an authority (by showing in earlier work a command of facts) tends to rely more on judgments (inferences) based on experience, and often on the clever use of language as well. As readers, when we read such writers, we should be alert for assumptions guiding the writer's thinking but not explicitly written down, and for words the writer is deliberately using in unconventional ways. By noting these words and by discovering these assumptions, we can better understand the writer's point and make a better-informed decision about whether or not we agree.

Exercise 12-4

Read the following editorial by Ellen Goodman of the *Boston Globe*. Circle all the words that are used in an unusual way, and when you've finished, try to explain, for each circled word, the difference between the usual meaning of the word and the meaning implied by the author. Also, try to locate any assumptions the author has about relations between men and women that are not stated but that clearly influence the author's point of view. Bring your notes to class, and compare your results with those of your classmates.

When Grateful Begins to Grate (1979)
Ellen Goodman

I know a woman who is a grateful wife. She has been one for years. 1
In fact, her gratitude has been as deep and constant as her affection.
And together they have traveled a long, complicated road.

In the beginning, this young wife was grateful to find herself mar- 2
ried to a man who let her work. That was in 1964, when even her college
professor said without a hint of irony that the young wife was "lucky to
be married to a man who let her work." People talked like that then.

Later, the wife looked around her at the men her classmates and 3
friends had married and was grateful that her husband wasn't threatened, hurt, neglected, insulted—the multiple choice of the mid-'60s—by
her job.

He was proud. And her cup overran with gratitude. That was the way 4
it was.

In the late '60s, when other, younger women were having con- 5
sciousness-raising groups, she was having babies and more gratitude.

You see, she discovered that she had a Helpful Husband. Nothing 6
in her experience had led her to expect this. Her mother was not married to one; her sister was not married to one; her brother was not one.

But at 4 o'clock in the morning, when the baby cried and she was 7
exhausted, sometimes she would nudge her husband awake (wondering
only vaguely how he could sleep) and ask him to feed the boy. He would
say sure. And she would say thank you.

The Grateful Wife and the Helpful Husband danced this same *pas* 8
de deux for a decade. When the children were small and she was sick, he
would take charge. When it was their turn to carpool and she had to be
at work early, he would drive. If she was coming home late, he would
make dinner.

All you have to do is ask, he would say with a smile. 9

And so she asked. The woman who had minded her p's and q's as 10
a child minded her pleases and thank yous as a wife. Would you please
put the baby on the potty? Would you please stop at the store tonight for
milk? Would you please pick up Joel at soccer practice? Thank you.
Thank you. Thank you.

It is hard to know when gratitude first began to grate on my friend. Or 11
when she began saying please and thank you dutifully rather than genuinely.

But it probably began when she was tired one day or night. In any 12
case, during the car-time between one job and the other, when she
would run lists through her head, she began feeling less thankful for her
moonlighting job as household manager.

She began to realize that all the items of their shared life were 13 stored in her exclusive computer. She began to realize that her queue was so full of minutiae that she had no room for anything else.

The Grateful Wife began to wonder why she should say thank you 14 when a father took care of his children and why she should say please when a husband took care of his house.

She began to realize that being grateful meant being responsible. 15 Being grateful meant assuming that you were in charge of children and laundry and running out of toilet paper. Being grateful meant having to ask. And ask. And ask.

Her husband was not an oppressive or even thoughtless man. He 16 was helpful. But helpful doesn't have to remember vacuum cleaner bags. And helpful doesn't keep track of early dismissal days.

Helpful doesn't keep a Christmas-present list in his mind. 17 Helpful doesn't have to know who wears what size and colors. Helpful is reminded; helpful is asked. Anything you ask. Please and thank you.

The wife feels, she says, vaguely frightened to find herself angry at 18 saying please and thank you. She wonders if she is, indeed, an ingrate. But her wondering doesn't change how she feels or what she wants.

The wife would like to take just half the details that clog her mind 19 like grit in a pore and hand them over to another manager. The wife would like someone who would be grateful when she volunteered to take *his* turn at the market or *his* week at the laundry.

The truth is that after all those years when she danced her part 20 perfectly, she wants something else. She doesn't want a helpful husband. She wants one who will share. For that, she would be truly grateful.

Active Reading

Exercise 12-5

In your reading thus far in this chapter I've told you what to look for. But each of us reads in an individual way, based on past reading experience and on past experience in general. Consequently, each of us draws unique inferences (you might prefer the term *insights*) from any work we read with care. While reading the following three selections—two brief poems and a description of a coal mine—underline in each whatever *you* think is important, and make at least five comments in the margins. (Your underlining indicates that you regard the author having written those words as a fact worth noting. Your marginal comments are readers' inferences that you're drawing.) In class, then, compare your comments with those of your classmates. How different was what you chose to mark from what they marked?

What inferences were the most thoughtful in the class? What was it that made those inferences stand out from the crowd?

In completing this exercise, you will see more clearly what you value when you read, and you will begin to discover what other readers, including your teacher, look for. Are some ways of reading better than others?

Airport: A Takeoff on a Poem (1980)
E. Ethelbert Miller

sitting in the airport
for about two hours
i finally landed a conversation
with an old white lady who looked
mulatto
she asked me if i was a student
at the university
i told her no
she asked me what i did
i told her i wrote poetry
she asked me what i wanted to do
i told her i had always
wanted to kill a large number of people
i told her of my desire to climb into
clocktowers and be a sniper
i told her that i had missed the draft
and was too proud to enlist
i told her about all the audie murphy
films i had ever seen
i told her that i was the type
that carried bombs inside luggage
when making short trips
i watched the old mulatto lady
turn white
there was no mistaking it now
she was a white lady and i...

well i have been sitting in this
airport for over two hours more
listening to the soft ticking sounds
coming from the case i carry my poems in

Smokestacks: 23 February 1942
L. Schwartz (1984)

Here in this place
    Where the air always has a damp chill,
    And the wind cuts through my scant clothing
    I work endlessly under their shadows.
No one looks at the smokestacks
    But all know they are there,
    Belching thick, nauseous smoke
    Which rises higher and higher
    And sails over the walls, free.
Day after day they smoke
    And are forever fueled—
    The supply never seems to dwindle
Today I allowed my eyes to be drawn toward the stacks,
    Toward the smoke that escapes over the gates,
    And longed to be free—
    To sail on the wind and out of Hell.

From *The Road to Wigan Pier* (1937)
George Orwell

Our civilization...*is* founded on coal, more completely than one re- 1
alizes until one stops to think about it. The machines that keep us alive,
and the machines that make the machines, are all directly or indirectly
dependent upon coal. In the metabolism of the Western world the coal
miner is second in importance only to the man who ploughs the soil. He
is a sort of grimy caryatid upon whose shoulders nearly everything that
is *not* grimy is supported. For this reason the actual process by which
coal is extracted is well worth watching, if you get the chance and are
willing to take the trouble....

It is impossible to watch the "fillers" at work without feeling a pang 2
of envy for their toughness. It is a dreadful job that they do, an almost
superhuman job by the standards of an ordinary person. For they are
not only shifting monstrous quantities of coal, they are also doing it in a
position that doubles or trebles the work. They have got to remain kneeling all the while—they could hardly rise from their knees without hitting

the ceiling—and you can easily see by trying it what a tremendous effort this means. Shoveling is comparatively easy when you are standing up, because you can use your knee and thigh to drive the shovel along; kneeling down, the whole of the strain is thrown upon your arm and belly muscles. And the other conditions do not exactly make things easier. There is the heat—it varies, but in some mines it is suffocating—and the coal dust that stuffs up your throat and nostrils and collects along your eyelids, and the unending rattle of the conveyor belt, which in that confined space is rather like the rattle of a machine gun. But the fillers look and work as though they were made of iron. They really do look like iron—hammered iron statues—under the smooth coat of coal dust which clings to them from head to foot. It is only when you see miners down the mine and naked that you realize what splendid men they are. Most of them are small (big men are at a disadvantage in that job) but nearly all of them have the most noble bodies: wide shoulders tapering to slender supple waists, and small pronounced buttocks and sinewy thighs, with not an ounce of waste flesh anywhere. In the hotter mines they wear only a pair of thin drawers, clogs and knee-pads; in the hottest mines of all, only the clogs and knee-pads. You can hardly tell by the look of them whether they are young or old. They may be any age up to sixty or even sixty-five, but when they are black and naked they all look alike. No one could do their work who had not a young man's body, and a figure fit for a guardsman at that; just a few pounds of extra flesh on the waistline, and the constant bending would be impossible. You can never forget that spectacle once you have seen it—the line of bowed, kneeling figures, sooty black all over, driving their huge shovels under the coal with stupendous force and speed. They are on the job for seven and a half hours, theoretically without a break, for there is no time "off." Actually they snatch a quarter of an hour or so at some time during the shift to eat the food they have brought with them, usually a hunk of bread and dripping and a bottle of cold tea. The first time I was watching the "fillers" at work I put my hand upon some dreadful slimy thing among the coal dust. It was a chewed quid of tobacco. Nearly all the miners chew tobacco, which is said to be good against thirst.

Probably you have to go down several coal mines before you can 3 get much grasp of the processes that are going on round you. This is chiefly because the mere effort of getting from place to place makes it difficult to notice anything else. In some ways it is even disappointing, or at least is unlike what you have expected. You get into the cage, which is a steel box about as wide as a telephone box and two or three times as long. It holds ten men, but they pack it like pilchards in a tin, and a tall man cannot stand upright in it. The steel door shuts upon you, and somebody working the winding gear above drops you into the void. You have the usual momentary qualm in your belly and a bursting sensation in the ears, but not much sensation of movement till you get near the bottom, when the cage slows down so abruptly that you could swear it is going upward again. In the middle of the run the cage probably touches sixty miles an hour; in some of the deeper mines it touches even more. When you crawl out at the bottom you are perhaps four hundred yards under ground. That is to say you have a tolerable-sized mountain on top of you; hundreds of yards of solid rock, bones of extinct beasts, subsoil, flints, roots of growing things, green grass and cows grazing on it—all this suspended over your head and held back only by wooden props as thick as the calf of your leg. But because of the speed at which the cage has brought you down, and the complete blackness through which you have traveled, you hardly feel yourself deeper down than you would at the bottom of the Piccadilly tube.

What *is* surprising, on the other hand, is the immense horizontal 4 distances that have to be traveled underground. Before I had been down a mine I had vaguely imagined the miner stepping out of the cage and getting to work on a ledge of coal a few yards away. I had not realized that before he even gets to his work he may have to creep through passages as long as from London Bridge to Oxford Circus. In the beginning, of course, a mine shaft is sunk somewhere near a seam of coal. But as that seam is worked out and fresh seams are followed up, the workings get farther and farther from the pit bottom. If it is a mile from the pit bottom to the coal face, that is probably an average distance; three miles is a fairly normal one; there are even said to be a few mines where it is as much as five miles. But these distances bear no relation to distances above ground. For in all that mile or three miles as it may be, there is hardly anywhere outside the main road, and not many places even there, where a man can stand upright.

You do not notice the effect of this till you have gone a few hun- 5 dred yards. You start off, stooping slightly, down the dim-lit gallery, eight or ten feet wide and about five high, with the walls built up with slabs of shale, like the stone walls in Derbyshire. Every yard or two there are wooden props holding up the beams and girders; some of the girders have buckled into fantastic curves under which you have to duck. Usually it is bad going underfoot—thick dust or jagged chunks of shale, and in some mines where there is water it is as mucky as a farmyard. Also there is the track for the coal tubs, like a miniature railway track with sleepers a foot or two apart, which is tiresome to walk on. Everything is gray with shale dust; there is a dusty fiery smell which seems to be the same in all mines. You see mysterious machines of which you never learn the purpose, and bundles of tools slung together on wires, and sometimes mice darting away from the beam of the lamps....

At the start to walk stooping is rather a joke, but it is a joke that 6 soon wears off. I am handicapped by being exceptionally tall, but when the roof falls to four feet or less it is a tough job for anybody except a dwarf or a child. You have not only got to bend double, you have also got to keep your head up all the while so as to see the beams and girders and dodge them when they come. You have, therefore, a constant crick in the neck, but this is nothing to the pain in your knees and thighs. After half a mile it becomes (I am not exaggerating) an unbearable agony. You begin to wonder whether you will ever get to the end—still more, how on earth you are going to get back. Your pace grows slower and slower. You come to a stretch of a couple of hundred yards where it is all exceptionally low and you have to work yourself along in a squatting position. Then suddenly the roof opens out to a mysterious height—scene of an old fall of rock, probably—and for twenty whole yards you can stand upright. The relief is overwhelming. But after this there is another low stretch of a hundred yards and then a succession of beams which you have to crawl under. You go down on all fours; even this is a relief after the squatting business. But when you come to the end of the beams and try to get up again, you find that your knees have temporarily struck work and refuse to lift you. You call a halt, ignominiously, and say that you would like to rest for a minute or two. Your guide (a miner) is sympathetic. He knows that your muscles are not the same as his. "Only another four hundred yards," he says encouragingly; you feel that he might as well say another four hundred miles. But finally you do somehow creep as far as the coal face. You have gone a mile and taken the best part of an hour; a miner would do it in not much more than twenty minutes. Having got there, you have to sprawl in the coal dust and get your strength back for several minutes before you can even watch the work in progress with any kind of intelligence....

It may seem that I am exaggerating, though no one who has been   7 down an old-fashioned pit (most of the pits in England are old-fashioned) and actually gone as far as the coal face, is likely to say so. But what I want to emphasize is this. Here is this frightful business of crawling to and fro, which to any normal person is a hard day's work in itself; and it is not part of the miner's work at all, it is merely an extra, like the City man's daily ride in the tube. The miner does that journey to and fro, and sandwiched in between there are seven and a half hours of savage work. I have never traveled much more than a mile to the coal face; but often it is three miles, in which case I and most people other than coal miners would never get there at all. This is the kind of point that one is always liable to miss. When you think of a coal mine you think of depth, heat, darkness, blackened figures hacking at walls of coal; you don't think, necessarily, of those miles of creeping to and fro. There is the question of time, also. A miner's working shift of seven and a half hours does not sound very long, but one has got to add on to it at least an hour a day for "traveling," more often two hours and sometimes three. Of course, the "traveling" is not technically work and the miner is not paid for it; but it is as like work as makes no difference. It is easy to say that miners don't mind all this. Certainly, it is not the same for them as it would be for you or me. They have done it since childhood, they have the right muscles hardened, and they can move to and fro underground with a startling and rather horrible agility. A miner puts his head down and *runs*, with a long swinging stride, through places where I can only stagger. At the workings you see them on all fours, skipping round the pit props almost like dogs. But it is quite a mistake to think that they enjoy it. I have talked about this to scores of miners and they all admit that the "traveling" is hard work; in any case when you hear them discussing a pit among themselves the "traveling" is always one of the things they discuss. It is said that a shift always returns from work faster than it goes; nevertheless the miners all say that it is the coming away, after a hard day's work, that is especially irksome. It is part of their work and they are equal to it, but certainly it is an effort. It is comparable, perhaps, to climbing a smallish mountain before and after your day's work.

   When you have been down two or three pits you begin to get some 8 grasp of the processes that are going on underground. (I ought to say, by the way, that I know nothing whatever about the technical side of mining: I am merely describing what I have seen.) Coal lies in thin seams between enormous layers of rock, so that essentially the process of getting it out is like scooping the central layer from a Neapolitan ice. In the old days the miners used to cut straight into the coal with pick and crowbar—a very slow job because coal, when lying in its virgin state, is almost as hard as rock. Nowadays the preliminary work is done by an electrically driven coal-cutter, which in principle is an immensely tough and powerful bandsaw, running horizontally instead of vertically, with teeth a couple of inches long and half an inch or an inch thick. It can move backward or forward on its own power, and the men operating it can rotate it this way and that. Incidentally it makes one of the most awful noises I have ever heard, and sends forth clouds of coal dust which make it impossible to see more than two or three feet and almost impossible to breathe. The machine travels along the coal face cutting into the base of the coal and undermining it to the depth of five feet or five feet and a half; after this it is comparatively easy to extract the coal to the depth to which it has been undermined. Where it is "difficult getting," however, it has also to be loosened with explosives. A man with an electric drill, like a rather smaller version of the drills used in street-mending, bores holes at intervals in the coal, inserts blasting powder, plugs it with clay, goes round the corner if there is one handy (he is supposed to retire to twenty-five yards distance) and touches off the charge with an electric current. This is not intended to bring the coal out, only to loosen it. Occasionally, of course, the charge is too powerful, and then it not only brings the coal out but brings the roof down as well.

After the blasting has been done the "fillers" can tumble the coal   9 out, break it up, and shovel it on to the conveyor belt. It comes out at first in monstrous boulders which may weigh anything up to twenty tons. The conveyor belt shoots it onto tubs, and the tubs are shoved into the main road and hitched onto an endlessly revolving steel cable which drags them to the cage. Then they are hoisted, and at the surface the coal is sorted by being run over screens, and if necessary is washed as well. As far as possible the "dirt"—the shale, that is—is used for making the roads below. All that cannot be used is sent to the surface and dumped; hence the monstrous "dirt-heaps," like hideous gray mountains, which are the characteristic scenery of the coal areas. When the coal has been extracted to the depth to which the machine has cut, the coal face has advanced by five feet. Fresh props are put in to hold up the newly exposed roof, and during the next shift the conveyor belt is taken to pieces, moved five feet forward and reassembled. As far as possible the three operations of cutting, blasting, and extraction are done in three separate shifts, the cutting in the afternoon, the blasting at night (there is a law, not always kept, that forbids its being done when there are other men working near by), and the "filling" in the morning shift, which lasts from six in the morning until half-past one....

Watching coal miners at work, you realize momentarily what dif-   10 ferent universes different people inhabit. Down there where coal is dug it is a sort of world apart which one can quite easily go through life without ever hearing about. Probably a majority of people would even prefer not to hear about it. Yet it is the absolutely necessary counterpart of our world above. Practically everything we do, from eating an ice to crossing the Atlantic, and from baking a loaf to writing a novel, involves the use of coal, directly or indirectly. For all the arts of peace coal is needed; if war breaks out it is needed all the more. In time of revolution the miner must go on working or the revolution must stop, for revolution as much as reaction needs coal. Whatever may be happening on the surface, the hacking and shoveling have got to continue without a pause, or at any rate without pausing for more than a few weeks at the most. In order that Hitler may march the goosestep, that the Pope may denounce Bolshevism, that the cricket crowds may assemble at Lord's, that the Nancy poets may scratch one another's backs, coal has got to be forthcoming. But on the whole we are not aware of it; we all know that we "must have coal," but we seldom or never remember what coal-getting involves. Here am I, sitting writing in front of my comfortable coal fire. It is April but I still need a fire. Once a fortnight the coal cart drives up to the door and men in leather jerkins carry the coal indoors in stout sacks smelling of tar and shoot it clanking into the coal-hole under the stairs. It is only very rarely, when I make a definite mental effort, that I connect this coal with that far-off labor in the mines. It is just "coal"—something that I have got to have; black stuff that arrives mysteriously from nowhere in particular, like manna except that you have to pay for it. You could quite easily drive a car right across the north of England and never once remember that hundreds of feet below the road you are on the miners are hacking at the coal. Yet in a sense it is the miners who are driving your car forward. Their lamp-lit world down there is as necessary to the daylight world above as the root is to the flower.

It is not long since conditions in the mines were worse than they 11 are now. There are still living a few very old women who in their youth have worked underground, with a harness round their waists and a chain that passed between their legs, crawling on all fours and dragging tubs of coal. They used to go on doing this even when they were pregnant. And even now, if coal could not be produced without pregnant women dragging it to and fro, I fancy we should let them do it rather than deprive ourselves of coal. But most of the time, of course, we should prefer to forget that they were doing it. It is so with all types of manual work; it keeps us alive, and we are oblivious of its existence. More than anyone else, perhaps, the miner can stand as the type of the manual worker, not only because his work is so exaggeratedly awful, but also because it is so vitally necessary and yet so remote from our experience, so invisible, as it were, that we are capable of forgetting it as we forget the blood in our veins. In a way it is even humiliating to watch coal miners working. It raises in you a momentary doubt about your own status as an "intellectual" and a superior person generally. For it is brought home to you, at least while you are watching, that it is only because miners sweat their guts out that superior persons can remain superior. You and I and the editor of the *Times Lit. Supp.*, and the Nancy poets and the Archbishop of Canterbury and Comrade X, author of *Marxism for Infants*—all of us *really* owe the comparative decency of our lives to poor drudges underground, blackened to the eyes, with their throats full of coal dust, driving their shovels forward with arms and belly muscles of steel.

From Drawing Inferences to Evaluating

When you write a paper or an essay exam about something you've read, your responsibility is not simply to summarize it but to do what we've been practicing throughout this chapter: draw inferences about it. But the inferences you'll be expected to draw in academic papers will be restricted a bit. *They can no longer be about the author, but must be about the author's craft.*

You may have inferred from George Orwell's writing, for example, that he was a strong man, despite his claims to the contrary. When we analyze reading in school, though, this kind of inference takes a secondary role to inferences about how well the writer has used the tools at his or her disposal. Words are of course the primary tools of a writer; every word and phrase has a history of use by others behind it and therefore a set of emotional meanings that we can interpret and comment on. But more abstract tools, the tools that you have been sharpening yourself during this course—*ethos, logos, and pathos*—are at every writer's disposal, of course, and the words that the writer puts on the page can be used by us as evidence of the writer's greater or lesser effectiveness in using *ethos, logos,* and *pathos.* One of the most straightforward ways to evaluate any piece of writing is to examine how effectively the author has used these three means of affecting readers:

Ethos	*Logos*	*Pathos*
1. Is the writer intelligent?	1. Are the facts used well chosen?	1. Does the writer show a concern for the needs of the reader?
2. Well-informed?	2. Are the author's inferences justified by the facts?	2. Does the writer make a skilled use of emotional appeal?
3. Fair?	3. Are the author's assumptions justifiable?	
4. A person of goodwill?	4. Is the piece well-organized?	
	5. Is its purpose clear?	

Your textbooks, your mail, and everything else you "read" (including ads, films, political speeches, and popular songs) can be judged by the same standards.

Rhetorical Analysis

Exercise 12-6

The following two selections were both originally speeches, one given to the faculty of the University of Maryland at College Park, the other to the graduates of Bishop Strachan School in Ontario, Canada. Read each carefully, noting how effectively you think it employs *ethos, logos,* and *pathos.* Decide how well crafted you think each is, and compare your results, and the evidence you have used to arrive at your results, in class.

You may want to expand this exercise into a full-fledged paper, or perhaps having practiced assessing *ethos, logos,* and *pathos* in these two speeches, assess them again in a nonfiction film, as suggested in Assignment 8 in Chapter 14.

The Idea of a University in an Electronic Age (1985)

Kathleen Hall Jamieson

On September 22, 1964, Americans faced a revealing choice. Would 1 they settle into their sofas to watch that embodiment of high culture known as "Petticoat Junction"? Alternatively, would they snuggle into the sin and seduction of "Peyton Place"? Or would they watch Dwight Eisenhower discuss the future of the world with Republican party nominee Barry Goldwater? Americans chose the Clampetts and clinches over conversation at Gettysburg.

An aberration? On November 4, 1979, another moment of decision: 2 on one channel, "JAWS," on the other, Roger Mudd's documentary on presidential aspirant Edward Kennedy. "JAWS" swallowed "Teddy." The pattern repeats itself each time Americans choose to watch reruns of moldy movies rather than live coverage of national political conventions.

The problem isn't a new one. Long before the invention of televi- 3 sion, Samuel Butler noted, "The public buys its opinions as it buys its meat, or takes in its milk, on the principle that it is cheaper to do that than to keep a cow. So be it, but the milk is more likely to be watered."

The triumph of "JAWS," "Peyton Place" and "Petticiat Junction" 4 would not warrant concern if Americans were reading position papers, listening to speeches by candidates, and digesting books about the issues central to the campaigns. But we aren't. Instead we get most of our political information from two sources: televised spot ads and news coverage. In practical terms that means that, with the occasional exception of a presidential debate, our direct exposure to those who would lead the country occurs in 15 or 60 second snippets. In the last general election, a typical network newscast contained only 15 seconds of each candidate speaking; the typical spot ad was 60 seconds long.

The length of political messages reaching the electorate has 5 steadily decreased. Where the thirty minute political speech was standard in the early days of radio, by 1956 the five minute televised ad had replaced it.

In 1964 the five minute ad gave way to the sixty second spot. The sixty second ad has held sway ever since.

The story of print messages is not much different. Where in the 6 nineteenth century, newspapers routinely reprinted the texts of important political speeches, with the occasional exception of the *New York Times* and the *Washington Post,* few now reprint even the entire text of the state of the union address. By contrast a number of newspapers reprinted Charles Sumner's 80 page long "Crime Against Kansas" speech. In pamphlet form, almost a million copies were sold. In the presidential campaign of 1856, that speech was circulated as a campaign document.

In presidential debates too, the tendency has been to squeeze messages into shorter and shorter time slots. The time for answering questions and for delivering speeches was twice as great in the Kennedy-Nixon debates as it was in the debates between Reagan and Mondale. Stump speeches too are shorter, down from an average length of over an hour in the nineteenth century to just over seventeen minutes in this decade.

In the electronic age, survival of the briefest has become a political 8 imperative. The costs of this compression are high. Speakers from Demosthenes through Churchill routinely traced the history of their ideas. In the process, they revealed how they saw the world. Today, history has little place in political discourse except when selectively marshalled to assert that a proposed policy is a mistake.

In the ages in which ideas governed length, not length ideas, 9 speakers spent time defining their terms, a process that forces assumptions into the open. It made a great deal of difference whether speakers in 1967 saw the Vietnam war as a civil war or an act of self-defense by the South against invasion from the North. At the point of definition, conflicting assumptions are made plain. Without this stage of discourse, we can talk past each other unaware that our primal premises are at odds.

In the past, speakers assumed the burden of laying out the range of 10 policy alternatives, scrutinizing each in turn. Only after showing the strengths and weaknesses of each and arguing the comparative advantage of the course they favored, did they conclude. Such speeches demonstrated that the speaker commanded the situation, understood the alternatives and could defend the choice of one avenue over others.

Formerly, speakers lovingly explored the range of available evi- 11 dence. Today, speeches argue by hitting and running: a single supposedly telling statistic, report, or anecdote is slung under a claim as if it constituted conclusive proof.

In the past, speakers developed and defended their positions. In 12 spot ads, newsclips, and two-and-a-half-minute statements in debates, candidates can do little more than assert the godliness of their own side. Consequently, the audience is invited to do one of two things: nod be-

cause the politician and they embrace the same stand for reasons neither has disclosed or endorse the idea because they endorse the politician and are willing to take the legitimacy of his undisclosed case on
faith. Neither alternative encourages contemplation; neither produces
conversion; neither is conducive to long term commitment.

By contrast, an audience that accepts a speaker's interpretation of 13
the history of a question, grants the definitions that she offers, weighs
the alternatives and with the speaker finds them wanting, sees the problem in memorable dramatized human terms and then reaches the
speaker's conclusion, is an audience likely to retain a commitment to
the position. The fickleness of the public and the volatility of public
opinion may be, in part, the byproducts of the politicians' reliance on
forms of communication incapable of either marshalling or sustaining
public commitment.

None of this means that a thirty second spot is necessarily simple- 14
minded or that a thirty minute speech is necessarily substantive. It does
mean that it is impossible to adequately warrant complex claims in 15 or
60 seconds.

A second spin-off of the age of compression is of note. Because 15
those best able to think and speak in quotable snippets are most likely to
appear on news, and because news time is to politicians what honey is
to bears, survival of the briefest becomes survival of the politician disposed toward concise hyperbole. By dramatizing, capsulizing and
shouting wolf, members of congress bid against each other for the
crumbs of network time left after the president has gotten his share. In
the world according to network news, politicians appear to be in a per-
petual state of "alarm," "dismay" or "outrage." "Calamities" abound. In
the process, complex ideas are transformed into parodies of their former
selves and the capacity of the language to express outrage is exhausted.

The compulsion to compress has then devalued political discourse 16
and denuded it of its power to reveal the substance of those who would
be president. As disturbing is the possibility that the world of 15 and 60
second bites is inhospitable to the candidacies of those whose positions
are highly nuanced, subtle and complex and hospitable to the candidacies of those willing, able and eager to simplify.

The causes of this cursed compression are complex. (The antidote 17
for this awful alliteration is not approaching.) Central among them are
the cost of broadcast time and print space and the explosion in the
amount of information trying to force its way into the channels of mass
communication. As educators, there isn't much we can do about either.
But there is a factor over which we exercise control. It was articulated by
a political consultant I interviewed while researching *Packaging the
Presidency.*

"Look lady," he said, "your job is educating the electorate. My job is 18 electing candidates. If you're graduating students eager to watch "Peyton Place" and disinclined to watch Goldwater, don't blame me. When the electorate wants political fast food, it would be suicidal for me to tell my candidates to serve a seven course meal. The day a political speech can compete with "Dynasty" or even "Dialing for Dollars" is the day speeches will return to television. Until then, it's spots they'll watch so it's spots they'll get."

We might rephrase his contention as a challenge: Why is an elec- 19 torate that is filled with an unprecedented number of college graduates so eager to avoid sustained encounter with political argument? Have we perhaps failed to teach our students the joy and the value of the sustained encounter with ideas?

A cynic might respond to the notion that we could change the 20 viewing habits of our students by paraphrasing H. L. Mencken: it is unreasonable to assume that one can teach a streptoccocus the principles of Americanism. What gives lie to Mencken's claim is our commitment to the belief that we are able to cultivate a disposition toward careful thought, reasoned argument and articulate expression. Even in an electronic age we still espouse the ideal expressed by Newman in "The Idea of a University" that a university is "a place where inquiry is pushed forward and discoveries verified and perfected, and rashness rendered innocuous, and error exposed, by the collision of mind with mind and knowledge with knowledge." What the physicists, pharmacists and philosophers in our intellectual community share with the chemists, the computer scientists and the scholars of communication is a dedication to the belief Francis Bacon expressed when he wrote that students and scholars should "read not to contradict and confute, nor to believe and take for granted, nor to find talk and discourses, but to weigh and consider."

We also understand that education is a powerful agent of social 21 stability and change. As Mark Twain put it, "Soap and education are not as sudden as a massacre, but they are more deadly in the long run." These shared beliefs invite the self-examination entailed by the question, to what extent are faculty members demonstrating and students learning the value of the sustained encounter with texts and ideas?

In an age in which knowledge is expanding faster than our librar- 22 ies, we have too much to teach and too little time in which to teach it. A sustained encounter with one idea or text means that other important stuff must be displaced. And so, like those we indict in the newsrooms and the campaigns, we compress big ideas into small units of time. Consequently, the closest many of our students come to a close encounter is probably in a movie by that name or in a popular class that studies the causes and consequences of another type of close though not necessarily sustained encounter. It's likely that some students receive appeals to

donate funds to the Alumni Association without ever having plunged
into an idea, frolicked and splashed about in it, felt the force of its cur-
rents and undertows, risked being lost in it, and struggled to the surface
having grown gills.

How could they? The texts of important works are abridged; 23
abridgements are anthologized. Although classes in rhetoric once spent
weeks dissecting Edmund Burke's masterful "On Conciliation with
America," one is now hard pressed to find a complete copy of a speech
text. Instead we have five page excerpts. To reduce "On Conciliation" to
five pages is akin to reducing the Mona Lisa to her left ear, Beethoven's
Fifth to the first four notes, $E = MC$ squared to...C.

Anthologies filled with abridgements are the spot ads of higher ed- 24
ucation. Sanctifying abridged speeches, plays, novels, and scores signals
students that in an electronic age it is appropriate to know a little about
a lot. T. S. Eliot phrased the inevitable indictment well when he asked,
"Where is the wisdom we have lost in knowledge? Where is the knowledge we have lost in information?"

The texts we choose provide models of inquiry telling students 25
how to consume, command and convey ideas. So too do the lives we
lead. Sam Schoenbaum's life-long devotion to Shakespeare or Louis Har-
lan's to Booker T. Washington are living testaments to the joy of the sustained encounter. The fact that Robert Manson Myers put years into
Children of Pride and Paul Traver has invested much of his adult life in
bringing song to the campus, the community and the country is an invitation to sustained encounter.

But is that the message we consistently convey? What are we say- 26
ing about the value of the sustained encounter with ideas and arts when
it is easier to secure tenure for a person who has published 20 niggling
articles on cabbages and kings than for the person who has published
two definitive essays on the nature of inquiry in a democratic state? Isn't
something wrong when we confidently tenure someone who has published often though not well but challenge the tenureability of someone
who has published well though not often?

We establish models of inquiry not only in our lives but also in the 27
tests by which we assess learning. When we use GRE scores as a prime
criterion for awarding fellowships, are we perhaps attracting only those
best able to promiscuously engage an idea a second? What of the student who in the middle of the exam finds herself captivated by an idea
that just won't let go? What has speed of response to do with scholar-
ship, anyway?

As I sat growling my way through GREs, I was reminded of "[an ep- 28
isode of] I Love Lucy" that took place in a bakery whose conveyor belt
was malfunctioning. Cakes began to speed past her. Finally she could
cope no longer. Cake stacked on cake. Cakes slid onto the floor. A met-

aphor for GREs: scramble from question to question, wiping one from the mind as the next approaches, moving at a faster and faster pace or your prospects for graduate school will wind up dripping and melting like huge globs of cake and icing.

As the conveyor belt speeds by us are we not devaluing sustained 29 encounter with ideas when we spurn essay exams for the more easily graded, less easily questioned, true-false, multiple choice and fill in the blanks exams? And aren't administrators guilty accomplices for telling us to increase class size, hence the likelihood of true-false exams, to protect existing lines and barter for new ones? How can we criticize the electronic media for shaving meaning into slivers of time when our assignments read: a paper of 5 to 7 pages, a paper of not more than 3500 words. Why are we not instead demanding that an important idea be engaged in an important way in however many pages or words that takes? Along similar lines, how can we fairly ask M.A. and Ph.D. students to compress the collective insights of their fields into 10–12 hours of one– and two–hour timed exams. While we're milking sacred cows may this be the time to ask, Why do we confront ideas in fifteen week units of three hours per week? Aren't there some topics that demand eighteen weeks and others that deserve only four hours? The units in which we process information are almost as unbending as those into which television slots its content.

I was wondering about all of this as I taught "TV and Politics" this 30 summer. "TV and Politics" is that horrible aggregation of nouns, the mass lecture class. The essay questions for the tests in that class contain the usual words we write into our questions: "Analyze and defend" "Consider" "Weigh the alternatives." When the luxury of teaching at night permits, I try to allay the fears that such questions engender by telling students that, although the class ends at 9:45 p.m., I will stay with them until they have answered the questions as thoroughly and thoughtfully as they reasonably can.

For the first time in 15 years, a student took me at my word this 31 summer. At 9:45 all of the other students had left for the Vous and the other places students go in the night to salve their wounds and wonder about their salvation. As 10:30 approached, I began to worry about my safety on the now dark, silent campus. At 10:45 uncharitable thoughts about the student encroached on my consciousness. "He doesn't command the material well enough to focus his answer," I thought. At 11, I considered the possibility that I might become the first professor in the history of the University to end a 7 p.m. class by saying good morning to an arriving 8 a.m. class. Hoping he would read and respond to nonverbal cues, I shifted restlessly. He was too lost in thought to notice. I contemplated the thought that he wasn't writing my exam at all, but rather the great American novel or a letter home asking for clean socks.

I cleared my throat. I wondered if a campus attorney would defend me from a breach of oral contract charge if I stood up and announced, "enough is enough." In an evil moment, I relished the thought of placing a large F on the exam that had deprived me of the comforts of family and food for over an hour. Finally at 11:05 he capped his pen and handed in the exam.

The next day I was astonished to find that his answers were perceptive, original, thoughtful and all of the other adjectives we secretly hope our colleagues will apply to our work. Rested and fed and in the light of day, I was relieved that my non-verbal signs of disapproval had not driven him from the classroom. At the same time I wondered how many other times, subtle, sensitive, sophisticated answers were left unwritten in the rush of timed exams. 32

In what will appear to be a non sequitur let me add that that experience helped me understand Adlai Stevenson. Stevenson's speeches never seemed to fit the pre-set times demanded by television. He was often speaking as the camera faded to black. Did it mean that he lacked discipline or that he secretly wanted to sabotage his chances to be president? Or, and this is the message that emerged from my close encounter with hunger and desperation in "Television and Politics," did Stevenson simply rebel at the notion that ideas should appear in pretimed, freeze dried units? Perhaps Stevenson was simply shouting "No" to the Procrusteans who demand that political ideas be stretched or cut to fit television's bed. Perhaps, our mission as a university in an electronic age is to educate an electorate that will stand up with the Stevensons of today and shout "no." Some ideas deserve sustained encounters. Certainly those about the direction of the country deserve no less. The electorate should both expect such encounters and elect those whose ideas can withstand the scrutiny such encounters invite. 33

But if we are to shout "no," we must reject the philosophy Sam Goldwyn immortalized in his observation, "I read part of it all the way through." As an alternative model let me suggest Isaac Newton. "If I have ever made any valuable discoveries," he noted, "it has been owing more to patient attention than to any other talent." Isaac Newton would have watched political conventions and political speeches, "Teddy" not "JAWS," Eisenhower not "Peyton Place." And were he writing about the electronic age, I suspect he might tell us that as the mass of the well-educated audience increases, so too does the gravitational pull that mass exerts on politicians and political programmers. 34

One of our missions as a university in an electronic age is engendering in our students such a love of the sustained encounter with ideas that they will demand it of us and of those who lead the university, the community and the country. And, if in the process, we produce an Isaac Newton or an Adlai Stevenson, I can't imagine anyone complaining. 35

What Every Girl Should Know (1973)
Robertson Davies

As a schoolboy I listened to many speeches on Prize Days from older persons whose good intentions were impeccable, but whose manner and matter were tediously patronizing and stuffy. When my own turn came I determined to be as honest as possible, not to talk down, and if possible to say something that was not usually said in schools. This is what I said to the girls of the Bishop Strachan School in June 1973.

During the years when my own daughters were pupils in this 1 school I attended many of these gatherings, and heard many speeches made by men who stood where I stand at this moment. They said all sorts of things. I recall one speaker who said that as he looked out at the girls who were assembled to receive prizes, and to pay their last respects to their school, he felt as though he were looking over a garden of exquisite flowers. He was drunk, poor man, and it would be absurd to treat his remark as though he were speaking on oath. I am not drunk, although I have lunched elegantly at the table of the Chairman of your Board of Governors; I have had enough of his excellent wine to be philosophical, but with me philosophy does not take the form of paying extravagant and manifestly untruthful compliments. Let me put myself on record as saying that I do *not* feel as though I were looking over a garden of exquisite flowers.

On the contrary, I feel as though I were looking into the past. You 2 look uncommonly as the girls of this school looked when my daughters were of your number. And in those days I used to think how much you looked like the girls who were in this school when I was myself a schoolboy, just down the road, at Upper Canada College.

I remember that boy very well. He was a romantic boy, and he 3 thought that girls were quite the most wonderful objects of God's creation. In these liberated days, when it is possible for anyone to say anything on any occasion, I may perhaps make a confession to you, and this is it: I never liked anything but girls. Nowadays it is accepted as gospel that everybody goes through a homosexual period of life. I cannot recall any such thing: I always regarded other boys as rivals, or nuisances, or— very occasionally—friends. I am rather sorry about it now, because in the eyes of modern psychologists and sociologists it marks me as a stunted personality. Nowadays it appears that there is something warped about a man who never had a homosexual period. But there it is. I stand before you with all my imperfections weighing heavily upon me. I always liked girls, and simply because of geography, the girls I liked best were the girls of BSS.

I have recovered from this folly. I have myself achieved some 4
knowledge of psychology and sociology, and it tells me significant but
not always complimentary things about you. I don't know how many of
you are here today, but statistically I know that during the next ten years
58.7 per cent of you will marry, and that of that number 43.4 per cent will
have two and a half children apiece, and that 15.3 per cent will be di-
vorced. Of the remainder, 3.9 per cent will be dead, 14.5 per cent will
have been deserted, 24.2 per cent will have spent some time in jail. One
hundred per cent of those who have married will have given up splendid
careers in order to do so, and of this number 98.5 per cent will have
mentioned the fact, at some time, to their husbands. These statistics
were compiled for me by a graduate student at OISE, and if you doubt
them, you must quarrel with her, and not with me. I accept no responsibility for statistics, which are a kind of magic beyond my comprehension.

I have said that when I was a boy I entertained a lofty, uncritical 5
admiration for the girls of this school. Our romantic approach in those
days was more delicate than it is today, when sexual fervour has
achieved almost cannibalistic exuberance, and I thought I was lucky
when I had a chance simply to talk to one of the girls from this school.
I never had enough of that pleasure; I yearned for more. Now here I offer
my first piece of good advice to you: be very careful of what you greatly
desire, in your inmost heart, because the chances are very strong that
you will get it, in one form or another. But it will never be just the way
you expected. You see what has happened? As a boy I wanted to talk to
the girls of BSS, and I always thought of doing this to one girl at a time,
in shaded light, with music playing in the distance. And here I am today,
talking to all of you, in broad daylight. The things I planned to say when
I was a boy would be embarrassingly inappropriate if I were to say them
now. Indeed, I don't want to say them; they have ceased to be true or
relevant for you or for me. I know too much about you to compliment
you, and in your eyes I am not a romantic object. Or if I am, you had
better put yourself under the treatment of some wise psychiatrist.

Here I am, after all these years, and Fate has granted one of my 6
wishes, in the way Fate so often does—at the wrong time and in whole-
sale quantity. What am I to say to you?

The hallowed custom, at such times as these, is that I should offer 7
you some good advice. But what about? It was easier in the days when
girls like yourselves thought chiefly about marriage. Nowadays when little girls play

Rich man, poor man, beggar man, thief,
Doctor, lawyer, Indian chief

they are trying to discover their own careers, not those of their husbands. Quite recently a very young girl told me that she did not intend to
bother with a husband; she would be content with affairs, because they

would interfere less with her career. That remark showed how much she knew about it. A girl who thinks love affairs are less trouble than a marriage is probably also the kind of girl who thinks that picnics are simpler than dinner-parties. A first-class picnic, which has to be planned to the last detail, but which must also pretend to be wholly impromptu, is a vastly more complicated undertaking than a formal dinner for twenty guests, which moves according to a well-understood pattern. Personally I have always greatly liked dinner-parties, and hated picnics. But then I am a classicist by temperament, and I think the formality and the pattern, either in love or in entertaining, is half the fun.

But you may have different views, so we won't talk about that. Let 8
us talk about something that will be applicable to your life, whether the love aspect of it takes the dinner-party or the picnic form. Let us talk about enjoying life.

Don't imagine for a moment that I am going to talk about that fool- 9
ish thing happiness. I meet all kinds of people who think that happiness is a condition that can be achieved, and maintained, indefinitely, and that the quality of life is determined by the number of hours of happiness you can clock up. I hope you won't bother your heads about happiness. It is a cat-like emotion; if you try to coax it, happiness will avoid you, but if you pay no attention to it it will rub against your legs and spring unbidden into your lap. Forget happiness, and pin your hopes on understanding.

Many people, and especially many young people, think that variety 10
of sensation is what gives spice to life. They want to do everything, go everywhere, meet everybody, and drink from every bottle. It can't be done. Whoever you are, your energies and your opportunities are limited. Of course you want to try several alternatives in order to find out what suits you, but I hope that ten years from today you will agree with me that the good life is lived not widely, but deeply. It is not doing things, but understanding what you do, that brings real excitement and lasting pleasure.

You should start now. It is dangerously easy to get into a pattern of 11
life, and if you live shallowly until you are thirty, it will not be easy to begin living deeply. Whatever your own desires may be, the people around you won't put up with it. They know you as one sort of person, and they will be resentful if you show signs of becoming somebody else. Live shallowly, and you will find yourself surrounded by shallow people.

How are you to avoid that fate? I can tell you, but it is not a magic 12
secret which will transform your life. It is very, very difficult. What you must do is to spend twenty-three hours of every day of your life doing whatever falls in your way, whether it be duty or pleasure or necessary for your health and physical well-being. But—and this is the difficult thing—you must set aside one hour of your life every day for yourself, in which you attempt to understand what you are doing.

Do you think it sounds easy? Try it, and find out. All kinds of things 13
will interfere. People—husbands, lovers, friends, children, employers,
teachers, enemies, and all the multifarious army of mankind will want
that hour, and they will have all sorts of blandishments to persuade you
to yield it to them. And the worst enemy of all—yourself—will find so
many things that seem attractive upon which the hour can be spent. It is
extremely difficult to claim that hour solely for the task of understanding, questioning, and deciding.

It used to be somewhat easier, because people used to be religious, 14
or pretended they were. If you went to the chapel, or the church, or a
praying-chamber in your own house, and fell on your knees and buried
your face in your hands, they might—not always, but quite often—leave
you alone. Not now. "Why are you sitting there, staring into space?" they
will say. Or "What are you mooning about now?" If you say "I am thinking" they may perhaps hoot with laughter, or they will go away and tell
everybody that you are intolerably pretentious. But you are doing very
much what you would have been doing if you were your great-
grandmother, and said that you were praying. Because you would be
trying your hardest to unravel the tangles of your life, and seek the aid of
the greatest thing you know—whatever you may call it—in making sense
of what will often seem utterly senseless.

I am not going to advise you to pray, because I am not an expert on 15
that subject. But I know that it is rather the fashion among many people who do pray to think that it is pretentious to pray too much for yourself; you are supposed to pray for others, who obviously need Divine assistance more than you do. But when I was a boy at the school down the
road, we were taught that prayer has three modes—petition, which is for
yourself; intercession, which is for others; and contemplation, which is
listening to what is said to *you*. If I might be permitted to advise you on
this delicate subject, I would suggest that you skip intercession until you
are a little more certain what other people need; stick to petition, in the
form of self-examination, and to contemplation, which is waiting for suggestions from the deepest part of you.

If I embarrass you by talking about praying, don't think of it that 16
way. Call it "pondering" instead. I don't know if you still learn any Latin
in this school, but if you do, you know that the word ponder comes from
the Latin *ponderare*, which means "to weigh". Weigh up your life, and
do it every day. If you find you are getting short weight, attend to the
matter at once. The remedy usually lies in your own hands. And in that
direction the true enjoyment of life is to be found.

There you are. I promised your Headmaster I would not speak 17
for too long. But I have done what a speaker on such occasions as
this ought to do. I have given you good advice. It is often and
carelessly said that nobody ever takes advice. It is not true. I have
taken an enormous amount of advice myself, and some of it was

extraordinarily helpful to me. I have passed on some of the best of it
to you this afternoon, and I have enjoyed doing so. Because, as I told
you, it was my ambition for years to have a chance to talk to every
girl in BSS and today I have achieved it. Not quite as I had hoped, but
then, in this uncertain world, what ever comes about quite as one
hopes? I have enjoyed myself, and for what I have received from you I
am truly thankful.

Reading, and Writing about, Fiction

The final two reading selections in this chapter are short stories, stories
invented (with more or less truth behind them) by their authors to entertain us and to make us think about what it means to be human. Fiction writers often select their materials the same way nonfiction writers
do: they look for the facts that will most readily convey their intentions
to the reader. (They have the advantage over nonfiction writers, of
course, of being able to invent facts if the facts they want are not available.) And works of fiction can be judged, like works of nonfiction, by
assessing the *ethos, logos,* and *pathos* that comes through as we read.
More commonly, though, when we think of the tools of the fiction writer,
we use a different vocabulary: character, setting, plot, tone of voice, distinctive uses of language, and theme. Since fiction writers immerse us in
a world in order to make us think about their meaning, we rarely hear
from them what the "thesis" of their work is. Even their titles are often
meant to be intriguing rather than self-explanatory. Therefore, deciding
what we think the theme or thesis of a work might be is an important
aim of any paper about a work of fiction. And deciding on that theme is
done in precisely the way we have done it with nonfiction materials
throughout this course: by looking at the words (facts), drawing inferences about them, and summarizing (with qualifications) those inferences in a thesis.
　　Papers about literature usually take one of three forms:

1. An explanation of several devices used by the author to achieve his or
   her overall effect.
2. An explanation of how one portion of the story helps the author to
   achieve his or her overall effect.
3. A comparison of one aspect of a story, for example, the theme or the
   setting, with the same aspect of another story.

All these tasks ask you, as you did in writing about nonfiction, to draw
inferences about the writer's craft. As with nonfiction, the more carefully
you've read and the more you know about the tools writers use to build
their works, the better a paper you can write.

Exercise 12-7
Drawing Inferences about Works of Fiction

Read the following two stories and draw two or three inferences (with references to the texts to substantiate them) about each of the major tools of the writer's craft: character, setting, plot, and distinctive uses of language. Then give your best judgment of what you think the themes of the two stories were meant to be.

God Sees the Truth, but Waits (1872)
Leo Tolstoy
(Translated by Louise and Aylmer Maude)

In the town of Vladímir lived a young merchant named Iván 1
Dmítrich Aksënov. He had two shops and a house of his own.

Aksënov was a handsome, fair-haired, curly-headed fellow, full of 2
fun and very fond of singing. When quite a young man he had been given
to drink and was riotous when he had had too much, but after he married he gave up drinking except now and then.

One summer Aksënov was going to the Nízhny Fair, and as he bade 3
good-bye to his family his wife said to him, "Iván Dmítrich, do not start
to-day; I have had a bad dream about you."

Aksënov laughed, and said, "You are afraid that when I get to the 4
fair I shall go on the spree."

His wife replied: "I do not know what I am afraid of; all I know is 5
that I had a bad dream. I dreamt you returned from the town, and when
you took off your cap I saw that your hair was quite grey."

Aksënov laughed. "That's a lucky sign," said he. "See if I don't sell 6
out all my goods and bring you some presents from the fair."

So he said good-bye to his family and drove away. 7

When he had travelled half-way, he met a merchant whom he 8
knew, and they put up at the same inn for the night. They had some tea
together and then went to bed in adjoining rooms.

It was not Aksënov's habit to sleep late, and, wishing to travel while 9
it was still cool, he aroused his driver before dawn and told him to put in
the horses.

Then he made his way across to the landlord of the inn (who lived 10
in a cottage at the back), paid his bill, and continued his journey.

When he had gone about twenty-five miles he stopped for the 11
horses to be fed. Aksënov rested awhile in the passage of the inn, then he

stepped out into the porch and, ordering a samovar to be heated, got out his guitar and began to play.

Suddenly a *trôyka* drove up with tinkling bells, and an official [12] alighted, followed by two soldiers. He came to Aksënov and began to question him, asking him who he was and whence he came. Aksënov answered him fully and said, "Won't you have some tea with me?" But the official went on cross-questioning him and asking him, "Where did you spend last night? Were you alone, or with a fellow-merchant? Did you see the other merchant this morning? Why did you leave the inn before dawn?"

Aksënov wondered why he was asked all these questions, but he [13] described all that had happened, and then added, "Why do you cross-question me as if I were a thief or a robber? I am travelling on business of my own, and there is no need to question me."

Then the official, calling the soldiers, said, "I am the police-officer [14] of this district, and I question you because the merchant with whom you spent last night has been found with his throat cut. We must search your things."

They entered the house. The soldiers and the police-officer un- [15] strapped Aksënov's luggage and searched it. Suddenly the officer drew a knife out of a bag, crying, "Whose knife is this?"

Aksënov looked, and seeing a blood-stained knife taken from his [16] bag, he was frightened.

"How is it there is blood on this knife?" [17]

Aksënov tried to answer but could hardly utter a word and only [18] stammered: "I don't know—not mine."

Then the police-officer said, "This morning the merchant was [19] found in bed with his throat cut. You are the only person who could have done it. The house was locked from inside, and no one else was there. Here is this blood-stained knife in your bag, and your face and manner betray you! Tell me how you killed him and how much money you stole?"

Aksënov swore he had not done it; that he had not seen the mer- [20] chant after they had had tea together; that he had no money except eight thousand rubles of his own, and that the knife was not his. But his voice was broken, his face pale, and he trembled with fear as though he were guilty.

The police-officer ordered the soldiers to bind Aksënov and to put [21] him in the cart. As they tied his feet together and flung him into the cart, Aksënov crossed himself and wept. His money and goods were taken from him, and he was sent to the nearest town and imprisoned there. Enquiries as to his character were made in Vladímir. The merchants and other inhabitants of that town said that in former days he used to drink and waste his time but that he was a good man. Then the trial came on: he was charged with murdering a merchant from Ryazán and robbing him of twenty thousand rubles.

His wife was in despair and did not know what to believe. Her chil- 22
dren were all quite small; one was a baby at the breast. Taking them all
with her, she went to the town where her husband was in gaol. At first
she was not allowed to see him, but, after much begging, she obtained
permission from the officials and was taken to him. When she saw her
husband in prison-dress and in chains, shut up with thieves and criminals, she fell down and did not come to her senses for a long time. Then
she drew her children to her, and sat down near him. She told him of
things at home and asked about what had happened to him. He told her
all, and she asked, "What can we do now?"

"We must petition the Tsar not to let an innocent man perish."   23

His wife told him that she had sent a petition to the Tsar but that it 24
had not been accepted.

Aksënov did not reply but only looked downcast.   25

Then his wife said, "It was not for nothing I dreamt your hair had 26
turned grey. You remember? You should not have started that day." And
passing her fingers through his hair she said: "Ványa dearest tell your
wife the truth; was it not you who did it?"

"So you, too, suspect me!" said Aksënov, and, hiding his face in his 27
hands, he began to weep. Then a soldier came to say that the wife and
children must go away, and Aksënov said good-bye to his family for the
last time.

When they were gone, Aksënov recalled what had been said, and 28
when he remembered that his wife also had suspected him, he said to
himself, "It seems that only God can know the truth; it is to Him alone
we must appeal and from Him alone expect mercy."

And Aksënov wrote no more petitions, gave up all hope, and only 29
prayed to God.

Aksënov was condemned to be flogged and sent to the mines. So he 30
was flogged with a knout, and when the wounds caused by the knout
were healed, he was driven to Siberia with other convicts.

For twenty-six years Aksënov lived as a convict in Siberia. His hair 31
turned white as snow, and his beard grew long, thin, and grey. All his
mirth went; he stooped; he walked slowly, spoke little, and never
laughed, but he often prayed.

In prison Aksënov learnt to make boots, and earned a little money, 32
with which he bought *The Lives of the Saints*. He read this book when it
was light enough in the prison; and on Sundays in the prison-church he
read the epistle and sang in the choir, for his voice was still good.

The prison authorities liked Aksënov for his meekness, and his 33
fellow-prisoners respected him: they called him "Grandfather," and "The
Saint." When they wanted to petition the prison authorities about anything, they always made Aksënov their spokesman, and when there were
quarrels among the prisoners they came to him to put things right and
to judge the matter.

No news reached Aksënov from his home, and he did not even 34
know if his wife and children were still alive.

One day a fresh gang of convicts came to the prison. In the evening 35
the old prisoners collected round the new ones and asked them what
towns or villages they came from, and what they were sentenced for.
Among the rest Aksënov sat down near the new-comers, and listened
with downcast air to what was said.

One of the new convicts, a tall, strong man of sixty, with a closely- 36
cropped grey beard, was telling the others what he had been arrested
for.

"Well, friends," he said, "I only took a horse that was tied to a 37
sledge, and I was arrested and accused of stealing. I said I had only
taken it to get home quicker, and had then let it go; besides, the driver
was a personal friend of mine. So I said, 'It's all right.' 'No,' said they, 'you
stole it.' But how or where I stole it they could not say. I once really did
something wrong and ought by rights to have come here long ago, but
that time I was not found out. Now I have been sent here for nothing at
all....Eh, but it's lies I'm telling you; I've been to Siberia before, but I did
not stay long."

"Where are you from?" asked some one.   38

"From Vladímir. My family are of that town. My name is Makár, and 39
they also call me Semënich."

Aksënov raised his head and said: "Tell me, Semënich, do you 40
know anything of the merchants Aksënov, of Vladímir? Are they still
alive?"

"Know them? Of course I do. The Aksënovs are rich, though their 41
father is in Siberia: a sinner like ourselves, it seems! As for you, Gran'dad,
how did you come here?"

Aksënov did not like to speak of his misfortune. He only sighed, and 42
said, "For my sins I have been in prison these twenty-six years."

"What sins?" asked Makár Semënich.   43

But Aksënov only said, "Well, well—I must have deserved it!" He 44
would have said no more, but his companions told the new-comer how
Aksënov came to be in Siberia: how some one had killed a merchant and
had put a knife among Aksënov's things, and he had been unjustly condemned.

When Makár Semënich heard this he looked at Aksënov, slapped 45
his own knee, and exclaimed, "Well, this is wonderful! Really wonderful!
But how old you've grown, Gran'dad!"

The others asked him why he was so surprised, and where he had 46
seen Aksënov before; but Makár Semënich did not reply. He only said:
"It's wonderful that we should meet here, lads!"

These words made Aksënov wonder whether this man knew who 47
had killed the merchant; so he said, "Perhaps, Semënich, you have heard
of that affair, or maybe you've seen me before?"

"How could I help hearing? The world's full of rumours. But it's 48 long ago, and I've forgotten what I heard."

"Perhaps you heard who killed the merchant?" asked Aksënov.   49

Makár Semënich laughed, and replied, "It must have been him in 50 whose bag the knife was found! If some one else hid the knife there— 'He's not a thief till he's caught,' as the saying is. How could any one put a knife into your bag while it was under your head? It would surely have woke you up?"

When Aksënov heard these words he felt sure this was the man 51 who had killed the merchant. He rose and went away. All that night Aksënov lay awake. He felt terribly unhappy, and all sorts of images rose in his mind. There was the image of his wife as she was when he parted from her to go to the fair. He saw her as if she were present; her face and her eyes rose before him, he heard her speak and laugh. Then he saw his children, quite little, as they were at that time: one with a little cloak on, another at his mother's breast. And then he remembered himself as he used to be—young and merry. He remembered how he sat playing the guitar in the porch of the inn where he was arrested, and how free from care he had been. He saw in his mind the place where he was flogged, the executioner, and the people standing around; the chains, the convicts, all the twenty-six years of his prison life, and his premature old age. The thought of it all made him so wretched that he was ready to kill himself.

"And it's all that villain's doing!" thought Aksënov. And his anger 52 was so great against Makár Semënich that he longed for vengeance, even if he himself should perish for it. He kept saying prayers all night but could get no peace. During the day he did not go near Makár Semënich nor even look at him.

A fortnight passed in this way. Aksënov could not sleep at nights 53 and was so miserable that he did not know what to do.

One night as he was walking about the prison he noticed some 54 earth that came rolling out from under one of the shelves on which the prisoners slept. He stopped to see what it was. Suddenly Makár Semënich crept out from under the shelf, and looked up at Aksënov with frightened face. Aksënov tried to pass without looking at him, but Makár seized his hand and told him that he had dug a hole under the wall, getting rid of the earth by putting it into his high bots and emptying it out every day on the road when the prisoners were driven to their work.

"Just you keep quiet, old man, and you shall get out too. If you blab 55 they'll flog the life out of me, but I will kill you first."

Aksënov trembled with anger as he looked at his enemy. He drew 56 his hand away, saying, "I have no wish to escape, and you have no need to kill me; you killed me long ago! As to telling of you—I may do so or not, as God shall direct."

Next day, when the convicts were led out to work, the convoy sol- 57 diers noticed that one or other of the prisoners emptied some earth out of his boots. The prison was searched and the tunnel found. The Governor came and questioned all the prisoners to find out who had dug the hole. They all denied any knowledge of it. Those who knew would not betray Makár Semënich, knowing he would be flogged almost to death. At last the Governor turned to Aksënov, whom he knew to be a just man, and said: "You are a truthful old man; tell me, before God, who dug the hole?"

Makár Semënich stood as if he were quite unconcerned, looking at 58 the Governor and not so much as glancing at Aksënov. Aksënov's lips and hands trembled, and for a long time he could not utter a word. He thought, "Why should I screen him who ruined my life? Let him pay for what I have suffered. But if I tell, they will probably flog the life out of him, and maybe I suspect him wrongly. And, after all, what good would it be to me?"

"Well, old man," repeated the Governor, "tell us the truth: who has 59 been digging under the wall?"

Aksënov glanced at Makár Semënich and said, "I cannot say, your 60 honour. It is not God's will that I should tell! Do what you like with me; I am in your hands."

However much the Governor tried, Aksënov would say no more, 61 and so the matter had to be left.

That night, when Aksënov was lying on his bed and just beginning 62 to doze, some one came quietly and sat down on his bed. He peered through the darkness and recognized Makár.

"What more do you want of me?" asked Aksënov. "Why have you 63 come here?"

Makár Semënich was silent. So Aksënov sat up and said, "What do 64 you want? Go away or I will call the guard!"

Makár Semënich bent close over Aksënov, and whispered, "Iván 65 Dmítrich, forgive me!"

"What for?" asked Aksënov.   66

"It was I who killed the merchant and hid the knife among your 67 things. I meant to kill you too, but I heard a noise outside; so I hid the knife in your bag and escaped through the window."

Aksënov was silent and did not know what to say. Makár Semënich 68 slid off the bed-shelf and knelt upon the ground. "Iván Dmítrich," said he, "forgive me! For the love of God, forgive me! I will confess that it was I who killed the merchant, and you will be released and can go to your home."

"It is easy for you to talk," said Aksënov, "but I have suffered for you 69 these twenty-six years. Where could I go to now? My wife is dead, and my children have forgotten me. I have nowhere to go...."

Makár Semënich did not rise but beat his head on the floor. "Iván 70

Dmítrich, forgive me!" he cried. "When they flogged me with the knout it was not so hard to bear as it is to see you now...yet you had pity on me and did not tell. For Christ's sake forgive me, wretch that I am!" And he began to sob.

When Aksënov heard him sobbing he, too, began to weep.   71

"God will forgive you!" said he. "Maybe I am a hundred times worse   72 than you." And at these words his heart grew light and the longing for home left him. He no longer had any desire to leave the prison but only hoped for his last hour to come.

In spite of what Aksënov had said, Makár Semënich confessed his   73 guilt. But when the order for his release came, Aksënov was already dead.

Hands (1919)
Sherwood Anderson

Upon the half decayed veranda of a small frame house that stood   1 near the edge of a ravine near the town of Winesburg, Ohio, a fat little old man walked nervously up and down. Across a long field that had been seeded for clover but that had produced only a dense crop of yellow mustard weeds, he could see the public highway along which went a wagon filled with berry pickers returning from the fields. The berry pickers, youths and maidens, laughed and shouted boisterously. A boy clad in a blue shirt leaped from the wagon and attempted to drag after him one of the maidens, who screamed and protested shrilly. The feet of the boy in the road kicked up a cloud of dust that floated across the face of the departing sun. Over the long field came a thin girlish voice, "Oh, you Wing Biddlebaum, comb your hair, it's falling into your eyes," commanded the voice to the man, who was bald and whose nervous little hands fiddled about the bare white forehead as though arranging a mass of tangled locks.

Wing Biddlebaum, forever frightened and beset by a ghostly band   2 of doubts, did not think of himself as in any way a part of the life of the town where he had lived for twenty years. Among all the people of Winesburg but one had come close to him. With George Willard, son of Tom Willard, the proprietor of the New Willard House, he had formed something like a friendship. George Willard was the reporter on the *Winesburg Eagle* and sometimes in the evenings he walked out along the highway to Wing Biddlebaum's house. Now as the old man walked up and down on the veranda, his hands moving nervously about, he was hoping that George Willard would come and spend the evening with him. After the wagon containing the berry pickers had passed, he went across the field through the tall mustard weeds and climbing a rail fence peered anxiously along the road to the town. For a moment he stood thus, rubbing his hands together and looking up and down the road, and then, fear overcoming him, ran back to walk again upon the porch on his own house.

In the presence of George Willard, Wing Biddlebaum, who for 3 twenty years had been the town mystery, lost something of his timidity, and his shadowy personality, submerged in a sea of doubts, came forth to look at the world. With the young reporter at his side, he ventured in the light of day into Main Street or strode up and down on the rickety front porch of his own house, talking excitedly. The voice that had been low and trembling became shrill and loud. The bent figure straightened. With a kind of wriggle, like a fish returned to the brook by the fisherman, Biddlebaum the silent began to talk, striving to put into words the ideas that had been accumulated by his mind during long years of silence.

Wing Biddlebaum talked much with his hands. The slender expres- 4 sive fingers, forever active, forever striving to conceal themselves in his pockets or behind his back, came forth and became the piston rods of his machinery of expression.

The story of Wing Biddlebaum is a story of hands. Their restless 5 activity, like unto the beating of the wings of an imprisoned bird, had given him his name. Some obscure poet of the town had thought of it. The hands alarmed their owner. He wanted to keep them hidden away and looked with amazement at the quiet inexpressive hands of other men who worked beside him in the fields, or passed, driving sleepy teams on country roads.

When he talked to George Willard, Wing Biddlebaum closed his 6 fists and beat with them upon a table or on the walls of his house. The action made him more comfortable. If the desire to talk came to him when the two were walking in the fields, he sought out a stump or the top board of a fence and with his hands pounding busily talked with renewed ease.

The story of Wing Biddlebaum's hands is worth a book in itself. 7 Sympathetically set forth it would tap many strange, beautiful qualities in obscure men. It is a job for a poet. In Winesburg the hands had attracted attention merely because of their activity. With them Wing Biddlebaum had picked as high as a hundred and forty quarts of strawberries in a day. They became his distinguishing feature, the source of his fame. Also they made more grotesque an already grotesque and elusive individuality. Winesburg was proud of the hands of Wing Biddlebaum in the same spirit in which it was proud of Banker White's new stone house and Wesley Moyer's bay stallion, Tony Tip, that had won the two-fifteen trot at the fall races in Cleveland.

As for George Willard, he had many times wanted to ask about the hands. At times an almost overwhelming curiosity had taken hold of him. He felt that there must be a reason for their strange activity and their inclination to keep hidden away and only a growing respect for Wing Biddlebaum kept him from blurting out the questions that were often in his mind. 8

Once he had been on the point of asking. The two were walking in the fields on a summer afternoon and had stopped to sit upon a grassy bank. All afternoon Wing Biddlebaum had talked as one inspired. By a fence he had stopped and beating like a giant woodpecker upon the top board had shouted at George Willard, condemning his tendency to be too much influenced by the people about him. "You are destroying your-self," he cried. "You have the inclination to be alone and to dream and you are afraid of dreams. You want to be like others in town here. You hear them talk and you try to imitate them." 9

On the grassy bank Wing Biddlebaum had tried again to drive his point home. His voice became soft and reminiscent, and with a sigh of contentment he launched into a long rambling talk, speaking as one lost in a dream. 10

Out of the dream Wing Biddlebaum made a picture for George Willard. In the picture men lived again in a kind of pastoral golden age. Across a green open country came clean-limbed young men, some afoot, some mounted upon horses. In crowds the young men came to gather about the feet of an old man who sat beneath a tree in a tiny garden and who talked to them. 11

Wing Biddlebaum became wholly inspired. For once he forgot the hands. Slowly they stole forth and lay upon George Willard's shoulders. Something new and bold came into the voice that talked. "You must try to forget all you have learned," said the old man. "You must begin to dream. From this time on you must shut your ears to the roaring of the voices." 12

Pausing in his speech, Wing Biddlebaum looked long and earnestly at George Willard. His eyes glowed. Again he raised the hands to caress the boy and then a look of horror swept over his face. 13

With a convulsive movement of his body, Wing Biddlebaum sprang to his feet and thrust his hands deep into his trousers pockets. Tears came to his eyes. "I must be getting along home. I can talk no more with you," he said nervously. 14

Without looking back, the old man had hurried down the hillside and across a meadow, leaving George Willard perplexed and frightened upon the grassy slope. With a shiver of dread the boy arose and went along the road toward town. "I'll not ask him about his hands," he 15 thought, touched by the memory of the terror he had seen in the man's eyes. "There's something wrong, but I don't want to know what it is. His hands have something to do with his fear of me and of everyone."

And George Willard was right. Let us look briefly into the story of 16 the hands. Perhaps our talking of them will arouse the poet who will tell the hidden wonder story of the influence for which the hands were but fluttering pennants of promise.

In his youth Wing Biddlebaum had been a school teacher in a town 17 in Pennsylvania. He was not then known as Wing Biddlebaum, but went by the less euphonic name of Adolph Myers. As Adolph Myers he was much loved by the boys of his school.

Adolph Myers was meant by nature to be a teacher of youth. He 18 was one of those rare, little-understood men who rule by a power so gentle that it passes as a lovable weakness. In their feeling for the boys under their charge such men are not unlike the finer sort of women in their love of men.

And yet that is but crudely stated. It needs the poet there. With the 19 boys of his school, Adolph Myers had walked in the evening or had sat talking until dusk upon the schoolhouse steps lost in a kind of dream. Here and there went his hands, caressing the shoulders of the boys, playing about the tousled heads. As he talked his voice became soft and musical. There was a caress in that also. In a way the voice and the hands, the stroking of the shoulders and the touching of the hair were a part of the schoolmaster's effort to carry a dream into the young minds. By the caress that was in his fingers he expressed himself. He was one of those men in whom the force that creates life is diffused, not centralized. Under the caress of his hands doubt and disbelief went out of the minds of the boys and they began also to dream.

And then the tragedy. A half-witted boy of the school became enam- 20 ored of the young master. In his bed at night he imagined unspeakable things and in the morning went forth to tell his dreams as facts. Strange, hideous accusations fell from his loose-hung lips. Through the Pennsylvania town went a shiver. Hidden, shadowy doubts that had been in men's minds concerning Adolph Myers were galvanized into beliefs.

The tragedy did not linger. Trembling lads were jerked out of bed 21 and questioned. "He put his arms about me," said one. "His fingers were always playing in my hair," said another.

One afternoon a man of the town, Henry Bradford, who kept a sa- 22 loon, came to the schoolhouse door. Calling Adolph Myers into the school yard he began to beat him with his fists. As his hard knuckles beat down into the frightened face of the schoolmaster, his wrath became more and more terrible. Screaming with dismay, the children ran here and there like disturbed insects. "I'll teach you to put your hands on my boy, you beast," roared the saloon keeper, who, tired of beating the master, had begun to kick him about the yard.

Adolph Myers was driven from the Pennsylvania town in the night. 23 With lanterns in their hands a dozen men came to the door of the house where he lived alone and commanded that he dress and come forth. It was raining and one of the men had a rope in his hands. They had intended to hang the schoolmaster, but something in his figure, so small, white, and pitiful, touched their hearts and they let him escape. As he ran away into the darkness they repented of their weakness and ran after him, swearing and throwing sticks and great balls of soft mud at the figure that screamed and ran faster and faster into the darkness.

For twenty years Adolph Myers had lived alone in Winesburg. He 24 was but forty but looked sixty-five. The name of Biddlebaum he got from a box of goods seen at a freight station as he hurried through an eastern Ohio town. He had an aunt in Winesburg, a black-toothed old woman who raised chickens, and with her he lived until she died. He had been ill for a year after the experience in Pennsylvania, and after his recovery worked as a day laborer in the fields, going timidly about and striving to conceal his hands. Although he did not understand what had happened he felt that the hands must be to blame. Again and again the fathers of the boys had talked of the hands. "Keep your hands to yourself," the saloon keeper had roared, dancing with fury in the schoolhouse yard.

Upon the veranda of his house by the ravine, Wing Biddlebaum 25 continued to walk up and down until the sun had disappeared and the road beyond the field was lost in the grey shadows. Going into his house he cut slices of bread and spread honey upon them. When the rumble of the evening train that took away the express cars loaded with the day's harvest of berries had passed and restored the silence of the summer night, he went again to walk upon the veranda. In the darkness he could not see the hands and they became quiet. Although he still hungered for the presence of the boy, who was the medium through which he expressed his love of man, the hunger became again a part of his loneliness and his waiting. Lighting a lamp, Wing Biddlebaum washed the few dishes soiled by his simple meal and, setting up a folding cot by the screen door that led to the porch, prepared to undress for the night. A few stray white bread crumbs lay on the cleanly washed floor by the table; putting the lamp upon a low stool he began to pick up the crumbs, carrying them to his mouth one by one with unbelievable rapidity. In the dense blotch of light beneath the table, the kneeling figure looked like a priest engaged in some service of his church. The nervous expressive fingers, flashing in and out of the light, might well have been mistaken for the fingers of the devotee going swiftly through decade after decade of his rosary.

13

The Writing Process: An Overview

English has always been a difficult subject, in that words get lost between the mind and the hand.

student

Books always amaze me, due to the fact that so many people can express themselves in writing without much difficulty.

student

The fun is not in writing; the fun is in HAVING WRITTEN.

Gene Olson

Writing is easy. All you do is stare at a blank sheet of paper until drops of blood form on your forehead.

Gene Fowler

I now write my first drafts like an optimist, assuming that people are interested in anything I have to say. I revise like a pessimist who figures that none of my ideas will get through.

student

Now when I know I have to write, I don't feel the task is against me, but on my side.

student

Reflections on the Writing Process

In this chapter, I'd like to give you some general advice about writing strategies gleaned from what I've learned from students, colleagues, and professionals. Much of this advice you will have found elsewhere in the book, but all of it is here, too, in this single chapter to which you can return as often as you wish. You may want to read it early in your course

256

to get your bearings, but if you read it again later in the course, it will mean more to you since you can then compare it with your own experience writing.

Exercise 13-1
Review of Your Writing Habits

Your attention will be sharpened if, before we begin, you write out answers to these two questions:

1. What do you hate most about writing?
2. What are the main differences you imagine between a professional writer and yourself?

I don't know anyone who thinks he or she has found the most efficient way to write. In fact, most of us are a little embarrassed about the way we go about it, procrastinating often and being irrationally attached to a special pen, or a yellow legal pad, or Oreo cookies to fuel the fire, or an oversized table in the basement. We also have never told ourselves, much less our teachers or our classmates, the details of our alternating despairs and satisfactions as we work on a paper.

Your Writing Process

Exercise 13-2

The most effective way to get over a vague fear of writing is to admit it and to spell out exactly what its sources are. Think of something you've written that you're proud of—a report from high school, a paper from this course, a difficult letter, something you've written on the job. Think about *how* you went about writing. What did you do while preparing for and writing it? What problems did you have? Record both the *physical* and the *emotional* steps you went through from the time you first thought about writing to the time you gave your work to someone. If you've never written anything you're proud of, make a record of how you went about writing some piece that you hated doing. In class, read the descriptions of several of your classmates. What do you all have in common? What new ideas have you picked up?

Your writing process may seem annoyingly complex to you, but that process will seem miraculously simple if you compare it with the filming process that any film director is faced with. Here is Satyajit Ray, the most prominent Indian filmmaker, explaining the process of creating just one short scene for *Pather Panchali* (Geduld 269–70):

> To me it is the inexorable rhythm of its creative process that makes film-making so exciting in spite of the hardships and the frustrations. Consider this process: you have conceived a scene, any scene. Take the one where a young girl, frail of body but full of some elemental zest, gives herself up to the first monsoon shower. She dances in joy while the big drops pelt her and drench her. The scene excites you not only for its visual possibilities but for its deeper implications as well: that rain will be the cause of her death.
>
> You break down the scene into shots, make notes and sketches. Then the time comes to bring the scene to life. You go out into the open, scan the vista, choose your setting. The rain clouds approach. You set up your camera, have a last quick rehearsal. Then the "take." But one is not enough. This is a key scene. You must have another while the shower lasts. The camera turns, and presently your scene is on celluloid.
>
> Off to the lab. You wait, sweating—this is September—while the ghostly negative takes its own time to emerge. There is no hurrying this process. Then the print, the "rushes." This looks good, you say to yourself. But wait. This is only the content, in its bits and pieces, and not the form. How is it going to join up? You grab your editor and rush off to the cutting room. There is a grueling couple of hours, filled with aching suspense, while the patient process of cutting and joining goes on. At the end you watch the thing on the moviola. Even the rickety old machine cannot conceal the effectiveness of the scene. Does this need music, or is the incidental sound enough? But that is another stage in the creative process, and must wait until all the shots have been joined up into scenes and all the scenes into sequences and the film can be comprehended in its totality. Then, and only then, can you tell—if you can bring to bear on it that detachment and objectivity—if your dance in the rain has really come off.

Most beginning writers want to skip this patient "editing" stage that is so important to the success of a film. They feel that "planning" and "shooting" a paper is the most they should be expected to do.

Another art closely related to writing is sculpture—listen to these descriptions of the French sculptor Auguste Rodin at work (Descharnes and Chabrun 236, 238):

> Nothing in Rodin's surroundings resembles the society studios of fashionable sculptors; no knick-knacks, no art objects calculatingly displayed for sale. Everything here reminds one of the craftsman, wearing wooden shoes, with dust and smears of clay on his garments.
>
> Rodin always carried some clay and something to draw with in his pocket and never seemed to spend more than five minutes, even

while talking or eating, without either sketching or modeling some shape with his busy fingers.

Rodin appeared to work slowly. When in 1898 he had to part with his *Balzac* to meet the Salon's deadline (he had put off the delivery of the statue as long as he could) he felt he was being hurried and was greatly upset. "They're snatching the work out of my hands," he grumbled, as the statue was removed from the Dépôt des marbres. "When will those idiotic officials understand that in order to turn out something good, one must have time to forget it?"

A careful writer gets her hands just as dirty as Rodin did, is just as alert to new ideas for her work, and is just as aware that the paper finally turned in could still use a little work.

Stages of the Writing Process

The writing process is never as neat and orderly as a cookbook process, but it can be usefully described in terms of stages. Every writing specialist will give you a different version of these stages. Their versions are more or less specific (four are shown below), and their categories overlap, but you'll find many different versions useful.

Richard Gebhardt (21)

1. Generating and focusing
2. Drafting
3. Revising

Michael Adelstein (120)

1. Worrying (15 percent)
2. Planning (10 percent)
3. Writing (25 percent)
4. Revising (45 percent)
5. Proofreading (5 percent)

Kenneth Dowst (4.2, 4.14)

1. Invention writing
2. Revision writing

Sharon Pianko (275–78)

1. Prewriting

2. Planning
3. Composing
4. Writing
5. Pausing
6. Rescanning
7. Rereading
8. Stopping
9. Contemplating the finished product
10. Handing in the finished product

This variety should remind us that even in this chapter, we should be looking not for a single writing strategy but, rather, for "workable strategies." Every writing assignment and every writing situation is slightly different; no advice about the writing process can give us ironclad, step-by-step instructions. All we can say of even the best advice is that it is *often* fruitful.

Collecting and Selecting

Everyone seems to agree that a person can't just start writing: writing requires preparation. But what that preparation should be is a matter of some dispute. Many student writers have been scared or misled by the rhetorical term for prewriting: *invention*. How am I to "invent" a whole five-page paper out of nothing? But *invention* (from the Latin verb *invenire*) means "to find, to discover." Our task is more manageable if we realize that we only have to *find* things. We are all capable of doing that. Or are we? If we have to find *ideas*, that's still a mystical task.

In many traditional writing courses, you practiced that mysticism, finding a topic (finding a topic meant finding the right-sized topic) and then choosing a pattern of organization to "develop" that topic. But this mysticism is quite unnecessary. Prewriting should begin not with topic analysis but with information. It then continues with interpretation of the information we want to pass on. Once we "find" the information, our creativity, our "invention," comes into play as we draw inferences from the information we have.

Once you've been given a problem or area to research, then, "invention" begins with observation, with a search for telling details. Writing is not worth reading if its subject has not been carefully observed. Why should any of us, even if we are teachers, go to the trouble of reading a piece by a writer who doesn't know his or her subject? The search for details, depending on the assignment, may begin with a careful look at a place, with research in a laboratory, with an interview, with the underlining of passages in books, or with note taking in a library. No matter where this fact collecting takes place, though, the writer will have along the tools of our trade—a pen (or pencil) and plenty of paper—to note whatever facts (details, statistics, quotations) seem pertinent. When drafting time comes, a fact on solid paper is worth ten in the writer's leaky memory. While collecting facts, a writer should also note down *any* ideas about those facts which come to mind. Ideas are even more slippery than facts we observe—they fly out of the head as fast as they fly in—so they must be noted down. (Most people need to practice this crucial step, for it isn't often natural—we're not used to listening to ourselves think.) If we later decide that an idea is harebrained or exaggerated, we can always discard or qualify it. Once we have maybe twenty-five telling details and maybe six or seven good ideas, we have the foundation for a three- to four-page paper, and we can consider beginning to write.

Such note taking requires starting early—no one can write an information-rich paper the night before it's due. As often as possible, you should start your work early enough so that you can bring your notes—not yet in the form of a first draft—to class and have them discussed for their value. Which of your notes would the teacher and other students like to see in a paper? Which would elicit the praise in a final paper "fascinating information" or "well thought through"? If you bring no raw material that's provoking to this session, no amount of coherence will glue a decent paper together by the due date.

Once you've taken some notes, you may want to try some timed writing like that you practiced in Chapter 4 to see what direction your writing might take. Setting a timer forces you to get a page or two or three written, and you may well discover in this kind of writing new aspects of your subject that you'd like to explore. Writing with a timer often allows us to see what we really want to say about a subject—and not just what we think we should say. Writing quickly but honestly temporarily frees our conscious minds from social restraints which cause us to fall into patterns rather than make a mark for ourselves. Later on, we may not be satisfied with what we've drafted, but we now have some raw material that we can work with.

Another alternative technique that can help us get our information and ideas on paper is called *clustering*. Clustering is a bit like outlining in that it is a record of what we might say, but it is not nearly as rigid as an outline and doesn't commit us to the order in which we will present our ideas. To begin a cluster, just write the only idea you have (if you have only one) on a sheet of paper and then circle it. The author of the reader analysis of *Everywoman Magazine* (1944) on page 284, for example, may have started a cluster, after reading once through the magazine, as follows:

Then he might proceed with his cluster, one circle at a time, until it looked like this:

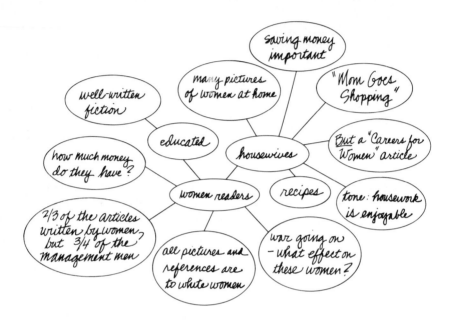

Such a cluster gives you plenty to work with when you start writing.

After collecting facts and inferences, doing some timed writing (if you wish), and building up a cluster (if you wish), you can look over the chaos of facts and ideas on the page and consider your first step well done. We can't begin unless we have some chaos to work with, as we're reminded by Mary Shelley, the author of *Frankenstein*: "Invention, it must be humbly admitted, does not consist in creating out of a void, but out of chaos" (7). To live with this chaos for a while severely tests the patience of most writers: "The mind doesn't like chaos; ordering is its natural activity." But "the aim of composing is not to tolerate chaos for its own sake but to learn to put up with it while you discover ways of emerging" (Berthoff 65).

The writer should now find, among the chaos of facts and ideas, the kernels she likes, and she should then ask some questions. For any isolated facts in the paper, she ought to anticipate a reader's asking "So what?" For any ideas or generalizations, she ought to anticipate a reader's asking "For instance?" Short written answers to these questions should (when combined with the original notes) start giving shape and density to the paper.

Incubation (Waiting)

Fortunately, not all our writing decisions need to be conscious. After doing some spadework for an essay, we can go play ball, do housework, or just go to sleep without feeling guilty, because we are allowing our subconscious mind to take its turn while the conscious mind goes fishing. Both our conscious and our subconscious minds have plenty to contribute. A paper written by choosing a thesis, writing an outline, and filling out the paragraphs is completed entirely by the conscious mind—the paper may be good, and time limits may occasionally make this way of writing necessary, but it is not the best we can do.

Donald Murray, a Pulitzer-prize-winning writer, has shown how we can put our intuitive strengths to work when we write. When we begin to see a shaping idea for a paper, we should pull away from it for a while, partly to see how new evidence that we come across fits with that idea, but partly just to await the ordering process of our mind, as it sifts and resifts the data we've collected in the light of this new "idea." We don't immediately make judgments about the idea—we test it, half consciously, half unconsciously.

The temptation, of course, is to let this part of the process go on indefinitely: "Writing which can be delayed, will be" (Murray, "Write" 375). Research is more fun than sharing research. It's a great pleasure to have our heads full of ideas, but it doesn't do anyone any good but ourselves. Murray suggests that at this point only force—a waiting audience or an approaching deadline—can make a writer write, can pull the writer out of this very satisfying state. I do think *ego* will also do it; fortunately for us as writers, our egos want credit for the ideas we have. Of all the kinds of force, though, deadlines are the most effective. Don't curse them. They are there to bring out the best in you. Satisfaction doesn't come until late in the writing process—though the pleasures of research come early. Without a deadline, most writers would prefer to bask in the early pleasure of learning. But when we allow ourselves to do so, we deny ourselves the opportunities for the genuine satisfaction that comes from presenting what we've found to others.

Ordering

Let's assume now that we're faced with a writer's dream—we have plenty of notes, and we've stopped for a day or two to think about them. What are we going to do with the information now that we have it? How are we going to organize it? The next steps we take are going to commit us in ways that are difficult to retrace, so it may be time to make sure of our own commitment. I find it useful to make, at this point, a statement of commitment:

I plan to [aim] for [readers] by [methods].

This statement sets our tone, our pace, our level of difficulty, and the question of whether we want to inform, judge, or persuade. It should help us see whether and what kind of further research is necessary. But if we have completed the necessary research, we can now simply sort through the information we've collected and see what inferences (assertions, claims) we want to make and can justify. A simple diagram based on those inferences, perhaps as they appeared in our cluster, can then serve as a provisional outline, which is all we want at this stage. The outlines we form now should only be rough sketches—outlines will play a larger part later in the writing process when we check our draft to see whether we've been systematic and whether we've kept our sense of proportion.

The structure we create in this way should not be considered a complete map of our finished paper. Much will be added during the actual writing. But if the structure seems only half or less than half complete, a writer might refer to some list of common organizing principles, or ways of filling out the plan:

1. Do I have enough information to justify each assertion?
2. Have I drawn as many inferences as I can safely draw from my information? Are my inferences bold enough? thoughtful enough?
3. Are there any contrasts that might highlight my subject?
4. Would some analogy make any of my points clearer to my intended readers?
5. Would my readers appreciate a historical context?
6. Do any of my key terms need defining?
7. Have I answered the readers' questions—Who? What? When? Where? (these four are important, but rapidly answered) and, more important, Why? and How?

Thus, the invention process continues, and it is perhaps more imaginative at this point than it is in the beginning of our work on a paper. By considering (and often rejecting) these options, we not only may stumble onto an organizing principle which solves all our problems; we also may discover what we don't yet know about our subject.

Planning at this point increases efficiency. An utterly unplanned draft may take so long to sort out that its value as "something on paper" is more than offset by the revision time it requires. A plan that we can refer to while drafting reduces the load on our memories, leaving our minds free to deal with each sentence as it comes.

Drafting

With rare exceptions, all of us would rather do anything than begin to write: no matter how many times a person has written and succeeded before, each time he starts, he faces a fear that nothing of quality will come out this time. In the face of this fear, our best ally is determination: we must make ourselves do what we have to do, when it ought to be done, whether we like it or not. But when we have done all the gathering and planning mentioned in the previous few pages, summoning the determination to begin is much less traumatic. We face no blank page. We have more than enough notes to complete our assignment. Three other things can help. First, we must realize that there is *no* rule in writing that can't be broken. Our materials, our purpose, our intended readers may require a strategy that we've never heard of. It can't hurt to try. We can always revise later. Second, as we write out our first draft, we must not even think about trying to make it perfect—"decent" is all we want; "playful," perhaps, but "decent" will do. We shouldn't allow ourselves to be slowed down by an attempt to find the "perfect" word or by a worry over a matter of grammar or spelling. Third, we need a deadline—if the teacher hasn't given us one, then we must impose one ourselves. Unless we're in the position of having readers waiting for our results, we won't very often start without a deadline. Flexible deadlines are, I would guess, the greatest cause of writer's block on our college campuses.

The other cause of writer's block is a fear that "style"—indeterminate, indefinable "style"—is what makes or breaks a paper. It's very difficult to write when we don't understand the grounds by which we might be judged. If we feel secure, though, that the quality of a piece of writing depends primarily on the quality of the facts we have selected and the quality of the inferences we have drawn from those facts, then much of the quality of a paper is established before the first draft begins to appear on the page—the first draft has thus shrunk to its proper dimensions.

Once writer's block has been shuttled aside, drafting becomes one of the easiest steps in the writing process. We should allow ourselves *some* revision during this stage. One good sentence often produces better sentences after it. One good paragraph often produces better paragraphs following. But it is important to remember that this is "only" a draft, so it's most important that we take some risks and try to convey to our readers the clear voice of a writer enjoying writing (revision is always waiting, prudently, to rescue us). We must be willing, too, to write much more than we will eventually need (thus allowing the reviser in us to choose later the better from the worse). As we write, we must keep in mind not only our subject but the questions our readers will have for us about our subject. The difficulties we can expect while drafting are that we'll have to start earlier than we want to, that our hands and fingers will get tired, that our ideas will tend to come faster than we can express them, and, worst of all, that we'll get discouraged because we'll lose faith that our work is original or that anyone will want to read it. All four difficulties are normal: but when we expect them, they don't hurt so much.

We should think seriously about completing this drafting step at a word processor, if at all possible. Some writers disagree with me here. Paul Theroux, author of *The Great Railway Bazaar,* argues that writing by hand is slower and thus allows more time for thought and for surprise. Many writers say they can think better with pen and paper than they can at the typewriter. But those same writers have adjusted very quickly to writing at a word processor. Professional writers have moved on to word processors; the rest of us should join them as soon as we can. The advantages of working at a word processor (or even a typewriter) are numerous, unless a person really can't "think" at either of those machines, in which case she'd best stay with pen and paper. A typed or processed draft is much easier to read objectively, much easier to make changes on while still remaining readable. When we write by hand and use the typewriter only as a "finishing machine" for producing a final draft, we become very reluctant to make any changes in that draft, which is a shame, since that typewritten draft gives us our first opportunity to really read our work carefully. Starting on a word processor will save you much time now, and it will allow you to develop better writing habits (primarily the willingness to revise) for your use in your future professions.

The most important thing to note about a draft, though, is not whether it's typed or written but whether the mind is engaged while it's coming into being. Donald Murray says that "the most accurate definition of writing, I believe, is that it is the process of using language to discover meaning in experience and to communicate it ("Internal Revision" 86). Thus he calls the first draft a "discovery draft," a very useful term. The writer has a plan before beginning that "discovery draft," but she is open to new ideas as she executes it, and she is disappointed if she hasn't "discovered" something as she's worked her way through it. We need room to breathe while writing. We begin with a sense of direction, yes, but we rarely know our final intention before we have finished the paper. If a writer doesn't learn much in writing a paper, the reader isn't likely to learn much from reading it either.

Revising (Making the Work Readable)

> When I say writing, O believe me, it is rewriting I have chiefly in mind. (Robert Louis Stevenson)

Revising begins almost as soon as a paper is first conceived, with the writer's first shift in ideas about what to include in or how to organize the paper. It continues with changes in the writer's first written sentence and with pauses for reflection and rereading as the draft is taking shape. But concentrated revising, beginning *after* a first draft, is the point at which a work either comes to life or falls dead. All the preceding steps of writing are relatively easy; the hard work begins here. The British writers Robert Graves and Alan Hodge tell us that "there should be two main objects in ordinary prose writing: to convey a message, and to include in it nothing that will distract the reader's attention or check his habitual pace of reading" (154). Collecting, selecting, waiting, and drafting focus on coming up with a message; revising focuses on getting that message, as clearly as possible, to the reader. Only when we have gathered and written out something both thoughtful and informative are we willing to go through this final process, which demands (admittedly) that we become a little fanatic about perfection. It may seem that as writers we spend a very long time to gain a very small end, but we might compare our efforts with those of filmmakers. How many thousands of hours do they spend to give us just two hours of entertainment?

Most people equate revising with cleansing, with seeing to it that what is written conforms to the conventions and rules, so that the written piece can be received and judged by the reader without the distraction of faulty punctuation, poor spelling, or other errors. Such cleansing is important, but revising is a much broader process. Seldom do we write down exactly what we meant to say. Only when we read through our papers can we judge whether our points have come out the way we thought they did. Once we've adjusted our draft so that it says what we meant to say, we must check also to see whether there are any points on which we've changed our minds since we started writing. And finally, once we are reasonably sure of what we mean, revising also entails reading to see whether we've made our meaning clear to others.

To revise successfully, a writer must first break away (we writers love breaks). A day is good, and an hour is essential, for the writer needs time to take off his writer's cap and put on his reader's cap. A writer's assumptions and background are necessarily different from those of any reader, and the writer must therefore try to read from that alien perspective. Much of revising lies in the writer's ability to read his writing as though he were an interested but uninformed reader. His job is much easier if he can get an honestly critical friend to read his paper. The foremost question that this reader should be asking is a question suggested by Aristotle: *Have I learned easily?* If not, why not? The comments of readers like this are often very helpful. But even if they aren't directly helpful, they may indirectly trigger new ideas for the writer. We all become fond of our own words and ideas (much as parents become fond of their own children, because they have gone to so much trouble to bring them up). But our ideas, like our children, still need to be disciplined into shape. Outsiders don't share our uncritical fondness, and they can help us sort out the best in our writing from the unnecessary.

If no reader is available, the writer should at least read her own work aloud until she is satisfied with the way it sounds. In ancient Greece, "all literature was written to be heard, and even when reading to himself a Greek read aloud" (Kennedy 4). Therefore, Aristotle took it for granted that "a composition should be easy to read or—which is the same thing—easy to deliver" (195). We, in the twentieth century, seem to have forgotten that words are written to be heard. But if, when we read our work aloud, we find ourselves halting or embarrassed, we should consider that embarrassment an invitation to revise:

1. We may see several places where we have hinted at, rather than specified, our meaning.
2. We may find that we need more details.
3. We may see that a briefer introduction or conclusion would better use our reader's time.
4. We may think of an introduction or conclusion which would make our intentions clearer.
5. We may see that our main point—the something that we wanted to achieve when we began—isn't clear (we may want to add an explicit thesis).
6. We may see that our coverage of issues isn't balanced and that some important matter needs more explanation.
7. We may find that a paragraph is too long and needs to be split or that several are too short and might well be combined.
8. We may find sentences that are clumsy or ungrammatical.
9. We often find that some of our sentences are not linked together well.
10. We may find that we've written lies or half-lies which we have to correct.
11. We may find clutter that distracts the reader from our message.
12. We may find that we've put our most important points in places where they'll receive little emphasis.
13. We may want to rewrite sentences to achieve a better sound or rhythm.
14. We ought to write a paragraph-by-paragraph outline to see whether the draft makes sense, and perhaps we need to add some direction-indicating sentences that will make reading easier.
15. Most important, we ought to check to make sure that a real author comes through clearly to the reader.

In short, we "must read with an eye to *alternatives* in content, form, structure, voice, and language" (Murray, "Internal Revision" 95). When we're finished, we should have few qualms about handing this piece to a reader.

Publishing

Only now are we ready to check spelling, punctuation, grammar, and neatness. We can forget, finally, what we've said; we can make sure (with a dictionary) that the words we're not sure of are spelled right, check (using the rules in Chapter 9) our punctuation, and look over the whole paper to make sure it looks clean. We don't want to leave in our work any unnecessary distractions from what we're trying to say.

Overview

We don't always spend all the time suggested here and go through all these stages as we write papers for school or reports outside school. As our writing intuitions develop, many of these steps will take place more quickly. But even with highly developed intuitions, writing is never easy, and it requires several blocks of uninterrupted time to be completed.

John Muir has said that the great thrill of exploring is that "we find more than we seek." That's the same thrill of the writing process, and that's what so often leaves us satisfied after so much work.

14

Suggested Assignments

One thing which could be done would be to make all the papers the students have to write interesting. Make the subject something students would be interested in writing about.

student

I always thought a description was very short.

student

The proposal paper brought a lot of emotion out in me. It enabled me to convince not only the reader but myself of what I wanted to propose.

student

The Assignments

This chapter offers several sample writing assignments:

1. Description of a Curious Place
2. Reader Analysis of a Magazine
3. Reader Analysis of Two Newspapers
4. Character Sketch
5. Study of a Historical Issue
6. Proposal
7. Persuading a Classmate
8. Film Evaluation
9. Literary Interpretation

The assignments suggested in this chapter are just a sample of the many kinds of assignments that would allow you to practice the many writing skills you have been developing in this class. These assignments should be clearly distinguished from the exercises in earlier chapters. Those exercises enable you to practice a skill or two (or even several). But these assignments place you as nearly as possible into a professional writing situation—that is, they demand that you collect and present information that will be helpful to your readers (teacher and classmates) or that will move them to action. Each assignment here directs you to a distinctive kind of material. Then you have the freedom, and the responsibility, to select, to organize, and to interpret that raw material. (The paper length called for in each case should be a clue to how much detail is expected.) Each assignment should stretch you, should ask you to do more than you initially think possible. Each will show you a new source of information so that you don't have to keep relying on yourself (a source too seldom replenished). Every time you write, then, you should be learning something new, acquiring a new perspective, a new understanding. Every paper you write should, in turn, serve to increase your readers' experience, and perhaps also their understanding.

The Sample Papers and Draft Review Worksheets

Each assignment in this chapter is followed by two sample student papers that I think are good responses to the assignment. No paper is ever "perfect," but these papers should give you some idea of what you are aiming for. Following these two samples for all but the final assignment are two more items—a Draft Review Worksheet and a third student sample, this time a seriously flawed one—that will be more valuable to you, I think, than the first two "good" papers.

I recommend that as you begin any of these assignments, you review each of these papers, particularly the flawed sample, using the accompanying draft review worksheet. Reviewing will be easier if you make notes to yourself on the papers as you read. And be sure to add your own questions to the worksheets if they don't ask the questions you think are most important.

After you practice on each of these papers, you'll be well prepared to spend a class day, before each paper is due, trading your draft with those of classmates, and making constructive suggestions based on the questions on the worksheets. On an assigned day, you bring your draft to class and exchange drafts with a classmate. Using a worksheet, read through the paper and make comments which will help the writer improve. If time permits, you can repeat this process with two or three papers, and your own paper will get two or three readings itself. You'll probably get several ideas for your own paper just by reading the papers of others, and you'll also be able to take home two or three pages of comments which you can consider as you revise. Using the suggestions of your reviewers and the experience you gain reviewing the papers of others, you should be able to make substantial improvements in your final drafts.

Assignment 1: Description of a Curious Place

Method of Research: Observation and Note Taking
Most Pertinent Chapters: 2, 13
Selected Details Due:
Clean Draft Due for Workshop:
Paper Due:

In this first assignment, your task is to bring a place alive on paper. Don't just describe the place for yourself. Think of your readers—your teacher and your classmates—as you write, and try to make them curious enough to want to see the place themselves. Show, in your description of the place, that you understand its social significance. Are the people who use the place rich, poor, or in between? What kinds of clothes do they wear? What does this place show about the way people treat others? Choose a place that people frequent, and include some characterization of those people in your description.

Past students have written about laundromats and auction houses, farmers' markets and decaying neighborhoods, museums and hospital emergency rooms, restaurants and department stores, junkyards and city centers, courtrooms and locker rooms. No matter how well you think you know the place you choose, *visit* it before the date your selected details are due, and plan to stay awhile (at least an hour). During this visit you'll do your research. Consider yourself a sound camera, and record the atmosphere and character of the place. If you have trouble noticing details, look for details that are contrary to your values or expectations, or think about similar places you know and look for the details that are different. If you are describing a fast-food restaurant, for example, and its rest rooms are labeled "gunslingers" and "señoritas," you have your first telling fact.

If time permits, it would be helpful to bring a list of details to class on a date assigned, and collect opinions on them from your classmates: Are they telling or unrevealing? After that class, select your best details, write a draft of your paper, and read the paper through to see if there are sections where you need more information. Then visit your place at least once more. You'll be much more receptive during the second visit, because you'll have a better idea about the direction that your paper is likely to take.

Your paper must be at least three typewritten pages. It will include a variety of details, but it should convey some distinctive character (e.g., nearly everything about Beltway Plaza is cheap). Use as many telling details as you can. Use your introduction to make your readers take notice. Provide historical and material background if you can.

When you're finished writing, before the final typing, have a friend or two read your paper for you. Ask them which parts they like best. See whether you've been able to catch their interest, and whether there is anything they don't understand. Ask them if there are any parts that seem boring or too obvious. And ask them if they can identify the distinctive character you intended to convey—if they can't, you'll want to go back to your draft for a while before you do your final typing.

At the end of your paper, list three facts that you collected but that you decided, in the end, not to use in the paper. Note why your paper is better off without them.

Sample Papers

A Culinary Illusion
Kristen Tokarek

Jardine's Farm Restaurant is located in the cozy village of Sarver, 1
Pennsylvania. The charm of this establishment is its hideaway location
in the rolling hills of farm country. People from all areas of Pittsburgh
travel many miles to visit Jardine's because it gives them a chance to escape the pressures of city life. As such customers sit down to enjoy a
leisurely repast of home cooked delicacies, they may envision Aunt Bea
of Mayberry types bustling about in a Grandma Moses style kitchen as
they prepare succulent down home treats. But these same customers
would be amazed to find, instead, a cadre of efficient restaurant personnel that would make Henry Ford's assembly line look primitive.

Like parts on an assembly line, all appliances in the kitchen are 2
made of durable, shiny silver metal. The floor is cream colored linoleum
with an array of brown, black, and white speckles. Cleverly camouflaged
on the floor lie spatters of greasy barbeque sauce. Located in the center
of the floor area is the expediter, called simply the expo-man, who begins the complicated process of preparing a "simple, home cooked
meal." His job is to inform the cooks and fryers of the items needed for
the customers' orders. Unlike the colorful, frilly aprons of yesteryear,
these kitchen employees wear austere white uniforms reminiscent of
garb worn by attendants in *One Flew Over the Cuckoo's Nest*. On a silver
counter convenient to the employees is a chafing bin filled with corn
that is coated with a delicious butter substitute called "Whirl." Nearby
are one-gallon institution-sized vats of mayonnaise and sour cream that
did not come from the old wooden ice box but rather from an eight-
wheeled semi with "Sexton Foods" emblazoned on its side.

Incongruously sharing the parking lot with the mammoth vehicle 3
is the hayride wagon and the trappings of a quilt show. The intricate
blankets are admired mostly by elderly women who compliment the
quilt makers on their skill. Several purchases are made by the adults
while a bored, whining child insists that he is starving to death.

Mechanically preparing food to assuage the barbaric hunger of 4
Atilla the Tot are three employees in the kitchen in orderly formation
behind a stark, stainless steel counter. The first is the fryer who begins
by filling the frying machine with five gallons of cold lard. The lard is
then heated until it is bubbly and spitting grease on the surrounding
metallic countertop. The other two employees are high school boys who
can prepare anything from barbequed ribs to succulent lobster tails.
Near these refugees from football training camp are two immense ovens
with a scuffed gray finish and rectangular viewing windows instead of a
friendly, black cast iron oven from a turn of the century farm kitchen.

And replacing mother's elbow grease is a tall can of generic oven cleaner which sits atop the massive gray ovens. In lieu of the old farm smoke house is a gleaming white commercial-size Kenmore refrigerator stocked full of meat and fish from all parts of the world. And Jardine's desserts are not made by little elves in a hollow tree. Instead, a refrigerated case holds commercially made coconut cream pies, cheesecakes, chocolate cakes, and, best of all, "home-made" apple pies. The industrial-looking freezer contains three-gallon jugs of chemically synthesized chocolate and vanilla ice cream, ice cream pies, and pecan balls, all magically created in a food laboratory setting instead of in an ice cream churn on the back porch.

The only function that an ice cream churn serves in the restaurant 5 is as a decorative item along with other antiques that lend a country atmosphere to the dining room. Family diners absorb the ambience of the setting, chatting comfortably with each other. At one of the large, highly polished oaken tables, a lady diner gently scolds her young, crying son that there will be no hayride for him if he doesn't behave and clean his plate.

Clean plates are hardly a problem at Jardine's. The final area of the 6 kitchen is the dishwashing apparatus. One employee, the scraper, removes all food from the dinner platters before they enter the huge machine. His system is quick and efficient; he grabs the dish in his left hand and makes a clean swipe across the plate with his bare right hand sending the waste flying into a large black garbage can. The can is filled with a colorful array of soupy sauces, chicken bones, baked potato skins, and unidentifiable remnants of country cooking. The dishes are loaded into tawny tote boxes and put on a conveyor belt that pulls them noisily into the monstrous machine. After the dishes undergo a cycle of washing, rinsing, and steaming, another employee separates the forks from the knives and spoons and places them in round plastic holders to air dry. He also groups like dishes in tall stacks so that they, too, can air dry. Clean dishes are then replaced in their proper area where they will be ready for quick use by other workers. At the end of the evening when all customers have gone, all of the kitchen workers clean and disinfect their working areas. Only when the floors are swept and mopped and the countertops sanitized do the employees rush to punch out their time cards and go home. And to think that Aunt Bea had only Opie and Andy in the kitchen to help her clean up!

Perhaps it is cruel to spoil the illusion held by hard-working city 7 folk living in the fast lane who yearn for the slower paced life style and down home cooking of days past. Why not let them believe that Aunt Bea is indeed alive and well and living in Jardine's kitchen in the little country village of Sarver, Pennsylvania?

Benson Animal Hospital
Rani Garrison

The sweltering mid-day summer sun dominates the day's activities: 1 people hurrying to and from their lunch breaks, children recklessly racing down the sidewalks on their bicycles and skateboards towards the neighborhood's video arcade, construction workers drowning out the usual business-day street noises with the constant piercing and throttling sounds of jackhammers as they tear up the road. Yet, in the midst of this daily chaos, a secluded world is confined within the walls of Benson Animal Hospital. The building has been situated in the heart of Bethesda, Maryland for almost three decades. From the street, it is a plain, one-story corner building, the brick recently painted a mustard-yellow. Usually, there is hardly as much as a single cigarette butt on the surrounding sidewalk.

Upon entering the hospital early in the morning, after the floors 2 have been freshly mopped, one cannot help but notice the potency of ammonia lingering in the air. This is the only time of day that the floors actually shine. Tile floors are used instead of carpeting for easier cleaning and less animal odor. Another advantage of having tile floors is that once an animal sees a doctor and decides to make a quick exit, the hard, smooth floor and a firm grip on the leash keeps him running in place. By early afternoon miniature tumbleweeds of hair begin to drift around on the floor, and eventually settle in the corner.

After a client and patient are checked-in at the front desk and their 3 record is pulled from the file cabinets, they wait, seated on long cushioned benches. Above and behind these benches are glass windows, eight feet tall. These windows occupy most of the area provided for two walls. Two sets of bent venetian blinds hang in front of the windows. The only portion of the blinds that isn't damaged is the part that is out of reach. The clients often lean against the windows, sandwiching the blinds between the glass and their backs. Most of the damage is caused by the patients, but sometimes excited puppies romp around the benches and crash into the blinds too.

One of the two remaining walls is paneled with thick boards of oak. 4 In that wall is a split-level door, like those in horse stables, which leads to the two doctors' offices. Dr. Benson's name plaque hangs on the wall by the door. Below it are bare spots where the name plaques of previous colleagues hung. Many new doctors and interns practice with Dr. Benson, then move on to their own businesses a short time thereafter. On the other side of the door is a glassless window with shutters, as a service window in a fast food restaurant might look. The shutters can be closed when necessary. They are frequently closed when other clients are either excessively curious or equally disturbed by the sight of animals in emergency situations.

On the other side of the doctors' offices is the "backroom." Due to ₅ the absence of air conditioning and the lack of proper ventilation, walking into the room is like walking into a steamroom except that it has a rather unpleasant stench of heated feces. The room is filled with cages lining all four walls, stacked three and four cages high. The "E. E. box" (excremental exercise box), otherwise simply known as "the box," takes up most of the area in the middle of the room. Looking into the box, you can usually see one or two dogs curiously sniffing the urine-soaked newspapers. In one corner of the room, between two walls of cages, is a stack of donated newspapers which are constantly in use. Another corner has three steps leading up to the rear exit. Next to the rear door are stacked cases of various prescription dog food, sometimes stacked six to seven feet high. At the bottom of the steps is a trashcan used to hide euthanized animals, each one placed in a trash bag, until they can be properly disposed of. In a third corner is a bathtub for bathing cats and dogs. Sticky jugs of flea shampoo are placed at random on the floor around the tub.

Behind the tub is a concealed lavatory. The door to this 4 ft. by 5 ft. ₆ room rests on its lower hinges. Inside the lavatory, a dusty toilet with a cracked seat and no lid is camouflaged by more cases of prescription dog food, as well as cat food. A window fan, in the same tiny room, slowly rotating in a breeze of muggy summer air, is temporarily placed in the window above the toilet. Outside that window is an alley where neighboring restaurants dispose of their refuse in huge dumpsters. Clouds of swarming flies and other pests feed on this collection of rotting scraps.

Leaving through the rear door into the alley, overwhelmed again by ₇ the summer sun, I felt a little guilty that in writing this paper, I'd be letting out a little more, probably, than Dr. Benson would want known.

Draft Review Worksheet:
Description of a Curious Place

Writer: _____   Reviewer: _____

1. Can you picture the place that the writer has described? What details best help you picture it? Note two or three sentences or words that are too vague to call up a picture.

2. Are there enough facts here to make you glad you read this paper? What kinds of facts do you feel are missing?

3. What strategy does the writer use in the introduction to catch our interest?

4. How does the writer's conclusion let us know that reading this paper has been valuable to us?

5. After reading this paper, do you feel that you understand the character of the place described? What character do you think the author intended to express?

6. Are there any changes you would suggest in punctuation, grammar, or spelling?

7. How has reading this paper given you a new perspective on the paper you are working on yourself?

Flawed Paper

Life in the Ghetto

Living in the ghetto, especially in Washington, D.C., is a great strug- 1
gle for many families, but they know that it will be an even greater fight
to survive.

When a stranger enters this area, the first thing that he notices is 2
that all of the buildings are four stories high and the color is a drab, old
and dingy brick red, trimmed in a pale green. They extend from Burns
Place, Southwest, to Minnesota Avenue, Northeast. Two of the buildings
are completely boarded up, because of two fires set by arsonists, which
claimed the lives of two young children.

There are two posters nailed to the boards, one advertising protest 3
against the Alan Baake decision and the other campaigning for the election of three government officials, who are Marion Barry, Walter Faun-
troy and Mayor Walter E. Washington.

On the right side of one of the buildings is a rusty twenty-gallon 4
garbage can, that was overfilled. When you walk past the garbage can,
your nostrils pick up a distinct odor of rotted vegetables, molded bread
and dead rodents. This odor is something that your stomach cannot adjust to. It creeps through cracks in the door, while you try to enjoy a
good breakfast consisting of fatback, fried potatoes, grits and biscuits.

The buildings are so badly infested with roaches and rats, you can 5
sometimes hear them in the basement at night, rumbling through the
trash. The plumbing is so inadequate, many families go for days without
hot water. When they complain to the rent office for months at a time,
they receive no response.

In the backyard there are two broken washers. One washer has a 6
blue dull color with paint scraped off the side to spell out a dirty word,
and the other washer is pink with the lid torn completely off. There are
sixty-seven trees surrounding the entire area, all of which are pine. The
residents complain, because it looks like part of Fort Dupont Park.

Parked on the curb is a 1969 brown Skylark, with the front window 7
broken completely out. The car was abandoned for two months by a
young boy, who hot wired it and went on a joy ride.

On Friday and Saturday nights, the air is filled with the sounds of 8
recording artists such as Ashford and Simpson, Peabo Bryson and Par-
liament, singing their gold record hits, as the neighbors tune in their radios to OK100. The sounds of arguing families make you an informed lis-

tener. It also keeps you from getting a good night sleep. The smoke of a freshly lit joint fills the lungs of dope users, as they get a "contact high."

During the Fourth of July, when you stand on the rooftops, you can 9 see the fireworks being shot off from the monument grounds.

The homes were built at the start of World War One. They were 10 used as off-base housing for military families. There is a sixty-foot pole in the backyard, which was used to hang flags on, by American soldiers. One section was used as a graveyard, but it is covered by bricks.

Four years ago, ground breaking ceremonies were held by Mayor 11 Washington for the building of the first recreational center in the southeast area. There are five outdoor basketball courts, a football field and three tennis courts. Two years ago, when a thunderstorm flooded the tennis courts up to the nets, the neighborhood kids went swimming in the water.

The area itself is ninety-nine percent black, but there is one white 12 man living in the ghetto. Jack Macy is forty-three years old with stringy brown hair, a broad nose and a protruding chin. He considers himself black, and if you challenged him, he would probably curse you out.

Every first of the month, Jack gets dressed up in his burgundy colored 13 polyester suit, cashes his check and gets drunk. When he returns home staggering drunk, he carries a brown paper bag tucked safely under his arm. The bag contains two six packs of Miller and Schlitz beer. Upon entering his apartment, he plays the only record that he owns, which is his Fats Domino record. Although Jack is a drunk, he is mechanically inclined. He is able to repair television sets, refrigerators and radios.

Assignment 2: Reader Analysis of a Magazine

Method of Research: Finding Significant Facts and Drawing Inferences from Them
Most Pertinent Chapters: 2, 3, 13
Clean Draft Due for Workshop:
Paper Due:

GOAL

To uncover and explain some of the magazine's assumptions about its readers and about the milieu, or the world, in which that audience lives or lived.

YOUR READERS

Those of us who are curious about the world our parents lived in, or curious about the readers of some of the unusual magazines we see in the stores.

SUGGESTIONS

1. Look at, read, and inspect your magazine carefully—any magazine published before 1945 or a current magazine addressed to people quite unlike yourself. Look at three or four consecutive issues or at one issue *very* thoroughly. Notice everything about the magazine—the kinds of articles, the style of writing, the advertising, the photos, the letters to the editor, the layout. Notice the kinds of articles, ads, and photographs that are *not* there too. Go into your investigation without a sense of what your thesis will be—with an open mind—*not* with a preformed idea about what you'll discover.
2. After you feel comfortable with the magazine, make a list of details about the magazine that strike you as interesting, unusual, or surprising.
3. About halfway through your note taking, look at the notes and see if you can find some patterns or trends. What assumptions does the magazine make about its readers and their world? What do we learn about the people who bought this magazine? about their values? their interests? their habits? their likes and dislikes? their education? economic level? social class? moral concerns? age? sex? political views? family life? Now you can start to form a tentative thesis.
4. Finish collecting your details, remembering that the details you observe in the magazine will serve as the evidence for your thesis.
5. To aid the reader and yourself, present your evidence—the details that support your conclusion—in systematic groupings, classes, or categories. Don't present information in the same random order in which you found it.
6. Be yourself when you write—straight, if you like; humorous if you like. Remember that you are a real person, and you are writing for a real audience. Read your paper aloud to make sure that it sounds recognizably human.
7. Catch us (your readers) with an introduction that will make us want to read on.

Sample Papers

Real Men Read *Soldier of Fortune*
Unknown Student Author

Are you interested in buying or selling guns, collecting military or 1 war memorabilia, or learning survival tactics? Would you enjoy reading stories of combat and guerrilla operations from those who participate? Have you ever wondered what it would be like to be a mercenary, a professional soldier for hire? Or, would you like perhaps an hour or so of comic relief? If so, then this is definitely the magazine for you!

Soldier of Fortune is a magazine devoted to the art of killing. It is a 2 weapons catalogue, an instruction manual, and a "journal of professional adventures" all rolled into one. Published monthly and distributed worldwide, it is a super-macho, ultra-right wing conservative refuge where women, children and liberals are not allowed. Yet, it does not cater to the seeker of cheap thrills; the "messy" side of battle is nowhere to be seen. Although written in a surprisingly high-quality, if biased format, its coldly technical, matter-of-fact style is as chilling as the subject matter itself.

Nearly all of the magazine's articles and features concern men and 3 their lethal toys (affectionately referred to as "she," use of the female gender almost always refers to weapons, not women), or the occasional profile for such "enemies of free democracy" as Jane Fonda or Henry Winston. Monthly features include spotlights on particular small-arms weaponry and accessories; a section variously titled "I Was There," or "It Happened To Me," a grab-bag of first-hand accounts of mercenaries and ordinary soldiers in combat situations; and "Bulletin Board," a collection of current interest items. In one recent issue, the "Bulletin Board" focused on a variety of subjects such as El Salvador and Nicaragua, British mercenaries jailed in Angola, the annual DOD publication "Soviet Military Power," counterpropaganda activities of Radio Free Kabul, the magazine's sponsorship of Vietnamese refugees, and the postwar Falklands situation. There is also a letters column titled "Flak," in which readers respond to articles in previous issues. Notably, all the letters are written by men, and most indicate more than a passing familiarity with weaponry or military operations.

Articles in the magazine include: a series of combat stories, such as 4 "Inside Free Angola," about anti-Soviet guerrilla fighters; "Intrigue in Africa," an account of Special Forces activities in Liberia; and a "frontline" report on strife in Central America. The magazine also lays heavy emphasis on Soviet and rebel warfare in Afghanistan, mercenary activities in third-world nations, and, for some reason, American Marines in combat in Vietnam, largely ignoring the contributions of the other military branches of service. Perhaps the editors are ex-Marines.

The photography is mostly of a dramatically glorified style; soldiers 5 and weapons are pictured in much the same way as are new cars in full-color layouts. One gets the feeling that the photographers coach their subjects into displaying stoic expressions in emotional situations. Men are shown crouching behind their weapons with an air of intense concentration, slogging through muddy rivers or over dry wasteland in atti-

tudes of seemingly joyful anticipation, or cradling their weapons in muscular arms while grinning at the camera as if to say, "this is child's play!"
Few civilians are photographed; when they are, it is usually as part of a
sympathetic article on a third-world nation.

The vast majority of advertisements concern the latest in foreign 6
and domestic small-arms weaponry, accessories, assorted military clothing and insignia. Most are available through mail order and include such
oddities as WWII German and Japanese memorabilia, Vietcong and NVA
military issue items, and everything from grenades to exotic knives to
airdart blowguns, steel ships, and ultra-sophisticated submachine and
anti-tank weapons. Fireworks and plastic explosives are also on order;
one ad goes so far as to offer instructions for making napalm! A striking
fact is that only small, portable weaponry is advertised; also, ads commonly found in male-oriented magazines such as TV's, stereo equipment, cars, liquor, etc., are nowhere to be seen.

A good number of the advertisements are so totally outlandish, in a 7
sick sort of way, that they are unwittingly funny. Some of the crazier ads
include offers of folding kayaks, copies of CIA ID cards, mercenary news-
letters, a manual outlining "dirty divorce tactics," tatooing supplies, a
"Boy's Marine Academy" summer camp (specializing in boot-camp drills
and physical training), and, especially, a cryptic appeal titled simply "A
Warrior's Religion! Odin and Thor Live!"

For the aspiring professional assassin or covert activities specialist, 8
there are mail-order ads for telephone bugs and anti-bugging devices,
cigarette-lighter microphones, electronic surveillance equipment and
"how-to" codebooks, frequency lists, etc. Of interest to the survivalist-
cum-paranoid are bullet-proof houses, body armor, trained attack dogs,
"safe" land in Canada and Alaska, survival caves, and nuclear shelters,
complete with food and fuel supplies. One ad, for home security systems, is headlined "Catch the Scumbags!"

A great number of books, films and catalogues are available, offering 9
everything from state and international law codes to video cassette re-
cordings of combat, Marine boot camp, the Soviet Army, and the Third
Reich. There are numerous ads for instruction in the martial arts, bounty
hunting, etc. There's even a "complete vacation package" at a "fun-filled
resort," offering hot-air ballooning, mountain climbing, simulated combat games, and survival training, in addition to tennis, swimming, horse-
back riding, and so forth. Not your typical get-away hot spot!

Lastly, the "open for hire" ads alone provide enough food for 10
thought to fill an essay on criminal psychology. Some of these ads are
quite specific about experience and skills offered (bounty hunting, courier service, bodyguards, electronic warfare specialists, even a "doctor
trained in general anesthesia"). Some list post office boxes, some give full
addresses, some merely list a phone number. They come from all over

America, Italy, Canada, even the Dominican Republic. Those that are signed are apparently all-male, usually using macho-type professional or nick-names, such as Buck, Thorn, Mad Dog, Spotter, Stringer, Joe, and Troy. Others apparently are "agencies," like "Omega" or "MacDonald Associates," which sound more like real-estate firms than mercenary or assassination organizations.

Overall, *Soldier of Fortune* is frightening, pathetic, and/or comical, 11 depending on the attitude of the reader. If the subject matter, including the freakiest of advertisements, were not treated with such utter seriousness, or if it did not contain so much solid reporting on military and para-military activities, it might be less threatening. In any case, it is sobering enough to consider that a magazine such as this evidently has the resources to provide such in-depth, technical information on modern weaponry and behind-the-scenes political intrigue; but especially, that it is available to anyone, anywhere in the world with three dollars to spend.

Everywoman's Magazine, 1944
Michael Parry

The time is November 1944, and a world war is raging across both 1 the Atlantic and the Pacific oceans. But not everyone is giving full-time attention to that war. An issue of *Everywoman's Magazine* gives us a good look back in time into the households of Americans at that time and lets us see what the values and interests of women were four decades ago. By carefully examining the magazine, we can get a good picture of the needs and desires of the audience of the magazine—women—as well as an overview of the country during that era.

A quick glance through this magazine will tell that it is geared to- 2 ward women, and more specifically, housewives. The table of contents lists articles such as "Children Can Make Housework Easier," "Mama Goes Shopping," "Thanksgiving Specialties," "Low-Cost Luncheons for the Family," "Diary of a Housewife," and "For a Becoming Winter Wardrobe." There are numerous pictures and drawings of women, children, food, and new fashions, while there are only three pictures of men—all drawings and all in fictional stories.

The interests of women are presented as the typical housewife's in- 3 terests: cooking, keeping a neat house, caring for children, and keeping up with the latest fashions. Seventeen recipes are included within three cooking articles as well as a turkey-stuffing article. Housework is assumed to be enjoyed and maybe even the highlight of a housewife's day. A quote like "Things get so dirty that it is a positive joy to clean them" does not seem out of place in this magazine. There are four articles about caring for and entertaining children, as well as three different photo essays on fashion covering six pages. Money appears to be of concern to all, and most articles are interested in the best-looking but most cost-efficient way of doing things.

By closer reading it is possible to find some further clues about the 4 magazine's readers. Three fiction short stories are placed at the front of the magazine. The articles are well-written and appear to be aimed toward a well-educated group of people. Although they are all about household situations, they are entertaining. Surprising for this period of time, women appear to be interested in working, probably because of conditions imposed by the war. An article entitled "Careers for Women" describes how to discover the things you really enjoy doing and how to market yourself for a job. I think women were becoming bored, with their husbands off at war, and were tired of being idle. In addition, many factories were in need of extra help during this period to produce war goods.

It is surprising to note that although this is a women's magazine 5 and two-thirds of the articles were written by women, three-fourths of the magazine's management is conducted by men. Only the editor of the magazine is female, while the president, managing editor, art director, and general manager are male. This could mean that women may not have had enough experience to run a magazine and that most women held jobs of less prominence.

One large group that seems to have been completely excluded from 6 this magazine is minorities. All (no exception) pictures, drawings, ads, and articles show white people, no minorities. As this is before the movements of the 1960s, there probably was a lot of prejudice surviving in America, and it could also be possible that most minorities had been denied an education, and could not obtain some of the better-paying jobs and luxuries that most middle-class families enjoyed.

If one puts this magazine in the proper time frame, it is almost sur- 7 prising to realize that America was helping to fight a world war. In reading this magazine, it is hard to tell. There are only three ads which (not-so-clearly) state that there is a war going on. The most obvious is an ad to buy war bonds, but it is buried on the second to last page. It shows two feet literally stamping out Nazism and Japanese Imperialism, and it states that war bonds will "give you that luxurious feeling of freedom that goes with a well-lined pocketbook." I'd say that was blowing it a little out of proportion.

The second and third war-related ads are to promote saving paper. 8 The reason given in the second ad for this is that paper and paper products were needed to ship items to Europe. Although in the second ad they mention the words *war, invasion,* and *ammunition,* one would never conclude a world war was being fought. The third simply states, "Paper is still essential—save it." The playing down of the war could mean that people were getting tired of hearing all the news of the war, since it had been going on for a few years, and were just interested in "bringing the boys back home." The first two of these ads are the only direct references to a war in the entire magazine.

Overall, this issue of *Everywoman's Magazine* can be seen as directed toward middle-aged housewives interested in cooking, house-cleaning, caring for children, and keeping up with the fashions. The world war presents a situation where women are looking for jobs while their husbands are away, are money-conscious, and are not too worried about keeping up with the latest war news. Finally, these women are well-educated, generally interested in reading articles about other households, and slightly prejudiced. 9

Draft Review Worksheet:
Reader Analysis of a Magazine

Writer: _____ Reviewer: _____

1. What does the writer attempt to do in the introduction to the paper? Does the introduction provide the background you need to understand the analysis that follows?

2. Do the facts and quotations cited help you sense the "flavor" of the magazine? Which quotation captures the flavor best? What single piece of information in the paper are you most likely to remember a week from now?

3. Did the writer draw at least four distinct inferences from the facts found in the magazine? List the inferences you find. Which inferences need to be made clearer or more specific?

4. What is the writer's overall opinion of the magazine? How do you know?

5. Does your reading get tedious at any point? Specify where.

6. Do you have any suggestions for improving spelling, punctuation, or grammar?

7. How has reading this paper given you a new perspective on the paper you are working on yourself?

Flawed Paper

Bass Master Magazine

Think of a boat that goes sixty miles an hour, reads depth level, pH 1
content, oxygen level, and water temperature. It is a sleek, streamlined
boat with cushioned seats high on pedestals, wall to wall carpeting and
aerated live-wells to keep fish alive. It sounds like a biologist's dream, but
actually it is a modern day bass fisherman's boat.

I found that today's bass fisherman has to be a fairly intelligent in- 2
dividual. Many articles describe how to use different gauges and contour
maps to paint a precise picture of a lake in scientific terms. Moon phases
and barometric pressure must also be considered. Tables show oxygen
level, water temperature and pH level that bass prefer. Learning and
knowing these things among others they suggest, will greatly increase
your catch.

There seems to be an ever growing number of professional bass 3
fisherman, some of whom make over fifty thousand a year. These men
fish two or three day tournaments which are held by the organization
who publishes this magazine. These tournaments are featured in the
magazine with the writer describing how every fish was caught.

Other articles describe new artificial lures, boating products and 4
fishing rods. One soft plastic lure is described as being mushy and flexible like a frog, fooling the bass into holding the lure and enabling the
fisherman to set the hook. Another lure is computerized, has a battery
pack and runs on its own on top of the water like an injured minnow.

Bass fisherman seem to be away from home quite a bit pursuing 5
the sport of fishing. In every edition of the magazine, there is a story on
the escapades of two fictitious characters named Harry and Charlie.
They are two die-hard bass fisherman who are "good ole boys" from the
South. Their wives are always nagging them to stay home. It seems their
every free moment is spent fishing or making plans to sneak out and go
fishing. On one occasion, they are in the local beer joint after unsuccess-
fully trying to launch their boat because of a large crowd at the boat
ramp. At the beer joint, they connive a plan to get their "old ladies" to let
them go away to a secluded fishing spot. While chewing tobacco and
drinking beer, they realize they are going to have to bring the "old
ladies" along. They decide to tell them it is a second honeymoon. As
things turn out, Harry's wife catches a huge bass and puts Harry to

shame. Stories with Harry and Charlie of this nature are in every issue. I
suppose most bass fishermen identify with these stories.

Bass fishermen, in general, are somewhat intelligent and spend   6
quite a deal of money on fishing and boating equipment. If they are exceptionally good at fishing, they can make a lot of money. Above all, they
must stay flexible, innovative and try new lures and techniques. They
must also make fairly good money since the average boat seems to cost
around six thousand dollars. However, there are ways to bass fish without a great deal of investment. One might consider buying a small, inexpensive aluminum boat or even fishing off of the bank of the lake or river.
Less area can be covered like this but this is precisely how many young
children get started.

In conclusion, one thing all fishermen have in common is that they   7
spend a great deal of their time fishing because it is a time-consuming
sport by nature.

Assignment 3: Reader Analysis of Two Newspapers

Method of Research: Finding Significant Facts and Drawing Inferences from
   Them
Most Pertinent Chapters: 2, 3, 5, 13
Fact-Inference Pairs Due:
Clean Draft Due for Workshop:
Paper Due:

An ethnographer studies what the people are like in a given area. The
first ethnographers studied societies like those of the Tibetans and the Eski-
mos because they thought these peoples were exotic. But recent ethnographers have decided that history teachers or presidential counselors or Chi-
cagoans can be just as exotic. In this assignment, your task is to act as an
ethnographer and, using only two newspapers as evidence, draw some contrasting conclusions about the readers those newspapers are published for.
In other words, you'll be trying to determine how two newspapers view the
readers in their respective communities.

To begin, find two newspapers that are likely to appeal to quite different audiences of readers. If you can find in your library local newspapers
from different parts of the country, say the *Seattle* (Washington) *Times* and
the *Rutland* (Vermont) *Herald,* or the *Fort Worth* (Texas) *Star-Telegram* and
the *Kenosha* (Wisconsin) *News,* that would be wonderful. If you can't get
papers from distant communities, though, consider some papers that are
available in most cities: *The New York Times, The Village Voice, The Na-*

tional Enquirer, The Christian Science Monitor, a local religious newspaper, or a propagandistic newspaper of any kind. Also, most libraries carry at least a few papers from around the country (or around the world), and you could do your research using two of those.

Begin your research by looking through your papers and jotting down facts about the newspapers that reveal something about their intended audiences. Use as evidence the types of stories included, the way stories are written, the placement of stories within the paper, the types and number of advertisements, the wording of headlines, the opinions expressed and implied, and anything else that strikes you as you read. Then, next to each fact you've noted, write out an inference you think you can draw about the audience. Here's what your notes might look like:

Facts	Inferences
There are several ads in *The Village Voice* for plastic surgery, transparent braces, electrolysis, clinics for baldness, dermatology, and weight reduction.	Readers are very concerned about their appearance.
Produce advertised in a September *Seattle Post-Intelligencer* is very cheap: 23 pounds of apples, $4.98; squash, 9 cents per pound.	The Seattle area must have a good climate for growing fruits and vegetables.
A first-page article in the *Rutland Herald* about oil drilling along George's Bank (off Cape Cod) concludes with two paragraphs about the plight of the fisherman.	Emphasis suggests that the paper expects its readers to side with the fishermen.

As with any other research, look for evidence that is contrary to your values or expectations, and you'll find evidence much more easily. Be bold in the inferences you draw, but remember that one fact is not enough to justify a bold inference, so look back to see whether there are any more facts that will help substantiate that inference.

At some point in your research, it will help if you bring your fact-inference pairs to class and discuss them with your classmates. Have your classmates evaluate your research by telling you whether they find your facts surprising rather than routine and whether they find your inferences thoughtful and not obvious. With that advice, continue to collect fact-inference pairs until you have thirty to forty; then decide on a thesis statement (a summary of your best inferences) about the newspapers' contrasting readers that you feel you can substantiate using the examples you've noted. Once you have decided on a thesis, write a three- to four-page paper using as much evidence as you think is necessary to convince your reader that your thesis is accurate and reasonable, that you have a legitimate, thoughtful assessment of the differences between the two sets of readers. If your emphasis changes as you write your paper, be sure to make adjustments in your thesis that reflect that change.

Sample Papers

The Good Life? Where?
Jeffrey Gagliardi

The New York Times and *The Seattle Post-Intelligencer* from April 1
22, 1984 are two very dissimilar papers. There are a substantial number of differences between the papers which reflect the differences of subscribers, and therefore, the purposes of the papers. The major contrasts deal with the lifestyles and economies of Seattle and New York.

The New York Times is a business oriented newspaper with a wide 2
subscription area. The business section is fifty-two pages long and is packed with national stock exchange and investment data, ads for office supplies, computer systems, and even more ads for managerial and high tech jobs from around the nation. The major section of the newspaper is mainly national and international news. As is characteristic of all newspapers, the *Times* has car ads in its classifieds section. A large number of the car ads, though, are from dealerships, which are generally expensive, and have the option to lease. Leasing is the standard way a business acquires company cars. Although the paper, and New York, seem to center around Wall Street and the business world, New York's ports and shipping industry are also important to its economy. Two articles attested to this.

The *Times* seems to have a very wealthy backing. On most of the 3
pages in the main section, over three-fourths of each page is advertisements. A majority of the ads are from the most expensive stores in the nation. Some ads are for products that only upper-middle-class or very rich people can afford, such as expensive jewelry, fashion wear, and luxury cars.

In the area of the arts, New York is an important place. Not only 4
does New York harbor thousands of musical and acting performances, it is also a major testing ground for the success of movies. In the Art and

Leisure section of the *Times,* there are countless advertisements and articles on stage and musical performances. Movie ads are the most prominent, though, sometimes running full or even double pages.

Although New York is a place of great opportunity and entertain- 5
ment, it is also a highly pressured environment for its inhabitants. In the
Times's travel section, there are a large number of ads for expensive
overseas vacations. This helps support my view that there are many very
wealthy people in New York, but it is the remaining ads which reflect the
true nature of New York life. I am referring to the abundance of inexpensive weekend trips that are advertised as being restful and only ninety
minutes outside of New York. These ads are meant to lure in average
workers, as opposed to the ads for the well-to-do. The number of these
ads points to the fact that New Yorkers like to get away from New York as
often as possible.

Politically speaking, it is obvious that New York and *The New York* 6
Times are mainstream Democratic. Not only did all the articles concerning the presidential campaigns favor Democrats, they supported and
promoted Walter Mondale, who is presently in the lead in the race for
the Democratic party nomination.

The purpose of the *Intelligencer* is drastically different from that of 7
The New York Times. Whereas the *Times* is a nationally subscribed-to
paper with a primary interest in the business world, the *Intelligencer* is
localized for the Seattle area. It seems that the Seattle area has a high
percentage of blue-collar workers. There are a large number of articles,
both national and local, concerning Seattle's major industries. The articles deal with the timber industry, agriculture, the shipping industry,
the effect of international grain embargoes on farmers and shippers, and
the recent drop in Washington state's unemployment from sixth to thirteenth in the nation. Shipping is probably Seattle's most important industry. There are a large number of articles on shipping and fishing, the
name of the baseball team is the Mariners, and the name of the football
team is the Seahawks.

The *Intelligencer*'s business section is only four pages long. The 8
employment and real estate ads are small too. With this in mind, it
seems that the Seattle area has a limited job market and low economic
opportunities. The *Intelligencer* is clearly meant to be a daily paper for
the average person. Articles frequently have informal titles like "Fewer
Couples Are Getting Unhitched," "Campaign Kitties Are Empty," and a
front page feature entitled "Today's Chuckle." There are also a page and
a half of games, eleven full pages of supermarket sales, several cooking
recipes, and five advice columns.

The people of Seattle seem to hold more traditional American val- 9
ues than New Yorkers do. One title to an advice column read: "Fix supper early and relax with your husband," which represents a traditional

view of the role of the female sex. The *Intelligencer* also has a religious
advice column by the evangelist Billy Graham.

After reading these papers I find myself wondering whether I 10
would rather live in Seattle or New York, based on the information I have
gotten from the two papers. Honestly speaking, I would like to live in
both Seattle and New York; both have qualities which I like. For economic reasons I would like to live in New York. Deep down, though, I
have a desire to live in America's past, with some of its old customs and
values. Seattle's farms and simpler lifestyle appeal to me more than the
hustle and bustle of New York life. Seattle leaves me with the impression
that it is a remnant of the Old West.

Vision: Local and Moderate or Liberal and International

Joseph Greenawalt

The *Seattle Post-Intelligencer* and the *Baltimore Sun* published on 1
September 25, 1984, are two very different types of newspapers. They differ greatly in their focus on international and national events, sports and
leisure events, and editorial preferences. These differences not only indicate the publisher's point of view on various issues, but also the type
of reader that each paper is attempting to reach.

First of all, the headlines of the two papers focus on two very dif- 2
ferent subjects. The *Seattle Post-Intelligencer* reserves a good portion of
its front page for its headline story dealing with the renaming of a Seattle
airport in honor of the late Senator Henry Jackson. The headline reads,
"SEA-TAC RENAMED FOR JACKSON." Since Jackson is primarily known
in the Washington state area, and because the news is only of local interest, it is evident that the publisher believes that significant local news
takes precedence over national or international news in the minds of the
readers of the *Intelligencer.*

In contrast, the *Baltimore Sun*'s headline, as well as the entire first 3
page, deals solely with national and international events. Two articles
deal with presidential news, including the headline, which reads,
"REAGAN DROPS PLANNED VISIT TO PHILIPPINES." Although an entire
section, entitled "Maryland," is later devoted to state and local news, local news is nonetheless subordinate. Also, because Baltimore is a port
city, the publisher recognizes that international events may have great
bearing on Baltimore based import/export companies.

In the business area, the *Intelligencer* and the *Sun* show some 4
sharp differences. The *Intelligencer* shares its business section with a
sports section, spending roughly five pages on business matters. However, the articles deal mainly with general subjects such as Internal Revenue information, Federal Reserve Board rulings, and Dow Industrial
and other stock averages. There are only two marginal articles discussing local Seattle business. However, the *Sun* deals with a greater number
of specific local business matters. Its main headline is of a local issue,
and reads, "TIRE PLANT GETS SOBER ASSESSMENT," while the headline
of the *Intelligencer* deals with national I.R.S. news. It seems that while
readers of the *Sun* are more interested in national politics, they are also
more interested in local business news.

The *Intelligencer* and the *Sun* differ also in their treatment of 5
sports. The *Intelligencer* and the *Sun* both have significant sports sections. However, the *Intelligencer* deals more with football and golf, only
reserving one article for its baseball team, The Seattle Mariners. This is
because the Mariners were not a very successful team this season. In
contrast, the *Sun* not only has three articles in its sports section discussing Baltimore's baseball team, the Orioles, but also includes a separate
eleven page section on their upcoming playoffs against the Chicago
White Sox. With the addition of this extra section, the publisher is evidently capitalizing on the increased popularity of the Orioles. He's hoping that more people will buy the *Sun* to read about the success of their
Orioles.

In the editorial page, the character of a newspaper and its readers 6
can be readily and dramatically observed. The *Intelligencer* and the *Sun*
seem to agree on basic political issues. In the *Intelligencer,* there are five
articles criticizing the Soviet way of life. It is evident that this paper is to
a degree anti-Soviet—but this does not mean that the paper is conservative or pro Reagan. Quite the contrary, for on the same pages, there are
two cartoons criticizing Reagan administration policies. One cartoon
shows how the Pentagon is using the Korean Airlines incident to acquire
more armaments. In fact, one editorial expands on this criticism and attacks Reagan himself for using his speech condemning the Russians as a
pretext for pushing his MX missile plan. The second cartoon criticizes
the militarist supported violent response to the KAL incident by the
American public. The paper has taken the position that moderate responses to the Soviets are appropriate, and that to build up the nuclear
arsenal as a response is impulsive and wrong. Also, to support this, one
editorial says America cannot retaliate to the Soviets because of the
threat of nuclear weapons, and only when this threat disappears can
America handle Soviet aggression. It seems, therefore, that the paper is
an advocate of the nuclear freeze, giving the paper a decidedly liberal
character.

The *Sun* also demonstrates, through its opinion/commentary page, 7
a liberal or Democratic character. Firstly, a lengthy piece in praise of
Democrat Walter Mondale appears. The article congratulates Mondale
for his recent victory in Maine's straw poll and goes on to tell of his direct and forthright campaigning methods. Evidently, the paper supports
Mondale and his Democratic ideals and hopes that he will defeat the
Republican candidate for the presidency in 1984. Also two letters to the
editor express dislike for Reagan policies. No pro Reagan letters or editorials
appear, reaffirming the liberal character of the *Sun* and its readers.

The content of a newspaper and its focus shows much about its 8
particular readers. Even though the *Seattle Post-Intelligencer* and the
Baltimore Sun share a similar liberal character and audience, they differ
greatly in their approaches to presenting the news. The *Intelligencer*
seems to be a locally oriented paper, with its readers preferring major
local news to international or national news. The *Baltimore Sun* seems
to present a broader view of the news to a business oriented subscriber
who needs to keep abreast of major national and international news developments.

Draft Review Worksheet:
Reader Analysis of Two Newspapers

Writer: _____ Reviewer: _____

1. Does the writer tell you enough about the newspapers so that you get a good sense of what the papers are like? Does the writer sound as though he or she knows the papers well?

2. Does the writer quote from the newspapers? Do the quotations help you sense the "flavor" of the newspapers?

3. Where does this paper need more evidence?

4. Which inferences need to be made clearer or more specific?

5. Which paragraphs don't proceed smoothly from the paragraph they follow?

6. What changes in spelling, grammar, or punctuation would you suggest?

7. What is your most important suggestion for revision?

Flawed Paper

Newspaper Comparison Paper

What is the first thing about newspaper that catches your eye? Is it 1
the title, the pictures or the front headline? In choosing my second
newspaper for this report it happened to be all three. "The Sun" happened to hit me as an uplifting title. One of the first headlines read, "Boo-
gieing with the Bird", corresponding with a color picture of the Oriole
mascot dancing with one of the cheerleaders.

Another picture was one of a dirty little boy with a sad look on his 2
face, standing next to an older sad looking man. This was also in color.
Both had enough pathoes in them to make anyone want to read the ar-
ticals which were found on the next page.

This is an example of how the editors figure that they will sell the 3
paper. They definitely want to catch attention through the appeal of pictures. It seems to me that the editors believe that it is pictures that sell
the paper, being that the two pictures on the front page are the only colored ones in the whole newspaper. To go on, the fact that there thirty-
seven photographs, more than half the number of articles, we could assume that the editors also believe that pictures tell a better story. The
pictures show and tell quite a bit about the story. There are detailed
shots of what the story behind them is about.

In compairing this to another newspaper, the Seattle Post Intelle- 4
gencer, this is quite the opposite. This paper has a total of sixty-three
articles to a mere twenty-three photographs, which out of all, only has
one colored picture in the last section. Maybe the editors of the Intellegencer believe that a paper should be just what the title suggests, to in-
telligize the readers, "cutting the crap" and getting straingt to the point.

This assumption can also be pointed out through the big difference 5
of advertisements and coupons in both papers. The Sun has a total of
105 advertising ads, almost twice as many as the Intellegencer, with a
total of sixty. In spite of this difference though, there is no way that anyone looking through these ads could not possibly notice that computors
are the most popular item on the market today.

Computor ads rank highest of all other, especially in the business 6
and finance section, which happens to be the thickest section in The
Sun. There are nineteen articles in this paper which out does the Intelligencer by ten articles. Besides the nineteen articles, there are four
pages of stock information. I would say that Baltimore is a much more

business orientated city than Seattle just by the amount of information that is put in the paper. Also I find it interesting that the food and liesure section of The Sun, is considerably thinner than the same section in the Intellegencer. In this paper, there are only five articles and the rest of the pages are coupons and advertising. The Intellegencer's section is the thickest of all the other sections. The only colored picture in the paper is on the front page of this section. It has twenty articles consisting of cooking tips, recipes, and a few articles on cooking traditions in other countries. I think this is very interesting and shows a treat deal just where the people of Seattle, Wash. and the people of Baltimore, Md. place their interests.

As far as the sports go, I think every newspaper has sufficient in- 7 formation and more on our beloved sports. The Sun only has six more articles than the Intellegencer has. Both only cover very local information on local teams. The reason for more articles in The Sun, might account for the success that the Maryland Baltimore Oriols have had in past seasons. Also the fact that one-fourth of the sports page was the Business section, limits the amount of space that the sports can use.

Local reports in Maryland are also half as much higher than in the 8 Seattle paper. This is most likely the case because Baltimore is an industrial and highly populated city. It is understandable that there be a lot of local information. In Seattle education seems to be a prime matter being that three out of eight articles deal with Seattle public schools. One could assume without knowing anything about Seattle, that it is a small city. If it weren't for the classified ads in this section, Local would be a single sheet of paper. (The classified ads are six pages of cars and other items for sale including one and a half pages of job openings. This fact can also lead to saying that Seattle is a smaller, less populated, and less business orientated city than Baltimore with nine pages of classified ads and four of those being job openings, mostly for computor processors and programmers.)

This now leaves us with world political issues which range just 9 about the same in both of the papers. This topic in the front page section of the papers seems to have less articles that any other section. The current topics are brief but well covered. I did notice, though that not one of the articles, in either of the papers, was put as as headline. This tells me that these papers are both basically local papers cobering limited amount of matters outside their own territory.

Just by examing the style and content of the papers it can become 10 a little obvious that they are from two cities in two different parts of the country. One, Seattle, being from the Northwestern part, where leisure time, food, and sports, seems to be the main interest of the people, and Baltimore, the home of the Orioles and the dwelling of the big businesses.

Assignment 4: Character Sketch

Method of Research: Interview
Most Pertinent Chapters: 2, 3, 4, 5, 7, 11, 13
Clean Draft Due for Workshop:
Paper Due:

In a crowd we all look alike. But even the most innocuous looking among us has had some adventures, endured some hardship, and tried to make a sensible plan for his or her life. The purpose of an interview is to ask perceptive enough questions to find the details that make a person distinctive. You've done research in earlier assignments by observing a place, by studying newspapers or magazines. This time you'll do your research—gather your facts—in an interview with someone you don't know. Again, you need to concentrate and gather the facts that will speak for themselves and convey an impression. In the paper you will write, you will offer us not a random series of questions and answers, but a thoughtful portrait of the person you interview. You may be asked to read your paper to the class so that your classmates can get to know the person you have chosen. The hardest part of this assignment is getting your nerve up to ask someone to be interviewed. But it won't be nearly as difficult as you think; people like to talk about themselves.

Your paper will be most successful if the person you interview is (1) someone over 40 years old or (2) someone whose occupation is one you don't know much about or (3) someone whose background is very different from yours. Don't bother to interview a person your age, or a member of your family, or a neighbor whom you know well. You won't learn much from such an interview. One of my students interviewed a housewife who rode a motorcycle as a hobby. Another interviewed a derelict in Annapolis and got him to talk about how much time he would spend in Purgatory. Another student—from Korea—sat at a bus stop until he found someone—an immigrant from Turkey who had, coincidentally, fought in the Korean War—willing to be interviewed. He rode the bus home with the man and finished the interview at his home. And you can always find someone to talk to at a nursing home. Decide, as soon as possible, whom you'd like to interview so that you'll have plenty of time to organize your notes and write your paper.

Before you go to the interview, prepare a list of questions. Once you've asked a few of those questions, though, and you find yourself comfortable with the person you're interviewing, you should find yourself asking spontaneous questions and forgetting those on your list. Take careful notes, for the person's own words will usually be more effective than your own. Before you leave, ask permission to call the person back in case you need more information. Also ask whether the person would like a copy of the interview. Typing up your notes *immediately* after the interview will help you remember everything you want to.

Remember these key elements when you organize your material for your first draft:

1. Your first obligation is to the person you interview—don't change the meaning of what is said.
2. Your second obligation is to the reader; choose quotations and information your readers are likely to be curious about.
3. Use the person's own words as often as you can in your writing; they will be more telling than your own.
4. Don't try to unify too soon. Try to see the variety in the person you interview.
5. In your introduction, let your readers know why this person is worth reading about.
6. Don't relinquish control in your paper to your interviewee or to your notes. You are the writer. You organize and paragraph the paper, and you do it for your readers' convenience.

Sample Papers

A Water Person: An Interview with John Hoffman
Diana Lambird

"Come on in, we're having an orgy," he said as he waved four more   1
girls onto the elevator. By the time the elevator came down seven floors and reached the lobby, John Hoffman had everyone laughing. A handsome stocky man, the only sign of his thirty-five years are his laugh lines that are there whether he smiles or not. A deep tan and a couple scars on his hands are the only visible casualties of having the life that most people only dream of—sailing around the Virgin Islands and the Chesapeake Bay year round. "I fell into the job. If you had told me a couple of years ago I would be sailing the islands for a living—I would have winked at you and said, 'sure.'"

Anyone can hire John. All you have to do is give him a call and he'll   2
answer the phone, "Hey, this is John. What can I do for you today?" Just let him know what you want, and he'll try to get it done for a "reasonable price." He'll take you sailing on a fifty-five foot sailboat "anywhere where the sun is shining and the wind is blowing." In fact, he's

leaving for St. Croix with a couple of "lady doctors" and plans on staying down in the islands until the eastern sailing begins again. He admits that business is getting harder to find, but he's not worried: "I used to be booked up all through the winter by now. But not this year. Things must be getting tougher for people." But it doesn't seem to be getting tough for John. He dresses as if he stepped out of one of the pages of *G.Q.*, drives a bright red 280Z T-top, and lives in an old house in downtown Annapolis.

The house is always occupied by his live-in maid and three Chesapeake Bay retrievers. "I don't find much time to live here, but I call it home." The house is filled with wood antiques and furniture he made himself. His favorite room is his bedroom, which is filled with unicorn artifacts. "The unicorns were all given to me by my friends—the ones that know me well." His close friends call him Uni because, he explains with a wink and a hug, "we're both fabulous animals." But the truth of the matter is his soon to be ex-wife pegged him with the nickname. During one of their frequent parties, "she told a good friend of mine that she saw me as frequently as she saw a unicorn—and that I was as horny as one when I finally did appear. Anyway, the name stuck." 3

He took this present job because his marriage was over and it gave him the freedom he needed. "Pepper and I went through a lot together. But we finally had to let the relationship go. We didn't love each other anymore. That's one person I failed. I tried, but sometimes, I don't know." Silence. "I guess I can't change that I failed someone." They met while in college at the University of Michigan. They lived together for four years when "she just suggested that maybe we should get married. Hell, we were together for so long I figured, why not. So we did." 4

During this time John and friends from college started the Brooks Construction Co. With this, he made his fortune: "My partners and I were quite good at what we did; we were all good businessmen." But as the business flourished, the friendship of the partners dwindled. "To make a long story short, one of my partners—he was also one of my best friends—embezzled money from the rest of us. Another close friend and business partner committed suicide as a result of many financial and marital problems. I sold my shares and got out," he said, which explains his wealth now. 5

He has always been accustomed to wealth. His parents are "well-off" and live in Houston, Texas. "I hate it there though. Can't really explain why because I love my parents, they're cool people. The other people there aren't like these people [people who sail]." "Water people" is what John calls people who like the water. "Water people are the greatest. They're open. Just ask anything of them and its done for you. I love 'em all." People are John's business, and he wouldn't go into another business unless he could work with them. "People are what make the 6 world. I've seen some pretty ignorant ones, but they still are the only thing worthwhile in this world."

"Sailing," he said, "is when people are themselves. People let down   7 their defenses under two conditions: when they're scared or when they're laughing. I like to do both. I like to make them laugh, and well, sometimes sailing can scare 'em a little." He doesn't plan to keep the job forever, though. He has plans to start and run a chartering business in Annapolis and to settle down again. But people are definitely in his future, "whether they're water people or not."

You Are Only as Old as You Feel
Robin Shaw-Maglione

Hal Saylor sits straight in his wheelchair, smoking his pipe. Swirls of   1 apple-scented smoke surround him. Although unshaven—"I think I might just grow a beard"—his clothes are of a recent style and his crystal blue eyes are clear and bright behind "bottleglass" spectacles. "Ah, you're here. That's good. I detest waiting for people—don't like to waste time."

We settled down in a cozy corner of the nursing home lobby near the   2 piano. A frail white-haired woman was softly playing chopsticks. "Used to play quite a bit," he said, nodding at the woman. "When I was young, my mother used to make me take lessons from every music teacher in town. Whenever she'd hear of a better teacher, I'd have to change teachers again. Once I had this teacher, Mrs. Maddox I believe her name was, who'd slam the piano cover down on my fingers if I made too many mistakes. Broke a finger once that way. Didn't want her as a teacher after that, but being as she was the best in town, I had to keep taking my lessons with her. After my finger 'n all, she started using a hat pin!"

Hal pursued his music and received his degree from the Cincinnati   3 Conservatory of Music. He spent one of his summers during college working on the "Chris Green," a riverboat on the Ohio River. "I started out in the boiler room shoveling coal. One day the Captain happened by and we got to talking. He found out that I could play the piano and promoted me up to the lounge where I played for the passengers. Some promotion, eh?"

He looked down at his hands. His right hand moved and lifted his   4 left hand into a more comfortable position. "You know," he spoke softly, "I spent eighteen years getting these fingers to play the major chords and now look at them. Useless. You might just say that I'm a one handed piano player." Hal had a major stroke thirteen years ago this January.

Recently his grandson, who is eight, asked him if he had ever walked. "I told him yes, but I don't think he believed me. Still and all, though, in and out of this chair, I've done a lot in life. Course, I haven't done it all yet, but I still have a few miles left in me. And if I don't get it all done—I'll just have to come back and do it."

After his music degree, Hal earned another degree in engineering. 5
"There were too many starving musicians." Already an accomplished ham radio operator, having received his first license at thirteen (the youngest ever in the state), he entered the police force to head a radio communications team. "We were just a bunch of gun totin' radio operators." From there, Hal entered the FBI. "We used to call it the Farm Boys Institute because so many of the boys were from Iowa and Indiana." He joined the FBI to be close to the war effort. "I was too young for WWI and too old for WWII." He became an agent and traveled to every state in the union and every country in South America and Europe. "Once I traveled to a town just south of London to deliver a message to Churchill. The message was engraved on the lenses of my glasses. You couldn't see it with the naked eye, you needed a microscope to decode it. Another time, using a device called an extortion package, we were attempting to capture a high-level banker involved in a blackmail racket. It (the E.P.) was thrown from a car window disguised as the money drop. It was equipped with a small tracking device that we could pick up by radio in the car. A faster beep meant that someone was close to it. It started to beep faster, so we went back to nab the guy. When we got there, there was this dog using it for a fire-plug."

When the war was over, Hal left the FBI for a job with less traveling. He 6
went to work for CBS as a sound engineer. "The first thing CBS did was send me to Europe!" He worked with many celebrities, including Lloyd Bridges, Peter Graves, and Guy Lombardo. "During one of the New Year's Eve shows Lombardo did, he wanted the violins to be highlighted at one particular point. He said he would signal me at the appropriate time. When I wanted to know why he didn't just mark it on the sheet music, he laughed. Lombardo couldn't believe that an engineer could read music!"

The time was nearly up. Hal had promised to talk to one of his ra- 7
dio friends. He has a complete ham radio set-up in his room at the nursing home. His friends at CBS installed the antenna on the roof for him. He's working on upgrading his ham license so that his equipment can reach out farther. "My world extends far beyond this nursing home. Where this wheelchair can't get me, the radio does."

We said goodbye, and I watched him wheel away to his room. On 8
my way out, I passed his room and there he was, talking to someone in West Virginia and practicing speeding up his morse code. Go for it, Hal. As you yourself once said, "There isn't anything a body can't do, if you set your mind to it."

Draft Review Worksheet:
Character Sketch

Writer: _____ Reviewer: _____

1. Does the character sketch you have just read make the person inter-viewed seem simple or complex? Too simple? Too complex? Explain.

2. The most effective interviewers let their subjects tell their stories in their own words. Which quotation in this paper best helps you understand the personality of the person interviewed. Point out any sections of the pa-per where the writer needs to add quoted material.

3. Does the writer include enough commentary and background informa-tion to show that he or she is in control of the material? Or has the writer allowed the person interviewed to do all the talking?

4. Has the writer grouped material into paragraphs of reasonable length? Find a paragraph that you think is either too long or too short, and ex-plain why you think so.

5. How does the writer's introduction convince you that the person inter-viewed is worthy of your attention? How does the writer conclude? What is your last impression of the person interviewed, and does it seem consistent with the writer's point of view?

6. Are there any questions that you think the writer should go back and ask the person interviewed?

7. Do you have any suggestions for improving grammar or punctuation?

8. What is your most important suggestion for revision?

Flawed Paper

Interview with John Morquay

He wasn't much to look at. In fact, if there was any athletic ability in   1
this aging man, it was very difficult to detect. He was a jockey, or still is,
depending on who you are talking to. A small man of about fifty who
grew up around the track and made horse racing his life. His name is
John Morquay.

John was born of Hispanic origin, but raised in America. The deep   2
South to be exact. He was raised in an impoverished environment where
his father worked some 12 hours a day at a local racetrack. John's father
had a big influence on his son. Often he would say, "You will have it better than me, John. Cleaning stables is no life for a son of mine." It was
hard for a young boy like John to see his father working so hard for nothing. When he would accompany his father to the track, he would notice
all the jockeys in their fine satin riding suits. This is when he decided
that racing was to be the life for him.

As he grew older, he moved from exercise boy to apprentice rider.   3
He was a small boy, but very agile and learned to be aggressive when he
rode. "This," he said, "was what owners and trainers liked to see. A rider
who was aggressive but who also knew when to be patient in a race."
These skills John acquired quickly and with his knowledge he soon became well-liked. All that was left for him was to finish his apprentice-
ship. At the age of 18 he was a full fledged jockey at the racetrack near
where he grew up.

The next 10 years of John's life were spent riding the circuit in Flor-   4
ida, South Carolina, North Carolina, and Georgia. This is the period in
his life that he says is the most important. He grew up not only physi-
cally, but mentally as well. He saw the hardships and realities of life.
Moralistic values were set and he found himself maturing to the point
where he was his own man. He mentioned morals specifically because
John was an honest man and looked with disfavor on corruption. Corruption, however, is what he saw. It would be no great surprise to be
told of races being fixed or horses being drugged to make them run
faster. These illegal activities surprisingly shocked John very much.
John's father protected him from seeing these things when he was
younger, but this sheltering proved harmful as he became older. Now he
had to make a choice. There was good money to be made by fixing a
race, but on the other hand, there were many risks involved. John heard

of jockeys losing their licenses to race and even going to jail. He knew he could not participate in these "shady" operations because for the first time in his life, he was going to plan for his future, to look ahead.

At the age of 26, John had taken a wife. He fathered two children, a 5 girl and a boy. Having saved a good deal of money, he decided to move up North. He did not want his children growing up in the same environment as he did. It was time for a change. New York was the place to go. Bigger tracks, more money, and greater exposure were also some reasons for moving.

Some twenty years later it happened. What John likes to call his 6 midlife crisis. That fear of getting old. His racing ability was slipping. He now had to rely on his cleverness and years of experience to combat the physical powers of younger jockeys. To compound his troubles there was a divorce. As with all separations of marriage there are many feelings and emotions that need to be dealt with. Since his children had already grown up and left home, he decided to get away, to take a year off from racing and collect himself. Well, one year grew to another and he had not raced in all this time. He had some money saved, but was growing bored with the apathetic life he was now leading. He needed the thrill of racing again, the competition, the danger. But how could he get his now soft body back into racing shape, and if he could, did he still have what it takes to win? These are questions he still asks himself.

It is hard to say whether he can do it or not. Sitting here talking 7 with him, I get the feeling he will try, that he's not a quitter, that there's still fight left in him. It will be interesting to see whether he makes it or not. As for myself, I am *betting* on it.

Assignment 5: Study of a Historical Issue

Method of Research: Finding Facts and Journalistic Views of Those Facts
    from Library Sources
Most Pertinent Chapters: 2, 3, 4, 5, 7, 10, 13
Probable Topic Due:
Possible Sources Due:
Clean Draft Due for Workshop:
Paper Due:

GOAL

To look at journalistic reporting of some person or event at least 18 years old, and to study either (1) the event and its place in history or (2) the way journalists interpreted the material they reported.

THE PROCESS

1. Locate, in your library's periodicals room, the microfilm version of *The New York Times* from the day that you were born (e.g., June 5, 1970). If you have never worked with the microfilm, ask a librarian or a student library worker for assistance. Read through the entire paper (using one of the microfilm scanners), and choose one article which especially interests you. If you can't find an article that intrigues you from the day you were born, look at papers from days near the day you were born. You may choose your article from any section of the paper except the sports pages, but I recommend that you choose from the first section.

2. Once you've chosen an article, think up a possible topic that you might like to write about that connects, closely or loosely, with your article. You might, for example, contrast some stories which indicate racial attitudes then and now; you might show how union and management stubbornness led to a long strike that neither side anticipated; you may be led to try to figure out why a certain event happened; you may show how several magazines or newspapers treated the same issue very differently. Readers of this kind of paper don't want you to tell them something that they could find out just as easily by looking in an encyclopedia. Your readers are curious about how people and events were viewed by the journalists of their own time.

3. On _____ (date), bring to class a sheet of paper with the following information handwritten on it:
   - Your date of birth
   - A summary of the article you have chosen to work with
   - A topic, connected with that article, that you think you'd like to write about
   - The kind of reader you imagine being interested
   - Why you think such a reader would benefit from your paper

   The class that day will compare potential topics, and suggestions will be made about where you and your classmates can find more information on the topics you've chosen. You'll learn a great deal by comparing your plans with those of your classmates. When you leave, you should feel confident that you have a topic that is not too broad so that you can research it thoroughly and still meet the deadline for the assignment.

4. Your next step is to check the library's indexes (your first stop should be *The New York Times Index* for newspaper articles, and the *Readers' Guide to Periodical Literature* for magazine articles) for sources of further information on your topic. Note down the sources you find in these indexes, and bring a list of ten possible sources of information to class on _____ . You probably won't use all these sources in your final paper, and you may well use some others that you come across as you work.

5. Find as many of these articles as you can, then, and begin taking notes on items that will serve the purpose of your paper. You'll undoubtedly

be noting facts (which of course must be acknowledged), as well as inferences made by the journalists you're reading (which also must be acknowledged). The quality of your paper will depend in part on your selecting these items carefully. But it will depend much more on the quality of the inferences (judgments, or conclusions) *you* draw about the facts and about the journalists' opinions. Your introduction, your conclusion, and the comments you make on each paragraph of material should show that you understand your material and that you, as a writer, are thinking and in control.

6. Before you begin writing, and as you sort through your notes, it may help to decide on an organizational pattern (cause-effect, comparison-contrast, narration, problem-solution) which best accommodates your evidence. Also, much of the information you've collected will have to be omitted. How will you decide what to include and what to omit?

7. Finally, you'll write your paper and bring it to class for your classmates to read on _____ . With their suggestions, you'll have _____ more days to rethink and revise your paper. Your typed paper is due on _____ .

Sample Papers

Why Weren't Atomic Bombs Used During the Korean War?

Soon-Kee Kim

The Korean War broke out with the invasion of Communist North   1
Koreans in June 1950, and ended in a truce in July 1953. It was only five years before the Korean War that the atomic bomb ended World War II against Japan. Then, why was not the same bomb used in the Korean War against the aggressors, the North Koreans and the Chinese, and why was the war allowed to last for more than three years?

An article in *U.S. News & World Report*, Dec. 8, 1950, answers the   2
question of what the atom bomb could and couldn't do in a war with North Korea and China: "It can strike terror, destroy thousands in cities. But it can't knock out the Communists armies. They are too scattered. There are no big mobilization centers; no concentration of war industry or transportation, few other good targets. As the war stands, other bombs can do the job better" ("A-Bomb" 23). According to this article, the reason an atomic bomb was not used during the Korean War is simply that it was not practical. The enemy troops were scattered along the 150 miles of the fighting front across the Korean peninsula. The potential

targets were mainly small basic industries such as railroads, bridges, factories, tunnels, and freight yards which could be destroyed effectively by conventional weapons. The two biggest cities in North Korea were its capital Pyungyang and Hamhung which were both railroad centers with some factories ("No" 50). The Hiroshima and Nagasaki bombs affected ten square miles, and it was not practical to use such a devastating bomb on small North Korean cities.

Another reason the atom bomb would not be effective in Korea was 3 its terrain: the battlefield in Korea was mostly rugged mountains which provided a considerable protection from the bomb. Ralph Lapp, in an article written late in the war, pointed out that a human being is harder to knock out than the average building and that more people died in Hiroshima and Nagasaki by the fragments of flying glass and the collapse of buildings and houses than from the direct impact of the atomic bombs (31). He further noted that the impact of the bomb was limited to less than one square mile if soldiers took proper cover like bunkers, which were widely used by the North Koreans and Chinese Communists. On the same subject, the earlier *U.S. News & World Report* article said that "A man or a building over the crest of a hill has almost complete protection, because earth takes up the shock" ("A-Bomb" 23).

The lack of good targets and the mountainous terrain in Korea and 4 China discouraged the use of the atom bomb during the Korean War. But it was President Truman who had the ultimate authority to decide on the use of the bomb, and who did not allow it. The pressure from Congress and the public to use the bomb was the greatest when 300,000 Chinese troops crossed the Korean border to help the losing North Koreans in November 1950, five months after the war broke out. But President Truman forbade the use not only of the atomic bomb but also of any conventional bombs in Chinese territory in order to avoid the possible involvement of Soviet troops.

President Truman's ban against bombing China angered many U.S. 5 military leaders. But President Truman did not allow any potentially dangerous remarks by them. When Air Force Major Gen. Emmett O'Donnell stated that all weapons, including atomic bombs, should have been used against the Chinese Communist aggressors and that "the U.S. had not learned a single important lesson in this war" (Hill 7), he was summoned to Air Force Headquarters and forced to reverse his remarks (White 5). Gen. Douglas MacArthur never made statements directly concerning the use of atomic bombs because he did not see the real need for it at the time. But he criticized President Truman's policy saying that it put the U.N. forces "under an enormous handicap without precedent in military history" ("McArthur Calls" 1). Not being able to support the president's cautious policy, Gen. MacArthur was relieved by the president on Apr. 11, 1951.

Though President Truman never really intended to use an atomic 6 bomb in Korea or China, he often warned the Communists that the U.S. might use it in order to discourage further possible aggression by the Soviet Union and to force the Communists to agree to a truce in Korea. The most direct warning by the president came on Dec. 1, 1950 after Chinese aggression. He said then that we would "settle for nothing less than a just and peaceful world" and that the U.S. would not hesitate to use an atomic bomb if necessary ("President Warns" 1). The indirect warning on the use of an atomic bomb came from Gordon Dean, chairman of the Atomic Energy Commission on Oct. 7, 1951. He warned that if the U.N. forces used atomic weapons against the aggressors within the appropriate destructive force, the moral obligation was upon the invaders, not on the defenders (Leviero 3).

When the Chinese Communists intervened in the Korean War to   7
help the North Koreans, the American public, who experienced the power of atomic bombs only five years before in Japan, thought this "miracle weapon" could be used again to end the war in Korea. It was hard for the American public to believe that the scattered targets and the mountainous terrain of Korea would make such a powerful bomb so ineffective. President Truman also did not want to risk another world war by using an atomic bomb in Korea. But the most important factor which made the atomic bomb less effective was that the U.S. was not a sole possessor of the atomic bomb and the possibility of a nuclear war was no longer unthinkable. When Stalin confirmed the experiment of the atomic bomb in the Soviet Union and proposed to continue the development of atomic bombs on Oct. 7, 1951, President Truman's choice became our only choice.

WORKS CITED

"A-Bomb Will Not Beat China." *U.S. News and World Report* 8 Dec. 1950: 23.

Hill, Gladwin. "O'Donnell Favors Using All Weapons." *New York Times* 19 Jan. 1951: 7.

Lapp, Ralph E. "Would the Atomic Bomb End the War in Korea?" *The Reporter* 6 Jan. 1953: 31–33.

Leviero, Anthony. "Dean Idea to Wage Atom War in Field is Held Significant." *New York Times* 7 Oct. 1951: 1,3.

"McArthur Calls Curbs a Handicap." *New York Times* 2 Dec. 1950: 1,4.

"No Worthwhile Targets of A. Bomb in North Korea." *Science Newsletter* 22 July 1950: 50.

"President Warns We Would Use Atom Bomb in Korea if Necessary." *New York Times* 1 Dec. 1950: 1,3.

White, William S. "McArthur Hearings End After 8 Weeks." *New York Times* 26 June 1951: 1,5.

Women in 1970: Pressed by Bias
Jennifer Lee

"This is not a bedroom war, this is a political movement..." 1
("Leading Feminist" 30), declared feminist leader Betty Friedan. Despite
the growing number of women leaving their homes and entering the
workforce prior to 1970, job opportunities and pay for women were still
limited compared to those for men. Working out of necessity or for ful-
fillment, many women were denied promotion and lacked adequate
child care (Charlton 20). Such problems were addressed and denounced
by the Women's Liberation Movement—"sisters", linked arm in arm,
staged demonstrations, sit-ins, and rallies, openly expressing their desire
to gain equal status with men. However, the press often dismissed feminist enthusiasm as "emotionalism" ("The Liberated Woman" 34). Writers' assumptions and presentation of facts and inferences in the 1970
New York Times show that the paper was very biased against women.

Articles often presented women as demanding nuisances. For in- 2
stance, a February article describing Senate hearings on changing the voting age mentions an outburst by militant feminists ("Bayh Optimistic" 20):

> The hearings were briefly disrupted in the afternoon when a group of
> militant women stood up and demanded hearings on an amendment
> granting equality to women.
>   Senator Bayh quieted the group with polite humor and the
> suggestion they meet with him after the hearings. His humor was not
> appreciated by the women but brought laughter from the large teen-
> age and young adult audience that followed the two days of hearings.

The writer placed major emphasis not on the women's reasons for mak- 3
ing their demands at that time but rather, that the women were not
taken very seriously. This passage suggests that the press often treated
women as spoiled children—militants were to be quietly calmed before
they could throw tantrums. The laughter of the young adult audience
further supports the press's opinion that the women were being ridiculous in their demands.

Another article discussing a sit-in at the *Ladies' Home Journal* ed- 4
itorial offices also illustrated the newspaper's attitude of annoyance toward women. The article suggested strong disapproval of the feminists'
tactics in gaining the right to publish a women's liberation supplement
of the magazine, describing how demonstrators "lunged" at the publisher and how "a half-dozen girls helped themselves to cigars from a
box on [publisher] Mr. Carter's desk and smoked them" (Lichtenstein
51). Reference to the feminists as "girls" alone, which would have elicited
more lunges from the women, implies the press's view that the women

were immature in their behavior. Yet, no mention was made of the specific significance of the feminists' victory in gaining the *Ladies' Home Journal* as a means of communicating their views—other than phrases from demonstration spokesmen commending the sit-in as "a historic beginning" and "one small step for womenkind" (Lichtenstein 51). Only mentioning the feminists' demand for a free on-the-job day-care center, much of the article discussed the feminists' demand to replace the publisher and editorial and advertising staff with women, a point which supported the *Times'* bias concerning the outlandishness of the women's demands.

The *New York Times* also assigned ulterior motives to the words 5
and actions of feminists, as seen in the same article on the *Ladies' Home Journal*. One of the demonstration leaders, Susan Brownmiller, stated that the *Ladies' Home Journal* was targeted for protest because "it is one of the most demeaning magazines towards women" (Lichtenstein 51)— the writer coupled this statement with the fact that the *Ladies' Home Journal* was one of the largest magazines, having a circulation of 6.9 million readers. The inference that the size of the *Ladies' Home Journal* was more of a determining factor in choosing the magazine as a target for protest may well have been true. However, the writer failed to either support or refute Brownmiller's charge of the magazine as demeaning with any examples. Displaying Brownmiller's view of the *Ladies' Home Journal* as possibly invalid, the *New York Times* preferred to present its view that the feminists were "publicity-seeking exhibitionists" ("The Liberated Woman" 34). Another example of feminist "exhibitionism" presented by the *Times* may be seen in a description of a women's lib movement complaint to the Federal Government charging *Newsweek* with "bypassing" women for writing positions (Lichtenstein 51). The *New York Times* immediately noted that the complaint was made at the time *Newsweek* printed their cover story on the women's liberation movement.

The *New York Times* seems to have felt that women spent excessive 6
time on their appearance. For instance, an article discussing feminist attendance at a Senate meeting on the Equal Rights Amendment focused more upon the clothing worn than on the issues discussed: "Women attired in everything from miniskirts to midifrocks filled the Senate Caucus Room" ("Women Fill Hearing" 38). Another article, titled "Leading Feminist Puts Hairdo Before Strike," described Betty Friedan's "last-minute emergency appointment with her hairdresser" before a radio interview (30). That the *Times* suggested that the feminists thought more about their looks than the movement indicates the paper's condescension toward women.

A further insight into the *New York Times'* bias against women may 7
be seen in an editorial article on "The Liberated Woman." The writer lik-

ened feminists to the suffragettes who were "often noisy and obstreper-
ous" (34). Although he conceded that the feminists' fight for equality had
"substance," the writer attributed the success of the revolution mainly to
"science and wealth" (34):

> Because Western societies are increasingly rich, they can afford to
> educate more of their women and provide them with leisure. Because
> science has eliminated most of the drudgery, if not the tedium, of
> farm work and household work, millions of women are free to leave
> the fields and the kitchens and work beside men in offices and
> factories.

In assuming that science had allowed women to escape the drudgery of   8
housework and enter the workplace, the writer forgot the women who
worked out of necessity (i.e. to contribute a second family income, to
provide as single parents)—for with increasing wealth and scientific
achievement came a higher cost of living. Furthermore, in concluding
his article with an unsupported assertion, the writer revealed his own
opinion of the woman's place in society (34):

> But many values will remain little altered. The family has proved to
> be a tough, durable human institution in many different social
> settings. Many women will continue to find their most satisfying
> fulfillment in bearing children and raising them.

Ironically, the writer had previously mentioned (briefly) how there could   9
be more women in nontraditional fields: "There could well be thousands
of additional women in engineering, architecture, medicine and other
traditionally masculine professions." The contradiction between this
viewpoint and that in his conclusion may indicate the writer's wish to
please both halves of his audience—the women who want to change
their lives and the majority of the men who want women to "stay in their
places."

The *New York Times'* biased coverage of the feminist revolution   10
during 1970 revealed its disapproval of the changing role of women from
that of passive homemakers to that of radical activists. For all their
"attention-getting antics," as the *Times* called them ("The Liberated
Woman" 34), the feminists did manage to gain the nation's "consciousness about the worth and dignity of women" (Salholz 58), if not
the total equality they had hoped for. And despite the growing problem
today of professional women juggling family and career, a Gallup poll
(*Newsweek*, Mar. 31, 1986) showed that 71% of women who responded
said that the women's liberation movement has improved their lives (Salholz 59)—this is the same movement that the *New York Times* had described as "a matter for careful legislating, not for emotionalism or political gestures" ("The Liberated Woman" 34).

WORKS CITED

"Bayh Optimistic on Voting Age of 18 After the White House Backs Measure." *The New York Times* 18 Feb. 1970: 20.

Charlton, Linda. "The Feminine Protest." *The New York Times* 28 Aug. 1970: 20.

"Leading Feminist Puts Hairdo Before Strike." *The New York Times* 27 Aug. 1970: 30.

"The Liberated Woman." Editorial. *The New York Times* 27 Aug. 1970: 34.

Lichtenstein, Grace. "Feminists Demand 'Liberation' in *Ladies' Home Journal* Sit-In." *The New York Times* 19 Mar. 1970: 51.

Salholz, Eloise, *et al.* "Feminism's Identity Crisis." *Newsweek* 31 Mar. 1986: 58–59.

"Women Fill Hearing on Rights Equality." *The New York Times* 6 May 1970: 38.

Draft Review Worksheet:
Study of a Historical Issue

Writer: _____ Reviewer: _____

1. A writer promises to do something. What does the writer promise to do in this piece of writing? Where is the promise made? Does the writer keep the promise?

2. Read over the introductory paragraph again. Does it introduce the subject adequately? Does it attract your interest? How? Read over the concluding paragraph. What emotion does the writer try to leave you with? Can you make any suggestions for improving either the introduction or the conclusion?

3. Describe the paper's organizational strategy, paragraph by paragraph. Which paragraphs don't proceed smoothly from the paragraph they follow?

4. Does the writer use quotations well? How well do they contribute to and support the thesis of the paper? Do any sections of the paper need more quotations for support? Where would you like more information?

5. Can you recognize the writer's voice, the writer's *ethos,* throughout the paper? In which sections does the writer sound more like an encyclopedia?

6. Are there any changes you would suggest in spelling, punctuation, or grammar?

7. After reading this paper, what thoughts do you, as a thoughtful reader, have about this topic? How has reading this paper affected your attitude toward the issue discussed?

Flawed Paper

John Kennedy

Presidential candidates are often charged with changing faces in 1
different parts of the country. This was a major accusation of Jimmy
Carter during his run for the Presidency. I am going to focus on four
speeches given by Senator Kennedy during his campaign against Vice
President Nixon.

Kennedy—on vacation after the Democratic convention nominated 2
him as their Presidential candidate—chose three men to head top slots
in the campaign, Byron R. White, John M. Bailey, and J. Leonard Reinsch.
Kennedy and his staff were planning campaign schedules, trying to decide if they should open the campaign on Labor Day with a speech in
Cadillac Square, Detroit, as other Democratic Presidential nominees had
done (*New York Times*, July 21, 1960).

Kennedy did open his campaign with a Labor Day speech in Ca- 3
dillac Square, Detroit (*New York Times*, September 6, 1960). The crowd
was enthusiastic and his first phrase would label the theme of his administration the new frontier, "I have come today from Alaska, America's
last frontier, to Michigan to state the case for America's new frontier." He
mentions his endorsement from the A.F. of L.-C.I.O. and asks labor for
their support. While he was discussing the economy he brought up a
figure dealing with car production, in this car producing city of Detroit.
He stated that the President had said, on August 10, that we had a fine
year in automobile sales even though a few years ago we produced
1,500,000 more cars than this year.

In this speech, given on November 1, in Philadelphia's Convention 4
Hall there was a confident Kennedy speaking (*New York Times*, November 2, 1960). During this campaign, Kennedy and Nixon held four television debates in which Kennedy appeared as an able and capable leader.
Today these debates are considered major turning points for Kennedy.
He started this speech with this comment, "This, unfortunately, is not
the fifth debate, but I am glad to be here and have a chance to express
my views on this occasion, and I wish the Vice President could have arranged his schedule to do likewise tonight." He went on with promises
for School Equality and for Fair Farm Prices. This was to try to get votes
from strong Republican midwestern States. He warned Americans that
Russia was spreading communism through Asia and Africa by sending
diplomats well versed in the language and customs of the country they

were being sent. He said in 1958 our ambassador to Moscow was the only United States ambassador to a communist country who knew the language of the country to which he was assigned. He brought the idea of the Peace Corps, young men and women trained in skills and taught the language and customs of the country they will be assigned. Kennedy was emphasizing the importance of learning foreign languages, in his speech he quoted Goethe, "A man who is ignorant of foreign languages is ignorant of his own." This emphasis on language was peculiar because Kennedy did not speak foreign languages. In *Conversations with Kennedy* Ben Bradlee noted that once during a French embassy dinner at the White House talk around the table was all French and he had a difficult time. Bradlee said that Kennedy spoke French with a Cuban accent.

In his last two speeches in San Francisco and Chicago had the sim-   5
ilar promises of the first two (*New York Times,* November 3 and November 5, 1960). In San Francisco he again attacked the administration for letting the United States fall behind Russia. In Chicago he told the audience that Mr. Nixon was running not Mr. Eisenhauer. He urges for Social Security with a Medical Care Plan tacted on. The farming issue came up again with Kennedy stating that the administration had driven income down and this caused nearly 11,000 people to lose work in Illinois.

Speeches during a Presidential election don't have much sub-   6
stance. Their purpose is to gain votes and stir emotion. Senator Kennedy did give moving speeches, his most memorable speech was his inaugural address. The debates served a greater service to voters than individual speeches. The two answered the same questions and the public could decide which was the most capable. The speeches bring an old cliche, easier said than done.

Assignment 6: Proposal

Method of Research: Studying an Audience and the Facts of the Case
Most Pertinent Chapters: 2, 3, 4, 5, 6, 7, 13
Clean Draft Due for Workshop:
Paper Due:

PRELIMINARY EXERCISE

Write down in your notebook a brief description of a problem—in your family, in this school, in your community, in society—that bothers you.

Now think of a worse problem, a problem that affects more people, and write a brief description of it.

Choose one of these two problems to be the subject of the proposal paper you'll be writing. Before you do any research, can you think of a method of attacking your problem? What's the cause of the problem? Have any solutions to the problem already been tried?

Finally, pair up with one of your classmates, and explain your proposal. After you've explained it, give your partner enough time to write out three possible problems with, or objections to, your proposal. Consider these objections as you write your paper.

OVERVIEW

Injustice rears its head daily in our experience, even when we belong to a society that tries to be just. There is always room, therefore, for proposals to improve matters. In writing a proposal you will be using writing not only to get people to listen to you as you explain something, or to agree with you about the value of some part of our culture, but to get them to do something about a problem that you think should be remedied. Think up a way to solve the problem that bothers you most. It may take a while to work out the details, but be patient and keep thinking. Keep in mind practical details like cost. And try to figure out how the solution will help everybody—not only you, the employee, for example, but also the boss and the whole company.

Write your solution in a letter to the people who would have the authority to make the change you are recommending. See whether you can make them happy that they received your letter.

SUGGESTIONS

In your letter, you will need evidence to show why there is a problem and how your solution is the best one available. Use your detective instinct to do your research: consider books, newspapers, journals, company papers, phone calls, interviews, observation. Use, in short, whatever material you need to make your case.

Remember to anticipate the objections your reader or readers will have. What will your readers not like about your plan? And how will you answer their objections? Assume that your readers are skeptical, but that they are not hostile and will at least begin to read your paper with an open mind and a sense of goodwill. Your problem is to wedge yourself into that slight opening and expand it as far as you can.

Remember, too, the importance of your own *ethos*. Not only do you have to know what you are talking about, you also have to be generous and understanding of your readers' position. You want to do everything you can to persuade them to say "Yes" to your proposed change.

Structure your essay so that it progresses smoothly, with each point building on the preceding one. You'll probably want to include the following elements:

1. Opening words that win attention and goodwill by introducing the problem in a tone expressing optimism about solving it
2. A history of the case, including possible causes of the problem
3. An acknowledgement of your readers' probable point of view
4. A concession to parts of that view and a refutation of other parts
5. A direct statement of your proposal, along with evidence that it is the
   best alternative and a detailed explanation of the good effects likely to
   be produced (it often helps to acknowledge constraints that would affect
   any solution to this problem)
6. A final, heightened appeal for support (you don't want your reader to
   sleep easily that night until your plan has, in some form, been accepted)

Sample Papers

Note: The following two papers, while strong in other respects, have not
acknowledged their sources of information as they should have. As you
read, decide where acknowledgements should have been included.

Protect the Protectors
Unknown Student Author

One of the biggest concerns of American citizens is crime on the   1
streets and, in particular, violent crimes where victims are stabbed or
shot. Every day there are stories in newspapers and on television about
someone who has been injured or killed during the commission of a
crime. Some of the victims are innocent bystanders who happen to be
nearby and are struck by a stray bullet. There is also a special class of
victims of these crimes who are usually not directly involved in the original act and they are not mere bystanders. These victims are police officers who, because of their oath and duty, must pursue and attempt to
apprehend violent people. Police officers are expected to get involved in
dangerous situations and to relieve citizens of the threat of violence. It is
because of this danger that a police officer faces that I address the Montgomery County Council.

In recent years there has been an increase in the number of law   2
enforcement officers killed or injured in the line of duty. Between 1960
and 1967, there was an average of 51 officers killed each year in the
United States. Since 1970 there have been at least 100 deaths reported
every year, and some of those years the figure was 125 or more. Most of
the officers were killed with handguns. A few were murdered with

knives, rifles, or shotguns. Four police officers have been killed in Montgomery County since 1972. Some of these deaths could have been prevented if the officers had been equipped with an inexpensive protective vest.

Protective devices for the chest are not new and unknown pieces of equipment for the police community. Bullet-proof vests have been used for years by police departments in special situations where there was an obvious chance of being shot. This equipment was always expensive, big, heavy, and cumbersome and could not be worn all the time. In the past few years a more compact, lightweight, and inexpensive vest has been developed and is now available for purchase. This newer vest can be worn at all times concealed under outer clothing and provides constant protection against stabbing or shooting. My proposal to the Montgomery County Council is that money should be immediately appropriated, under emergency legislation, to purchase one of the new bullet-proof vests for every officer on the county police department.

Several brands of chest protectors are on the market, but an average description can be given to describe them. Newer models weigh approximately two and a half pounds. They cover an area of about twelve inches by sixteen inches on the chest and back. Construction is of various lightweight synthetic materials that are sewn together in layers and hang from shoulder straps over the chest and back. Elastic straps on the side of the body pull the front and back together but are not restraining and allow freedom of movement. Tests have been conducted by the manufacturers and by the Law Enforcement Assistance Administration of the Department of Justice. These tests have shown that the vests will stop almost all handgun bullets including the powerful .44 caliber magnum. Repeated forceful thrusts with knives have failed to penetrate the protectors. Only a relatively small number of thin sharp-pointed objects and bullets were able to go through the material. Overall, the modern bullet-proof vest has shown in tests that it provides good protection from knives, handguns, and other low velocity weapons such as small rifles and shotguns. Statistics show that most murdered police officers die from wounds in the chest or back inflicted by these kinds of weapons.

The cost of buying a bullet-proof vest for every officer is low, especially when compared to the benefit derived. The average price is approximately $100.00 per vest when purchased by an individual officer, but a discount could probably be obtained if a large order was placed with one of the manufacturers. At the price of $100.00 per unit, every officer on the police department could be equipped with a vest for about $75,000.00. The murder of the lowest paid officer in the department would cost the county at least a quarter of a million dollars in death benefits. If just one life was saved by a bullet-proof vest, it would also save far more money than the initial cost to the taxpayer.

One possible drawback has been suggested if every officer were to be given a protective vest. Some people feel that the officer would have a false sense of security and would take chances that he or she would not take without the vest. Even if this is true, I suggest there is no way to measure the possibility or predict that it will happen with a particular police officer. Valuable life-protecting equipment should not be withheld from a person merely because it will make the person feel secure. Also, because some officers may not wear the vest, it is felt, by some people, that the equipment should be bought by the individual. I agree that some police officers may refuse to wear the vest because, at times, there is a slight discomfort from excessive heat, but the major reason is that many officers cannot afford the purchase. The Montgomery County government has the money to buy bullet-proof vests that could eventually save far more than the initial investment.

Bullet-proof vests are efficient and inexpensive protection for police officers. They are light enough to be worn at all times and do not hinder normal movement. Cost is low to supply every officer with a vest and a cash outlay now could possibly prevent a far more costly loss in the future. Extensive testing has shown that bullet-proof vests will provide protection against the wounds that usually cause the death of police officers.   7

Now is the time to take a bold step to provide protection for the police officers of this community and to show that someone cares about the welfare of the men and women who try to shield others from aggression. The duty of a police officer is to provide protection and to assume the danger that a citizen might have to face. This duty cannot be ignored, but there should also be the duty of the citizens of a community to furnish basic protective equipment to the police. These men and women who serve are just mortal humans who can bleed to death, and this fact is being proven with greater and greater frequency. Right now, without hesitation, let's do something that will help shield our police.   8

To: Dr. J. P. Stewart, Principal of Buchanan Academy
Tracey E. Landis

She is the one at the end of the welfare line, holding in her arms a dirt-smudged one-year-old. She rolls her eyes as she realizes the baby is wet, and she blows a puff of smoke into his round, dirty face. He cries; she hits him. Fifteen years old, this mother would probably rather be outside throwing a frisbee, or roasting corn on a beach with a bunch of   1 friends, but she is just one of the one million teenage girls who became pregnant in 1978 and could be one of the ten girls who became pregnant while attending Buchanan Academy in the last five years. Unable to return to school, and painfully aware of the difficulties of getting a good job without a diploma, she depends on the small check she receives each week to pay the rent, buy diapers, and provide food for the two of them. She didn't plan on getting pregnant, and there is a good chance, had she known how, she would have prevented it. But her parents never told her about contraception, and the school she attended offered no classes on the subject.

Her school did have a sex education class on puberty, pregnancy, heredity, and V.D., but prohibited discussion of contraception, abortion, homosexuality, and masturbation. Like most of the schools in the country, the course taught the students about gonorrhea, syphilis, and chancroid, they warned them of venereal warts, dreaded lesions, and blindness, but they never told them how to prevent them. After endless diagrams, films, and lectures, all the students really knew about sex was how to "identify the parts." Speaking with Laura Jackson, Director of Health and Physical Education at Buchanan Academy, I learned of the students' lack of information. "These teenagers do not know the first thing about contraception. They think an I.U.D. is something like an IOU, that all jellies are made by Welches, and that a prophylactic shield is a piece of armor used in the holy wars by the ancient men of Prophylon." She went on to tell me of one pregnant sixteen-year-old who came for counseling. After asking the girl if she had taken "precautions," the wide-eyed girl assured her, "Of course, we were afraid someone would find out, so Joe shut all the windows and I locked all the doors. We were real careful...." Although amusing, this student's "misconceptions" should be corrected, and because this duty is sometimes neglected by forgetful or embarrassed parents, I propose that you, Dr. Stewart, add this type of sex education to the curriculum at Buchanan Academy.

A four-week mandatory course could easily become part of the health education class which is already required for graduation. Those teaching the course will decide on a standard course description and syllabus including the four major units:

1. Understanding the sexual functions of the human body.
2. Pregnancy prevention and alternatives.
3. Venereal disease and its prevention.
4. Making responsible decisions.

The first unit should include a brief explanation of the anatomy of sex and pregnancy, followed by the second unit which could include contraception and abortion. The third unit would solely be devoted to V.D.

and its prevention. Diminishing the emphasis on the anatomy of sex, the teacher could bring contraceptive devices into the classroom for the students to see, and would answer questions on abortion, masturbation, and homosexuality. The fourth unit should attempt to correlate the first three units with the student's need to be able to make a responsible decision. It is in this fourth and final unit that the teachers should try to make the student understand that owning a body and having the ability to function sexually do not give the student free license to use these assets indiscriminately.

Because some embarrassed students have difficulty asking questions they think they should already know the answer to, a shoe box could be set by the door and students could place, as they exited, their written questions into a slot, ensuring the students' anonymity, preventing wide eyes, dropped jaws, and embarrassed giggles, and allowing the teacher time between classes to answer the questions adequately. **4**

Lest the mention of practical sex education conjure up in the minds of fretful parents images of Fourteenth Street, *Hustler* magazine, and Farmer's Daughters jokes, a Friday night parent-teacher assembly could be arranged to tell the parents exactly what their children will be taught. During this meeting, the parents could ask questions and offer any suggestions they felt would improve the course. **5**

The present Health Education Directors at Buchanan Academy could teach the class as part of the health class, avoiding hiring new teachers and the burden of extra hours and rescheduling. The cost of the course would vary, depending on the cost of audio-visual media, samples, and teacher's text, but could initially be held to a small sum, a minimal amount if we are to consider the $10,000.00 bill the state must foot for the delivery, postnatal care, and welfare of a single jobless mother. The class will try to give all the students a sense of responsibility and make them aware of the decisions that they must make as adults. But even if the program were to reach just one person and help keep her from becoming pregnant, the program would have justified itself monetarily, as well as reaping the unmeasurable rewards of saving a student from the trauma of an unwanted pregnancy. But for this program to work, the course must be mandatory. There may be some students who are adamantly opposed to listening to "things they already know," but even if they answer to the name Masters or Johnson, there are always more questions to be asked. It is often the ones who swear to having read *The Joy* ten times who ask the fewest questions, yet know the least about preventing V.D. and conception. Working this course into the already mandatory sophomore health class solves the problem of insuring 100% enrollment. **6**

Parents attempting to shield their "innocent" children from this subject may, for religious or personal reasons, question the course's ne- **7** cessity and ethical value. Addressing the question of necessity, Northern Urban Area studies show that the mean age for the boy's first sexual intercourse is twelve years old and that by the age of sixteen, one in five girls has had sex. Each year there are one million pregnancies, and 300,000 abortions. These figures are not being lowered, and the problem of teenage pregnancy and V.D. are not diminishing. We, as parents, administrators, and concerned citizens, cannot erase the millions, but we can do something to help the small percentage coming from our school. Neglecting to inform these teenagers about sex is obviously no guarantee that they will not have intercourse, yet informing the students increases the chance that they will think twice before they do have sex, and if they decide they want to, they will know enough to make an intelligent decision.

To satisfy those who for religious reasons will not want their children learning about contraception and abortion, the teacher could make it clear that the alternatives to pregnancy may not be desirable for all, but simply that these alternatives exist. It is similar to the class on evolution presently taught in your school. The teacher does not in any way imply evolution to be the preferred view: in fact, the teacher is a creationist, but the students are taught that other views exist whether they choose them as their own or not.   8

I realize that the subjects of contraception and abortion have been traditionally taboo, and there may be difficulty in getting the school board to even discuss the matter, much less appropriate money, but I feel that this subject has been too long ignored by the people who have the power to make a change. If Buchanan Academy were to initiate this type of program and if it were successful, not only would the school gain recognition and added respect, but it might set a precedent for other schools in the county.   9

The proposed course could save a young couple from being forced into marriage, eliminate the pain of a parent who might otherwise have been devastated, and prevent the heartbreak of a child who might have grown up unwanted and unloved. As a parent and a school administrator, don't you think that it is worth it?   10

Respectfully yours,

Tracey E. Landis
Class of 1979

Draft Review Worksheet:
Proposal

Writer: _____ Reviewer: _____

1. Does the writer make you feel that the problem is significant? What examples, illustrations, or statistics does he or she use to convince you? If there are not enough facts, how could the writer research this issue more thoroughly?

2. Will the author's suggested solution work? Why or why not? What is one way it might break down?

3. What about the writer's *ethos?* Is the writer an "expert" on the subject? Has the writer been fair to the other side?

4. What are two possible objections that the writer has not taken into consideration? If you were in the position of power, would this proposal make you take action? What priority would you give it?

5. Describe the paper's organizational strategy, paragraph by paragraph. Is there any point where the structure becomes unclear?

6. What is your most important suggestion for revision?

Flawed Paper

To Whom It May Concern:*

   This letter is written in behalf of myself, a personal property owner 1
in Huntington Village since 1968, although its contents may affect most
of the other 308 owners, who I suspect will not wish maltreatment in the
callous and unethical manner that I was. I request—no, I demand—the
opportunity to appear at the Huntington Village Community Association
Board of Directors next meeting to present my grievance and receive answers to my questions. I provide the following details in advance so that
you may reasonably prepare your responses, a consideration that was
denied me.

   On 24 March 1982 an employee of your nursery contractor ruth- 2
lessly and effectively cut off at the ground seven mature and living but
dormant butterfly bushes that paralleled the rear fence of my property.
He was merely executing orders and I have no grievance with that man.
In my effort to determine responsibility, however, that night the Architecture Committee chief confided that she was the one responsible. I
pursued several direct questions, to which I insist I am entitled to a reasonable answer. The first question was why my bushes were cut down.
I was informed that, in accordance with the publicized *Herald* of
September/October 1981, they were *not* "my" bushes if they were outside
the fence. I do not challenge that technical point further at this time, but
I suggest it has suspect legality. Proceeding on, I asked why *these* particular bushes were removed; she provided three plausible reasons.
First, home owners have been planting on common ground bushes and
trees that are not compatible with Huntington Village decor and that vi-
olate public and personal rights; this assessment is a factual one but it is
inapplicable in my case, since my bushes were planted there by the
Huntington Village developer in 1968, with some frail bushes subse-
quently having been replaced by me. The second reason given was that
many bushes in Huntington Village are eyesores and detract from the
community decor; if that be the case, and I seriously doubt that it is the
sole reason, why then has it taken thirteen years for someone (?) to decide their unacceptability? And why were mine the only offensive butterfly bushes? (More on this subject later.) The third reason given was

*This time I've included a letter written by a condominium owner rather than a student
paper because it offers so much to comment on.

that some overhanging bushes interfere with the mowing of lawns by contractor personnel; in my humble opinion, anyone who endorses that it is *right* to *destroy* living plants for the convenience of lawnmowing or other similar activity has a peculiar sense of values. I STILL DO *NOT* KNOW WHY MY BUSHES WERE DESTROYED. My second question was what would now be done to correct the horrible eyesore created by the removal of the bushes; you are invited to examine the ugly brown fence (standard for Huntington Village, when not partially hidden by foliage), the dead grassed area, and the tree stumps which were previously hidden. The initial answer was that nothing more will be done; eventually, though, she acknowledged that sod may be brought in and the stumps removed. My third question pertains to an aspect of this entire experience that is by far the most distressing. Why was this heinous act perpetuated without even the decency to notify me that something was allegedly unacceptable and that corrective action was imminent? She will have to provide you her own rationale, since I do *not* want to misquote what she told me.

In my subsequent inspection of Huntington Village, and you can 3 believe I have made a thorough one, I found that the dormant butterfly bushes to the rear of my fence and two of them across the roadway at the playground (along Clover Road) were decapitated on 24 March. I found that *green* bushes along Clover Road were *not* touched. I found a proliferation of dormant butterfly bushes along other property in Oxford and Cambridge Courts which were *not* touched. I have found *no* other evidence of "corrective surgery." I come to the inescapable conclusion that for some reason I have been selected for discrimination, and I don't really appreciate it one bit!

I do not deny the need for community standards, nor do I chal- 4 lenge the Board's responsibilities and rights for correction of deficiencies and nuisances. In the discharge of those functions I would trust that my Board would perform in a reasonable and legal and professional manner.

The following facts apply: 5

1. I have incurred damages, both tangible and intangible. The destruction of the bushes, whoever's they may have been, constitutes a loss in immediate resale value of my property. The eyesore newly created has a deleterious effect on all Huntington Village property, for that matter. The removal of the bushes denies my family the degree of privacy formerly provided by those bushes blocking the spaces in the alternately-slatted fence. This whole unsavory and uncompassionate experience has caused extreme mental anguish to my family.
2. This entire experience, with all applicable acts, has been highly selective in nature and prejudicial against one person: me.

3. Common and uncommon criminals such as Charles Manson and John Hinckley are accorded rights that insure they be confronted by their accusers, be informed of alleged indiscretions, be properly judged and then, and only then, be punished if found guilty. I have been deprived of comparable rights. I am waiting for someone to inform me of my alleged indiscretions (property nuisance features, if that be the case) that have warranted the premature and unwarned corrective/destructive action against me, for which the Board is responsible.

Lastly, I will not tolerate a recurrence of this selective maltreatment, nor do I wish to witness similar wanton actions against my fellow neighbors. 6

Assignment 7: Persuading a Classmate (Taylor 507–10)

Method of Research: Studying the Classmate's Opinion, Then Finding Information and Further Opinions in the Library and Elsewhere
Most Pertinent Chapters: 2, 3, 4, 5, 6, 7, 10, 13
Clean Draft Due for Workshop:
Paper Due:

Your assignment this time is to use writing to its fullest potential—that is, to change someone's mind, even if only slightly.

Stop for a moment.

Fill out, in as much detail as possible, a copy of the opinion sheet following this assignment. When you've finished, hand your opinion sheet to another student, and you'll receive one in turn.

In your paper, your writing task will be to show the student whose opinion sheet you received that the issue he or she commented on is more complicated than he or she might think. Or if you prefer, you may take a position directly opposed to the position taken by this student. In order to better understand your classmate's views, take fifteen to twenty minutes to question her or him about those views. Then allow yourself to be questioned by the writer who will be writing for you. Before you leave, exchange phone numbers so you can ask follow-up questions. If, after this interview, you find yourself forced to write a paper you see no hope for (for example, defending the South African government), ask your partner to fill out another opinion sheet or two until you are comfortable with your assigned task.

This paper will allow you to show almost all the skills that you've practiced in this course—using facts to back up an opinion, using library resources, conducting interviews (if you wish), writing effective introductions and conclusions. In addition, this paper will force you to become clearly aware of your reader, another crucial writing skill.

You may structure your paper any way that suits your material, but you may find your research proceeding more clearly if you keep in mind the following format:

Introduction of the problem
Concession to your reader's point of view
Advancement of your own argument
Conclusion

As you write, you may want to consider any of the following common methods of persuasion:

1. Use of facts, statistics, and examples found through research
2. Use of examples from your personal experience
3. Definition of terms in a way in which your reader does not usually define them
4. Discussion of possible causes or effects
5. Appeals to authority (combined with evidence that the authority deserves to be listened to)
6. Description of a similar situation and its results

My guess is that as you do your research, you'll consult about ten sources (remember that you'll be researching both sides of the question), and that your final paper will acknowledge at least three.

Opinion Sheet

Name: _____

1. Issue that you have strong feelings about:

2. Statement of your views on that issue:

3. Reasons (three) for holding your views:

4. Authorities (at least two) who agree with you or whom you have learned from:

5. Why you consider these people authorities:

6. Examples of incidents which have helped develop or reinforce your view:

Sample Papers

Capital Punishment: A Good Idea Despite Its Flaws
Dahlia Shaewitz

Capital punishment is defined as the death penalty for a crime. A   1
'capital crime' can be aimed against one person, several people, the government, or property when a person's life is at stake ("Capital Punishment" 435). These are the simple facts, perhaps the only simple facts
that remain constant throughout the highly controversial debate of
whether to continue, or abolish, capital punishment.

My personal stand is for capital punishment, and I also agree with   2
the fundamental belief in retribution, retaliation, and deterrence
("Capital Punishment" 435). However, my classmate, Monique Moore,
has some strong feelings about this subject, and her views are directly
opposite to mine. She advocates an abolishment of the death penalty for
several reasons. Her most important arguments are that capital punishment entails a too long and drawn out process, that imprisonment is a
better punishment, and that class and racial inequality and unfairness
are rampant in our judicial system. Although there are several other reasons that also might be used in opposition to my arguments, these three
are serious challenges to anyone who defends capital punishment.

To begin with, one must realize that proponents of the death pen-   3
alty have three important reasons which they feel support their position.
A majority of the public feels that criminals are not punished as often or
as deservedly as they should be (Janigan 12). These people also demand
the highest form of retribution for the most hideous crimes—capital
punishment. As a Canadian spokesperson for Citizens Responding to
You, Joyce Wilson speaks for many when she says that "any cold-
blooded murderer has forfeited his right to live" (Janigan 11). Retaliation
is not only a choice, but the right choice for many people like J. Wilson.
Deterrence, as the third basis of the pro-capital punishment stand, is its
only weak point. Statistics do not prove or disprove capital punishment's
effects on crime (Janigan 8). Regardless of the statistics, though, seventy-
three percent of proponents would continue to support capital punishment, even if it were not a deterrent (Stout 46).

The first argument against capital punishment is that imprison-   4
ment—and rehabilitation—is the best choice. Of course, it would be
wonderful if all persons convicted of heinous crimes and murders could

be sent to prison, taught to behave correctly in society, and then released. But this is not always so; for if it were, there would be no need for either extremely long term prison sentences or the death penalty. Thus, the only real choice is over what type of punishment to impose. In fact, there is only one possible, logical punishment—the punishment that fits the crime. In this case "a life for a life" (Janigan 10).

Approximately 250 men and women are issued the death sentence 5
each year (Deiter 11). Nonetheless, only twenty-five persons were executed in 1987, only eighteen persons each in 1986 and 1985 (Begley 64). Richard C. Dieter, who writes articles in support of the abolition of capital punishment claims that about "half of [those executed are] minorities, and almost all of [them are] poor" (Deiter 12). It seems, as Monique says, that the handing out of justice is not fair and equal.

Still, I strongly believe that mass murderers and serial killers de- 6
serve the death penalty, and seventy percent of all other Americans agree (Deiter 11). However, when a black man is sentenced to death for killing a white woman, as opposed to a white man receiving merely a prison sentence for killing a black woman, then something is wrong. Two inmates on death row, Billy Sinclair and Wilbert Rideau, know well that although a higher proportion of murder victims are black, "it is unlikely that anyone, Black or white, will be given the death sentence for killing a Black" (Rideau and Sinclair 136). Indeed, reports show that the black killers of white victims are approximately four times as likely to be executed as those (black or white) who kill blacks (Lacayo 80). Almost half the persons on death row are black, even though blacks represent only eleven percent of the population (Begley 64). Obviously, punishments are not always meted out fairly or justly, no matter how neatly they may fit the crime. However, in the case of "Ga. vs McCleskey," the Supreme Court ruled that there was no racial prejudice in deciding his case (Gest 54). This ruling indicates that there may be other factors which account for the astounding numbers above. Racial discrimination permeates our lives, so it is fair to say that it is also a part of our judicial system. The problem is not capital punishment so much as it is the prejudices and inequalities present in our culture. Justice Lewis Powell of the Supreme Court wrote, "It is the legislatures, the elected representatives of the people, that are constituted to respond to the will and consequently the moral values of the people" (Lacayo 80).

Whether or not we blame ourselves for the disproportionate num- 7
bers gravely presented to us from death row is something we must decide. To change for the sake of equality and fairness is something we can do. But one thing we must not do is to let cold-blooded murderers serve a few years in jail and then go back to the streets. J. C. Shaw and James Terry Roach raped a young immigrant girl from Columbia in 1987, then proceeded to kill her and her boyfriend (Stout 48). Did these two men

deserve to live long healthy lives after taking two others without reason? What about Paula Cooper? She is a young woman who ran out of coins to play the video machines with. She and her friends conned their way into Ruth Pelke's home and Paula proceeded to stab the 78-year-old woman to death. She stabbed the elderly Bible-studies instructor thirty-three times. Then she took the thirty dollars she found and returned to her video games (Bruning 13). No one's life is worth thirty dollars of spare change. Murderers like these, the ones who send chills up your spine, deserve a punishment equal to their crime.

Finally, Monique makes the point that capital punishment is a long **8** drawn out process. After being sentenced to death, a man or woman may join the nearly 2,000 men and women across the country who await their final days on death row (Begley 64). Some of them have been waiting for years and years (Lacayo 80). Prisoners may continue to appeal a decision of death as more information comes out. Many times it seems similar to the television commercials announcing "no sale is ever final," except in this case the word is not "sale" but "final decision." This process of sentencing can be costly and time consuming, but sentencing and life imprisonment is also expensive. Time is not such a bad thing, though, when one considers the consequences of a quick decision and punishment. If a long time elapses between sentencing and execution, then evidence found later could still help the prisoner, making the long wait more of an advantage than a disadvantage.

The capital punishment issue is continually debated. In my sup- **9** port of the death penalty, I do not regard the facts lightly; instead, I have weighed both sides and have come up with what I feel is the better answer. The process of capital punishment is time consuming, but for the benefit of the prisoner. Yet, the execution of killers seems the best way to handle the problem, rather than supporting the life imprisonment of a murderer. The only real problem to be faced is that of racial discrimination in the judicial system. Indeed, this is a grave matter that the American public must face. But prejudice is not only a characteristic of capital punishment, it is also a factor in many other processes. We must overcome our racial problems and deal with our capital punishment questions as two different issues. Capital punishment is the most fitting punishment for the most horrendous crimes.

WORKS CITED

Begley, Sharon, et al. "The Slow Pace on Death Row: A System No One Likes." *Newsweek* 8 Feb. 1988: 64.

Bruning, Fred. "Countdown to the Electric Chair." *MacLeans* 16 Mar. 1987: 13.

"Capital Punishment." *Dictionary of American History,* 1976 ed.

Deiter, Richard C. "The Death Penalty Dinosaur: Capital Punishment Heads for Distinction." *Commonweal* 15 Jan. 1988: 11–14.

Gest, Ted. "Death Penalty Again Haunts Supreme Court." *US News and World Report* 14 Nov. 1983: 54.

Janigan, Mary. "Capital Punishment: The Death Vote." *MacLeans* 16 Mar. 1987: 8–12.

Lacayo, Richard. "Clearing a Path to the Chair." *Time* 4 May 1987: 80.

Rideau, Wilbert and Billy Sinclair. "An Inside View: The Death Penalty." *Essence* July 1982: 136.

Stout, David G. "The Lawyers of Death Row." *New York Times Magazine* 14 Feb. 1988: 46–60.

The Necessary Role of United States Marines in Lebanon

Joseph Greenawalt

Since the death of over 230 Marines in Beirut, an increasing 1 amount of attention has been focused on the role of the United States in Lebanon. Supporters of the U.S. role in Lebanon argue that the Marines are a necessary symbol to friends and foes alike and that the United States is committed to backing the government of Lebanon and attaining peace in the volatile Mideast region. Opponents like my classmate Claudia Gelzer argue that the Marines complicate an already complicated situation. Both views, though, voice a concern for the people of Lebanon and share a common desire to gain a fast and lasting peace in the region.

Opponents have emotionally demonstrated a rightful concern for 2 the innocent lives lost in Lebanon in recent months, especially after the massacre of hundreds of Palestinian refugees at Sabra and Shatila in early 1983. They say that everyone sympathized with the United States when the Marines were massacred, but we all have ignored for a long time the daily hardships and the death of hundreds of innocent Lebanese people. This is of great concern to all of us, but the withdrawal of U.S. troops, as the opponents of the U.S. role have called for, is not a way to end the senseless killings in Lebanon. On the contrary, the U.S. presence is designed explicitly to stabilize the region. The U.S. Marines are not causing the killing—they are attempting to stop the killings. The opponents also believe that the United States should let the Middle East People solve their own disputes. This may seem a viable way of handling the conflicts in the area, but it is, in reality, a simple and naive solution to a complex problem. The people of the Mideast have consistently demonstrated their inability to solve their own problems. Time and time again, the government of Lebanon has called to outsiders to solve their internal problems. This in fact is why the United States is in Lebanon today.

The basic internal strife in Lebanon has existed for hundreds of 3 years—it is the fundamental conflicting beliefs between Christians and Moslems that arose following the Crusades in the 11th through 13th Century. These different religious groups, despite their individual identities, have lived together for centuries and have been united as Arabs sharing a common bond to the land in which they live. However, the immediate problems in Lebanon can be directly traced not to the fundamental religious conflicts that exist in the area, but to a census and unwritten agreement in 1943 that pointed out anew these differences (Smith 32). This agreement established that a Christian would be president of Lebanon while a Moslem would be Prime Minister. However, this agreement has led to increased religious tension in the area, for Moslems in 1983 are dissatisfied with their subservient role to a Christian President and want a larger share of political power. The Moslems today, called Druze, have sided with anti-Lebanese government forces to win increased power. These anti-governmental forces include Syrians, the strongest Arab allies of the Soviet Union.

The United States has rightfully accused the Syrians of using the 4 desires of the dissatisfied Lebanese Moslems as a pretext to gain their foothold in the region, thus increasing the Soviet sphere of influence in the Mideast. "Any action taken by the Syrians," said Secretary of State George P. Shultz, "must be seen as Soviet supported and promoted" ("This Week").

The U.S. reaction is therefore to support in the strongest possible 5 way the traditional and legitimate Lebanese Government headed by its elected President, Amin Gemayel. The U.S. not only supports Lebanon against the Syrians but also against the Palestinian Liberation Organization, who received substantial amounts of Soviet support themselves (Schultz 15), and who have for years been the agents of instability in the region. Amin Gemayal says, "We are sincere and genuine in saying that we are talking about the survival of a democracy in Lebanon. We are fighting for values—values we have in common with the United States who is helping in this fight for Democracy with us" ("Fighting" 37). Susan King of Channel 4 News adds, "The government of Amin Gemayal would not exist without the U.S. presence in Lebanon" ("Channel 4 News").

The presence of U.S. forces in Lebanon is not simply to rightfully 6 promote democracy by supporting the Gemayal Regime, but also to protect vital U.S. interests in the region from hostile and radical forces. The Middle East is by far the largest importer of U.S. weapons, constituting billions of dollars in annual sales (Schultz 17). These sales greatly strengthen the U.S. economy, and the U.S. Marines in Lebanon are a symbol that the U.S. is willing and able to protect its economic as well as its political interests.

For many valid and important reasons, the U.S. Marines are sta- 7 tioned in Lebanon. The Marines are there first to support the democratic regime of Amin Gemayal against hostile and sometimes Soviet supported anti-Democratic forces. Second, they are there to protect U.S. economic interests which are vital to ensure the stability of the United States economy. The most important aspect of the U.S. role in Lebanon, however, is that the Marines were invited as *peace keepers* by the Lebanese Government. After all, as the leader of the free world, the United States must answer the distress calls of those democracies that are under siege.

WORKS CITED

"Fighting for Western Values." *Time* 3 Oct. 1983: 37.

King, Susan. "Channel 4 News." WRC, Washington, D.C. 1 Dec. 1983.

Schultz, Ann. *Current History* July/Aug. 1979: 14–17.

Smith, William E. "Helping to Hold the Line." *Time* 3 Oct. 1983: 26–36.

"This Week with David Brinkley." ABC. 4 Dec. 1983.

Draft Review Worksheet: Persuading a Classmate

Writer: _____ Review: _____

1. What, judging from this paper, is the point of view of the classmate whom this writer is trying to persuade? What is the point of view of the writer? If you are the person to whom this paper is directed, has the writer succeeded in changing your mind at all?

2. Does the writer use a variety of sources of information? Does the writer seem well-informed about the issue? Note here some remark made that seems to be superficial.

3. Describe the paper's organizational strategy, paragraph by paragraph. Did you get lost anywhere as you read? Note every point in the paper where you were temporarily confused. Explain two such places here.

4. How would you characterize this writer's *ethos*. Cite examples from the paper to explain your characterization.

5. What uses does the writer make of *pathos?* Do you find them effective?

6. Do you have any suggestions for improving grammar or punctuation?

7. How has reading this paper given you a new perspective on the paper you are working on yourself?

Flawed Paper

To Draft or Not To Draft...

The re-implementation of compulsory registration for the draft in 1
1980 was a highly controversial decision. Like most of my peers, I have
numerous and mixed emotions on this policy. On one hand, I recognize
the need for a stand-by force which would be activated in the event of a
major conflict. However, I am concerned about being forced into a situation like Vietnam, an area where the United States should have never
become involved in. The solution of how to defend our country is a very
complex one. At one point in time an all-volunteer service was sufficient
to defend ourselves; but over the intervening years the ability of the
armed services to defend the country has come under serious delibera-
tion.

During the years after World War II and up to the Vietnam War the 2
U.S. was able to adequately defend itself soley on the strength of an all-
volunteer service. However, after the Vietnam War the ability of the service under an all-volunteer system has been severly tested. There are
two major factors which have led to this predicament. The first reason
was our basis for becoming involved in the Vietnam War. The second
reason is the fact that the salaries being paid by the armed services are
not keeping pace with the ever-increasing cost of living. This leads to
many highly trained servicemen leaving the service for better paying jobs
in private business (Marmion 9). As a result of the previously mentioned
problems the size of our combat-ready troops has been severely de-
pleted. It is now at the point where the United States would have trouble
executing any sort of large-scale mobilization of troops. The major reason for the inability of the U.S. to mobilize troops is the inability of the
National Guard and the Reserves to maintain their minimal levels of
strength. This problem becomes even more serious when you realize
that these two agencies would be responsible for the initial mobilization
of troops. These troops would have to provide a defense system for at
least 120 days. This is the time period required to implement and carry-
out a draft of the proportion necessary to supplement a major conflict. A
second problem facing the armed services is the inability of the individual reserve pools (the Individual Ready Reserve, the Standby Reserve,
and the Retired Reserve) to fulfill their personel requirements. These
preceeding situations are a result of several factors. The first is a miscal-
culation as to the number of individuals entering these institutions. The

second is the alarming drop in the rate of reenlistees. However, there are solutions to these problems.

The solutions as to how to correct the problems of diminishing re- 3 enlistees and the lack of new recruits entering the armed services are numerous. Such things as enlistment bonuses, educational assistance, and other new extras are definitely worth considering (Coffey 15). Consideration also should be given to extending non-pay incentives. For example, tuition assistance, death gratuities, auto license tag discounts, and state tax benefits. Individuals in the reserves could be provided with post exchange (PX) priveledges, life insurance, family medical and dental care, and some form of educational benefits. Although these benefits may not cure the problem this will most definitely have a positive impact which will increase this nation's ability to react more rapidly and forcefully in the event of a major conflict.

The problems of troop mobilization previously mentioned are sig- 4 nificant. It is in the best interest of the nation for its citizens to take appropriate measures to correct this situation. The various improvements and adjustments mentioned earlier would reduce the scope of the problem, but they will not eliminate them. To fully accomplish this task, a return to Selective Service induction, the adoption of a special IRR draft, or the expending of billions of dollars for new recruiting incentives would be required.

Due to the very strong opposition to the draft during the Vietnam 5 War, a return to compulsory service in any form is not a realistic possibility, at least in the foreseeable future. It also seems as though the government will not be willing to spend the additional billions that would be necessary to persuade more men and women into enlisting or extending their service in the nation's armed forces. Even if the additional funding was approved there is no guarantee that the expenditures would be able to entice the required number of individuals away from the many competitors in the employment market.

If these conclusions prove to be true, then the nation's lawmakers, 6 in their eagerness to abandon the draft and adopt an all-volunteer system, may have created even greater problems than were present during the draft years. The Selective Service policies may have caused lasting problems within our society. However, the all-volunteer system may have permanently lowered our nation's ability to mobilize our defense system. When the American people agreed to end the draft, they also agreed, to a reduction in the nation's ability to mobilize. If they remain opposed to the reinstation of any form of compulsory service or to the spending of additional billions of dollars for enlistment incentives, they are allowing for an increased possibility of both an armed conflict between the members of NATO and of the Warsaw Pact countries and the use of nuclear weapons (Daly 33).

WORKS CITED

Coffey, Kenneth J. *Manpower for Military Mobilization*. Washington, D.C.: American Enterprise Institute for Public Policy Research, 1978.

Daly, John Charles. *How Should the U.S. Meet its Military Manpower Needs?* Washington, D.C.: American Enterprise Institute for Public Policy Research, 1980.

Marmion, Harry A. *The Case against a Volunteer Army*. Chicago: Quadrangle Books, 1971.

Assignment 8: Film Evaluation

Method of Research: Studying a Film's Use of Subject, Language, Music, Shot Sequence, and Camera Angle to Determine Whether or Not the Film is Ultimately Effective

Most Pertinent Chapters: 2, 3, 4, 5, 6, 7, 12, 13

Clean Draft Due for Workshop:

Paper Due:

PRELIMINARY EXERCISE

Fill in the blanks in the following sentence:

As _____'s go, _____ is one of the worst.

Having filled in the blanks, specify three criteria by which you judge a "good," or at least a "not-so-bad," whatever-your-first-blank-filler-was. Compare your statements, and your criteria, with those of the rest of the class. Which criteria are well thought through and based on common sense?

When you write an evaluation, keep in mind that your judgment must be based on criteria. Your statement that "Almond Joy is a good candy bar" is merely a reflection of personal taste until you specify that (1) chocolate, (2) nuts, and (3) a nourishing base—like coconut—are the essential criteria for a good candy bar. Now your evaluation is publicly useful and can be discussed.

If you have completed this exercise carefully, you should be prepared to see the form your film evaluation will take:

1. _____ is a good (or bad) persuasive film.
2. What criteria must be met for a film to be persuasive?
   - Effective *ethos*
   - Effective *logos*
   - Effective *pathos*
     or, perhaps
   - effective plot

- effective characters
- effective photography
- effective tone
- effective music
- effective connection with real life

3. How well does this film meet these criteria? (The answer is likely to be at least slightly mixed—some aspects of the film will be effective, others not so effective.)

SUGGESTIONS FOR THE PLANNING STAGE

1. Films make their points using a wide variety of techniques unavailable to books, newspapers, or magazines. They use words, to be sure, but also music and a great number of pictures (shots) that vary in content, time exposed, camera angle and distance, and juxtaposition with other shots. So, in order to pick up on the visual strategies and others beyond the obvious ones, view the film at least twice—if possible, three or more times. At the first viewing, try not to be too critical. Just ask yourself, after viewing, whether you were persuaded to accept the filmmaker's point of view. If not, why not? If so, why so? Or if the audience did not include you, did the filmmaker persuade his or her audience? Your answer here will establish the basis, or thesis, of your evaluation (how effective was the film?).

2. Use your second and subsequent viewings to make notes about *types of strategies* the filmmaker employs to convince you. Look for the following:
   - *Logos:* What verifiable facts does the filmmaker present? What assumptions does the filmmaker make? Does the filmmaker use an organizational structure that helps persuade, or fails to?
   - *Ethos:* What strategies does the filmmaker use to convince us of his integrity, that his argument is ethically sound and that he has our best social and moral interests in mind? Consider, for instance, the choice of a narrator, the choice of words in the narration, the biased or unbiased selection of material, and the choice of any other authorities who appear in the film.
   - *Pathos:* What strategies have been used to evoke a subjective response by appealing to our feelings rather than to our logic? Keep an eye out especially for visual and sound effects here.

3. It is not necessary to be an expert on film in order to do this assignment. But try to observe and analyze some of the basic cinematic techniques used: for instance, dramatic editing (juxtaposition of scenes, movement from one scene to the next), the use of unusual camera angles, dramatic lighting, pacing, or use of music. *These will not be obvious from your first viewing.*

As you write, think of your readers as being skeptical of your point of view (it will help you to respond to that skepticism if, sometime while you're planning the paper, you write a paragraph or two explaining the reasons your readers might have for being skeptical). In your introduction, give us the facts about the film, offer your sense of what the filmmaker's aim was, make clear the criteria by which you'll be judging the film's effectiveness, and offer your judgment of its effectiveness. After that you can organize the paper any way you wish. However, keep your thesis (effective or ineffective) in mind as you write. And be specific—citing dialogue, noting music, describing shots—in supporting all your points.

Sample Papers

Nuclear War: A Guide to Armageddon
Soon-Kee Kim

One of the biggest threats to the modern world is a nuclear war. We **1** all have heard about the destructive force and the deadly effects of nuclear weapons. But how much do we really know about their power? How can we warn ourselves most realistically without actually experiencing them? *Nuclear War: A Guide to Armegeddon* is a film which brings the viewers close to that real experience. In order to persuade the viewers, *Nuclear War: A Guide to Armegeddon* uses a realistic assumption and a logical organizational structure, presents a reliable narrator, and appeals to the viewers' emotions.

The film *Nuclear War* is based on the assumption that a single **2** one–megaton nuclear weapon has exploded one mile above St. Paul's Cathedral in London. Then, the film shows the effects of the nuclear weapon in various places in London beginning from ground zero, St. Paul's Cathedral. Among the many places the film follows are St. James's Park, the Wimbledon tennis courts, and Hampton Court Palace, which are 2, 7, and 12.5 miles away from the assumed ground zero. By selecting a specific city for the assumed nuclear bomb explosion and by following specific places to find the effects of the bomb, the film makes the supposed experience appear much more realistic to the viewers.

The organization of the film *Nuclear War* is also very clear and per- **3** suasive. The film is divided into 3 sections—"The Heat," "The Blast," and "The Fall-out"—which are the three main effects of a nuclear weapon. Each section of the film shows how devastating and deadly the effects of the bomb are. For example, the narrator begins "The Heat" section by

saying that the temperature of a one–megaton nuclear fireball at the moment of detonation is 20 million degrees, which is equivalent to the temperature of the center of the sun. The narrator then notes that the temperature at St. James's Park, which is within a 2-mile radius of St. Paul's
cathedral, will be 4000 degrees at this time, and this will be hot enough
to ignite trees, scorch away grasses, boil the shallow part of the lake, and
leave the lake beds dry and steaming.

    The film does not end with showing the effects of the heat, the 4
blast, and the fall-out. It further assures the viewers of the fatefulness of
nuclear war by showing how useless the various civil defensive recom-
mendations proposed by the British Home Office are. One recommendation concerns digging an 18-inch-deep trench within a 3.5 mile radius,
a task that would take two adults a long hard weekend. The narrator
says that this trench will save the couple from the heat, but that the blast
will be 4 times more powerful than the force the trench is designed for.
Another nuclear shelter shown in the film is a sophisticated,
professionally-built steel tube which is buried 6 feet under the ground.
The narrator says that this steel tube is reasonably safe at the moment of
blast if a nuclear war involves a single warhead, but that he doubts that
a single warhead will be used. He says at least 30 warheads will explode
in a real war and this costly shelter will be useless in such a case.

    The end of the film follows a couple who somehow survive the ex- 5
plosion of the nuclear bomb. But the film presents still another obstacle
for the survivors: coping with the completely ruined world in which they
might be the only ones breathing. By showing that the various defensive
devices are useless in a real emergency and by gradually building to a
climax, the film assures the viewers of the hopelessness of survival in nuclear war.

    The narrator of the film *Nuclear War* appears as a well-informed, 6
sympathetic, and convincing person and this makes the film very effective in assuring the viewers of the disastrous effects of nuclear weapons.
From the beginning of the film, the narrator establishes himself as a well-
informed character. In order to emphasize the vulnerability of the human body to external force, he gives specific examples. He says that a
large fragment of broken glass travelling at 35 miles per hour will penetrate and lacerate the human skin, and that a skin temperature of 70 degrees Celsius will produce serious burns in less than a second, and that
even brief exposure of the human skin to strong radiation will cause
bleeding and loss of hair and blood cells. By providing detailed examples
which are indeed mild conditions compared to the condition in case of
a nuclear explosion, the narrator appears as a well-informed person and
the viewers begin to trust him.

    The narrator also appears as a sympathetic as well as a convincing 7
character. When he describes the destructive force of nuclear weapons

on trees and buildings, he constantly reminds the viewers how destructive such force will be on human beings. The narrator says that the heat of nuclear explosion within a 3-mile radius is hot enough to melt the sheet metal of buses. Then, he asks, "What is the effect of this incredible heat on the people who walk by?" When he says that the blast effect of a nuclear weapon is powerful enough to blow up any ordinary houses within 50 square miles, he asks the viewers again, "What is the effect of this blast on an unprotected human body?" These questions show that the narrator is very concerned with the hopeless situation of human beings in case of a nuclear bomb explosion.

After asking these fearful questions, the narrator actually shows the 8 effects of the heat and the blast on the screen and convinces the viewers of their devastating outcome. To the question concerning the effect of extreme heat on people, he answers that the human body behaves like meat hanging in a butcher-shop. Then he shows the meat whose tissue is slowly being charred to black carbon. For the question concerning the blast effect, he says in a convincing voice "This is what flying glass can do to pumpkins," and shows, in a slow motion, the endless fragments of flying glasses virtually demolishing one side of a pumpkin as if it is a human face. By showing these devastating effects of the nuclear heat and blast on screen, the narrator legitimates his fear and gains the viewers' trust.

The film *Nuclear War* uses audio-visual effects well and succeeds 9 in appealing to the viewers' emotions. The film begins with ballet dancers who are practicing with accompanying piano music. The scene is slow, soft, and peaceful and the music is sad. The first words of the narrator are "A human body is a fragile thing," and these words are followed by lists which explain the vulnerability of the human body to the blast, the heat, and the radiation of a nuclear bomb. As the narrator starts talking about the hypothetical condition of a one–megaton nuclear bomb exploding over the dome of St. Paul's cathedral, the ballet scene suddenly changes into a flame and the gym and the ballet dancers in it are destroyed completely. The sad piano music changes into a sharp, threatening, and loud noise. This juxtaposition of the peaceful and the violent scene emphasizes the powerlessness of human beings in case of a nuclear war and rouses deep fear and pity in the viewers.

The end of the film follows a couple who stay in a 36-inch-wide 10 trench for two weeks in order to avoid the deadly effects of fall-out. Imagining the wretched condition of the couple who stay in such a cramped place in utter darkness for two weeks, the narrator constantly asks trying questions: "Could you remove broken glass from your cut if you had to? How would you cope with the conditions of vomiting and diarrhea which are the symptoms of radiation sickness? Could you resist the temptation to go out and look even if you knew there existed radiation? And if you did come out after two weeks, what would you find?" As the narrator asks these shuddering questions, the camera moves out of the bunker and shows a field in complete ruin. Then, an organ music which is much like a funeral song begins. The camera continues to move, showing skeletons of buildings and buses and catching a glimpse of a telephone receiver, a policeman's badge, and a baby bottle in a burned wreckage. The narrator's voice is heard again: "How much of the complex world which you took for granted will be there? Sanitation? Water supply? High technology medicine? Doctors? Electricity? Communication? Who would tell you what's happening? Where would you find food?" As the narrator asks these questions with emotion, the camera moves further and further away and gives a long shot of the endless field of the wreckage. Nothing is recognizable. The final words of the narrator are "Maybe, your real problem is just beginning when you crawl out of your bunker." The death-reminding organ music, the endless ominous questions, and the presentation of still another obstacle at the end all evoke an enormous fear in the viewers' mind. The nuclear war indeed appears to the viewers as the end of the world.

Nuclear War: A Guide to Armegeddon is a very persuasive film. Its 11 organizational structure is clear and logical. It is full of details and narrated by a reliable person. It appeals to the viewers' emotions. By combining all these techniques, the film leaves a powerful impression on the viewers in a short 32 minutes: the absolutely devastating effects of nuclear war. *Nuclear War: A Guide to Armegeddon* showed to me that a film is the best device to present the appalling effects of nuclear war to the people since it can visualize the destruction directly to the viewers in a way that neither a book nor an audio cassette can.

Brace Yourself...for a Shock: A Look at the Film *Future Shock*

Jeff Green

We are being overthrown. Our civilization is crumbling. Our entire 1 way of life is being shaken by the foundations. Even our way of thinking is being tragically bent toward destruction. The ironic thing is that this is all being caused by what we have always considered our greatest friend, yet has indeed proved to be our overthrower—technology.

This is the warning presented to us in the film version of Alvin Tof- 2 fler's *Future Shock*. The movie shows how America is quickly going into "future shock," a state caused by "the premature arrival of the future."

The movie presents this ominous prophecy with great clarity, and it can be easily understood why people shook with fear after seeing this movie when it first came out in 1974. There are three main aspects which made this film so believable: the style in which the film presented each idea, the technological advances and modern trends used as examples of "the future getting out of control," and the strategies used by the producer to strike a nerve in the viewer.

The movie begins immediately with an interesting film technique 3 designed to capture the viewer's complete attention. It starts out with a pleasant scene of a couple walking alone in the woods. Suddenly a scene of sheer violence in a city street flashes on the screen, followed by the serene woods again with the silhouetted couple coming ever-so-slightly closer. The scenes rapidly switch back and forth between the peaceful woods and the terror-filled city until suddenly the couple is upon the viewer, and much to the viewer's horror too, for this couple, which seemed like a pair of peaceful lovers, is in fact a pair of grotesque-looking robots. Add to this the monotone voice of a narrator, and you leave the viewer in a state of utter confusion, which is just where the producer wants him.

The narrator of the film is none other than Orson Welles, and with 4 his rough, monotone voice he makes the ominous thought of society's downfall seem very believable somehow. Throughout the movie, Welles wears a dark, heavy overcoat which seems to show a lack of permanence, as though he's ready to leave at any time. This supports one of the major points made in the movie concerning the lack of permanence in today's society.

Another interesting point about the film's style is the camera usage. 5 Throughout the movie, the camera is constantly moving and pivoting and changing its focus. This gives the viewer a slight feeling of insecurity which the producer immediately thrives on by presenting his ideas as soon as this feeling appears. The best example of this is when the camera takes the viewer through two stores, first a supermarket and then a bookstore. The camera switches from item to item, aisle to aisle, floor to ceiling, doing complete 360° turns in order to show how far we have come in terms of choice. But the choice is so great it overwhelms us, leaving us staggering in indecision.

The second main aspect which makes the film seem frightfully be- 6 lievable is the technological advances and modern trends cited. The first and foremost trend cited is that of moving. More than ever before, Americans are packing up their belongings and moving. The movie shows how this is destroying our concept of the family and community. It explains how to kids today "home is just a place to leave." It also explains how the telephone directory is rewritten daily, showing further that "where we live means less and less."

The film also focuses on modern medical advances. These include 7
artificial limbs, artificial kidneys, and heart bypass surgery. It singles out
the case of Carl Schaefer, who, after suffering a stroke, was given eight
hours to live, but who was saved through a heart bypass operation. This
in turn prompts the idea that the body is slowly becoming replaceable
and, in a way, "disposable."

The film also discusses the case of Verlin Cobb, a prematurely 8
wrinkled lady who decided to get a face-lift, suggesting that "even faces
are temporary." Finally, Dr. C. Epstein discusses the feasibility of repro-
ducing human embryos within a test tube. This shows that "even motherhood is becoming obsolete," and if we don't gain control of technology
soon, we will find ourselves "baby shopping in babytoriums or genetic
supermarkets."

But medical advances are not the only new changes discussed in 9
the film; also noted are changes in basic, traditional institutions, including religion and marriage. The film discusses the cases of group marriages, commune living, and homosexual marriages, which for many are
truly shattering to the foundations of these institutions. These new
changes, according to the film, are the setting for "a quiet revolution,"
which in turn is "part of a bigger revolution." This big revolution can be
seen forming through such new developments as the battle for homo-
sexuals' equal rights, constant strikes against traditional methods, ideas,
and values in various occupations, and the battle for women's equal
rights.

The producer combines the mind-controlling film style with the 10
awe-inspiring data and then mixes in the final touch, an appeal to the
viewer's raw emotions, making the movie undeniably effective. This appeal is first seen when Welles is discussing everything's lack of permanence. A little girl walks into a toy store carrying a beaten-up doll and
trades it in for a different one. As she leaves, we see the shopkeeper
dump the old doll into a garbage can while Welles narrates, "Even old
friends don't last forever."

Another appeal to the viewer's emotions is a scene showing people 11
of the future getting up in the morning. When the male wakes up, he
takes a quick energy pill and then plugs himself into a socket for some
instant happy stimulation. He then plugs his wife in and gives her a
good morning kiss. The thought of this horrifies the viewer.

The final and most effective appeal to the viewer's emotions comes 12
in the final scene. It not only does the best job of reaching the viewer but
actually puts a cap on the film and sends the viewer away ready to act
against this terrible plague called "future shock." It shows a baby lying
alone on a vast beach with the narrator saying, "Our children—will we
save them from future shock? The choices we make will determine the
outlook of *their* world. There is still time...."

Draft Review Worksheet: Film Evaluation

Writer: _____ Reviewer: _____

1. Can you tell from the introduction of this paper whether the writer considers the film an effective persuasive film or not?

2. Does the writer examine the film's *logos, ethos,* and *pathos?* Which is examined most superficially?

3. Is there enough evidence in the paper to substantiate the writer's opinion? Which evidence of the writer's do you find most persuasive?

4. Describe the paper's organizational strategy, paragraph by paragraph. Which paragraphs don't proceed smoothly from the paragraph they follow?

5. Do you feel you understand the film better now than you did before you read this paper? What is the most interesting thing you learned about film technique?

6. Do you have any suggestions for improving grammar or punctuation?

7. How has reading this paper given you a new perspective on the paper you are working on yourself?

Flawed Paper

Red Nightmare—Is It Really True (Or Just a Red Headache)?

The first frame, "This program has been declared obsolete within   1
the issuing agency", sets the tone for this 1960s United States Deptart-
ment of Defense scare film, *Red Nightmare*. The director tries to convince the viewer of the evils of Communism, but the harder he tries, the
more humorous the film becomes. If the lack-luster plot were improved,
and the editing made more cohesive, the film might make the point it is
trying to make more effectively. The purpose of the film is to show the
viewer how bad life in a Communist system really is. The director uses
many tactics to try to make the 'Communist threat' manfest, but only
one of them works.

The only technique that even makes overtures at being effective is   2
the narrator. The script of the narrator, Jack Webb, proves effective when
coupled with graphic shots exemplifying the subject. For example, when
the narrator says "freedom", a shot of the majestic Statue of Liberty as-
sails the viewer. When the narrator speaks of "the freedom to study our
own chosen vocation", the halls of Congress and the White House take
on an ominous presense. These two things the director uses, I feel, give
the narrrator the burden of having to make the film serious, because the
rest of it certianly detracts from any legitimacy the film might otherwise
have had.

The plot of the film is the part that tends to make the film humor-   3
ous. It is not the actual plot that does this, but rather, the way the plot
and supporting points are presented. The plot of the film is that an
American, Gerry Donovan, who "takes his freedoms for granted", is
transported from his usually quiet dreams to a 'typical' Russian town,
where "freedom doesn't exist". His loving wife and children turn against
him, and the whole world becomes propagated with lies. He stands
'trial', and is given an opportunity to "confess his crimes". He refuses,
claiming he does not know what crimes he committed, nor against
whom. He is found guilty and sentenced to death. At Mr. Donovan's execution, he receives another chance to confess his crimes. Instead, he
says how evil the Communist system is, and how the Russians "can't
even fool [their] own people". Just as he is shot, he wakes up, and suddenly becomes a 'model' American.

In order to keep the film from becoming a Communist-bashing   4 comedy of errors (oops—too late), I would make the plot more realistic. The realism should be the main thing that keeps the film from being too funny, and keeps it realistic; too many cooks spoil the broth—well in this case, too dramatic creates too much humor and room for ridicule. For beginners, the town should be more realistic. There should be more lines around stores and fewer solders walking around armed with automatic weapons. This would probably show the more day-to-day differences between the United States and Soviet Union. I would use this film not as a scare film, as the Dept. of Defense has tried to do, but rather as a more realistic educational film.

Another major thing that could be done to improve the film would 5 be to change the way the music is used. Whenever the film starts to build to a climax, the music does likewise, but either it is dubbed badly or just is not cohesive with the rest of the film. For example, during the trial, the music climaxes twice, even before the verdict and sentencing. If only the director could make up his mind as to when the climax of a given scene occurs.

Finally, the transition from scene to scene could be much 6 smoother if the cutting and editing had been better planned out. Whenever the narrator appears in a scene, there is an immediate cut from the previous scene, regardless of whether or not there should be some kind of pause or not. In the other scenes, the vast majority of the cuts are also immediate cuts. The only scenes that fade into the next are those where a minor point was made and the director probably felt needed no support—one of the few times the viewer is given a chance to digest information; otherwise the audience is constantly being bombarded.

The film *Red Nightmare* is not what it claims; instead, it should be 7 retitled Red Headache (that is, for the viewer). As the plot proceeds, the situations become more and more absurd, and the point that is being drawn from the film becomes more and more humorous. The acting, the directing, and the representative facts should be made more factual, and should be redone. This film is like a rough draft. If the Defense Department really thinks this film worked, I shudder to think of the type of film the Soviets could use to tell its people of the "evils of America".

Assignment 9: Literary Interpretation

Method of Research: Careful Reading, Underlining, and Note Taking
Most Pertinent Chapters: 2, 3, 4, 5, 7, 12

ASSIGNMENT

1. Read a work of fiction, either on your own or with the rest of the class.

2. Take reading notes as you read, giving special attention to the ways in which parts of the book are connected to each other and (ultimately) to the purpose of the book as a whole.
3. Write an essay in class on _____ (date).

SUBJECT OF THE ESSAY

Select a favorite part or parts of your book and show how these parts contribute to the overall aims of the book's author. Assume that your reader is skeptical about the connection or connections you see. If you choose a single portion of the book to focus on, bring in a least two other sections for purposes of comparison, contrast, illustration, or elaboration of your point.

BRING WITH YOU TO CLASS

- More than one pen or pencil
- Your book
- A dictionary (if you wish)
- An outline of what you plan to write (The key to success with in-class writing when you are given the question in advance is *preparation*. Carefully plan your paragraph outline, and choose possible supporting quotations.)

ABOUT YOUR ESSAY

Make your writing show that you've mastered this course's priorities:

Observation	Organization	Clear connections
Selection of details	Telling quotations	Tightening
Thoughtful writing	Introduction	Conclusion
Purpose	Paragraphing	

WHEN YOU THINK YOU'RE FINISHED

Look over your whole essay and cross out (and replace, if necessary) any sentences that don't add something important.

Sample Papers

Note: Since these essays are written in class I don't require that page references accompany quotations.

Alice Hindman and the Special Problems of Women

Woienshet Kebede (written in class)

"Adventure," in *Winesburg, Ohio,* is the story of Alice Hindman. The 1
story, like almost all the other stories in this book, is about the problems
of communication. In addition to the communication problem which all
people in *Winesburg, Ohio* face, Alice also faces a problem due to her sex
(female).

Alice, when she was sixteen years old, met Ned Currie. She 2
wanted to marry him. But Ned only wanted to care for her. His idea of
only caring for her changed just before he left Winesburg to look for
another job. After that they did things they would not have done otherwise. Anderson puts it this way: "It did not seem to them that anything that could happen in the future could blot out the wonder and
beauty of the thing that happened." Ned left the next day. For a while,
since he was lonely, Ned wrote to Alice. But once he made friends in
the city, he forgot about her.

Alice, though, did not forget Ned. She felt lonely, but she thought to 3
herself that she should stay without friends. She did not try to make
friends. Anderson says about this as follows: "For all her willingness to
support herself she could not have understood the growing modern
idea of a woman's owning herself and giving and taking for her own
ends in life." She believed she had to be devoted to her husband and not
to anybody else. Her loneliness, despite her attempt to put up with it,
did not go away. Because of this she began to be attached to inanimate
objects. Finally she tried to give in a little bit and walked along with Will
Hurley. In the darkness she tried to touch his coat. But, she still did not
change her mind about Ned. In fact she did not want the clerk to walk
with her anymore.

Alice in some way is like Elizabeth Willard. Elizabeth married Tom 4
because society pushed her to do so. For example, "Other girls of her age
in Winesburg were marrying men she had always known, grocery clerks
or young farmers. In the evening they walked in the Main Street with
their husbands and when she passed they smiled happily." Alice, like
Elizabeth, was not able to make another friend, because there was always the notion that she was Ned's girl. Again here society made life difficult for the young woman.

In some other ways Alice is not like Elizabeth nor like Kate Swift. 5
Elizabeth, for example, had tried to do things that society does not allow
her to do. "Once she startled the town by putting on men's clothes and
riding a bicycle down Main Street." Elizabeth does this which is not expected of a female. Kate Swift also tried, despite what the society ex-

pected. For example, "The people of the town thought of her as a con-firmed old maid because she spoke sharply and went her own way."

Alice, when compared to the men, is like Wing Biddlebaum, who is 6 lonely and walks on his veranda *hoping* George Willard will come. Alice was also *hoping* Ned would come. She is also like Enoch, who later on did not want any people except his paintings. He was married once. He also had friends. But he could not get his message through to them. He preferred to be with his paintings. Alice did the same thing too. She began to like her furniture rather than humans.

When compared with all the above characters, Helen stands out as 7 knowing better than them all. Helen, in the story of "Sophistication," distinguishes between her interest and that of society. Her mother, for example, wanted her to marry her college instructor. But she did not do what her mother wanted her to do. She also did not leave with George. In the story of "Departure," George left Winesburg in search of a better place. But Helen's staying behind indicates her being independent. She did not have to be devoted to a man like Alice did.

Is Respect Possible for Women?
Jill Swackhamer (written in class)

Even today women are not considered as man's equal. *The Color* 1 *Purple*, by Alice Walker, addresses this issue but takes it one step further: black women are mistreated by whites and blacks alike. This book has several dominant women who demand respect for themselves (Shug, Sofia, Nettie), yet the majority of women are trapped in the traditional role of subservience which their community has come to expect (such is the case with Celie, Squeak, and Tashi).

One of the book's clearest models of the attitude men have towards 2 women is explained by Nettie who is trying to cope with the culture shock of African attitudes. In her new environment, Nettie is told how women are expected to behave. Tashi, the native friend of Olivia, "has tried to please her father, never quite realizing that, as a girl, she never could." Furthermore, Tashi's mother decides not to remarry after the death of her spouse: "since she already has five boy children,...she has become an honorary man."

The whole lifestyle of the Olinka people places the man in the top 3 authority position. The man is allowed (even expected) to have more than one wife, but this is never a choice for women. This practice makes

Samuel in particular uncomfortable because, as a missionary, he wants the Africans to accept the biblical instruction that a man should only have one wife so that they may become as one flesh. Samuel himself is a good model of such a relationship, first with Corrine, then with Nettie.

However, the Olinka women do not even choose their own mate 4 since they "were promised to old or middle-aged men at birth." Their lives only consist of their work and their children since even their husband must be shared. In their society, a woman cannot even have "a man for a friend without the worst kind of ostracism and gossip." Yet, Olinka women continue to "praise [their husbands'] smallest accomplishments," thus reinforcing their own subservience and worthlessness. The Olinka husband even "has life and death power over the wife" if she is unfaithful or suspected of witchcraft.

Although most black women in America at this time were also sub- 5 servient to their husbands, they at least were given the respect deserved by any human being. These differences are very subtle, however. Albert, for instance, took Celie as his *only* wife, yet he practiced infidelity with Shug as if he weren't even being disrespectful of Celie. Until things begin to change, Albert, too, shows his dominance over his black wife by saying to her, "You pore, you ugly, you black, you a woman...you nothing at all." In the hierarchy of both social cultures, black women were barely considered above the level of animals.

Regardless of such general similarities, there were times when 6 black women in America rose above their oppression, if only for a short while. Americans at least regarded male and female children of equal worth. Albert's statement that "the woman that brought Sofia into the world brought something" shows that boy children are not prized over girl children in this country. It also shows his current respect for Sofia as a human being and member of society.

In the United States, although it was customary for the woman to 7 submit to the man, Shug Avery shows her dominance over Albert as well as over all the other men and women in her life. She is said to "act more manly than most men...she upright, honest." Shug is respected for her singing ability and beauty as well. Albert describes her as "just like Sofia. She bound to live her life and be herself no matter what." Celie tries to absorb some of Shug's courageous characteristics so that she can break away from Albert's hold on her. Only then will she be able to gain more self-respect so that she will not tolerate his physical or others' emotional abuse of her.

As *The Color Purple* progresses through the stages of Celie's matu- 8 rity, the reader is shown how this one weak, feeble woman becomes her own person. Celie gains the strength to leave her husband Albert because of the many ways he has abused her. She establishes a new hope for the future through her companionship with Shug and her new business as a designer of pants. Celie is able to imitate the boldness modeled by Shug leaving Albert, Sofia and Squeak (Mary Agnes) leaving Harpo, and Squeak's decision even to leave Grady in Panama.

Through the metamorphosis of these courageous women, Alice 9 Walker seems to be saying to her audience that women are indeed special human beings worthy of God's love and, therefore, worthy of their fellowman's respect (both black and white). Nettie is the ultimate example of this ideal woman. She had the motivation to run away from Pa, the faith in God to become a missionary in Africa, and the self-respect by which her husband Samuel treated her as his partner and "beloved companion." Nettie really comes through when she stands up for women's rights while speaking with Tashi's father in Africa. She tells him, "It is no longer a world just for boys and men." Nettie, therefore, symbolizes women's hope that they no longer need to be considered "an object or pity and contempt" because they can demand the respect of others which God has taught them to expect.

15

What Next?

No, I didn't like the textbook. To me, all English books rank right down there with The Scarlet Letter.

student

I don't think this course requires a book. This course only requires pencil and paper.

student

I never liked to write much and I still don't like to unless it is necessary. But I think I now have more power to write.

student

This was a tough course to take while on academic probation. It involved a lot of time. Now it is slightly more enjoyable to write, but it still is a pain at times.

student

I'd still rather work with numbers but I do think I learned how to write better.

student

A blank piece of paper isn't as frightening to me any more.

student

I feel more comfortable about writing, but I still have a lot of room for improvement. I wish I could take this class again so that I could keep improving my writing skills.

student

Few are taught to any purpose who do not become their own teachers.
Sir Joshua Reynolds

Taking Stock

Exercise 15-1

You are now finishing a course which was designed to help you become a more correct, more effective, and more confident writer. You certainly have not solved all your writing problems—nobody ever does. But you have made some progress. Take a few minutes to take stock, now, of your current writing ability.

What kind of writer would you call yourself now? In what areas have you made the most improvement during this course? What problems do you still have as a writer? *Why* do you think you still have those problems? Can you think of methods you can use to help solve your remaining problems?

Recommended Books

In this book, I've tried to address writers who are skeptical of their own writing ability, and skeptical about whether writing can help them in their careers and in their lives. I hope now that you are less skeptical, that you've tasted the pleasure of teaching yourself and of profiting from the advice of your teacher and your classmates. I hope now that you'll take your writing education into your own hands and try to find the books that can help you learn more fully what the resources of our language are. I recommend highly:

1. A college dictionary (at least 50,000 words). When you don't know a word, the only way to make it part of your vocabulary is to write it down and look it up in the dictionary right away. No one looks up every unfamiliar word, no matter how much teachers have advised us to do so; very few of us do it as much as we say we do. But try doing it during your summers. Or for a week at a time during the school year. Surprisingly quickly, your determination will pay off in increased word and thinking power.
2. William Strunk and E. B. White's *The Elements of Style,* 3rd edition (New York: Macmillan, 1981). An inexpensive, brief review of all the basics of writing, including differences I haven't even mentioned in this book, like those between *lend* and *loan, allusion* and *illusion, flammable* and *inflammable.* This book is deservedly the most widely consulted book about writing.
3. H. W. Fowler's *A Dictionary of Modern English Usage,* 2nd edition, revised by Sir Ernest Gowers (New York: Oxford University Press, 1983), whose 700 pages cover thoroughly and delightfully almost every nuance of the English language. Once you decide that writing is a craft you want to excel in, you'll certainly want a copy of this book.
4. Robert Pirsig, *Zen and the Art of Motorcycle Maintenance* (New York: Bantam, 1975). Even if you're not interested in Zen (I'm not), and even if you're a hopeless motorcycle mechanic (I am), this book is an excellent introduction to the kinds of practical and critical thinking that

are so important for writers. Besides, it's a good story of a motorcycle trip.

5. Reginald Bragonier, Jr., and David Fisher, *What's What: A Visual Glossary of the Physical World* (New York: Hammond, 1981). This picture book identifies the component parts of everything from chain saws (guidebar, guidebar nose, spark-arresting muffler) to front doors (center stile, butte stile, lock stile) to flagpoles (finial, truck, staff) to electric guitars (bridge, frets, pickguard) to fire hydrants (bonnet, hose nozzle cap, cap chain). Just browsing through this reference book will help you think more clearly and develop a better eye for detail.

Strengthening Intuition

Having taken this course, you should now realize that writing helps us remember; it helps us make sense of our experience; it helps us work out our passions and frustrations; it gives us the power to make a mark, for better or worse, on the world around us. You know that learning to write is—far more than we might expect—learning to understand other people. You know that writing, not just for you but for everyone, is work, but that the satisfaction of a finished paper—well-observed, well-organized, and well-written—can make all that work worthwhile.

You have practiced many individual skills in this course, from observing to inference drawing to paragraphing to organizing to punctuating. Successful writing won't result from keeping those skills in the front of your mind all the time. The limitations of remaining fully conscious of your technique are illustrated in a story told about Walter Hagen, a golfer who won many of the top tournaments in the 1920s and 1930s, including four or five PGA championships in a row. Hagen was a notorious carouser, and in one of those PGAs, he showed up for the final round hung over, unshaven, and red-eyed. His opponent—it was match play—was one of those sweet-swinging, cold-blooded types, and just before they teed off, Hagen said to him, "You know, you've got the most beautiful swing I've ever seen. That little pause at the top of your backswing really works. How do you do it?" By the time the poor kid had figured out what Hagen had done to him, Hagen had won—five holes up with four holes to play. Skills are more useful after they've become intuitive than they are when we remain fully conscious of them.

I hope this course has strengthened your observation, your thoughtfulness, your organization, your sense of audience, your sense of self, and your ability to bring all of these to bear on your writing. The course has been designed to help you strengthen all these skills both consciously and intuitively—we hope fast enough for you to do well in this course. But even if you haven't done as well as you would have liked in this course, your intuitions have made some progress, and if you continue to nurture and strengthen them, they will eventually serve you well.

Works Cited

Adelstein, Michael, "Writing Is Work." In *The Practical Craft*. Ed. W. K. Sparrow and D. H. Cunningham. Boston: Houghton Mifflin, 1978: 116–25.

Aristotle. *The Rhetoric of Aristotle*. Ed. Lane Cooper. New York: Appleton Century Crofts, 1932.

Beisanz, Mavis Hiltunen, and John Beisanz. *Introduction to Sociology*. 3rd ed. Englewood Cliffs, N.J.: Prentice-Hall, 1978.

Bernstein, Carl. "Graduation Speech from the Bottom of the Class." *The Kenosha News* 7 June 1979: 5.

Berthoff, Ann. *Forming, Thinking, Writing*. Rochelle Park, N.J.: Hayden, 1978.

Bibliographic Index. Ed. Laurel Cooley. New York: Wilson, 1982.

Britton, James. "The Composing Processes and the Functions of Writing." In *Research on Composing*. Ed. Charles R. Cooper and Lee Odell. Urbana, Ill.: National Council of Teachers of English, 1978: 13–28.

Browne, Sir Thomas. *The Religion of a Doctor*. New York: Dutton, 1969.

Buel, Joy Day, and Richard Buel. *The Way of Duty: A Woman and Her Family in Revolutionary America*. New York: Norton, 1984.

Carson, Rachel. *Silent Spring*. New York: Houghton Mifflin, 1962.

Cowley, Malcolm, *The View from 80*. New York: Viking, 1978.

Cowley, Malcom, ed. *Writers at Work*. Vol. 1, New York: Viking, 1959.

Crosby, Harry. "Titles, A Treatise On." *College Composition and Communication* 27 (1976): 387–91.

Davies, Robertson. "What Every Girl Should Know." In *One Half of Robertson Davies*. Harmondsworth: Penguin, 1977.

Descharnes, Robert, and Jean-Francois Chabrun. *Auguste Rodin*. Secaucus, N.J.: Chartwell Books, 1967.

Dickens, Charles. *A Tale of Two Cities*. Harmondsworth, England: Penguin, 1970.

Dillard, Annie. *Pilgrim at Tinker Creek*. Harper and Row, 1974.

Dowst, Kenneth. *Basic Writing*. Pittsburgh, Penn.: The U of Pittsburgh, 1977.

Ellis, Robert, and Denny Gulick. *Calculus with Analytic Geometry*. 2d ed. New York: Harcourt, Brace, Jovanovich, 1982.

Faigley, Lester, and Thomas P. Miller. "What We Learn from Writing on the Job." *College English* 44 (1982): 557–69.

Farmer, Richard N. *Introduction to Business*. New York: Random House, 1972.

360

Finch, Vernor C., and Glenn T. Trewartha. *Elements of Geography.* New York: McGraw-Hill, 1936.

Flower, Linda, and John R. Hayes. "Problem-Solving Strategies and the Writing Process." *College English* 39 (1977): 449–61.

Frazier, Kendrick. *The Violent Face of Nature.* New York: William Morrow, 1979.

Fussell, Paul. *The Great War and Modern Memory.* London: Oxford University Press, 1975.

Galbraith, John Kenneth. "Writing, Typing, and Economics." *Atlantic* Mar. 1982: 102–05.

Garrison, Roger. *How a Writer Works.* New York: Harper & Row, 1981.

Gebhardt, Richard. "The Writing Process." *Freshman English News* 9 (1980): 19–22.

Geduld, Harry M., ed. *Filmmakers on Filmmaking.* Bloomington: Indiana U P, 1967.

Graves, Robert, and Alan Hodge. *The Reader Over Your Shoulder* New York: Random House, 1978.

Hall, Carla. "The Radical Voice of Moderation." *The Washington Post* 14 Mar. 1983: B1.

"Harper's Index." *Harper's* Jan. 1988: 11.

Harris, Art. "The Wild Bunch, Heros Once More." *The Washington Post* 4 Nov. 1983: D1–D2.

Hayakawa, S. I. *Language in Thought and Action.* 2d ed. New York: Harcourt, Brace, and World, 1963.

"How To Win at Wordsmanship." *Newsweek* 6 May 1968: 104.

Hymans, Edward. *The Changing Face of Britain.* St. Albans, England: Paladin, 1977.

Jamieson, Kathleen Hall. "The Idea of a University in an Electronic Age." *Precis* 4 Nov. 1985.

Kearns, Doris. *Lyndon Johnson and the American Dream.* New York: Harper and Row, 1976.

Kennedy, George. *The Art of Persuasion in Greece.* Princeton, N.J.: Princeton U P, 1963.

"Kenosha, Wisconsin" *Encyclopedia Britannica,* 1974 ed.

King, Leonard. Class handout. The Maret School, Washington, D.C.

Kolb, Harold. *A Writer's Guide.* New York: Harcourt, Brace, Jovanovich, 1980.

Lash, Joseph P. *Eleanor: The Years Alone.* New York: Norton, 1972.

LeSueur, Meridel. "I Was Marching." In *Women Working: An Anthology of Stories and Poems.* Ed. Nancy Hoffman and Florence Howe. Old Westbury, N.Y.: The Feminist Press, 1979: 228–40.

"Letters." *Los Angeles Times* 12 Nov. 1983: B2.

Linton, Calvin. *Effective Revenue Writing.* Washington, D.C.: U.S. Government Printing Office, 1962.

Macrorie, Ken. *Telling Writing.* 2d ed. Rochelle Park, N.J.: Hayden, 1976.

McPhee, John. *Basin and Range.* New York: Farrar, Straus, and Giroux, 1981.

McPhee, John. *The Curve of Binding Energy.* New York: Farrar, Straus, and Giroux, 1974.

McPhee, John. *The Pine Barrens.* New York: Farrar, Straus, and Giroux, 1967.

Mitchell, Henry. "The Waugh to End All Waughs." *The Washington Post* 18 Jan. 1982: C1.

Mill, John Stuart. *On Liberty.* Indianapolis: Appleton Century Crofts, 1947.

Moon, Truman J. *Biology for Beginners.* New York: Holt, Rinehart, and Winston, 1921. Rpt 1981.

More, Thomas. *A Dialogue of Comfort against Tribulation.* Ed. Louis Martz and Frank Manley. Vol. 12 of *The Complete Works of St. Thomas More.* Ed. Richard Sylvester. New Haven: Yale U P, 1963.

Murphy, James T. *Physics: Principles and Problems.* 2d ed. Columbus, Ohio: Charles E. Merrill, 1977.

Murray, Donald. "Internal Revision: A Process of Discovery." In *Research on Composing.* Ed. Charles R. Cooper and Lee Odell. Urbana, Ill.: National Council of Teacher of English, 1978: 85–103.

Murray, Donald. "Write before Writing." *College Composition and Communication* 29 (1978): 375–81.

New York Times Index, July-August-September 1916. New York: Bowker, 1965.

Pianko, Sharon. "Reflection: A Critical Component of the Composing Process." *College Composition and Communication* 30 (1979): 275–78.

Pirsig, Robert. *Zen and the Art of Motorcycle Maintenance.* New York: Morrow, 1974.

Plato. "Cratylus." In *The Dialogues of Plato.* Oxford, England: Oxford U P, 1892.

Public Affairs Information Service Bulletin. Ed. Lawrence J. Woods. New York: Public Affairs Information Service, 1982.

Ram, Hari. "The Path Down the Bhotia Kosi River in Nepal." In *A Book of Travellers' Tales.* Ed. Eric Newby. New York: Viking Penguin, 1985: 318–19.

Raymond, James and Ronald Goldfarb. *Clear Understandings.* New York: Random House, 1982.

Readers' Guide to Periodical Literature, March 1957–February 1959. Ed. Sarita Robinson. New York: Wilson, 1959.

Reed, Fred. "Lean, Healthy and Forty-Five." *The Washington Post* 29 Sep. 1979: D1.

Riekehof, Lottie L. *The Joy of Signing.* Springfield, Mo.: Gospel Publishing House, 1978.

Rogers, Carl. "Communication: Its Blocking and Its Facilitation." In *Rhetoric: Discovery and Change.* Richard E. Young, Alton L. Becker, and Kenneth L. Pike. New York: Harcourt, Brace and World, 1970: 284–89.

Ross, Nancy. "Guide Offers Hints to Bring Markets to Inner Cities." *The Washington Post: Business* 7 Dec. 1981: 5.

Segal, Bernice G. *Chemistry: Experiment and Theory.* New York: Wiley, 1985.

Shelley, Mary. *Frankenstein.* New York: Pyramid, 1957.

Smith, George Rose. "A Primer of Opinion Writing for Four New Judges." *The University of Arkansas Law Review* 1967.

Sterne, Lawrence. *Tristram Shandy.* Ed. Howard Anderson. New York: Norton, 1980.

Stoltz, Craig. "Doing Archaeology." Unpublished manuscript, 1983.

Taylor, Pat Ellis. "Teaching Creativity in Argumentation." *College English* 39 (1977): 507–510.

Thomas, Lewis. "The Art of Teaching Science." *New York Times Magazine.* 14 Mar. 1982: 89.

Tolstoy, Leo. "God Sees the Truth, But Waits." *Twenty-Three Tales.* Trans. Louise and Aylmer Maude. Oxford, England: Oxford U P, 1906: 1–11.

Toulmin, Stephen. *The Uses of Argument.* Cambridge, England: Cambridge University Press, 1958.
Worsley, Peter. *Inside China.* Harmondsworth, England: Penguin, 1975.
Zinsser, William. *On Writing Well.* 2d ed. New York: Harper & Row, 1980.

Acknowledgments

For permission to use the selections reprinted in this book, the author is grateful to the following publishers and copyright holders:

Sherwood Anderson, "Hands," from *Winesburg, Ohio*. © 1919 by B. W. Huebsch; © renewed 1947 by Eleanor Copenhauer Anderson. Reprinted with the permission of Viking Penguin, Inc.

Mavis Hiltunen Beisanz and John Beisanz. *Introduction to Sociology*. © 1978. Selections reprinted with the permission of Prentice-Hall, Inc.

Michael Berheide, "Brief Guide to Revision." Reprinted with the permission of the author.

Joy Day Buel and Richard Buel. *The Way of Duty: A Woman and Her Family in Revolutionary America*. © 1984. Selection reprinted with the permission of Norton, Inc.

Robert Farrar Capon, *The Supper of the Lamb*. © 1967, 1969. Selection reprinted with the permission of Doubleday & Company, Inc.

Rachel Carson, *Silent Spring*. © 1962. Selection reprinted with the permission of Houghton Mifflin, Inc.

Malcolm Cowley, *The View from 80*. © 1978. Selection reprinted with the permission of Viking Penguin, Inc.

Harry Crosby, "Titles, A Treatise On." *College Composition and Communication*. Dec. 1976. © 1976. Selection reprinted with the permission of the author.

Robertson Davies, "What Every Girl Should Know." © 1977. Reprinted with the permission of Viking Penguin, Inc.

Vernor C. Finch and Glenn T. Trewartha. *Elements of Geography*. © 1936. Selections reprinted with the permission of McGraw-Hill, Inc.

Kendrick Frazier, *The Violent Face of Nature*. © 1979. Selection reprinted with the permission of William Morrow, Inc.

Paul Fussell, *The Great War and Modern Memory*. © 1975. Selections reprinted with the permission of Oxford University Press.

Harry Geduld, *Filmmakers onFilmmaking*. © 1967. Selection reprinted with the permission of Indiana University Press.

Ellen Goodman, "When Grateful Begins to Grate." © 1979. Reprinted with the permission of the Boston Globe Newspaper Company and the Washington Post Writers Group.

"Harper's Index." © 1987. by Harper's Magazine. Reprinted from the January 1988 issue by special permission.

S. I. Hayakawa, *Language in Thought and Action.* 2d ed. © 1963. Selection reprinted with the permission of Harcourt, Brace, Jovanovich, Inc.

Kathleen Hall Jamieson, "The Idea of a University in an Electronic Age." © 1985. Reprinted with the permission of the author.

Harold Kolb, *A Writer's Guide.* © 1980. Selection reprinted with the permission of Harcourt, Brace, Jovanovich, Inc.

Los Angeles Times, selections © 1944 and 1983. Reprinted with the permission of the Los Angeles Times, Inc.

Ken Macrorie, *Telling Writing.* 2d ed. © 1976. Selection reprinted with the permission of Hayden Book Company.

John McPhee, *The Pine Barrens.* © 1967. Selections reprinted with the permission of Farrar, Straus, and Giroux, Inc.

E. Ethelbert Miller, "Airport: A Takeoff on a Poem." © 1980. Reprinted with the permission of the author.

Truman J. Moon, *Biology for Beginners.* © 1921. Selections reprinted with the permission of Holt, Rinehart, and Winston, Inc.

James T. Murphy, *Physics: Principles and Problems.* 2d Edition. © 1977. Selections reprinted with the permission of Charles E. Merrill, Inc.

George Orwell, *The Road to Wigan Pier.* ©1936. Selection reprinted with the permission of Harcourt, Brace, Jovanovich, Inc.

Fred Reed, "Lean, Healthy and Forty-Five." *The Washington Post* 29 Sep. 1979. © 1979. Reprinted with the permission of the author.

Jewell Rhodes, "When Your Sense of Humor is Your Best Traveling Companion." *MS* Mar. 1983. © 1983. Reprinted with the permission of the author.

Nancy Ross, "Guide Offers Hints to Bring Markets to Inner Cities." *The Washington Post: Business* 7 Dec. 1981. © 1981. Reprinted with the permission of the Washington Post Company.

L. Schwartz, "Smokestacks: 23 February 1942." Reprinted with the permission of the author.

Bernice G. Segal, *Chemistry: Experiment and Theory.* © 1985. Selections reprinted with the permission of John Wiley and Sons, Inc.

Craig Stoltz, "Doing Archaeology." Selection reprinted with the permission of the author.

Pat Ellis Taylor, "Teaching Creativity in Argumentation." *College English.* Dec. 1977. © 1977. Selections reprinted with the permission of the author.

Lewis Thomas, "The Art of Teaching Science." *New York Times Magazine* 14 Mar. 1982. Selection reprinted with the permission of the author.

Leo Tolstoy, "The Three Hermits." *Twenty-Three Tales.* Trans. Louise and Aylmer Maude. © 1906. Reprinted with the permission of Oxford University Press.

Richard Wright, *Native Son.* © 1940 by Richard Wright; © renewed 1968 by Ellen Wright. Selection reprinted with the permission of Harper & Row, Publishers, Inc.

Jeffrey Gagliardi, Rani Garrison, Jeff Green, Joseph Greenawalt, Aletha Hendrickson, Woienshet Kebede, Soon-Kee Kim, Diana Lambird, Tracey Landis, Jennifer Lee, Michael Parry, Robin Shaw-Maglione, Dahlia Shaewitz, Jill Swackhamer, Kristen Tokarek. Papers reprinted with the permission of these authors.

INDEX